the politics of lust

the politics of lust

john ince

Prometheus Books
59 John Glenn Drive
Amherst, New York 14228-2197

Published 2005 by Prometheus Books

Inquiries should be addressed to
Prometheus Books
59 John Glenn Drive
Amherst, New York 14228–2197
VOICE: 716–691–0133, ext. 207
FAX: 716–564–2711
WWW.PROMETHEUSBOOKS.COM

09 08 07 06 05   5 4 3 2 1

Library of Congress Cataloging-in-Publication Data

Ince, John.
    The politics of lust / John Ince.
        p. cm.
    Originally published: Vancouver, BC : Pivotal Press, 2003.
    ISBN 1–59102–278–9 (pbk. : alk. paper)
    1. Sex. 2. Sex role. 3. Sex customs. 4. Social change. 5. Sex in popular culture.
I. Title.

HQ21.I549 2005
306.7—dc22

2004027132

Printed in the United States of America on acid-free paper

Contents

To the erotic spark
in everyone

Introduction

OUR CULTURE APPEARS to be enthusiastic about sex. According to pollsters most people enjoy lovemaking and do it regularly. Almost every currently popular woman's magazine prominently features the word "sex" on the cover. Novels, television shows, and movies explore the nuances of erotic life. Sex saturates the internet. Explicit entertainment is a billion-dollar industry. Sex-positive attitudes seem prevalent in modern western society.

But appearances are deceiving. I contend that most people in our culture are highly ambivalent about sex. Opposing our in-born erotic hedonism are powerful irrational fears about our own sexuality and that of other people. Social scientists call such fear *erotophobia*. This book examines this largely unrecognized condition, its impact on our lives and culture, and the fascinating political system that imprints it in our minds.

Examine almost any dimension of human sexuality in our culture and you will find this sexual fear. Consider the widespread discomfort many people experience even speaking about sex. Though the media relentlessly reports sensational details of the intimate sex lives of celebrities, most of us have enormous difficulty talking openly about the subject. We suffer from a "sexual language barrier," according to Steven Carter and Julia Coopersmith, authors of the book *What Really Happens In Bed*.[1] Most people feel more comfortable sharing body fluids than words about the event.

Children soon learn of adult discomfort with sexual discourse. As sex researcher John Money puts it: "In the world in which we live today, no child can grow up without becoming acquainted with the taboo on talking about sex. No matter how open the conversation may be at home, or among age-mates, every child discovers sooner or later that certain everyday sexual words are absolutely forbidden in school, at church, on television and elsewhere."[2]

Most parents feel uncomfortable giving their children even rudimentary sex education.[3] Most children come of age without knowing the correct names for human erotic organs. In a society which values intelligence
and learning, almost every female will reach adulthood without knowing
the name of her erotic pleasure center, the clitoris.[4] Similarly, most teenaged boys masturbate regularly yet hear not a word from their parents
about this critically important early sexual behavior.[5] Most parents I
know would feel more comfortable jumping off a bridge than openly discussing autoerotic pleasure with their children.

The focus of sex education in our culture is on avoiding disease and
pregnancy; learning about creative ways to experience pleasure is completely unknown. Our schools teach our children how to paint, make music, play sports, and learn about their bodies in countless non-erotic ways,
but neglect erotic education. The result is that most people reach adulthood profoundly ignorant about sex, especially its pleasure potential.

Erotophobia also prompts the exclusion of genital imagery out of the
mainstream media and into pornographic ghettos. A similar phobic attitude prohibits any sort of live sex in public areas. Wrestlers are free to
beat each other senseless in vast public spectacles, but no one is allowed
to make love in a quiet corner of a park.

Irrational sexual fears also restrain our enjoyment of erotic pleasure.
Consider the widespread aversion to masturbation. Autoeroticism risks
no sexual disease or unwanted pregnancy, yet tens of millions of people in
our culture are uncomfortable with it. The most comprehensive survey of
American sexual behavior reports that half of the people who masturbate
feel guilty about it. The researchers believe this figure underestimates the
amount of masturbation negativity, because those who are highly uncomfortable with the act stop performing it.[6]

Our behavior with our sexual partners also reveals our sexual ambiva-
lence. The average sexual encounter is quick and routine. Sexual surveys
indicate that, as sex researcher Seymour Fisher reports: "Although relatively unlimited opportunities for coitus are available, couples level off at
about 1 hour a week, 4 hours a month, or the equivalent of about six
8-hour days a year. This is not a picture of much sexual action."[7]

Most of us have a very narrow erotic repertoire, a short sequence of erotic acts that varies minimally from day to day, partner to partner. We fear any form of sexual experimentalism or originality. While we seek out the new in movies, books, food, travel, fashion, computers, and so on, our sexual expression remains bland and repetitive. Further, while the deliberate and disciplined cultivation of non-erotic sensuality is very popular in our culture—evident in the proliferation of cooking schools, dance classes, music lessons, and other sensual projects—rare is the individual who devotes much attention to the erotic arts.

While young people today are less erotophobic than their baby-boomer parents, who are far less fearful about sex than the generation born prior to World War II, the idea that a "sexual revolution" in modern North America (or western Europe) has swept away all primitive inhibitions is often expressed, but is false.[8]

Dr. Bernie Zilbergeld, author of a leading work on male sexuality, says, "I have yet to meet a man or a woman who I think is totally comfortable with sex, and that of course includes myself. We all seem to have hang-ups of one kind or another."[9] Children suffer the same anxieties, according to Dr. Elaine Yates. "In my many years as a pediatrician and child psychiatrist, I have come to understand that virtually every child in my country [the United States] over the age of five has already concluded that sex is dirty, that genitals are shameful and eroticism a patent 'no-no'."[10]

Unnoticed Fear

While philosophers have long recognized the existence of negative attitudes towards sex, and words such as "prudery," "puritanism," and others have been used to describe such feelings, the subject of sexual fear has attracted little serious thought. Only a handful of mostly American social scientists have studied the condition.[11] But their body of work is small and lacks much of a perspective on the complex political process that produces erotophobia. The term itself is largely unknown; it does not appear in any popular dictionary nor in the standard psychiatric texts.

Though sexual fear is prevalent, it is hard to detect for several reasons. First, it usually coexists with positive attitudes towards sex. Only a very few extremely erotophobic individuals see all sex in a negative light. Most of us enjoy eroticism in specific contexts. In the same way that some anti-Semites deny that they could be racist because "some of my best friends are Jewish," most of us cannot see our erotophobia because we know we have some positive sexual feelings. Hence I often hear statements like: "I couldn't be erotophobic; I've had so many lovers I've lost count," or "How could I fear sex? I'm doing it all the time."

Second, the process by which erotophobia is learned is often highly unconscious. We acquire this fear in much the same way we acquire the accent in our speech. We absorb it subliminally in our early years through countless social interactions that are so normal and pervasive that everyone takes them for granted. Adult experience defuses some of our irrational sexual fears, but reinforces others. Schools, religion, the media, and the legal system set policies that imprint senseless sexual fears in millions of minds, yet are completely ignorant of this effect.

Third, many irrational sexual ideas are so deeply entrenched in the culture that they are difficult to recognize as nonsensical. For example, a widespread phobic belief is that the sight of adult recreational nudity harms children. Such an idea is regularly propounded but has no empirical basis. A delusion that is often expressed and rarely disputed is largely immune from rational challenge. That is why few whites in colonial America could recognize that their ideas about black genetic inferiority lacked any sense.

Systematic Irrationality

Human events that occur repeatedly and imprint baseless sexual fears in millions of minds are not random or accidental. They recur because powerful political forces drive them. Describing the complex but fascinating system that produces erotophobia is another key task of this book.

As all systems that generate mass irrationality are somewhat similar, throughout the book I borrow from the study of racism and sexism to gain insight into erotophobia. Reciprocally, our study of irrational sexual fear casts light on the traditional forms of prejudice. When you become aware of the subtle political processes that make you fear your own sexuality, you will become more sensitive to the way in which anyone can acquire delusional attitudes towards Jews, blacks, women, or Americans.

To understand erotophobia we must be familiar with its closely linked causes and effects. This book is organized around the causes of the condition, and a brief overview of them will give you an idea of the path ahead.

By far the most important cause is a group of behaviors that I label *antisexualism*. It consists of any negative response directed at sex organs and at harmless sex expression. Antisexualism has much in common with intolerant behavior aimed at racial or religious minorities. In the same way that racism promotes racial prejudice, antisexualism breeds erotophobia.

For example, I show how a very specific type of antisexualism, parental hostility towards nudity in the home, virtually ensures that a child will acquire specific phobic beliefs about genitals. A related type of antisexual conduct, the constant censorship of genital imagery by the mainstream media, reinforces the child's embarrassment and shame in relation to genitals. The law's prohibition of recreational nudity in all public space is yet another type of antisexualism that further supports phobic attitudes towards sexual body parts. In the same way that the effect of countless small acts of racial discrimination in racist cultures helps breed widespread racial prejudice, the cumulative impact of many single antisexual events produces irrational sexual fear throughout our community.

Further, like other types of irrationality, sexual fear is contagious. Erotophobia in the mind of one person motivates antisexual action, which in turn causes more erotophobia. For example, a parent anxious about masturbation will likely discourage a child from autoerotic play. Through exposure to the parent's phobia-inspired antisexualism the child internalizes similar phobic attitudes towards masturbation. Similarly, a school teacher who falsely believes that no teen can engage in responsible sex will favor an antisexual education program that teaches only about sexual abstinence and nothing about healthy erotic play. Such educational policy in turn helps teens learn phobic attitudes toward harmless sexual exploration. This *infection cycle* is a key reason for the prevalence of sexual fear in our world today.

The next thirteen chapters—the bulk of the book—examine the common varieties of antisexualism aimed at: nudity, nudity images, non-marital sex, contraception, masturbation, oral and anal sex, childhood sexuality, sex education, sexual fantasy, adultery, sexual discourse, visible live sex, pornography, prostitution, and homosexuality.

The second cause of erotophobia consists of harmful sexual acts that I label *nasty sex*, such as rape, violent pornography, unhappy sexual initiation, and sexual conduct causing disease or unwanted pregnancy. Sadly, despite medical technology and improved education, nasty sexual expression is still prevalent in modern culture, and it promotes phobic anxieties about sex, as Chapter 14 discusses.

A specific type of personality trait is the third cause of erotophobia, and it is the subject of Chapter 15. Through genetic predisposition and specific lifestyles, some individuals acquire a condition called *rigidity*, characterized by chronic physical tension, personal insecurity, and the inability to enjoy playful, spontaneous experience. Rigid personality traits produce a phobic aversion to the normally pleasurable physical sensations of sex. The rigid individual perceives sexual charge as physically uncomfortable or emotionally threatening, or both. Another reason erotophobia is prevalent in our community is because many people possess such traits.

Sex and Politics are Linked

One macro social force lurks behind the three causes of erotophobia: *hierarchy*, a power structure based on a pecking order of status divisions. It is found both in personal relationships and social organizations. The final chapter examines the fascinating coexistence of hierarchy and erotophobia.

For example, in a patriarchal family where a man dominates a wife and children, the incidence of sexual abuse is higher than in a family of equals. Similarly, in a culture where women are legally denied equality with men, or where masters dominate slaves, many privileged men abuse their power by sexually victimizing their subordinates. In contrast, in a family or culture of equals, sexual predators are more likely to encounter organized resistance, as in laws that ban marital rape and allow children to testify against adults, which reduce the prevalence of sexual assault and, in turn, erotophobia.

Pecking orders also tend to breed a special type of antisexualism motivated not by sexual fear but by opportunism. For instance, the leaders of the Roman Catholic Church discovered long ago that sexual prohibitions help segregate a society into separate groups, which in turn enhances authoritarian rule. Thus the rule requiring Roman Catholic priests to be celibate helps elevate them above the copulating masses. Similarly, people who favor family relationships based on strict boundaries between men, women, and children, tend to favor a range of sexual prohibitions as a way to maintain patriarchal roles. Further, denying children sexual information helps render them obedient to adult commands. The more hierarchic any social organization, the more likely it will engage in antisexual conduct and produce more erotophobia.

Hierarchic culture is also conducive to rigid personality traits that also cause erotophobia. Pecking orders create tension, anxiety, and the need for compulsive self control, all of which breed the fear of sexual pleasure.

What causes social hierarchy? Pecking orders are the result of many diverse forces, such as war and environmental stress, but as I shall show, erotophobia also plays a role. The final chapter shows that the more powerful our sexual fears, the more likely we will favor hierarchic relationships in our family, religion, or government.

For example, we cannot feel good about ourselves when we fear our own sexuality. In the grip of such insecurity we are less confident and more dependent, and that makes us more open to the control of others.[12] Erotophobia engenders obedience to the authority of parents, spouses, religions, government, and the media. Damaged self-esteem also breeds the need to stigmatize social minorities, and engenders an attraction for narrowly defined family and gender roles. (Islamic terrorists exhibit the classic indicators of erotophobia!)

Because social inequality and erotophobia are so intimately related, we can predict the existence of one where we find the other. Thus if you grew up in or are now a member of a patriarchal family, or a fundamentalist religion, or the police, the military, or a hierarchic corporate bureaucracy, you are more likely to be gripped with greater erotophobia than people inhabiting more egalitarian social environments. Reciprocally, if you harbor many and powerful erotophobic attitudes, chances are high that you also favor hierarchic relations: such as rigid gender roles, racial segregation, authoritarian leaders, and the strict discipline of children.

The prevalence of erotophobia in modern culture is a sign that our authoritarian roots run deep.

Overcoming erotophobia is an important step on the road to a truly democratic society. Sexual fear is a barrier to social equality. That is why I am so concerned to advance the rights of nudists or sexual entertainers; why I believe so strongly in sex education, or the right of consenting adults to engage in whatever type of sex they choose. While such rights most immediately serve the interests of a relatively few sexually adventurous people, such rights also ultimately serve a much bigger agenda, making our society more rational and humane and the relationships between all people more healthy. As sexual historian David Allyn aptly says: "Our willingness to examine our sexual attitudes—or our determined refusal to do so—will always remain a useful measure of our commitment to a truly enlightened society."[13]

The Message of the Fig Leaf

I believe an influential authority endorses the gist of these ideas. The Book of Genesis in the Old Testament distills into a few pithy paragraphs thousands of years of insight into the human condition. An important message of this mythic tale involves one of the key types of erotophobia, phobic attitudes towards nudity and genitals. The mere fact that an aspect of erotophobia should appear in this story is powerful evidence of the significance of the condition.

The very first reference in the Bible to human psychology, to our emotional life, involves the reaction of Adam and Eve to the sight of each other's genitals: "Now they were both naked, the man and his wife, but had no feeling of shame towards one another."[14] The Scriptures could have examined many other features about the human psyche in Eden, such as how Adam and Eve felt about God, or the beauty of the Garden. Instead, in a critically important passage the Bible focuses on negative attitudes towards genitals and tells us that in paradise such anxiety is unknown.

Erotophobia figures prominently a few lines later, in the dramatic events involving the serpent and the Tree of Knowledge. Adam and Eve eat the forbidden fruit and acquire a new consciousness: "The eyes of both of them were opened."[15] What did they see? "They discovered that they were naked."[16] Their world was full of fascinating things to attract their notice, but instead the Bible informs us that their attention was pulled immediately to their erotic organs. Adam and Eve now feel shame and hide their genitals behind fig leaves.

Genital fear thus appears twice in the western world's creation story. The Bible consumes precious mythological resources to prominently emphasize only one aspect of the human psyche: its attitude toward sex organs. This focus of the creation myth of western civilization is no poetic accident. The repeated reference to negative feelings about genitals conveys a clear message: that such attitudes are profoundly important.

Yet this message has been largely ignored. While Genesis has been exhaustively studied and re-studied for centuries, the fact that it repeatedly focuses on attitudes toward erotic organs and pays no similar attention to any other feature of human psychology or anatomy has been almost overlooked. Bibliographies of books and periodical articles dealing with the story of Adam and Eve contain hundreds of publications. I have sampled fifty of these works but found not one that explores why the Bible's creation story should give such key attention to genital shame, and not to love or hope or aesthetic beauty.

Not only does the Bible express the idea that attitudes to genitals are profoundly important, it goes further and suggests why. The Bible shows that while genital shame is unknown in paradise, it does occur in an environment of conflict and fear. Its cryptic language tells us that inner erotic attitudes correlate with specific external conditions. The harmony of Eden is associated with the absence of shame and no urge to don fig leaves. The hierarchic world of conflict, of disobedience and punishment, pain and anxiety, is associated with the existence of erotophobia and the impulse to hide pubic organs.

Biblical commentators have also overlooked this message about the correlation of specific erotic attitudes with specific external conditions. Genesis hails our attention and points us in a direction that few have chosen to travel. This book follows that road less traveled. It shows that the biblical correlation is amazingly accurate. Erotophobia tends to be absent from social environments that are harmonious and peaceful, and tends to afflict cultures that are conflicted and authoritarian.

The Path Ahead

The next thirteen chapters examine the main cause—and effect—of erotophobia: antisexualism. Such negative conduct comes in many different varieties, which I identify and discuss. The first of these, *fig-leafing*, consists of deliberately concealing one's own genitals, and is the subject of the next two chapters. Chapter 1 examines *solitary* fig-leafing, hiding the pubic region even when completely alone. Chapter 2 examines *social* fig-leafing, genital concealment when other people are present.

1 / Solitary Fig-Leafing

I AM NOT CONSCIOUS OF ever hiding my genitals from myself. I first became aware that other people did when I was a young adult. Oral sex gave me a good view of women's genitals and I discovered that two of my lovers had unusual features. The labia of one of the women were highly asymmetric, and the other woman had a sizeable mole. But both women were unaware of these features. They had never taken a good look at their own organs.

I met the first of these women while traveling in Italy after graduating from law school. Alice was an exchange teacher from Baltimore and we happened to stay at the same hotel in Siena, famous for its medieval architecture. She was an adventurous woman who had traveled much of Europe alone, bedding several men, and then me.

But she was inhibited about exposing her genitals. She refused a joint shower and came to bed wrapped in a towel. She insisted that we make love with the drapes closed and the light turned out. She was an inhibited lover. Several nights into our holiday fling I persuaded her to light a candle while we made love. In the flickering light I was able to see the beautiful folds of her vulva, one side much bigger than the other, and mentioned that her pussy was too pretty to hide away. "Yuk! Its gross down there," I heard her say. I asked her if she had ever really looked at her erotic parts. "Absolutely not," she answered.

I told her about *Our Bodies, Ourselves*, a popular self-help guide that encouraged women to examine their sexual anatomy. I offered her my travel mirror. She rejected that idea as "perverted."

While at first I thought she was shy about exposing her body to me, I realized that she hid her genitals from everyone, including herself. Fig-leafing spared her the anxiety of looking at something that made her uncomfortable.

A day or so later, I asked her why she was so reluctant to view her own genitals. She was obviously uncomfortable discussing the subject or even referring to her genitals by name, for she called that area of her body "the hole in the donut." She rejected the inference that her visual inhibitions were unusual or unhealthy. "Even Adam and Eve didn't want to see those parts," she said.

Alice's negativity toward the sight of her own genitals is not rare. The latest edition (1998) of *Our Bodies, Ourselves* still advocates genital self-examination, but notes: "It has taken a while for some of us to get over our inhibitions about seeing or touching our genitals."[1] Mainstream medical self-help books such as *The Good Housekeeping Illustrated Guide to Women's Health* recommend self-examinations for breast and skin cancer, but say nothing about inspecting erotic organs.[2]

The writers of the popular television series *Sex and the City* recognize genital anxiety as worthy of attention. In one episode Charlotte discloses to her friends that she has vulvodynia (causing her vulva to sting) and that doctors usually treat it with antidepressants. She also reveals that she has never inspected that region of her anatomy. "I don't want to look. I think its ugly." One of her friends replies, "Maybe that's why your vagina is depressed."

A response closely related to solitary fig-leafing is the reluctance to touch one's own genitals. A woman quoted in *Our Bodies, Ourselves* says,

When someone first said to me two years ago, 'You can feel the end of your own cervix with your finger,' I was interested but flustered. I had hardly ever put my finger in my vagina at all and felt squeamish about touching myself there, in that place 're-served' for lovers and doctors. It took me two months to get up my nerve to try it . . . .[3]

A friend of mine recalls a similar reaction. Coming of age in the 1970s, she and many of her peers were sexually promiscuous. Yet she noticed that when she washed her genitals her face always contorted into a grimace. Thereafter, she deliberately trained herself not to react that way.

Gynecologists are well aware of negative attitudes toward female genitals. Dr. Christiane Northrup says, "Over the years, many patients of all ages and backgrounds have asked me during their pelvic exams, 'How can you do this job? It's so disgusting.'" She adds: "The most common reason that women douche, moreover, is their mistaken belief handed down from mother to daughter, that this area of the body is offensive and requires special cleaning."[4]

What accounts for such genital inhibitions? Why are females more prone to it than males?

The Harm Test

The first step in answering this question is to determine whether fig-leafing flows from rational motives. When we react negatively to something that is truly harmful, and where our response prevents such harm, we can infer that our rational mind is in control.

The sight of one's own genitals is obviously harmless. The penis or vulva cast no dangerous rays. But fig-leafing one's own genitals *does* cause harm. Compulsive covering wastes physical energy. It inhibits cleaning that region of the body and delays discovery of genital diseases.

It also denies the many advantages of occasional nudity. When the temperature allows, nudity is sensually stimulating. Our skin enjoys moderate exposure to the warm rays of the sun or a cooling breeze. Our bodies relish the freedom of movement unrestrained by clothes. Without belts or bras our circulation flows more easily; we can breathe deeper. Nudity also promotes a sense of full-body integrity. Covering specific zones of the body sets them apart; the naked body cannot be so mentally compartmentalized.

No rational motive could prompt solitary fig-leafing. It is the product of a *genital aversion*, a key type of erotophobia. Such a condition almost certainly afflicted Alice in Siena. The same aversion also prompts attacks on recreational nudists and pornographers, because they expose genitals to view.

A brief overview of the unfamiliar psychology of aversions is helpful here. The discussion in the next few pages sets the foundation for the examination of other types of sex aversions in later chapters.

Emotional Cognition

You slice your finger and immediately cry out; you see a gorgeous sunset and swoon with delight; you smell the scent of your lover and feel lust arise within you. During each of these events a simple stimulus—somatic, visual, or aromatic—enters your brain, is instantly assessed, and an emotional response automatically ensues. Such cognition is reflexive, the emotional equivalent of the knee-jerk. No thought or deliberation occurs: the perception triggers the response. A simple neural program recognizes the stimulus as emotionally relevant and then immediately prompts a specific response, such as fear, joy, or lust.

Psychologists have discovered that the neural organs involved in such instant appraisal are located in an archaic region of the brain, often called the "limbic system." It evolved long before our species developed the more complex neural hardware that is key to thought and reason, known as the neo-cortex.

Experiments suggest that information entering the brain forks in two directions, down into the primitive limbic system where it is processed by emotional software, and up into the neo-cortex where more advanced neural programs analyze it. The limbic system has the ability to recognize only a relatively small array of information, but its responses are instantaneous. In contrast, the advanced system can process huge volumes of information, but it operates far more slowly. The result is that stimuli recognized by the primitive system will elicit an emotional response before the advanced brain has finished processing data.[5]

Our instantly appraising limbic system can operate entirely unconsciously. In psychological laboratories researchers have been able to train volunteers to react emotionally to visual and auditory stimuli that the volunteers were not conscious of ever seeing or hearing.[6] In contrast, the advanced cognitive system requires thought, analysis, and deliberation, all of which engage our conscious awareness. Hence, we tend to be much more aware of the responses triggered by our advanced cognition than of those triggered by our primitive appraisal system.

Aversions

An *aversion* is a primitive emotional attitude that commands instant *negative* feelings and related behaviors, such as fear, disgust, avoidance, and attack. An aversion is at work when a burning ember lands on your skin and you instantly wince and shake it off, or when you accidentally look into the rays of the sun and suddenly blink or look away.

Evolution imprinted a vast range of valuable aversions in our genes. The smell of a rotting corpse provokes innate disgust responses; a loud and sudden noise will prompt an innate startle reaction. Nature programmed these aversions into our brain because the stimuli that trigger them either cause pain directly or flow from things like the bacteria in a rotting corpse that tend to cause harm. Innate aversions are thus functional.

Evolution cannot imprint aversions to all the stimuli that signal instant danger. Fortunately, nature provided the primitive learning process called *fear conditioning*. Picture a mouse drinking at a creek. It hears the swoosh of the wings of a diving hawk, but does not react because it has no innate aversion to that sound. The bird's talons rip into the mouse and the rodent feels extreme pain. But it wriggles away and survives. This experience is likely to imprint in the rodent's brain a primitive new program that associates fear with the mere sound of a hawk's dive. The new aversion is functional because that sound signals a real threat.

This process was first discovered to occur in humans in 1920 in one of the most famous psychological experiments ever conducted. John Watson, the father of behaviorism, conditioned a young boy to fear the sight of furry objects and animals to which the child previously had no aversion.[7] The experimenters achieved this by frightening the boy with a sudden loud noise every time he played with the animal. "These early studies" says author Ronald Kleinknecht, "were further bolstered by virtually thousands of subsequent fear conditioning studies that clearly showed that fear and anxiety reactions could be conditioned to previously neutral stimuli."[8]

Not every distressing experience imprints a new aversion. But there is no doubt that fear and pain can produce new aversion programs. This is especially so when the negative event occurs in a person's youth, or when it involves a person's first contact with the neutral stimuli. The greater the pain or anxiety we suffer, the more likely fear conditioning will occur. Single events that involve very high trauma, such as a humiliating assault, are more likely to imprint an aversion than single events involving minor discomfort. But conditioning can also occur when minimally distressing events occur over and over in the face of a specific type of stimulus. Each incident can escape notice, but collectively they can imprint a very powerful phobic aversion.

Phobigenic Conditioning and Genitals

Phobigenic (phobia-causing) conditioning occurs when neutral stimuli projected by *harmless things* happen to be perceived at the same time as a person feels frightened or upset.[9] Visual aversions to genital organs are the product of such dysfunctional learning.

Constantly observing other's antisexual reactions towards genitals is the most common cause of the aversion. Many parents punish children who harmlessly play in the nude or play "doctor" with their peers. Such negativity distresses the child precisely when genitals are visible. Other types of subtle and repetitive conditioning can have a similar effect. For example, genitals can smell bad if they are not cleaned regularly. Smells from the anus can also be mistakenly attributed to the genitals. A child who is not regularly cleaned may only see his or her genitals at the same time that he or she smells offensive odors. If this occurs often enough, the child's emotional mind may acquire an aversion that triggers feelings of disgust when genitals are in view.

Similarly, because genitals are so often dark and moist they can breed infections, causing pain, itch, and discomfort. Menstruation exacerbates this problem. The genitals are also a common transmission point for venereal diseases like herpes that cause sores and more pain. If such negative experience is either very repetitive or very traumatic, phobigenic conditioning can result, producing a visual genital aversion. Because genitals are more naturally disposed to problems than most other parts of the body, they are much more frequently the targets of phobic aversions.

Genital aversions are also the product of sexual abuse, as I discuss further in Chapter 14. Consider a girl who is regularly forced by her father to perform oral sex. The trauma arising from such abuse occurs when the child's own genitals (or her father's) may be in view. Repeated over and over, the pairing of pain and humiliation with the sight of her genitals can cause her emotional mind to acquire the visual aversion. Because more girls than boys experience sexual abuse and suffer genital irritations, girls tend to be more averse to the sight of their own genitals.

Defusing Aversions

Positive experiences that occur while genitals are in view help imprint positive attitudes toward genitals. If a parent tells a child that his or her genitals are beautiful, or if the child is allowed to play in the nude, the child's emotional brain can learn to associate positive feelings with the sight of genitals. Even if an aversion has already been imprinted, subsequent positive experience with genitals can reduce the potency of the aversion or even extinguish it entirely. Sex therapists have discovered that systematic positive conditioning (often called *desensitization*) is very effective in treating most sex aversions.[10]

Organized social nudism, such as in the public baths common to many cultures or in the naturist movement in North America and Europe, offers such positive conditioning. Children and adults alike see their own genitals in a relaxed atmosphere. They acquire positive genital attitudes that defuse genital aversions.

Positive conditioning is another reason why boys tend to be more comfortable with the sight of their own genitals than girls. The penis is more visible than the vulva. Boys more than girls are likely to see their sex organs during relaxed experiences such as bathing.

As a result largely of nudity prohibitions imposed by adults, many children experience more negative than positive conditioning when their genitals are in view. Adulthood generally brings the reverse. Grown-ups usually see their genitals in safe or happy circumstances. Thanks to the effects of this positive experience, most people are not averse to the sight of their own genitals. But significant numbers of adults, such as Alice, never experience such positive conditioning and reach maturity with an aversion, even in safe settings.

Genitals in the Mind's Eye

The "mind's eye" has the ability to create mental pictures. We can close our eyes and visualize any scene, including genitals and sex. To the brain, these imaginary stimuli look like real visual stimuli. That is why we can salivate just thinking about chocolate mousse, or get sexually aroused when we imagine being in bed with our lover.

Because imaginary visual stimuli appear to the emotional brain to be much like real visual stimuli entering from outside, people averse to the sight of their own genitals can react negatively just thinking about those organs. Their imaginations alone can trigger their aversion. Many other sex aversions work the same way. This book provides many examples of people reacting negatively to sex stimuli they never actually see, but simply imagine.

One reason Alice did not want to talk about her genital aversion is that such discourse causes her mind to picture that region of her anatomy. Her emotional brain will then "see" the aversive stimuli and prompt a negative reaction. People who have visual aversions thus find it difficult to think about the subject of their fear. That people avoid thinking about things that provoke anxiety is well documented.[11] This is one reason highly erotophobic people are very ignorant about sex. Many clinical studies show that erotophobia impairs a person's ability to think clearly when sex is an issue. The more potent a person's genital aversions, the less likely they will be able to make intelligent decisions about contraception, pregnancy risk, and sexual ethics.[12]

The Effects of the Genital Aversion

The genital aversion lies dormant in the memory banks of the brain until it is triggered into action by genital stimuli. The first outcome of any sex aversion is usually a purely *emotional* response: fear, offense, shock, disgust, or anger. Alice's exclamation "Yuk!" when I mentioned her labia reveals such an emotional response.

Negative feelings are usually followed by *behavioral* responses aimed at avoiding the aversive stimuli. Some actions are so subtle they are entirely unconscious. For example, in a series of experiments a researcher used a device to track people's eye movements as they looked at several images, including the outline of a woman's breast. Some individuals consistently avoided looking at that specific image. Days later they had no recollection of any sexual content in the material.[13] A psychologist comments: "We are tempted to conclude that the avoidance is not random but highly efficient—the person knows just where not to look."[14] While averting one's eyes is one way to avoid an aversive stimulus, hiding it is even better. People with genital aversions engage in solitary fig-leafing to spare themselves the discomfort of seeing their own crotch.

These behavioral outcomes of the genital aversion have, in turn, several psychological effects on the person with the condition. The first is to reinforce the aversion. For instance, every time Alice covers her loins with a towel, clothes, or a bathing suit, she will experience the relief arising from hiding her genitals. This amounts to dysfunctional positive conditioning; her emotional brain learns to associate the act of fig-leafing with a sense of comfort. She now favors hiding her genitals not only to avoid aversive stimuli, but also because it feels good in itself.

Note also that his behavior also prevents positive genital conditioning. Because Alice constantly hides her genitals, she never sees them when she feels good, and thus her aversion is never defused. The outcomes of erotophobia prevent healing the condition.

Rationalizing is another important psychological outcome of the genital aversion, or any other sex aversion. It works as follows. Sex aversions are usually unconscious, the product of many negative events that escape notice. Yet the reflexive negative feelings and behaviors that the aversions generate are often too pronounced to ignore. People who are conscious of feeling bad usually look for a reason for their upset.

Most of us fancy that we are rational beings. Indeed, surveys indicate that most folks think they are more intelligent, fair-minded, and less prejudiced than the average person.[15] Negative feelings are only rational and functional when provoked by something harmful. Hence most of us have a bias to look for harm when we detect that we are frightened. The apt title of a scholarly paper expresses the gist of the idea: "If I feel anxious, there must be danger: the fallacy of ex consequentia reasoning in inferring danger in anxiety disorders."[16] When alarm is provoked by an unconscious sex aversion, no harm is actually present. So we invent it.

The simplest and most popular way to rationalize an unconscious aversion to genitals or sex is to attribute some negative or harmful feature to them. Alice imagines that her genitals are "gross," and that looking at them is "perverted." The first idea concerns genitals *per se*, while the other involves *seeing* genitals. Alice invokes such defective ideas to try to make sense of her otherwise senseless responses.

But such rationalizing has another phobigenic outcome. She now acquires a new erotophobic attitude, a *false belief* about her genitals and about looking at them. What begins as a primitive emotional program—an aversion—expands like a malignant tumor into something more dangerous, a genital *delusion*.

Because rationalizing is not a logical process but rather a primitive attempt to avoid anxiety, the delusions it produces make little sense, and are usually devoid of much concrete meaning. Vague concepts such as "gross" or "perverted" are favorites of rationalizers. So too are "unnatural," "immoral," or "indecent." Such terms suggest danger and harm without explicitly spelling it out.

Note also that rationalizing helps conceal the underlying unconscious phobic aversion. The rationalizer is able to explain the negative response to genitals on the basis of purported harm. The fact that the alarm was stimulated by small bits of *harmless* stimuli remains unconscious.

Genital aversions are the product of phobigenic conditioning while genital delusions result from much more complicated learning processes of which rationalizing is our first example. As you will discover, every erotophobic attitude is either an aversion or a delusion, and distinguishing between the two is important. The collective term I use to refer to both genital aversions and genital delusions is *genital phobia*. As the next chapter shows, both types of the condition motivate another type of fig-leafing more common than the solitary variety: hiding one's own genitals in *social* situations.

2 / Social Fig-Leafing

WHILE MOST PEOPLE do not hide their genitals from themselves, fig-leafing is almost universal in social situations. Nudist organizations estimate that less than 2% of the population practices regular social nudism.[1] Even most dedicated nudists cover themselves while at home.

Nudity enhances many social recreational activities such as sunbathing, swimming, or relaxing in a hot-tub or sauna. Yet the vast majority of people in English-speaking nations and most other countries never engage in nude recreation. Polls indicate that over 80% of Americans have never tried mixed-gender social nudity.[2] Of course many people simply have no opportunity to do so. Public nudity is illegal almost everywhere, and most communities lack private nudist clubs.

But even when people have the opportunity to socialize without clothes, they deny themselves that experience. Visit the rare public beach where local authorities allow nudity and you will find substantial numbers of people who still refuse to take off all their clothes. In clothing-optional hot-tubs at retreat centers and resorts, the same compulsive fig-leafing is common. Many people who could relax in the water free of clothes, prefer to wear bathing suits. Such social fig-leafers have always fascinated me. In the company of mostly nude people, their genital hiding stands out. Their minority status must generate some discomfort, yet it obviously is less than their anxiety about baring all.

Even in the privacy of the family home, fig-leafing is almost universal in modern western culture. Most social authorities oppose family nudity. The late Ann Landers, one of the most widely syndicated journalists in the world, opposed family nudity for decades. Consider her response to a woman who complained that when her children need attention in the night her husband, who sleeps in the nude and feels there is "nothing wrong with the naked body," goes to them "stark naked." Landers labels the man an "idiot" for leaving his bedroom without clothes and says: "Dear Readers, we have gone round and round about this issue before, and I maintain that nudity by the opposite-sex parent can lead to problems when the kids get older. I am ready to take on the abusive letters once again saying I am crazy."[3]

Even *Playboy* magazine supports family fig-leafing: "Unless they're nudists or under the age of three most family members, no matter how close, don't romp around in the buff."[4] A survey of 255 law enforcement and social workers in Virginia revealed that 75% believe that child welfare authorities should take action against parents who often appear nude in front of five-year-old children.[5] Forty per cent of the male respondents of another survey reported that they would be embarrassed being seen naked by their brother; 58% of the female respondents said they would be uncomfortable if seen without clothes by their sister.[6]

Fig-leafing would make sense if the visibility of genitals (or female breasts) caused harm. Does it? Consider some of the common allegations against social nudity.

Innate Offense

Many people contend that social nudity is innately offensive, that the sight of the genitals of other people will naturally disgust any normal person. They don fig leaves to spare other people offense, and they insist that everyone do the same.

The idea that nature could have programmed an innate aversion to the sight of normal body parts or even sexual functions seems very unlikely. Nudity is the social norm in many cultures, as the early European explorers discovered. Captain Cook was astounded to find an utter lack of shame amongst the aborigines of Australia: "They go quite naked both men and women, and without any manner of clothing whatever. Even the women do not so much as cover their privates."[7] The Spanish friars who made contact with the Pueblo Indians in Mexico had the same reaction, noting how the Indians walked about "stark naked without any . . . indication of self-consciousness."[8]

The much better explanation for the offense that social nudity provokes in many people is a genital aversion acquired through conditioning. From infancy most of us see lots of social negativity directed at naked genitals (or breasts) whenever they appear in the home, in public, or in the media. Such conflict produces stress precisely when erotic organs are in view. Repeated over and over it imprints a primitive emotional reflex—the visual genital aversion—that prompts negative feelings whenever genitals again appear. A person who feels uncomfortable simply upon seeing nudity, or merely thinking about it, can make sense of their stress by attributing some false negative characteristic to genitals or genital visibility. Rationalizations that genitals are "disgusting" flow from such a process, as we saw in the last chapter.

The fact that millions of people do find nudity offensive seems to confirm that rationalization; the prevalence of such offense suggests that it is innate. At the height of the slavery era in America, when visual aversions to black skin were very common in white people (also as a result of conditioning), a person offended by the sight of a black person in a park or restaurant would observe that all of his or her white peers reacted the same. The prevalence of the aversion made it seem innate. The delusion that nudity aversions are innate flows from the same phobigenic processes.

Titillation

Social nudity is also attacked on the ground it is by nature sexually arousing. This is the allegation made by prominent opponent of family nudity, the late Dr. Benjamin Spock. His classic child-rearing text *Baby and Child Care* has sold over fifty million copies since its first printing in 1945 and continues to sell today. In it he claims that young children get upset by regularly seeing their parents naked. A boy may find the sight of his mother "a little too stimulating." Little girls react the same way if they regularly see their fathers without clothes. He concludes: "I think it's a little wise for parents to keep reasonably covered and to keep children out of the bathroom while a parent is bathing or using the toilet."[9]

The idea that nudity is *innately* arousing both to children and adults is very popular, but it is false. Cross-cultural studies show that in places where nudity is routine, the sight of genitals is not considered erotic.[10] That is why people in naked tribal cultures are not in a constant state of arousal. Doctors and members of nudist clubs can also attest that exposure to nudity does not automatically prompt desire.

Nudity is often perceived to be arousing because of an interesting conditioning process. In the same way that fearful experiences imprint new aversions in the brain, sexually arousing experiences can produce new erotic circuitry. Such *erotic conditioning* occurs when our erotic passions are aroused through touch, sight, or smell, and at the same time we are exposed to stimuli that is not innately arousing.

Consider an actual example of how this can occur in ordinary life. A boy was given a toy fire truck and fireman's clothes, including a yellow raincoat. As part of his daily play he put on the raincoat and then straddled the toy fire truck to maneuver it around the room. This motion produced pleasant erotic sensations in his groin. The combination of repeated sexual arousal while seeing the yellow rain gear conditioned a visual fetish for yellow raincoats. The new erotic program was so powerful that years later he sought professional treatment to overcome compulsive masturbatory rituals involving such a garment.[11] Several clinical tests demonstrate that men can be erotically conditioned.[12]

Erotic conditioning also occurs when boys and men habitually use sexually explicit imagery depicting naked women who have the highly atypical physical proportions of a Barbie doll. As Gary Brooks discusses in *The Centerfold Syndrome*, the result is a very powerful visually oriented erotic program that can so narrow a man's sexuality that he finds average women sexually unappealing.[13]

In a culture in which fig-leafing is common and casual social nudity rare, most people see a naked adult body only during part of a sexual interaction, such as during lovemaking, or viewing strip shows or sexual media. In such circumstances sexual arousal accompanies the sight of genitals. Repeated over and over, that experience will help imprint an erotic program triggered just by the sight of genitals.

In contrast, in a community where family nudity is common and fig-leafing rare, genitals and female breasts are observed in contexts involving little or no sexual arousal, such as while making meals or playing games. The greater our exposure to genitals and breasts outside an erotic context, the less likely that the sight of such organs will sexually excite us. Any titillation caused by nudity is not an innate response to the sight of erotic organs, but rather a by-product of social fig-leafing.

Harm to Children

Some say that social nudity harms children psychologically. This allegation originated in the work of Sigmund Freud, who contended that when a boy observes nude females he would conclude that girls originally had penises but forcibly lost them, and that he is similarly liable to such a catastrophe. Freud also believed that the size of an adult male penis is threatening to boys; further, that girls acquire "penis envy" when they see they lack that organ.[14] These ideas have taken deep root in our society.

Fortunately, they are unfounded. Freud had little experience with children, no empirical evidence to support his claims, and no access to cultures in which nudity was common.

Children are not stupid. They understand that adult body parts are bigger than theirs and that as they age they will acquire adult proportions. Hence they do not feel inferior simply by observing the larger size of adult hands and heads. If as Freud alleges the sight of nudity causes children castration anxiety or penis envy, parents can quickly dispel such fears by telling children that males and females by nature have different bodies and that these differences are entirely normal and wonderful.

Several empirical studies have been conducted to determine the effects of nudity on children, in 1966, 1979, and 1988. A 1995 review of all three concludes that none of the data supports the child-harm hypothesis.[15] Given that an adult can quickly dispel any childhood delusions about nudity, no reasonable person would conclude that hiding nudity from children makes sense.

Indeed family nudity has many benefits. In a study of children raised on communes where nudity is common, pediatric researchers concluded: "The only significant difference between their experience and that of most traditionally raised children was their frequent contact with and comfortableness with both adult and child nudity."[16] Other studies have found that children from nudist families consistently score higher than non-nudist children with respect to body acceptance and self-concept.[17]

The idea that the sight of genitals harms children is caused in part by rationalizing the genital aversion. A mother who is averse to the sight of her own genitals can make sense of that negative emotion by inventing the idea that nudity causes harm to her kids. Perhaps a similar process occurred in Freud's mind. Genital aversions were widespread during the repressive era in which he grew up. It is likely he too had a compulsive need to hide his own genitals, and an easy way to make sense of that negative need was to invent the idea that the sight of genitals harms children. As many examples in this book show, adults frequently rationalize their own senseless fears by inventing ideas that the genital conduct in question harms kids.

Fig-Leafing Motives

No rational evidence shows that social nudity causes harm. Phobic attitudes are the main motive behind the urge to cover our loins in social situations. Because these fears are so deeply ingrained and common, most people never question them. In contrast, most nudists have to confront these fears when they first disrobe socially, and thus discover the power of these irrational feelings. Here are reports of some first time experiences:

PAUL: [The first time at a nude beach] I removed my shirt and sat down on the towel, trying to gather up my courage. There were so many butterflies in my stomach, my scalp tingled and my throat went totally dry . . . I did not want to be branded a gawker, so I decided to count to three, then take off my trunks. 1,2,3, Nothing! I was frozen in place. 1,2,3, still frozen! I must have counted to 90 by threes . . . After sitting on my towel like a stone statue for about 20 minutes, I finally got up the courage to carefully ease my trunks off without getting up . . . I was now sitting completely naked among a hundred or more other people. The sky did not fall! My first reaction was one of relief. My second reaction was, Hmmm, this does feel pretty good . . .

FRAN: With only a few Women's Only swims under my belt it was time for me to go full social, and I was very scared and nervous. Everyone at *Cybernude Chat* did their best to ease me with it. They all understood my feelings and were so nice about it.

Even after all their encouragement I did find that I was still uneasy. I did the 'should I go' or 'should I not go" all week long up
until the swim and then something inside me was pushing me to
go. So on a Tuesday evening I found myself at the pool in the
girls' changeroom, nude and very unsure of myself. And then it
happened, swallowing my fear I stood up and showered, and
walked towards the door and opened it a crack . . . I swallowed
hard again, told myself, "let's do it" and bounded out the
door . . . I felt a relief coming over me and I knew that I was now
a nudist.[18]

Though phobic anxiety is the key motive prompting social
fig-leafing, it is not the only one. Non-phobic motives can also prompt
the same inhibitions.

For example, a very popular body-type ideal for men is a large penis,
and for women full and firm breasts. Because few people have the ideal
body-types, masses of people believe that their bodies are inadequate.
Cosmetic surgery on breasts and even penises is a billion-dollar business.
A less drastic and cheaper remedy is to cover up the imagined faults. A
man who thinks he has a small penis will fig-leaf his loins. A woman who
feels her breasts are too small or saggy will rarely appear without a top.

Another non-phobic attitude common to children also causes
fig-leafing. Children have a strong need for acceptance by other children
and want to conform to group norms, which are often highly arbitrary
and unnatural. During puberty the young person's erotic organs undergo
profound change, and these changes vary with the individual. At twelve,
some girls have mature breasts and others none at all. Some boys of the
same age have genitals of adult proportions and some boys not a single
pubic hair.

If a young person fears that his or her body is maturing too quickly or
too slowly compared to the peer group, he or she will feel uncomfortable.
This concern is magnified by the fact that few children have a good idea
of the range of physical development that is normal for their age. To
avoid discomfort, or some of it, children hide their genitals and exhibit
enormous embarrassment when others see them in a locker room or at
the toilet.

Much social fig-leafing is also prompted by the normal desire to avoid the unwanted attention of others. Intolerant laws require everyone to cover their loins in almost every public recreational area; intolerant parents insist their children do the same, even in the privacy of their home. Many nudists hide their genitals simply to avoid legal attack and not because they harbor any genital phobia. Many women refrain from recreational nudity not because they feel uncomfortable with it, but rather simply to avoid unwanted male attention. Such fig-leafing is not phobic.

Fig-Leafing Causes Genital Phobia

Regardless of the motive that inspires fig-leafing, *all* such conduct helps cause genital phobia in persons who observe it. When we see someone hiding their genitals, a self-deceptive process occurs that is very similar to rationalizing. It differs only in that it involves the attempt to make sense of the negative reactions of *other* people rather than our own negative responses.

Consider how it occurs. Most of us want to believe that other people, especially people we trust, are rational beings. An easy way to make sense of a fearful response of a trusted person is to jump to the conclusion that the object of their fear is harmful in some way. That automatic assumption is generally correct. Trusted authorities usually are rational and usually act negatively only to things that really are harmful. The fearful reactions of adults help children identify real threats.

The collective fears of the community at large similarly influence most individuals. As Thomas Gilovich, author of *How We Know What Isn't So: The Fallibility Of Human Reason In Everyday Life*, explains: "Other things being equal, the greater the number of people who believe something, the more likely it is to be true; the more people who do something, the more we are well-advised to do the same."[19]

However, intelligent and authoritative people and even whole communities do suffer irrational fears, or act negatively toward people for completely spurious reasons. To conclude in such cases that the object of fear or attack must be harmful is to deceive oneself. This is another form of rationalizing, much like that discussed in the last chapter except that the self deception is triggered not by the rationalizer's own emotional responses, but rather by the reactions of other people.

This type of rationalizing is a key cause of racial prejudice. A child growing up in a racist community will observe his parents and other respected people react negatively when they see members of racial minorities (as a result of visual racial aversions). An easy way for the child to rationalize such negativity is to conclude that members of minorities are worthy of fear. Adults do not even have to specifically say, "The racial minority is dangerous," for the child to acquire prejudice. Merely observing the consistent wordless negativity is enough to engender racist ideas in the child's mind.

Similarly, a child who observes that the vast majority of people cover their pubic region virtually all of the time, even when they could go nude, will make sense of that fig-leafing by imagining that nudity is somehow harmful. Even in the absence of direct statements such as "genitals are offensive" or "nudity harms children," the child will invent similar delusions. Merely observing the prevalence of fig-leafing is phobigenic. The more antisexual conduct we observe, the greater our erotophobia. Because all of us grew up observing enormous amounts of fig-leafing at home and in public, few of us are free of genital delusions.

The Scope of Delusions

A child observing fig-leafing may invent the specific delusion that "seeing genitals is bad." The child might also generate the *broader* phobic idea that "genitals are bad." The narrower delusion attributes harm only to the exposure of genitals; the broader delusion casts aspersions on the organs themselves.

The act of hiding promotes broad delusions because concealment naturally suggests that the thing hidden is objectionable. We hide features about our body that we do not like, such as scars and blemishes, and features of our personality that we do not like, such as vanity or greed. Australian aborigines wore no clothes and resisted the western practice of fig-leafing because to their aboriginal kin hiding inferred genital disease. For that reason, aboriginals actually felt shame covering their genitals. To our children, the fact that so many adults in western culture are reluctant to expose their genitals is powerful evidence that sex organs are somehow tainted, in a special inferior class, unlike hands, ears, or feet.

The same delusioning process is also at work in many other sexual contexts. Children see images of war, crime, and the violence of fake wrestling matches on prime time television, but they never see normal sexual behavior. They are apt to conclude that not only sexual *images* are somehow dangerous, but that the unseen sexual *acts* are also improper. Sex expert Bernie Zilbergeld describes the child's conclusion: "Kids aren't stupid. They get the point: There's something wrong with sex."[20]

The Infection Cycle and its Catalysts

At the heart of the complex system generating irrational sexual fear is an infection process: phobia in the mind of one person causes behavior that transmits the phobia to the minds of others. *Phobic* fig-leafing is precisely such a behavior. Consider a mother who hides her genitals and breasts around her children because she is averse to the sight of them, or because she erroneously believes that her nudity will harm her kids. Through the rationalizing process discussed above, her fig-leafing helps her children acquire phobic attitudes towards genitals. Phobic fig-leafing is thus a *virus* of genital phobia, and one that spreads entirely without words.

Each of the next eleven chapters provides many other specific examples of similar infection cycles involving genitals and sexuality: an irrational fear prompts an intolerant response to genitals or sexuality, which in turn helps other people to acquire similar phobic attitudes. This *infection cycle* is the main engine of the erotophobia system.

Note that the infection cycle operates only *after* someone has first acquired the condition. Some force other than erotophobic conduct must breed the first cases of irrational sexual fear. I call those *non-phobic* behaviors *catalysts*.

Many such forces breed genital fear. As I discuss in detail in Chapter 14, the pain and trauma from sexual abuse or sexually transmitted disease can produce genital aversions. Such phobic attitudes will in turn prompt the victim to compulsively fig-leaf, and when that is observed by the victim's children and others, they are likely also to acquire similar genital fears. Genital assault and disease catalyze an infection cycle.

Another catalyst of genital phobia is fig-leafing prompted by motives other than genital aversions or delusions. For example, imagine a father who has a small penis and does not want anyone to see it. The man's son observes his father's fig-leafing and rationalizes it by inventing the idea that genitals are "dirty" and thus best hidden. What begins in the father's mind as concern about the *size* of his penis produces a different attitude in the child's mind, a phobic idea that genitals are inherently tainted.

Genital phobia is common in most cultures because the genital assault, disease, and non-phobic fig-leafing that breed genital fear separately from the infection cycle are very common. These forces tend to target women's genitals more than men's; hence genital phobia tends to be more pronounced in females than males. Similarly, because these forces involve genital organs rather than other body parts such as ears and toes, genital phobia is common while irrational fears about ears and toes are very rare.

Like genital organs, many types of sexual conduct, such as masturbation or anal sex, are subject to peculiar phobigenic catalysts operating independently of any pre-existing phobia about such conduct, and I examine these forces in detail in later chapters. Such forces help breed the first cases of irrational fear toward the sexual conduct in issue, and spur the infection cycle into operation, which breeds more and more of the same phobia. Similar forces do not target other human activities, such as singing, laughing, or running. That is why irrational fears about sexual conduct are prevalent while irrational fears about singing, laughing, or running are almost unknown.

3 / Genital Purdah

NOT EVERYONE IS a compulsive fig-leafer. Most young children are fond of playing in the buff. Some adults enjoy wearing no clothes and would do so often if there were no social resistance. But the opposition to social nudism is enormous. I call such a policy *genital purdah*, for it is equivalent to the conservative Moslem tradition that requires women to cover their faces.

In some very rare cases social nudity is harmful and deserves prohibition. The pubic region is a source of bodily discharges and thus should not directly contact areas that other people touch. A naked person sitting on a park bench or bus seat poses hygienic risks. However, our culture's regime of genital purdah does not target real harm. It is aimed solely at the harmless *visibility* of genitals or female breasts. Genital purdah is a type of social intolerance.

Parental Prohibitions

My first experience with genital purdah occurred when I was three or four, while I was visiting a friend. The weather was hot and my companion had removed his clothes and was running back and forth through the spray from the lawn sprinkler in the backyard of his home. I was taking off my clothes when his mother stormed out of the house and angrily demanded that he put on a bathing suit. He did so, and I can still remember the puzzled look on his face as he struggled to make sense of his mother's behavior.

The most severe cases of such parental attacks are physical, as in the following case.

> When I was about twelve or thirteen when everybody was asleep and I was in bed, I would take off my pajamas because the sheets felt so good. Once my mother came in and found that I didn't have

any pajamas on. She ripped off the covers, spanked me, and made me put my pajamas back on.[1]

Adult negativity is also common when children are found "playing doctor"—examining each other's genitals. I can remember several such incidents. The first occurred when I was five or six, when a female neighbor of my age went with me behind a bush. We each dropped our pants to the ground and gazed at each other's crotch. Unfortunately for us, the girl's mother was watching from an upper floor window and when we emerged from the bush she came out and confronted us, livid with rage. The girl began crying and I remember shaking with fear. We both lied about what we had done, but the mother lowered the girl's pants and showed that her white underwear was marked where it had touched the earth. I ran home ridden with shame.

Parental prohibitions against childhood nudity are enforced with more vigor against girls than boys. From a young age most girls are punished or shamed for allowing their brothers, fathers, or any male to see their pubic area. Consider the following reports two people gave to the sex journalist Dr. Ruth:

When I was growing up, I could see my mother naked and my mother could see me naked, but my father wasn't permitted even to see me in my underwear. My mother wouldn't allow him to see his granddaughters in their underwear.[2]

In my family, being without clothes on was always wrong. We always had to cover up. It was considered shameful. We were told this by my mother. Since there were two girls and a boy in the house, I was not even allowed to walk out of my bedroom in a nightgown. I had to put a robe over the nightgown. I could walk around naked in front of my mother if I wanted to, but I had to be fully covered around my father and brother. I began to feel that what my mother considered shameful was our bodies.[3]

These are but a few examples of informal attacks on the nudity of children. Most of us, both girls and boys, were exposed in our youth to similar intolerance, although we have forgotten most of the detail of it. One study shows that 40% of American college students recall warnings, scoldings, and punishments about nudity by parents, mainly the mother.[4]

Criminalizing Nudity

The law is a key instrument of genital purdah. Most places in the world criminalize harmless public nude recreation. Such policy has a long history in the United States.

Private nudity

In decades past, the American legal system attacked even *private* recreational nudity. Organized nudism was introduced to America in the late 1920s from Europe, where it had been popular for centuries. Although the American nudist pioneers confined their activities to enclosed places, the police constantly harassed them. On the second anniversary of the "American League for Physical Culture," police invaded a meeting at an indoor gymnasium in New York and arrested everyone, on the complaint of one anti-nudist. The case generated nationwide publicity around the country, prompting the opening of several nudist resorts. Because criminal laws against "public indecency" were so vague and unenforceable on private property, local politicians all over the country passed municipal by-laws prohibiting private nudism. For example, in 1939 the county of Los Angeles, one of the most desirable areas for nudism in the United States, outlawed nudist resorts. That prohibition was in effect for almost thirty years, until set aside by the courts in 1968.[5]

Nudity in private places is still under attack. In Kansas, for instance, a Republican state representative introduced a bill that declared nudist camps and resorts in the state a "nuisance" if they operated within five miles of a residential area. Constitutional law experts condemned the proposed law as a serious violation of privacy rights. The bill was drafted in such broad terms that it effectively prohibited anyone except married couples from appearing nude in the presence of another person, whether inside a nudist camp or not. The bill was ultimately abandoned.[6]

In San Diego authorities refused a license for Elbert Popell's nude church, then busted his nude social club, and raided his nude spa, throwing the former butcher in jail. He sued his tormentors and won. A federal jury awarded him $200,000 after concluding the police and civic officials had engaged in malicious prosecution and harassment. In refusing to order a new trial, U.S. District Judge John Rhoades ruled that while "a large

segment of the population views the plaintiff's activities as morally repre-
hensible" and that the plaintiff was "a creepy purveyor of indecency,"
Popell had a constitutional right to do what he did.[7]

These attacks on private recreational nudity are relatively rare in the
western world today. But harassment of nudists on private property who
are visible to third parties is still common. A seventy-seven-year-old nudist, Robert Norton of Pekin, Illinois, was sentenced to a year in jail for
walking in his yard in the buff. He had been arrested at least twenty times
since 1962 for the harmless act of enjoying his own property on hot days
without the inconvenience of clothes.[8] Because of such legal harassment,
few recreational nudists dare to bare all if outsiders can see them, even
within the confines of their own property.

Public nudity

Discrimination against nudists in *public* areas is very common in all but a
few countries of the world. If on a warm day you spread a towel on the
ground, take off all your clothes, and lie down to simply soak up the sun in
Hyde Park in London, or Central Park in New York, or the beaches
along the Los Angeles coastline, you can expect that sooner or later
armed men in uniforms will arrest you and haul you off to jail, the same
way they treat a thief, rapist, or murderer. And all because you simply exposed your pubic region to the rays of the sun.

For example, New York state law prohibits appearing in a public
place in such a manner that the "private or intimate parts of the body are
unclothed or exposed, including the portion of the breast which is below
the top of the areola for females."[9] In Canada the federal Criminal Code
prohibits "public nudity" anywhere in the country.[10] In these jurisdictions nudity is a crime even if nobody is offended by it.

In some places legal officials attack nudity only when somebody takes
offense. Rangers in California State Parks allow nudity in "traditional"
clothing-optional areas within state parks, but if one person reports a
complaint, the nudist must put on clothes for the remainder of the
day—or face charges. The process resets on the following day, allowing
nudism until somebody complains.[11] Many other jurisdictions informally
tolerate some public nudism, but only as long as nobody complains.

While complaints are essential to police action, the complainant's motives are irrelevant. Whether the complainant regards the nudist as "immoral," or "harmful to children," or simply ugly, the authorities are still obliged to act.

Arrests, charges, court hearings, and even new laws specifically aimed at nudists on public property are a constant feature of our legal system. The monthly newsletter of The Naturist Society, a North American nudist advocacy group, documents the seemingly endless attacks on nude sunbathers by police officers, prosecutors, and other agents of the state. Consider some recent examples of the campaign against nudity waged by legal officials in the United States:

- In Florida's Santa Rosa county, undercover officers wearing swimsuits and posing as sunbathers or fishermen arrest eight people for nudity at a local beach. A county ordinance prohibits nudity.[12]
- At the traditional clothing-optional "Black's Beach" near San Diego, officials suddenly begin to enforce a city anti-nudity ordinance that had been dormant for two decades.[13]
- The city council of Huntington Beach, California, debate an ordinance aimed at nude juice bars which would additionally ban all nudity in the seaside town. The hysterical preamble to the ordinance states: "Rioting has occurred after females exposed their breasts before a crowd in the Pier area of Huntington Beach. Their actions excited the crowded and triggered mob acts of violence and vandalism."[14]
- In Jefferson Country, Texas, a dozen sheriff's deputies use unmarked vehicles and a helicopter to arrest nude sunbathers on an isolated stretch of Bolivar Beach.[15]
- In New York City, officials try to stop photographer Spencer Tunick from photographing over 100 nude volunteer models. Police arrest the lensman for "promoting the exposure of a person." The city's legal case against the photographer ultimately collapses and Tunick re-assembles the nude group and takes the photos.[16]

American civil courts have ruled that public officials may be legally compelled to prohibit nudity on public property even where no legislation prohibits it, if sufficient numbers of local property owners are offended. The Oregon Court of Appeals held that extensive public nudity on beaches along the Columbia River managed by the State Department of Fish and

Wildlife constituted a nuisance to surrounding landowners. The mere sight of genitals was found to be so "intrusive" that the private owners were entitled to pursue their claim for an injunction against the State.[17]

Legal discrimination against nudists is common outside the U.S. as well. For example, in Brazil police suddenly began to enforce a vague law that they say prohibits female toplessness on public beaches. A national controversy ensued when a woman who refused to don a top at a beach in Rio was hauled off to jail by gun-toting police who then smashed her companion in the head with a club, all of which was caught on film by a national television network. The Roman Catholic Church supported the ban and the local Archbishop of Rio stated: "The human body is sacred. We cannot expose it for the purpose of sin."[18] Most Brazilians were horrified by the conduct of the police, not the sunbathers. After days of protests, politicians agreed to rescind the ban.

In Canada a sixty-four-year-old grandmother was convicted and jailed for baring her breasts at a municipal pool in Regina, Saskatchewan. Pool officials asked the woman to leave and when she refused she was arrested on "mischief" charges. The court ruled that the municipality had the right to enforce a topless prohibition that applies only to women.[19] In Toronto, Ontario twenty police officers arrested seven men for public nudity when they walked naked in the city's annual Gay Pride Day parade. The charges were later dropped when a prosecutor determined that no conviction was possible as the men were not totally naked during the parade—they wore shoes.[20]

I emphasize that these are only a few examples of the continual legal campaign in the modern world against nudity and topless females.

Phobic Motives

Attacks by parents and the law on social nudity would be sensible if anyone were harmed seeing genitals. But nothing supports that conclusion. Indeed exposure to nudity has beneficial effects, even to those who do not want to engage in it. It teaches about the diversity of the human body, helps de-eroticize genitals, and defuses genital phobia.

Genital purdah is largely the result of phobic attitudes towards nudity and genitals. Often the reasons given for enforcing genital purdah are exceptionally vague, revealing the signs of rationalizing. *Cosmopolitan* magazine conducted a survey on whether females should be allowed to go topless at public beaches.[21] Approximately 32% of the respondents said "no" for the following reasons:

AMY, 28, fashion assistant: "There's enough weirdness out there without throwing nudity into the mix."

TRACY, 34, flight attendant: "Women should be able to put up with a tiny piece of cloth for the sake of public decency."

MOLLY, 23, production coordinator: "Society's standards are permissive enough as they are. If anything, we should practice more restraint."

RUTH, 28, paralegal: "Public beaches aren't the Garden of Eden. It's bad enough to see women and worse—men—running around in thongs. Now they want it to be legal for women to go topless? You have to draw the line somewhere."

Indeed some people believe that allowing women to have the same right as men to bare their breasts in public undermines the status of women. A female broadcaster contends that going topless "devalues women" because it suggests "there is no particular beauty about their breasts or that female breasts have no unique function or purpose when compared to the male chest."[22]

The assumption that exposing breasts devalues their beauty or function is ludicrous; we expose our nose or hands, but that says nothing about our valuation of them. While exposing something expresses no negative message about it, hiding something does convey meaning. Concealment is a universal sign of devaluation, which is why the Bible records Adam and Eve as hiding the genitals when they felt genital shame.

Community Standards

Governments often try to justify nudity prohibitions on the basis of "community standards." The idea is a simple one, and is based upon the core democratic principle of majority rule. It holds that standards of public conduct are valid and proper as long as most people in the community support them. Because the majority of our community finds public nudity offensive, anti-nudity prohibitions are democratic.

The duty of tolerance

Though such ideas are very popular, they are based on a simplistic and thoroughly discredited theory of democracy. The concept of majority rule has long been tempered by another equally important democratic precept: the *duty of tolerance*. The concept of "live and let live" has been recognized for thousands of years, but it never emerged as a coherent ethical philosophy until the nineteenth century. Its classic expression is in *On Liberty* written in 1859 by the great English philosopher John Stuart Mill. The spur to the development of the philosophy of tolerance was the emerging multiculturalism of Europe, especially the rise of religious sectarianism flowing from the Protestant challenge to the overwhelming dominance of the Catholic Church. Ethical systems were relatively simple when there was only one moral authority, but a society of diverse and often contradictory moral perspectives required a new and more complex moral order.

Mill developed a supreme moral standard: the greatest good for the *whole society*, not just any temporary majority. Groups or individuals are free to craft moral rules to govern their *own* behavior, but they must not impose those moral rules on everyone in society unless such rules clearly benefit the collective interest of a nation of diverse moral viewpoints. Individual behavior can be prohibited by the state, but only if it clearly violates the interests of everyone, rather than the idiosyncratic morality of the majority. The duty of tolerance requires that individual behavior be free of social control unless it causes such real harm.

Mill was the first to clearly show how the duty of tolerance benefits everyone in the long term. By tempering the principle of majority rule, diverse groups can flourish; personal freedom is maximized yet everyone is protected against real harm. Tolerance secures the social stability that formerly had to be ruthlessly imposed by a dominant group or belief.

Thanks in part to the example of Nazi Germany, today no western culture recognizes majority opinion *per se* as a basis for social prohibitions.[23] The duty of tolerance is now enshrined in the ultimate moral document of western nations, their constitutions. The laws of most western nations forbid majorities from discriminating against anyone on the basis of race, religion, gender, and several other criteria. As Mill and other ethical theorists showed, such equality rights are a key part of the duty of tolerance, and the violation of such rights is always contrary to the long term collective interest.

Perhaps the most famous example of the duty of tolerance imposed on a large population is the action of the American Supreme Court in striking down racial segregation laws prevalent in many American states in the 1950s. Such laws enjoyed the mass support of the white population of most southern states. But the court struck down those laws because they violated the equality guarantees in the American Constitution and thus clearly harmed the common good. Today anyone proposing racist social policy on the grounds that local "community standards" supported it would be instantly and widely recognized as an enemy of democracy, even if a majority of the local community in fact favored such racist action.

Phobic community standards

Justifying nudity prohibitions on the basis of "community standards" violates the duty of tolerance because it allows the highly idiosyncratic sexual attitudes of a majority to be imposed on everyone in society. Nothing in the "community standards" doctrine requires that the majority's sexual morality be rational or clearly serve the long term collective interest. The test is simply whether *for any reason* a majority of the community opposes nude sunbathing in public. This is patently undemocratic.

Why is our society so much more inclined to respect the duty of tolerance in the realm of ethnic and religious expression, but not nudity? The answer must lie in the prevalence of genital phobia. Because racist and ethnic irrationality are less common than genital phobia in our culture, and because those prejudices are widely recognized to exist, community negativity aimed at racial or ethnic minorities is immediately suspect on democratic grounds. But the notion that an equivalent *genital* prejudice exists has almost no intellectual history. Further, the idea that masses of intelligent and educated citizens could harbor false beliefs about genitals and nudity is not easily accepted in a culture that claims to be enthusiastic about sex.

Further, as mentioned in Chapter 1, genital phobia impairs the ability to think clearly when genitals are in mind. Clear thinking is required to enforce the duty of tolerance. Our society recognizes the community standards doctrine as unethical with respect to religious or political expression, but not nudity. Erotophobia blinds the community to the ethical error inherent in the community standards doctrine.

The courts are a community's ultimate protection against its own irrationality, but when a community becomes infected with an irrational condition, its judges are likely to acquire it as well. For example, for over a century the American Supreme Court upheld overtly racist laws aimed at black people, notwithstanding that the American Constitution guaranteed equality for all. Judges eventually transcended their racism, but the modern judiciary has not yet been able to transcend its erotophobia.

But there are glimmers of change. In a case in Rochester, New York, several women who protested anti-nudity laws by removing their tops in a town park were successful in fighting anti-nudity charges. Two of the six justices of the appeal court ruled that long-standing stereotypical notions of the differences between the sexes simply could not serve as a rationale for a law prohibiting female toplessness. The court said that laws that reinforce "archaic prejudice" could not be used to protect public sensibilities.[24] However, elsewhere in America police continue to arrest women for topless protest activities.[25]

Opportunistic Motives

Purely opportunistic interests also prompt genital purdah. Parents sometimes demand that their children wear clothes simply to exert authority over them. Social dominance is powerfully expressed when underlings are forced to obey commands that make no sense. This is especially so when the prohibition involves denying subordinates control over their own bodies. Forcing children to wear clothes when they would rather be nude is a cogent sign of their powerlessness.

Attacking nudists also offers political rewards in a community hostile to nudity. At the very least, it gets the name of the anti-nudity activist in the news. In the above-mentioned arrest of nudists at Bolivar Beach in Texas, the local sheriff alerted the news media in advance, allowing him an on-camera photo opportunity.

In Canada, a politician who campaigned for new national laws to prohibit women from going topless in public, on the specious grounds that topless females "are harmful to children and could promote sexual assaults,"[26] earned headlines across the country. A church minister in Wisconsin whose followers blockaded a road leading to a nude beach received enormous publicity due to a statewide anti-nudity radio marathon. His opponents doubt that he was really agitated by public nudity, characterizing his action as a self-promotional stunt.[27]

More complex political motives also generate nudity prohibitions. Social nudity helps erode social boundaries. Clothes are powerful visible cues of social division: between the rich and the poor, the trendy and the unfashionable. Nudity is like a uniform, signaling the most inclusive of all forms of membership—our humanity. Yet this primal uniform is at the same time ultimately individualistic, revealing the very essence of our physical idiosyncrasies. Thus the shedding of clothes simultaneously promotes social equality and personal authenticity, a sense of community and a sense of individuality.

Those who favor a society based on roles and status will not be comfortable with social nudity—they recognize the egalitarianism in it. Such complex motives play a role in the hostility of elitist groups, such as the hierarchy of the Catholic Church, to earthy social nudism.

Phobigenic Effects

Genital purdah is highly phobigenic. For example, consider how parental intolerance towards social nudity produces genital *aversions*.

Psychologists have long recognized that emotions are contagious. Merely observing fear, laughter, or sadness in another person can elicit the same response in us, because we have the innate tendency to reflexively mimic the emotional responses we observe. We are especially likely to experience fear when we observe it in trusted caregivers such as parents. When we see our mother or father react with alarm at the sight of nudity, we will experience some of the same anxiety, and if that occurs repeatedly it will imprint an aversion to the sight of genitals. Psychologists call that process *observational conditioning*. It is so powerful that experts who have studied it advise parents who have strong fears or phobias to "avoid confronting their phobic object as much as possible in the presence of their children."[28]

Nudity prohibitions also promote genital *delusions* through the process of rationalizing. An easy way for children to make sense of constant parental negativity toward harmless nude play is to leap to the false conclusion that nudity is somehow harmful.

That phobigenic effect results even when parents have good reason to force clothes on their kids, such as to protect them from the intolerance of others. I recently observed such an event at a beach where a young mother was playing with her two young toddlers. An elderly man walked over and within earshot demanded that the children put on clothes. He claimed that allowing children to play in the nude was "immoral" and that he would call the police if they did not leave or put on clothes. In response the mother dressed the kids in bathing suits.

A child not permitted to frolic nude in a park because of the negativity of others will be influenced by the mother's capitulation. Unless the third party's harassment is identified as such, the mother's action communicates negative messages to the child about genitals and genital exposure. While children need to be aware that some people do react negatively to nudity, they also need to be told that the real problem is not nudity, but the phobic attitudes producing the negative response. Jewish parents in Nazi Germany had to teach their children an analogous lesson. The children knew that many Germans considered Jews offensive. But they also learned that the problem was not their Jewishness, but rather the prejudice of the Germans. Unfortunately, few children in our culture learn that attacks on nudity are motivated by a similar prejudice. Kids therefore blame nudity for the adult negativity, and thereby acquire the same phobic attitudes as their elders.

Criminalizing nudity also has powerful phobigenic effect. When the police swoop down and arrest nude sunbathers, or when criminal laws prohibit women from baring their breasts anywhere in public, they promote the self-deceptive rationalizing process in the minds of ordinary people. Virtually everything else the law prohibits is truly harmful; the legal harassment of nudists helps breed the false idea that somehow nudity causes harm. Whether caused by genuine erotophobia or purely opportunistic

interests, nudity prohibitions are an important part of the system generating irrational attitudes toward not only the exposure of genitals, but
also genitals *per se*.

As the concept of erotophobia is more widely understood the courts
will begin to apply the ethic of tolerance to protect recreational nudists.
Courts may well grant governments a transitional period during which
public recreational nudity will be gradually integrated into society, first
by designating large numbers of official clothing-optional areas (this has
occurred in a few areas in North America and is commonplace in Scandinavia), and ultimately by eliminating all legal restraints against hygienic
nude recreation.

Such action will help reduce genital phobia. Removing nudity laws
communicates the message that public nudity is harmless. Further, the
absence of nudity prohibitions allows nudity greater visibility in relaxed
public environments such as at the beach or a park, which will help defuse
phobic aversions and erase phobic beliefs. In the same way that we wonder today how generations of whites in the southern U.S. could have excluded black people from parks and universities, children who grow up
seeing nudity as normal and natural in public places will wonder how previous generations could ever have thought nudity offensive or somehow
morally dangerous.

4 / Genital Censorship

IN THE SAME WAY that genitals (and female breasts) are rarely visible in "real life," they are absent from the mainstream media. This chapter examines the enormous amount of negativity aimed at nudity *images*: depictions of nakedness and genitals in a *non-sexual* context, such as photographs of nude sunbathers, classic paintings of Adam and Eve, or anatomical illustrations. A later chapter discusses intolerance aimed at *sexual* images that are designed to elicit lust, such as pornography.

Harm Analysis

Exposure to in-the-flesh nudity causes no harm. Therefore, images of nudity cannot cause harm either, except in rare circumstances such as an explicit billboard that might attract the attention of drivers near a dangerous intersection. But very little of the negativity aimed at nudity images involves such exceptional circumstances.

The vast majority of nudity images not only do not cause harm, they have many social benefits. Nudity depictions in the mass media help expose the diversity of human body types, and especially genital types. By desensitizing us to the exposure of genitals, nudity images also reduce the potency of visual genital aversions. If such pictures were more prevalent in our homes, workplaces, art galleries, or streets, unhealthy genital aversions would be less common.

Images of nudity also help prevent the eroticizing of genitals. As discussed in Chapter 2, hiding genitals helps eroticize them, because most people see those organs only in erotic contexts, such as during lovemaking or while watching pornography. People conditioned in this way cannot remain relaxed and unaroused in the company of nude people. The more often genitals appear in the media outside a sexual context, the less we will associate those organs with sex.

Intolerance aimed at nudity images is itself harmful, amounting to intrusive meddling in the affairs of others. It also causes unhealthy stress. If you falsely believe that photos of breasts and genitals are harmful, you will be uncomfortable every time you see them. Such distress is dysfunctional; it can even threaten lives. Researchers at the University of Florida discovered that images of breasts often found in brochures describing breast self-exams interfere with the ability of many women to comprehend the accompanying written words. The researchers concluded that an erotophobic attitude toward images of breasts was the source of the problem, inhibiting women from getting the information they need to check for breast cancer. Women free of such fear valued the images as an important part of the information package.[1]

Intolerant reactions to the sight of harmless nudity images are not rare in our society, as the following examples show.

Informal Censorship

Self-censorship

We deliberately flee stimuli that disgust us. Many people know that they are distressed by images of genitals and breasts and hence consciously avoid them. Consider the response of a newspaper columnist in a suburban weekly who reports that one evening he and his wife were channel surfing and happened across a documentary on a women's television network showing average women talking about and revealing their breasts. "We didn't stick around to learn much about what the show was attempting to prove," the columnist reports, but he felt safe concluding that "such nudity reflects a decline in standards not only on TV but also in society as a whole."[2] His headline reads "Caution: channel surfing can be hazardous," and its caption proclaims: "TV immorality getting out of hand." Yet the columnist never describes the "hazard" such "immorality" causes.

This man obviously has an aversion to the very specific visual stimuli of naked breasts. Had the women in the documentary simply talked about their breasts and not exposed them, or displayed them covered with a bikini top, he would have ignored the show. He has no aversion to the sight of fully clothed women or of bikinis. He has no idea of his genital aversion, but he does know that he feels uncomfortable seeing breasts on television. To spare himself that stress he flees the show. Instead of acknowledging his reaction as purely emotional and subjective, he seeks to validate it with meaningless allegations of harm that are so vague they cannot be refuted. This allows him to maintain the illusion that his negative response is rational and valid. His phobic aversion remains undetected.

Children, too, engage in similar self-deception. I recently witnessed an example of this when I was walking along the street with a friend and her child. Through the window of an apartment we observed a large and prominently-lit painting depicting a reclining nude. The child covered his eyes with his hands, and then commented that the art was "sick." When I asked, "What type of sickness?" he replied: "The clothes-off disease."

Imposed censorship

Many parents censor their own access to nudity images and seek to deny their children the same. I recall such an incident from my childhood when a friend and I were seated at his kitchen table studying a photograph in a *National Geographic* magazine that depicted bare-breasted African tribal women and pubescent girls. My friend's mother snatched the magazine away and told us we had "dirty minds."

Because of the proliferation of the media today, censorious parents have a much tougher job. But technology can assist them. Software found in internet browsers and programs such as Cyber Patrol help parents control what their children view on the internet. The television V-chip, which the U.S. Federal Communications Commission requires as a standard feature in all new televisions with screens larger than thirteen inches, gives parents similar power. Such "blocking technology" is based on ratings of the content that media producers must provide. "Nudity," "female breasts," and "genitals" are always part of the ratings criteria.

The criteria of the Internet Content Rating Association, used by many web blocking devices, includes "genitals" and "female breasts" as suitable for censorship, even if depicted in art or a documentary and for purely scientific or educational purposes. The organization's website states:

> A parent can choose to allow "female breasts" in an artistic context, but block "erections" in an artistic context, thus allowing the *Birth of Venus* but blocking ancient, artistic depictions of erections.[3]

Private individuals also become informal agents of censorship when they complain to regulatory agencies and media organizations about harmless nudity images. Typically these busybodies say not only that *they* are offended by nudity, but also that such a response is the only natural and proper one. That was the argument of a man who complained to the U.S. Federal Communications Commission (F.C.C.) about a broadcast on two Michigan television stations of the Hollywood movie *Schindler's List*. A brief scene in the film about the Nazi holocaust showed full frontal nudity. The man wanted the F.C.C. to charge the television stations with a violation of its regulations against "indecent broadcasts." His complaint states: "There is nothing in human existence, short of death, severe injury, or legal obscenity that is more disturbing to the mind or emotions that [sic] the uninvited sight of adult frontal nudity."[4] To justify his own aversive reaction to frontal nudity the man leaps to the absurd idea that such a scene is innately disturbing. The F.C.C. ultimately dismissed his complaint.

Media Self-Censorship

While images of nudity are no longer completely absent from the media mainstream, they are still heavily censored. Consider several examples.

News media

Nudity is often in the news because events involving the naked body interest many people, even those who oppose nudity. When a nudity activist stages a public protest, when nudists begin frequenting a public beach, or when erotic art is publicly displayed, news reporters usually cover the story. Sometimes photographers accompany the reporters and capture film or video images of the newsworthy nudity. Yet the visuals that are published or broadcast rarely show genitals. The photographers design the shot so that pubic areas (or female breasts) are obscured by other parts of the body or objects. Or media editors simply conceal the erotic organs with digital "blurs" or black marks.

I saw a striking example of this type of news censorship in a tabloid newspaper on a recent trip to Mexico. One Spanish language paper in a line of many at a newsstand drew my attention because the front page had a large photo of the mutilated body of a teenage drug dealer, shot and tortured by a rival gang. I had never seen such explicitly gruesome material in any daily English language paper. But I was amazed at the sight of a much smaller picture on the same page of an unusual protest by striking street cleaners: they were naked. Their nudity garnered them front-page attention. When I looked carefully at the photo I observed that the crotch region of each of the protesters had been obscured behind a censorship bar, the patch newspapers usually use to conceal the eyes of people charged with but not convicted of a crime. The paper exposed the images of a mutilated body of a boy, but not images of healthy genitals—the appearance of which in the protest was the very reason the paper had covered the story.[5]

Similarly, photographs of nudity activists at nude beaches or swimming pools rarely reveal genitals or female breasts. Consider a few examples. A photo in a metropolitan newspaper shows an obviously naked man giving a speech at a beach, but conceals his genitals behind an informal podium.[6] Another photo from the paper shows a bare-breasted woman who favors being topless in public; the image conceals her breasts behind a censorship bar.[7] Interestingly, while images of women with their breasts exposed are still taboo in most newspapers, images of the breastless chests of women who have had mastectomies *are* sometimes displayed.[8] In the same national publication that shows such an image, editors digitally censored the penis in the photo of a male "streaker" running across the ice at a hockey game.[9] Even publications aimed at an alternative youth market, such as *Rolling Stone* magazine, are uncomfortable with genital images. In a photograph of members of the rock band Rage Against The Machine shown standing naked on a stage, a censorship bar conceals their genitals.[10]

Artistic representations of nudity also catch the eye of news media censors. Consider the *New York Times Magazine* story about "the last cool school in the art world," consisting of four so-called "Bad Girl" visual artists from New York with "sex on the brain." Accompanying the story are photos showing the work of each artist, but every photo is defaced with a huge censorship bar concealing genitals and breasts.[11]

Photojournalists are especially conscious of the media's appetite for guts and gore, yet also its antipathy to human erogenous zones. For example, news photographer Paul Watson was in Somalia during the skirmish involving U.S. helicopter gunships. An American airman was killed and his body was dragged around Mogadishu by an angry mob. The airman's underwear had been pulled to one side and his genitals were visible. The photographer took a series of six photos and his driver sped away. "I was sitting in the back of the car and realized that the first excuse any editor's going to use not to run these things is that his genitals are showing," he later told a magazine. The journalist risked his life returning to the mob to take another set of photos free of genital images. One of his shots earned him a coveted Pulitzer Prize.[12]

Genital censorship is especially common in the television news media. The Emmy-nominated series *The Human Sexes* hosted by Desmond Morris (author of *The Naked Ape*), which appeared on The Learning Channel, presents a serious discussion of sexual issues yet censors images of genital organs. One segment shows a man in the Philippines having plastic pellets implanted in his penis by an informal "backyard surgeon." (The man believed the operation would enhance his sexual appeal.) Even in this scientific, newsy context, the actual image of the penis is concealed behind a blurry digital veil.[13] The award-winning PBS investigative journalism show *Frontline* resorts to the same censorship. For example, its show on the American pornography industry masked images of frontal nudity.[14]

The censorship policies of television companies are a serious problem for producers of sexual documentaries. The Danish producers of *North of Eden*, a documentary about the sexual revolution in Scandinavia, had a tough sell at an international trade show because television executives from around the world objected to the full frontal nudity in the film. "You could almost hear the cheque books slam shut," is how a journalist described the reactions of potential buyers who saw a seven-minute video preview of the film.[15]

Examples of such overt censorship in the mainstream news media abound. Anyone who wants further evidence of the phenomenon will see it regularly on the television or in the press. Such censorship is more prevalent today than in the past, because nudity is becoming more common in public. In art, theater, movies, pranks, protests, and recreation, genitals and female breasts are appearing more frequently than ever before, and hence the news media has more nudity stories to cover. Ironically, genital censorship is more visible today than ever before.

Unethical censorship

The self-censorship by the news media violates the first principle of journalistic ethics: to "seek truth and report it," as the Code of Ethics of the Society of Professional Journalists describes it. The same code requires journalists to:

- never distort the content of news photos or video,
- tell the story of the diversity and magnitude of the human experience boldly, even when it is unpopular to do so,
- examine their own cultural values and avoid imposing those values on others.[16]

Similarly, the Code of Ethics of the Radio-Television News Directors Association requires journalists to "pursue truth aggressively and present the news accurately, in context, and as completely as possible" and to avoid techniques that "distort reality."[17]

The news media breaches these duties when it deliberately and openly conceals genitals. It denies its viewers access to the visual information that is usually the key reason the media covered the story. According to two media commentators, "A content-altered photograph with or without an explanatory caption is untruthful. Whether or not the reader is aware of the alteration doesn't matter because his judgment and perception of the photo is influenced and manipulated just the same." They add: "Any photojournalist who alters photos is not acting as a responsible steward of the freedom of expression."[18]

Further, defacement of genital imagery legitimizes the practice of censorship, which the free press has for centuries opposed. The black ink that defaces images in the *New York Times* and other publications is an advertisement for the propriety of hiding the truth, an idea no ethical journalist could favor. But perhaps worst of all, such censorship harms society by spawning yet another source of genital phobia.

Entertainment media

Prior to the 1960s, images of the human body rarely appeared in the mainstream entertainment media without a full set of clothes. That blanket censorship of the sight of human skin included all genital images, hence erotic organs were not specifically targeted for concealment. Today flesh is more openly exposed in the entertainment media, yet images of genitals still rarely appear, although female breasts sometimes do.

In prime time television shows such as *Baywatch*, actors often appear in skimpy bathing suits, but the pubic region is always concealed. In television hits such as *Friends* or *Seinfeld*, scenes occur in beds, baths, and showers, but erotic body parts are still unseen. Even late night television is squeamish about showing genitals. When *The Tonight Show with Jay Leno* scheduled the two men who perform the stage act *Puppetry of the Penis* to appear on the show, NBC executives prohibited the pair from performing their "genital origami", in which they stretch and twist their erotic parts to resemble real-life objects.[19]

The mainstream movie industry makes the same use of such censorship. The very popular "Austin Powers" comedy movies are filled with images of naked people, but their genitals are always concealed. The movie in fact mocks crotch censorship through an exaggerated use of it. Even film dramas about the pornography industry, such as *Boogie Nights* and *The People vs. Larry Flynt*, avoid any genital content. The former, set in the 1970s in California, tells the story of a young man who becomes a star in the X-rated film business. Given the subject matter, images of genitals and sex would seem to have a natural place in the story. But they are absent, except for a bizarre clip at the very end of the movie just before the credits roll, in which the lead actor drops his pants and an enormous penis appears – not a real penis, a plastic one. The image of a real flesh and blood phallus even in a movie about pornography is still taboo. *New York Times* critic Stephen Holden accurately identifies the final scene as "one of the saddest, most anti-sexual images ever filmed."[20] The movie about Larry Flynt is similarly lacking in genital images, except for a few brief shots of the pubic region of Flynt's wife, who is dead and submerged in the bathtub.

Such genital censorship in the movies is partly the result of the Hollywood ratings system. "Nudity," even in a non-sexual context, is one of the key criteria used to classify a movie. Generally speaking, the greater the exposure of genitals, the more restrictive the ratings classification. A movie rated G, which people of any age can view, must have no nudity at all, while only brief nudity scenes are allowed in PG (parental guidance suggested) and PG-13 (parents strongly cautioned).

Even niche cable and satellite services that advertise "uncensored" movies cannot resist the urge to censor genital images. The cable firm Trio touted June 2002 as "uncensored month," yet digitally concealed behind a "dancing red dot" the full-frontal nudity in Marlon Brando's film *Last Tango In Paris*.[21]

French Filmmaker Michel Ocelot knows well the aversion of the mainstream English-speaking media to nudity. He produced an animated feature *Kirikou and the Sorceress*, based on a West African tale. The film, meant for all ages, shows the female characters topless. Although his film was a success in France, Ocelot had trouble finding a distributor in the U.S. "It's about the breasts," he was told. Distributors urged him to cover the breasts of the African tribeswomen with "colorful bikinis," but Ocelot objected. "For me this is very discouraging because I think putting western clothes like brassieres and panties on these beautiful, natural bodies would have been obscene. And yet they tell me I'm obscene if I don't. This is crazy." The BBC also refused to show the movie because of the naked breasts.[22]

Advertising

Ads for perfume and fashion often display models who are completely or partially undressed. Yet their erotic organs are rarely visible, hidden by body positions or on-set props. Look at any fashion magazine and you will observe this pattern repeatedly. The human body is in full display, including even intimate details such as birthmarks, pores, and sweat, but the erogenous zones are never included as a result of genital censorship rules established by the advertising industry. In most developed countries advertisers must obey a formal code of ethics that regulates advertising content. The main purpose of these regulations is to protect the public from false or misleading claims, sexist and racist stereotypes, and other harmful messages. But the codes also regulate the "taste and public decency" of ads, and this opens the door to genital censorship.

For instance, the Canadian Code of Advertising Standards provides that advertisers must not "exploit sexuality" in a way which is "offensive to generally prevailing community standards." The private bureaucrats who enforce such standards have determined that almost any type of nudity image is "offensive," and deserves censorship. Even images merely suggestive of genitals rile the advertising censors. Consider their response to a complaint filed by a grand total of three people about a billboard advertisement showing a banana wrapped in partially unzipped denim jeans. The caption read "Manager Jeans. The only jeans with xxx-rated stitching." That ad appeared on billboards for three months in several cities. Thousands of people saw it. Three people complained. The enforcers of the advertising Code ruled that the ad "symbolically exploited sexuality in a manner offensive to prevailing standards."[23] Imagine the reaction of these censors if a real penis had been depicted.

The Motion Picture Association of America (MPAA) controls movie advertisements and frequently demands that posters and other ads delete images of erotic organs, or even replicas of them. The MPAA required the producers of the violent movie *Titus* to remove a faux nipple on the metal breastplate worn by Jessica Lange in a print ad.[24] Bus companies often prohibit nudity images appearing on ads on municipal buses.[25] Many websites have similar restrictions.

Some newspapers refuse ads for non-pornographic but genitally explicit movies. For example, the *Seattle Times* banned ads for the acclaimed Spanish film *Sex and Lucia*, which had received awards at the 2002 Seattle Film Festival. The ad was rejected solely because the *film* (not the ad) contained explicit content.[26]

An American supplier of bottled water aroused controversy when it placed a billboard in New York City showing a baby nursing at its mother's breast. Later it ran an ad in a magazine in Belgium that showed a naked baby boy urinating in the reader's direction. The ad caused no stir. The company decided not to run it in the United States. The firm's managing director explained, "What is seen as innocent and natural in Europe, we feared, would be denounced by some in America as child pornography . . . . In the United States, the problem is not that sex is pervasive—and it is—but that Americans refuse to see it in a positive light."[27]

Censorship Outside the Media

Schools and colleges

Nudity images have important educational value. Yet often school and college officials attempt to exclude such material from handbooks, texts, and displays, denying students access to the information such images contain. For example, art gallery staff report that when nude paintings are exhibited on their walls, teachers sometimes deliberately route their tour of the gallery to avoid exposing such images to their students.[28] Consider a few other recent examples of similar action.

The Texas Board Of Education, which buys all high school texts for school students in that state, demanded changes to a health handbook produced by publisher Holt, Rinehart and Winston. The board wanted the publisher to delete several clinical illustrations, including one showing a self-examination for testicular cancer. Publishers usually cooperate with the Board in the production of school texts because the Texas market is huge, and once texts are approved there, they are marketed nation-wide. However, in this case Holt courageously refused, contending that the proposed changes "are potentially injurious to the students of Texas."[29]

In Lynchburg, Virginia, the local school board ordered a page removed from a science textbook because it had an illustration of a vagina. A committee of parents, teachers, and students had earlier approved the book. One member who supported the censorship said the issue was "appropriateness and modesty." But the decision was widely attacked. The local newspaper called the action "a textbook case of sexphobic censorship." Over 100 parents and other interested citizens attended a school board meeting and eventually the Board voted 5-4 to approve the book.[30]

In Muskogee County, Georgia, a school superintendent ordered the removal of the pages in an elementary school text showing a reproduction of the classic painting of George Washington crossing the Delaware River.[31] The official fretted that a young mind might see in Washington's ruffled clothing something resembling a penis. School workers spent weeks removing pages from the text. The president of the local parent-teacher group supported the move, saying the illustration could elicit an inappropriate reaction from fifth graders. Anti-censorship groups were appalled; the deputy legal director of People Of the American Way urged the superintendent to "go to the blackboard and write 2,300 times, 'I will not deface textbooks.'"[32]

The chair of the Ethnic Studies Department removed from a public display at the University of California at Berkeley, the cover of a book showing an artistic collage of a car, bear, man, truck stop sign, and the back of a naked body of a person of unknown gender. The cover had been displayed for months until five students complained about the abstract nude figure. The department chair withdrew it, saying, "I too am sick of naked ladies—and men, for that matter—in the media."[33]

High school officials are also big fans of censorship whenever a female breast or genital appears in student art. Officials in upstate New York prohibited nude drawings in the annual student art show, but when the artists put black strips over the breast and genital areas, the drawings were allowed. "Schools expect opposition to anything remotely off-center. It's become the nature of society, not just here," said one of the student artists.[34] In another similar case, teachers near Chicago ordered the removal of a self-portrait by a high school student that exposed her left breast. When the artist concealed that area of the painting with a fluorescent green patch, the administrators relented. "Censoring me was a ridiculous act, so I countered with an equally ridiculous act," the artist explained.[35]

Employers

Laws aimed at prohibiting "sexual harassment" in the workplace have enabled many attacks on nude images. Some employees claim that simple nudity in photos, art, or cartoons is offensive or bothersome in some way and that posting such images on walls or cubicles at the office or factory constitutes sexual harassment. Because the legal definition of "sexual harassment" is unclear, employers often react to such complaints by removing the offending nude image. One of the most famous examples of such a reaction occurred at Penn State University.

A female professor demanded that Goya's *Naked Maja* be removed from her classroom: "I felt as though I were standing there naked, exposed and vulnerable . . . . After my initial embarrassment passed, I became angry because I knew none of my male colleagues would ever find themselves in a similar situation, nor would the male students in the class." University officials agreed that the painting created a "chilly climate" and thus could be considered harassment. The painting was removed. After much controversy, the art department reinstated the image.[36] The case highlighted the chilling effect not of classic nude art, but rather sexual harassment law.

A civic employee in Murfreesboro, Tennessee, complained that a painting hanging in the City Hall was sexually harassing. The city took the painting down because the city attorney believed the city had to comply with sexual harassment law: "I feel more comfortable siding with protecting the rights under the Title VII sexual harassment statutes than I do under the First Amendment," the attorney said. "We wouldn't permit that type of drawing or picture to hang in the fire hall. As far as I'm concerned, a naked woman is a naked woman."[37]

Public agencies
Many visual artists find the naked body a fascinating subject, hence paintings and photos of nudity are a common product of art studios everywhere. But, though regularly produced, nude art is far less commonly displayed, because nudity images often generate controversy when they appear in public. Consider some recent examples.

American Senators have banished nude art from the walls of the Russell Senate Office Building rotunda. The lawmakers refused to allow a collection of nudes in an art show dealing with people who have orthopedic conditions. Senator Mitch McConnell (R-Ky.) imposed the ban because, as a member of his office told one of the artists: "A lot of adults might not appreciate being put in the position of having to explain what's in the artwork."[38]

In Erie, Pennsylvania, a theater displayed an exhibition of the work of local artists for the opening of the Erie Philharmonic's new season. One of the paintings depicted a naked man. The executive director of the philharmonic removed the watercolor at a rehearsal because the opening was a "family event" and he was "protecting the interests of the Philharmonic and the people that come here." He allowed three works depicting female nudity to stay. A group of artists protested the censorship, but the result of the incident was a future ban on all nude work. "What we didn't do was say at the start that there could be no nudity. In the future, we'll be stating that up front," said the philharmonic director.[39]

In Springfield, Illinois, managers of the state fair removed a painting by a local Cuban-American artist. It showed a nude woman descending a staircase with her arms cradled as if holding a baby, and another woman ascending the stairs with a baby in tow, apparently pulled by its umbilical cord. The state fair bureaucrats defended their decision to pull the painting: "Families with small kids could have brought up some question that they may not have been ready to answer or really want to answer at days at the fair." Governor George Ryan supported the move: "It might be all right in an art institute—some place where adults go. But this is where families and kids go." The painter was appalled by the move: "It is ironic to me that people from Cuba came to the United States to be able to express themselves through their artwork, and here in the U.S. I'm being told that I can't express myself."[40]

The Police

Until the modern era, law enforcers often targeted art and photos depicting non-sexual nudity. As late as the 1960s the American Post Office refused to handle magazines for homosexuals containing images of naked men.[41] Today, nudity images are far less likely to attract the attention of a legal official unless they depict children without clothes. While the police sensibly attack images depicting nude children performing sexual acts, they also seize images simply because nude children are depicted. The problem arises because statutes aimed at child pornography are vaguely worded. American law defines "child pornography" to include "lascivious exhibition of the genitals or pubic area."[42] Because the concept of "lascivious" is vague, while the term "exhibition of the genitals" is clear-cut, the practical test to determine "child pornography" used by police officers, child-welfare officials, and lab technicians is simply to look for images of genitals plus anything slightly unusual. There are many recent examples. Consider some of them.

In Montclair, New Jersey, police charged a sixty-five-year-old social worker and doting grandmother with "endangering the welfare of a child" when an employee at a film processor found images of her naked granddaughters, ages three and eight. The photos showed the two girls dancing around the bedroom, totally unembarrassed. Police arrested her, searched her home, and seized her computer. Her employer, the local school system, immediately suspended her. "Yes, the kids were nude," she told the *New York Times*. "I didn't have sexual intent. It never entered my mind that I shouldn't take these pictures." The local police chief said that though the photos were not pornographic, they were "provocative," and commented, "I wouldn't pose my children like that." A woman who knew the accused for nearly five decades described her as an overprotective grandmother, someone incapable of exploiting her granddaughters for profit or titillation. "These allegations are absurd," the friend said. No trial or conviction ever occurred because the grandmother reluctantly agreed to a year of probation. She was angry about the emotional and financial costs of the ordeal. "I'm going to be paying for this for the rest of my life."[43]

A mother in Ohio with a penchant to document the life of her child in photos discovered the same scary reach of child pornography laws. A photo lab developed images of her eight-year-old daughter rinsing off her genital area with a shower spray. Police were called and the mother was charged. Prosecutors and a grand jury said the photos were "lewd," to which one of the mother's friend's commented: "Only someone with the most contaminated imagination could construe these as pornographic." Ultimately, charges against the mother were dismissed, but only after she agreed to have the photos destroyed, take counseling on sexuality, and demonstrate an understanding of what constitutes sexually-oriented material. The case prompted the Thomas Jefferson Center for the Protection of Free Expression to give to the prosecutor in the case the "Jefferson Muzzle" award for censorship.[44]

In Ottawa, Canada, police charged a father with making child pornography when photo lab employees discovered four nude photos of his four-year-old son. One shows the boy crouching with his buttocks towards the camera. Child protection authorities removed his two children from his home, but then returned them to the custody of his wife on condition that he move out. Ultimately the police dropped the charges because there was no reasonable chance of conviction. His lawyer called the police action "hysterical and exaggerated…. My client suffered great public embarrassment, while nobody took a sober second look at what was happening."[45]

The giant Wal-Mart retail chain refuses to develop any photos containing nudity in any context, adult or child. But they will snitch to police when they find photos of near-naked children. For example, managers in a Kansas store called the cops after developing photos depicting a three-year-old girl playing topless in the family's kiddie pool with her father. Police detained and then released the mother of the child and never laid charges. The mother sued the retail giant for invasion of privacy.[46]

Censorship Motives

Erotophobia is a key cause of genital censorship. The visual genital aversion plays an important role and is revealed when people react to the very specific stimuli of genitals or breasts and when they cannot explain that response.

For instance, ponder the case of a manager for Coca-Cola who posted nude photos of himself on the internet. His website did not refer to his employer. The images violated no law. Janet Parshall, author, broadcaster, and policy analyst for the Family Research Council, a conservative think tank, attacked both the employee's action and the company's refusal to discipline him. "This man stepped into the public in this way to get a response. That is deviant behavior…. The dollar is a very effective tool and if a corporation turns a blind eye and deaf ear to morality, people will walk away. As a consumer I would run from a product knowing that this is not the kind of corporation to support with my money. It's called trickle-down morality."[47]

One would think that a policy analyst for a think tank could provide some cogent reason to support the boycott of a company that tolerated its employees performing lawful behavior on their own time. But she does not. She simply bandies vague terms such as "deviant" and "morality" and assumes that they are sufficient to justify her intolerant response.

A child psychologist who commented on the same case reveals similar psychology. He says, "What this guy is doing is irresponsible. It's not like he is going into his bedroom and pulling the shades. Certain jobs and professions have greater responsibility. When you are exposing yourself to the world there is something wrong."[48] Note again the extraordinary vacuity in the definition of harm. The psychologist obviously *feels* strongly against the Cola-Cola employee, but cannot articulate rational grounds for his subjective emotional response.

These same phobic attitudes affect many media managers, educators, police officers, and public officials. Editors at the *New York Times* say that they forbid nudity images in part because the newspaper is "widely read in schools and at the family breakfast table."[49] The inference is that they believe the sight of a breast or genital is somehow harmful to children, a patently false notion.

Most censors of nudity images are not prepared to admit that their subjective feelings or beliefs are the source of the nudity ban. More often they justify their censorship on the perceived hostility *of others* to genital imagery. But even this justification usually lacks evidence. Genital censors often imagine that some audience would be offended.

This was the case when Canadian advertising censors ordered the removal of a billboard image of a banana in jeans. They admitted they could only guess at "community standards." They concluded that the billboard in that case violated these standards, even though thousands of people had seen the display and only three complained. Such evidence would seem to indicate that the ad in question did not violate community standards, yet the advertising censors concluded precisely the opposite.

Similarly, classifying Hollywood movies under the MPAA ratings occurs without testing actual public opinion. The chair of the classification agency says: "We make an educated estimate as to what most parents think. It is not clear like in the old days when one nipple was an R . . . . But the system does have consistency: we judge films according to what we think most parents feel."[50]

Censors easily miscalculate community attitudes because the only people motivated to publicly comment when nudity images are displayed are those who react most negatively, and their complaints to media managers, police officers, or politicians can severely distort the perception of actual community opinion. For example, editors at *The Virginian-Pilot*, a newspaper in Norfolk, Virginia, ran a photo of a naked man mowing his lawn. The naked yard work landed the clothing-optional activist in court with a charge of indecent behavior. Sixty irate readers of the paper complained about the photo. Faced with this barrage of protest, the editors might have concluded that the community opposed the nudity image, but they decided to conduct a poll on the issue, logging over 4000 calls to their telephone information service! Most of the readers—65%—in fact were not offended, though over 1,500 did support the original sixty complainers.[51]

Because nobody protests the *absence* of nudity images, media managers will capitulate to intolerant complainers. Even after the editor of *The Virginian-Pilot* determined that the majority of the community supported his decision to publish the nude photo, he said he would run a smaller picture of the nudist if the situation occurred again.

Although the main motive behind the censorship of nudity images is genital phobia, non-phobic motives also play a role, and the censorship policies of the *New York Times* provide a good example. When I asked executives of the *Times* to explain their prohibition of genital imagery, they indicated their desire to maintain the "character" of the paper, and referred me to a passage from the *New York Times Manual of Style and Usage* which states: "The *Times* differentiates itself by taking a stand for civility in public discourse, sometimes at an acknowledged cost in the vividness of an article or two, and sometimes at the price of submitting to gibes."[52]

If genitals and images of genitals are perceived as something disgusting and illegitimate, then a newspaper that censors genital images will indeed be perceived as having "character." But to any non-erotophobic editor or community, the overt censorship of genital images is a sign of poor journalistic character, a breach of elementary news media ethics. Further, regardless of the motive for such antisexualism, it causes real harm by reinforcing irrational attitudes to nudity images, nudity, and genitals.

Censorship Causes Genital Phobia

Surveys indicate that we tune in to media for fully one half of our discretionary time.[53] In the average American household the television is on for approximately 7.5 hours per day.[54] Nobody in our culture fails to recognize that nudity images are deliberately censored in the media. From a young age children observe images about all aspects of life, except human erotic organs. The censorship of erotic body parts is so ordinary and common that it goes unquestioned.

All of this has significant phobigenic effect. Most people make sense of the constant censorship of nudity images by rationalizing, inventing false ideas to explain the prevalent censorship. When schools disapprove of illustrations of genital self-examinations, when arts administrators remove nude art from walls, when police arrest parents simply for taking photos of their own naked children, negative conclusions about genitals and genital images are inevitable.

Consider also the phobigenic effect of "warnings" about nudity images commonly issued by the entertainment media. Any warning implicitly conveys the idea that the subject of the warning is somehow alarming or dangerous. Imagine if the media warned viewers that a show contained images of "Jews" or "Hispanics." The racist message is obvious, and any intelligent person would object to such a warning. But in our culture the same harmful warning targets harmless nudity, yet virtually nobody protests. Under the guise of helping children, phobic attacks on nude imagery actually harm young people, infecting a new generation with genital phobia. These phobigenic effects reinforce those flowing from fig-leafing and genital purdah.

While no one incident of such intolerance may amount to much, its constancy and consistency effect a brainwashing that no totalitarian regime could match. Amazingly, this occurs completely unconsciously. Champions of freedom subvert their cherished principles yet fancy they are doing good.

Constitutional rights to free expression are available only when a *government* agency attempts censorship. In the modern era, the state only rarely attacks nudity images. Most censorship of that kind is imposed by the private sector, mainly private media. Its end will come sooner if people who recognize such intolerance make their voices heard. As long as media managers and other decision-makers hear few protests about their genital censorship, yet receive a barrage of complaints when the rare nudity images do appear, genital censorship will continue.

Pandering to irrational prejudice is never a proper response for an ethical media executive. Some principles are higher than mere self-interest or pleasing an audience. That is why advertising codes prohibit racist or sexist advertising, even if the local community wants such content. In time, the codes of media organizations will recognize that censoring genital images has the same harmful effects as racist and sexist content, and will ban such censorship too.

5 / Lust Phobia

THE ENGLISH LANGUAGE lacks a single term for the somatic dimensions of sex, such as the itch of sexual desire, the tension of full-blown sexual arousal, and the release of orgasm. To abbreviate the discussion I refer to all such experience as lust. Although that word often refers just to sexual desire, I take poetic license to use it in a broader sense, to include the full spectrum of sexual sensation.

Lust is innately pleasurable. Our genes want us to reproduce and thus have programmed us to enjoy the sensations of sex. Ask most people whether they find sex pleasurable and they will answer, "Of course!" Yet I intend to show that most of us are comfortable with only a narrow range of sexual feeling. Outside that comfort zone the sensations of sex prompt fear, which I call lust phobia. It is one of the most important types of erotophobia, similar to but more complex than the genital phobia discussed in the previous four chapters.

Lust Aversions

Even though we are innately attracted to sexual sensation, we can acquire phobic aversions to it. Such learning occurs when we simultaneously experience sexual arousal and high trauma. For example, victims of sexual assault often experience sexual sensations during the attack, and many will acquire aversions to the very feel of sex. Similarly, parental negativity toward masturbation causes many children to feel shame during their autoerotic play. The constant pairing of sexual charge and low-level upset is conducive to an aversion to the very feel of sexual sensation. Intolerance aimed at "playing doctor," teen sexual experimentation, homoerotic activity, and other types of sexual play have the same phobigenic effect. Noted sex therapist Helen Singer Kaplan says, "In our sexually ambivalent society, such negative associations are likely to be repeated on countless occasions, which leaves few of us entirely free of sexual conflict."[1] Yet because this phobigenic conditioning process is both commonplace and unconscious, we have trouble accepting the idea that lust aversions are prevalent.

The lust aversion is also the product of rigid personality traits, a complex process that is the subject of Chapter 15. Individuals with such personality traits might never have been raped, or punished for youthful sex play, yet will still acquire the lust aversion as a by-product of their rigidity.

Lust Delusions

Lust phobia also includes delusions, which were more openly expressed in the past than in the present day. For instance, great thinkers in many historical traditions have denigrated sexual desire. Plato in *The Laws* expresses the belief that the world would benefit if the sexual impulse was starved.[2] St. Augustine exalted the "chaste majesty of continence" and referred to sexual desire as "evil."[3] Martin Luther said that intercourse was "horribly marred" by "the hideousness inherent in our flesh, namely the bestial desire and lust."[4] Immanuel Kant believed that sexual desire was innately degrading: "That is why we are ashamed of it, and why all strict moralists, and those who had the pretensions to be regarded as saints, sought to suppress and extirpate it."[5] Modern philosophers recognize these ideas as devoid of ethical validity.[6]

Another common lust delusion holds that lust is "unspiritual." The idea is that sexual experience distracts us from the religious path, which is superior to any path involving sex. This fallacy is perhaps most openly expressed in India and motivates the Hindu concept and practice of brahmacharya, of which Gandhi was the most famous modern proponent. The idea is not that sex is inherently evil, as some Christian philosophers contend, but that "if energies are to be moved in one direction they should not be sent flowing, at the same time, in another," says a famous student of Indian philosophy, Heinrich Zimmer.[7]

The notion that sex is inherently incompatible with spiritual development has no rational support. While periods of sexual abstinence, like periods of fasting, can provide powerful spiritual insights for some people, there is no evidence to suggest that sexual experiences interfere with the spiritual growth of all people all the time. The error of brahmacharya or any other tradition that denies the spirituality of sexuality flows from its overgeneralism. Cross-cultural evidence shows that sexual expression can be a tool of spiritual development and that sex is not inherently unholy. Tantrism and Taoism recognize sexual expression as worthy of the same deliberate cultivation and delight as any other part of God's creation,[8] and a burgeoning literature from the Christian perspective accords sexual pleasure a central position in its spiritual ethic.[9]

Another common lust delusion is the idea that sex is by nature uncontrollable and barbaric. Ascetics of all stripes are vigorous proponents of this view. Thus in the culture of the desert fathers of the early Christian tradition, male sexuality was considered a volcano ready to erupt with the slightest provocation. Peter Brown, the leading expert on early Christian sexuality, gives an example of such an attitude. "For a nun to simply pat the foot of an elderly, sick bishop was considered enough provocation to cause both of them to fall instantly into fornication."[10] Some people do experience their sexuality as disruptive. Some people may even be described as sex addicts. But the idea that sexuality is a demonic force within everyone is simply false.

Today most lust delusions are far more vague than those just mentioned. They consist of highly inarticulate ideas that sex is "bad" or "immoral" or "dirty." How do all such notions get into the heads of intelligent people?

Causes of lust delusions

The most direct way we acquire these beliefs is through exposure to the lust delusions of people we respect. A person who venerates the great Christian philosopher St. Augustine, who taught that sexual desire is inherently illicit, is apt to be influenced by such ideas. If you revere Gandhi as a modern saint and listen as he advises that we must choose between sex and spiritual development, you are more likely to perceive lust as a threat to God.

Lust delusions are also the product of rationalizing the negative feelings prompted by the lust aversion. Recall that scientists have discovered that humans have an innate tendency to fabricate the idea that something is dangerous merely because it provokes our fear. We can make sense of an aversive response to the very feel of sex by imagining that such sensations are somehow immoral or impure, or that they are inherently unspiritual or uncontrollable. Because few people are conscious of their lust aversions, they never imagine that a primitive emotional program prompts their anxious reaction to sex. So they invent seemingly logical reasons to justify their fear.

Observing social negativity aimed at sex is also conducive to lust delusions. The natural inference to be drawn from the hostility of religions, the law, and most ordinary people to a vast range of lustful expression is that lust is somehow illicit. A child who never hears his or her parents discussing sex, who never sees sex, who is attacked for sexually experimenting with peers, is bound to conclude "sex is bad."

Lust delusions are also a product of observing a recurring *pattern* in social responses to sex: the greater anything elicits lust, the more intensely it is attacked. Fore example, such a pattern is clearly evident in legal and corporate sex censorship policies. The more openly any sex image depicts sexual arousal or pleasure, the more likely the law or private media companies will censor it. The image of a man in the distance lying naked on a beach attracts one level of censorship, while the close-up image of his erect penis will attract more. A "cum-shot" photo of his ejaculating penis will attract the most censorship of all. Anyone producing sexually explicit media is intimately familiar with such patterns of sexual negativity.

The same antisexual pattern is readily observable in the conduct of most individuals. Listen carefully when people talk about sex and you will observe greater and greater discomfort the more sexual pleasure or arousal enters the discussion. Teenage males, for example, are far more likely to talk about sex as "conquest" or "scoring" than about the physical gratification in the act. Teenage females are likely to discuss the relational significance of sex, rather than how wet their vaginas get when they are aroused. Absent from their world is what one sex researcher aptly calls the "discourse of desire."[11]

Most of us are familiar with such a pattern, although we often recognize it unconsciously, the same way we recognize grammatical rules without being aware of them. Observing the constant subtle negativity aimed specifically at lust, we cannot avoid internalizing the vague idea that the sexual part of ourselves is illicit.

Effects of Lust Phobia

Cognitive corruption

Anxiety numbs the mind. In the same way that genital phobia undermines the ability to think clearly about genitals and genital visibility, lust phobia prevents rational thought about sex. A great mind like Kant uttered nonsense about sex probably because he harbored unconsciously conditioned aversions towards it. Kant lived a long life, but died a virgin. He philosophized about sex, but never had any actual experience of it. The result is very bad philosophy about sex.

If sex anxiety can cripple great minds, it must have an even greater impact on the cognitive abilities of normal people. Lust phobia has impaired our entire culture's ability to think about sex. As the sexual historian Paul Robinson explains, "In fact, throughout most of European and American history, sexual 'thinking' has amounted to little more than an assortment of popular prejudices, sometimes codified by medical authorities or exploited by pornographers, but rarely achieving the coherence and dignity that one associates with the word 'thought'."[12] Racist prejudice has the same effect on the minds of racists. They cannot think clearly about racial minorities and fall prey to ludicrous racist beliefs.

Shame and anxiety

While the lust aversion prompts fleeting primal responses like instant fear or offense, lust *delusions* produce much more complex and lasting emotional states. The most important of these is a sense of *shame*, the feeling that the lustful part of the self is bad or harmful. If, for instance, you hold the idea that sexual desire is inherently "illicit" or "bad," you cannot help but devalue your own erotic desires. Such shame is prevalent in all corners of the world. The International Reproductive Rights Research Action Group recently conducted surveys in seven countries in Asia, Africa, the Middle East, and the Americas, and found that a majority of women everywhere believe that to express a need for sexual satisfaction, much less a right to it, is shameful.[13]

While society has an interest in generating shame in the minds of people who cause real harm, shame about lust *per se* is a social scourge. A rich modern literature describes in detail the harmful psychological and social effects of any type of irrational shame. It damages an individual's self esteem and causes an array of self-destructive behaviors, such as unsafe sexual practices, alcohol and drug abuse, workaholism, consumerism, and social conformity.[14]

Many people plagued with lust phobia experience great shame about their sexual lives but still indulge in sex. Consider the enormous anxiety about masturbation. Surveys indicate that half of the Americans who engage in the act feel guilty about it.[15] Unlike virtually any other sexual act, masturbation has no purpose other than stimulating lust; the prevalence of negativity toward solo sexuality reveals the prevalence of lust phobia.

Shame about sexual desire and pleasure exaggerates the significance of lust, which in turn can give rise to the delusion that human sexuality is uncontrollable. American sex researchers John Gagnon and William Simon contend that sex anxiety causes most of us to overestimate our sex drive:

> [T]here is little evidence that there has been any reduction in the anxiety associated with masturbatory practices by the young who are beginning their sexual lives. Indeed, it is possible to hypothesize that it is the existence of this anxiety about masturbation that supports our experiential belief that the sexual drive is one of extreme potency. We presume that we are experiencing a biologically powerful experience when in fact it is the guilt and anxiety associated with arousal identified as sexual which is provoking our sense of intensity. We mislocate the source of the intensity, attaching it to a bodily state rather than to the psychological states that accompany the physical experience.[16]

When lust phobia takes root in our youth, the erotic shame it causes is not easily escaped. According to sex therapist Lonnie Barbach, this is a serious problem for women:

> Somehow, after years of practice at turning off sexual feelings both outwardly and inwardly, each of us is supposed to miraculously

emerge as a turned-on passionate woman when a legitimized adult sexual relationship materializes. Sally, one of the [sex therapy] group members, realized that she desired sex more and felt more sensations at sixteen than she did ten years later when she entered the group . . . . Even if our initiation into sex occurred on the wedding night, totally sanctioned by society and our parents, it may not have been easy to erase all the earlier negative messages that kept us anxious, uptight, and over-controlled.[17]

Similarly, women guilty about sex are reluctant to willfully engage in it, and require their partners to overwhelm them, a very common phenomenon which author Carol Cassell discusses in detail in *Swept Away*.[18]

This shame shows up in the content of female sexual fantasies. Author Nancy Friday conducted extensive research into such erotic daydreams and discovered that they are heavily infused with domination and abuse. Women fantasize about being sexually violated because it allows them access to pleasure without admitting that they are "bad." As Friday writes in the 1998 introduction to *My Secret Garden*, "The rape fantasy fools them into thinking the loss of control isn't their fault." Friday holds that this fear of sex is as alive today as a generation ago:

What tribute to the power of the unconscious that in the day of the internet, of pornographic videos, not to mention of the erotic assaults on the television, that with all this seeming permission, there is still a nay-saying voice that requires answering before we can reach orgasm.[19]

Professor Mary Krueger, author of a study of the sexual attitudes of teen girls makes a similar point:

Once girls reach adolescence, the messages not to allow themselves to become sexually aroused, or to acknowledge or act in response to arousal, are ubiquitous and powerful. Deborah Tolman, a member of the Harvard project on the Psychology of Women and the Development of Girls, found that adolescent girls internalize erotophobic scripts to such a degree they are unable to "admit" even to physiological indices of sexual arousal, much less the psychological experience of sexual desire.[20]

Inhibition

Lust phobia provokes various forms of antisexual inhibitions. The most extreme form is complete celibacy. For example, because of Christian teaching during periods of western history, sex became so disgusting to large numbers of both single and married people that they renounced sexual relations.[21] But even when people have sex, lust phobia undermines its passion and intensity. By keeping arousal levels low, an individual averse to lust obtains some of the benefits of sex, especially the social rewards, but avoids provoking the lust aversion. Stella Resnick, author of *The Pleasure Zone* contends that most of us suffer from this sexual syndrome, which she calls "pleasure-anxiety": an unconscious fear of being overwhelmed by sexual excitement. She says, "Most of the time we may not be in touch with our pleasure barriers because, generally, we don't go anywhere near the intensity of pleasure that would test our limits."[22]

There are many ways of minimizing the pleasure in sex. One way is to focus on the non-erotic dimension of the experience, such as the physical intimacy or the sensual rather than sexual sensations arising from cuddling and other close contact. Another way is to perform sex for entirely non-sensual reasons, such as to consummate a marriage, reproduce, affirm one's attractiveness, or earn money. By focusing on the valued outcome, and not the aversive sensations, we avoid discomfort. Sexual philosopher Russell Vannoy notes, "Each of these instrumental uses of sex is perfectly compatible with the disdain of the sex act itself at least in its physical sense."[23] Sado-masochistic sex offers similar benefits to a person with lust phobia, focusing attention on pain and the "head-trip" of s/m protocols, and away from the fearful rush of sexual pleasure.

Another form of phobic inhibition is to keep erotic encounters brief. Most people in western culture devote little time to sex. Kinsey's survey of the sexual habits of Americans reported, "For perhaps three-quarters of all males, orgasm is reached within two minutes after the initiation of the sexual relation."[24] In Britain doctors say that three minutes is the average length of time from penetration to orgasm.[25] Lust phobia helps make sex a rush to its endgame, without pausing to indulge in the passion that precedes release and promotes a very common male sexual problem, premature ejaculation.

A publication in the *Journal of the American Medical Association*, based on a carefully conducted national survey of over 300 people aged eighteen to fifty-nine, reveals that 43% of women and 31% of men had a sexual dysfunction over several months in the previous year. The most common problem reported was a lack of interest in sex.[26] A large majority of men report more occasional worries about their ability to have or maintain an erection. As male sexuality expert Bernie Zilbergeld concludes: "There's nothing abnormal or unusual about men being anxious about sex."[27]

By inhibiting the passion in sex, lust phobia helps make it boring and routine. David Snarch, author of *Passionate Marriage*, says: "After talking with thousands of people at public presentations and professional workshops, while teaching medical school, and during two decades of clinical practice, I've concluded that lots of people are bored and frustrated with their sex life."[28] *Time* magazine says, "The sex lives of most Americans are about as exciting as a peanut-butter-and-jelly sandwich."[29] Dr. Jean Marmoreo writes in a regular column on the lifestyles of people at mid-life, "The fact that many of my patients are having sex once a year (that is correct—once a year) so terrifies them that they're too paralyzed to even talk about it with me."[30] The late sex researcher Seymour Fisher reports: "[M]ost couples settle into a rather inhibited sexual state."[31]

The notion that ours is a sexually hedonistic culture is clearly a myth. Lust phobia helps marginalize our sexuality, pushing it outside the mainstream of our lives.

Social antisexualism

If you harbor delusions that lust is inherently sinful you will likely not want other people to experience it, just as you would not want them to be greedy or dishonest. Lust phobia also motivates attacks on the people who wantonly elicit lust for profit or attention. Prostitutes, pornographers, and even scantily-clad pedestrians attract the scorn of those who fear carnal desire.

As I discuss in later chapters, much more specific phobias pertaining to specific types of sexual expression can also motivate similar negativity toward such people. For example, *prostitution phobia* prompts opposition to sex workers, and *homophobia* prompts attacks on gays. But the same negativity can also be the product of a much more generic hostility toward lust *per se*.

A case in point is the law against prostitution. In much of the world a prostitute commits no crime if he or she confines the physical contact to non-genital areas, such as legs, face, or arms. No crime is committed when a prostitute puts a diaper on a client and lashes him (consensually) with a whip. Only when *genital pleasure* enters the transaction do the police intrude. To our legal system, the very worst part of the commercial sex is genital pleasure *per se*. Lust phobia is behind this irrational social policy.

Similarly, anyone harboring lust phobia will favor prohibitions against the mere visibility of sex. Recall that our emotional brain tends to mimic the reactions we observe in others, which is why we often feel sad when we observe another's grief, or chuckle when we hear them laugh. Seeing people engaging in lustful activity will often produce lustful feeling in us. Anyone who believes that lust is "bad" will attack anything that makes sex visible (or audible). Consider two examples of how lust phobia generates attacks on pornography.

The first is from the biography of the famous English censorship advocate, Mary Whitehouse. At a newsstand at a hotel in Copenhagen she opened what she thought was an "innocent" magazine. She was shocked to find it full of explicit sexual photographs. According to her biographer: "She admits that the images were so pervasive and corrupting that she found them hard to discard from her mind, she was so upset . . . that on her return home she asked the Lord to cleanse her. She felt absolutely degraded and could picture the effects such photographs might have on the minds of her adolescents."[32]

Such an intensely emotional response is a good example of an aversive reaction. Whitehouse's admission that the images were "corrupting" and that she needed "to cleanse," probably indicates that they triggered her sexual feelings. To anyone free of lust phobia, such arousal would trigger no alarm. But she reacts with intense self-loathing. Her negative response in turn inspires her to advocate vigorous media censorship, thus denying other people access to the same material.

Consider also the story of Raymond Gauer, one of the executives of Citizens for Decent Literature, an American censorship organization active in the modern era. One day in the 1960s Gauer was window-shopping on a street in his Hollywood neighborhood when he noticed that a new store had opened, and that it sold sexual toys, erotic books, and magazines. Gauer gazed at the titillating covers of the magazines and "felt a stirring of excitement, a loathsome awareness of illicit desire."[33] He returned home, but could not dispel the images from his mind. He was restless all night. In the midst of his agitation, he felt a summons from the Lord to "overcome the demonic allure of the despicable pornographers."[34]

Gauer's distress, more obviously than Whitehouse's, is provoked by a lust aversion. Gauer's distress arises when he detects "illicit desire," the physical sensations of lust. His arising anxiety in turn prompts a complaint to the police about the store; they raid it and the store closes. Thus began Gauer's career as an advocate of sex censorship.

Intolerance toward porn, erotic dancing, or public sex can also flow from *genital* phobia rather than *lust* phobia, because genitals are often prominently displayed when sex is visible. Reciprocally, negativity aimed at nudity or other genital display in a non-sexual context is often the product of lust phobia because the mere sight of genitals arouses many people. Intolerance toward the sight of overt sex is always more vigorous than toward the sight of nudity because overt sex triggers more lust than nudity. Thus the law in most places punishes public sex more harshly than mere public nudity; the mainstream media censors graphic sexual content much more than mere nudity. Lust phobia is a key factor in such antisexual patterns.

Lust phobia also motivates much more informal antisexualism. Psychologists have long recognized that people who feel shame about some aspect of themselves will relieve their self-directed negativity by attacking other people who display the same traits. Such externally directed negativity offers relief by venting some of the pain that would otherwise be directed internally.

The classic example of such *shame displacement* is the latent homosexual who knows that he or she is sexually attracted to people of the same gender but also believes that such desire is immoral and wrong. As psychiatrist Martin Kantor discusses in detail in *Homophobia: Description, Development And Dynamics Of Gay Bashing*[35], a common way to release the discomfort of such shame is to attack homosexuals. Similarly, many scholars of Catholic history have observed a form of prurience in the passion with which priests enforced sexual rules on their flock. In *Sacred Pleasure*, Riane Eisler notes that confessors regularly inquired into the sexual lives of their parishioners and developed highly detailed penances for specific sexual acts. This allowed the priests to obsess about sexuality while still claiming to be pure.[36]

Similarly, in *Sex, Power and the Violent School Girl*, Sibylle Artz discusses how negative feelings about sex lead to "slut bashing." She reports how the violent young females she works with are often uncomfortable with sex:

> The girls summed up sex in one word: 'gross'. They struggled with mixed feelings about whether or not they wanted to engage in sex, and had harsh things to say about girls who were sexually active . . . . Similarly, whenever they heard of others engaging in sex, they felt righteously angry—particularly with the girls involved. They later used their knowledge and their anger as justification to harass, threaten, and beat such girls.[37]

"Dirt Lust"

Lust phobia has one other bizarre effect. It can prompt our mind to eroticize anxiety, humiliation, and shame. A person with such an erotic appetite will deliberately seek out negative sexual experiences. D. H. Lawrence called this attraction "dirt lust."[38] How is it acquired?

Imagine a boy who has acquired delusions that masturbation is unhealthy or unmanly. But he continues to masturbate. Every time he does so his mind is flooded with a potent mix of sexual arousal and fear. Such an experience is conducive not only to an aversion to the somatic sensations of sex (as discussed above), but also to an erotic attraction to fear. By continually masturbating when he feels distress, his emotional mind will associate sexual charge with sexual shame, the same way that continually masturbating with a yellow raincoat can eroticize the yellow raincoat, as described in Chapter 2. Now the boy's guilty feelings are a spur to his arousal!

Every phobigenic conditioning event in a sexual context is conducive to the same effect, breeding not only genital aversions or lust aversions, but also an attraction to fearful or degrading sex. Therapists who specialize in treating victims of sexual abuse are familiar with this process. Ellen Bass and Laura Davis, authors of *The Courage to Heal: A Guide for Women Survivors of Child Sexual Abuse*, explain:

> The context in which we first experience sex affects us deeply. Often there is a kind of imprinting in which whatever is going on at the time becomes woven together. So if you experienced violation, humiliation and fear at the same time as you experienced arousal and pleasurable genital feelings, these elements twisted together, leaving you with emotional and physical legacies that link pleasure with pain, love with humiliation, desire with an imbalance of power.[39]

Repeated exposure to antisexualism involving far less trauma than rape can have the same erotic conditioning effect. Many of us experienced such routine conditioning and thus acquired "dirt lust." Jack Morin, in *The Erotic Mind*, calls it the "naughtiness factor."[40] Morin's surveys indicate it is especially prevalent in Catholics.[41] Freud recognized the same phenomenon in 1912 in his essay "On the universal tendency to debasement in the sphere of love."[42] He noted that many men of his generation could not achieve full sexual potency except with what he called a "debased object," such as a mistress or wife from the "lower classes."

Pornography producers are well aware that many people sexualize anxiety and shame. By describing their material as "nasty" or "dirty" and by producing images of unhappy or distressed people engaging in sex, porn producers deliberately generate negative feelings in the minds of their customers and thereby enhance the turn-on potential of the material. Such toxic conditioning is so common in our culture that for most people the word "naughty" or "dirty" are euphemisms for sex.

"Dirt lust" is a serious problem only when it dominates an individual's sexual repertoire, so that normal, loving sexual experiences have no appeal. Ritualized sado-masochistic sexual encounters provide such people with a safe way to satisfy their lust for degradation and domination. In extreme cases, "dirt lust" can produce sexual predators who sexually assault innocent victims because the negativity of the event stimulates their erotic charge.[43]

Religious Lust Phobia

Rare is the religion that celebrates erotic pleasure. In most spiritual communities sex is approved only for non-lust ends, such as procreation or the consummation of marriage. Today religious leaders rarely attack sexual desire or pleasure directly, but they never endorse it. Catholic sexual policy is an obvious case in point. According to Catholic thought, masturbation is immoral; so is premarital sex; so is marital sex where contraception is used. Absent from Catholic dogma is any celebration of erotic pleasure as worthy and noble in its own right.

In the fundamentalist Christian community today a rich literature exhorts believers to control any sexual impulse not directed toward their spouses. The books are filled with page after page of anti-lust ideology as their titles suggest, such as: *The War Within: Gaining Victory in the Battle for Sexual Purity*; *When Good Men Are Tempted*; *Pure Desire: Helping People Break Free from Sexual* Struggles; Faithful *and True: Sexual Integrity in a Fallen World*.

Religions often seek to impose their antisexual dogma on both their own followers and the community at large. For example, many groups in the Christian, Moslem, Jewish, and other religious traditions have long favored legal attacks on pornography of any type simply because it provokes lust. Anti-porn religious activists deny themselves access to such material and seek to prevent anyone else from having it too.

This secular application of phobic religious attitudes violates the duty of tolerance that is key to democratic life. Recall that the principle of "live and let live" holds that we tolerate social diversity and that we attack others only when their conduct clearly violates the long-term collective interest. Outside the sexual arena, the duty of tolerance is widely respected, even by fundamentalists. Thus even though Christian doctrine teaches that a Hindu, Moslem, or Buddhist is worshipping a false God, rare is the Christian who attacks Hindus, Moslems, or Buddhists for their violation of the Bible's religious morality. Even the vast majority of fundamentalist Christians limits the application of Biblical authority so as not to attack those who have different religious views. The duty of religious tolerance largely prevails, at least in western cultures. Yet with respect to sex, religious moralists of most faiths try to impose their sexual rules on everyone.

They are also often inconsistent in their application of their own religion's moral rules. Thus in the same Old Testament book of Leviticus that declares homosexuality an "abomination"[44] and adultery a capital offense,[45] the meat of the pig is declared unclean; shellfish, too, is taboo.[46] Leviticus also says, "When any man reviles his father and his mother, he shall be put to death."[47] Rare is the Christian who avoids eating pork or favors the death penalty for disobedient children, but many Christians still dogmatically assert the sexual ideology found in their Scriptures, such as the statement of Jesus that a man commits sin simply looking at a woman with lust.[48]

Both types of moral inconsistency—in selectively practicing the duty of tolerance and in selectively following the moral rules of one's religion—are not accidental or random. They are the result of lust phobia.

Erotophobia gives powerful emotional incentives to inconsistently embrace religious antisexual dogma while rejecting other religious rules. Scriptural antisexual dogma legitimates erotophobia, makes it seem moral and valid. Further, such dogma insulates erotophobic attitudes from rational debate. Because God's law ranks above mere human reason, religious antisexual dogma does not have to make sense, and hence neither do the erotophobic sentiments it supports. Therefore, even if no antisexual moralism appeared in Holy books, erotophobic religious people would have powerful emotional reasons to put it in, or to interpret religious precepts in an antisexual way.

The existence of erotophobic attitudes in western culture is often attributed to antisexual Christian theology. That is only partially true. For example, Biblical injunctions against homosexuality have undoubtedly increased the amount of homophobia in western secular culture. But the impact of religious sources of erotophobia can be overstated.[49] *Secular* culture is also highly conducive to erotophobia. A religious fundamentalist can acquire erotophobia simply by watching the mainstream media. Religious sexual moralism is as much influenced by secularly-produced erotophobia as antisexual secular policy is influenced by erotophobic religion.[50]

6 / The Enemies of Playful Sex

SEX CAN BE ENORMOUS FUN, and many people practice it as a form of play, like a game of tennis, a yoga session, or a swim. But many people in our culture want to take the glee out of sex, make it heavy or dull. They insist that all erotic activity be confined to marriage, that it occur without birth control protection, and be performed only in the missionary position. This chapter examines intolerant attacks on non-marital sex, contraception, and three popular types of purely playful sex: masturbation, oral sex, and anal sex.

Non-Marital Sex

"Fornication" is the archaic term for sexual conduct between parties who are not married to each other. Does sex deserve attack just because it occurs out of wedlock?

Restricting sex to marriage has two key benefits. It identifies the father of any offspring, and it minimizes the transmission of sexual disease. But neither pregnancy nor sexual disease are the inevitable result of non-marital sex, and never have been. For example, there are many types of sexual contact, such as mutual masturbation, that involve no risk of pregnancy and very slight risks of the transmission of sexual disease. Further, in the modern age, condoms and other forms of protection substantially reduce the chances of sexual diseases or unwanted pregnancies. Unmarried people who take those precautions cause no harm having sex. There is no rational basis to attack sex simply because it involves unmarried persons. These attacks are intolerant.

Such antisexualism has many ill effects. It pressures people to enter marriage without any sexual experience and sexual compatibility is a key determinant of the happiness of a marriage. Further, it encourages people to marry before they have the necessary maturity or life experience to ensure a happy partnership. By the teenage years most people have surging sexual needs. If they can fulfill those desires only within marriage, then they will tend to rush into marriage. Such a system cannot optimize marital happiness. It simply pushes up the divorce rate.

Traditionalists argue that fornication prohibitions are necessary to ensure marriage and protect women, and cite the adage: "Why buy the cow if you can get the milk for free?" A modern exponent of this view is the youthful author of the conservative bestseller *A Return to Modesty*, Wendy Shalit: "In the past, women secured the chances of lasting love by forming a kind of cartel: they had an implicit agreement not to engage in premarital or extramarital sex with men. This made it more likely that men would marry and stay married to them." Shalit, a foe of sex education and co-ed bathrooms in college dorms, claims that the modern tolerance of non-marital sex is harmful to women: ". . . in breaking up this cartel of virtue, we spoiled things, ultimately, for ourselves."[1]

But the idea that women need to withhold sex to get men to marry is false. Marriage is still popular despite the fact that non-marital sex is common. Men marry for reasons other than sex, including companionship, economic benefits, having children, and the inherent rewards of a long-term relationship. Prohibitions on non-marital sex simply induce premature marriages.

Informal intolerance

Although their numbers are shrinking, many people will still not have sex unless they are married. In a survey conducted by the largest lobby group for retired people in the United States, approximately one third of women between forty-five and fifty-nine agreed that "people should not have a sexual relationship if they are not married," compared with half of women sixty to seventy-four and two thirds of women over seventy-five. Such attitudes contribute to the sexless lives of large numbers of elderly people. In the words of the report:

Perhaps the saddest truth embedded in the numbers in this study is that for most older widows, the loss of a husband translates into the end of sex . . . . For a woman who might want a man in her life but does not wish to remarry—the position of many older widows—the belief that sex outside marriage is morally wrong is likely to pose an insurmountable barrier to any erotic relationship.[2]

Some young people adopt the same view as their grandparents on this issue. Recent American surveys of people eighteen to twenty-four reveal that one quarter believe that sex before marriage is "always" or "almost always" wrong, twice as many than in 1972. Market researchers call this conservative trend "neo-traditionalism." "Picture Eisenhower but with a pierced eyebrow," is how one observer put it.[3] Even in non-religious youth circles, virginity is a source of pride, not embarrassment.

Many people not only deny themselves any non-marital sexual outlet, they also insist that others do the same. For example, some parents oppose the idea of their children living with sexual partners outside marriage. A generation of young adults in the late 1960s and 1970s who decided to live "common law," had to cope with parental negativity towards "living in sin." Many of the friends I grew up with fought their parents over the co-habitation issue. Several friends gave in to the parental pressure and got married. Most but not all parents are more tolerant today. In some families the negativity only surfaces when unmarried couples travel to a parental home on holidays and find that they must sleep in separate rooms, even though the couple may have been co-habiting for years.

Adult children can act with similar intolerance toward the sexual conduct of their parents. As operators of nursing homes can attest, adult children often object to their widowed parent having a sexual relationship. Many eldercare facilities deal with this wrath from antisexual offspring and others by denying seniors private places to engage in sex.[4] In one facility, a nurse called 911 when she found two elders happily in bed together.[5]

Institutional intolerance

According to the Bible, fornication is a sin and its practitioners lose favor with God.[6] Those ancient commandments are still a prime but often unstated force prompting the "abstinence until marriage" programs in many school sex education programs, discussed in the next chapter. They also are behind rules at many religious schools, colleges, and even universities that require students to abstain from all non-marital sex. For example, at Milligan College in Tennessee "student conduct guidelines" state:

Any form of sexual immorality is prohibited. This includes but is not limited to pre-marital sex, adultery, and homosexual behavior. Cohabitation (living/residing with a non-related person of the opposite sex) outside the bonds of marriage is prohibited.[7]

School administrators regularly expel students who violate such rules. Brigham Young University kicked out a co-ed who revealed on MTV that she shares living quarters with a man;[8] a suburban Christian high school suspended its star basketball player when his girlfriend got pregnant.[9]

Even *secular* schools punish teens who engage in premarital sex. School districts exclude qualified students from the National Honor Society who lose their virginity. Because pregnancy is a sure sign of sexual activity, girls are the main victims of this policy. For example, in Kentucky two seventeen-year-olds with outstanding scholastic achievements were denied membership in the Honor Society when they got pregnant. School officials stated, "The admissions committee did not feel that someone who had engaged in premarital sex should be held up as a role model for the rest of the students to emulate, whether male or female."[10]

Many churches refuse membership or church rites to individuals who are "living in sin." Official policy of the Catholic Church authorizes priests to withhold communion to anyone having sex with another person out of wedlock. Fornicators are not welcome in the pews at most fundamentalist churches. The largest Protestant organization in the United States, the Southern Baptist Convention, recently reaffirmed its position that good Christians must not practice sex out of wedlock.[11]

Secular legal systems are the source of the same type of antisexualism. The criminal laws of over a dozen American states prohibit fornication. A Minnesota law provides: "When any man and single woman have sexual intercourse with each other, both are guilty of fornication, a misdemeanor." North Dakota law makes it a crime to "live openly and notoriously with a person of the opposite sex as a married couple where the cohabitants are not married."[12] In 2003 the North Dakota state Senate voted to keep that law! "It stands as a reminder that there is right, and there is wrong," said Sen. John Andrist. The law criminalizes the living arrangements of thousands of unmarried couples in that state.[13]

The American Supreme Court has never dealt directly with the constitutionality of the fornication prohibition, but one justice has said that the validity of such laws was "beyond dispute."[14] A few such laws have been struck down as contrary to a constitutional right to privacy but other cases have applied the comment of the Supreme Court judge and upheld the prohibitions.[15] Fornication is therefore still a crime in some American states. Officials in Georgia applied the law until 2003, when the state Supreme Court voided it. A teen who had been convicted of fornication for having consensual sex with his girlfriend, successfully challenged the law as an unconstitutional invasion of privacy.[16]

A senior official of Phyllis Schlafly's Eagle Forum, a right-wing lobby group, says: "I'd like to outlaw premarital sex." She admits, "there's an enforcement problem—invasion of privacy. But I see no problem with having it on the books."[17] Officials in Gem County, Idaho, have gone further. Dusting off their 1921 law prohibiting sex between unmarried people, they now charge pregnant teenagers with the crime. Officials identify pregnant girls and their boyfriends by using teachers, family members, or social workers as informers, and then haul both youths off to court. Most charged with the crime plead guilty.[18]

Judges in Charlotte, North Carolina, still routinely enforce the fornication ban on the books in that state by refusing to release on bail any accused person who is cohabiting out of wedlock. Defendants must agree to get married, move out of the house, or have their partner leave.[19]

Even when not directly enforced, fornication prohibitions carry a punch. For example, courts allow landlords to refuse to rent to unmarried couples. In some places a mother can lose custody of a child for ignoring criminal prohibitions against fornication. The Internal Revenue Service denies dependency exemptions to unmarried cohabiting taxpayers living in states with such prohibitions.[20]

The infection cycle: specific and generic
Fornication phobia is the most specific attitude behind attacks on non-marital sex, and consists of the false idea that just because sex occurs

outside marriage, it is in some way harmful. That specific phobia is in turn a product of intolerance aimed at non-marital sex. When trusted institutions such as the Church or the law make sex outside marriage a sin or a crime, people who trust those institutions are likely to engage in rationalizing, and falsely conclude that fornication is somehow harmful and deserving of attack. This is a *specific infection cycle* at work: fornication phobia causes intolerance aimed at non-marital sex, which in turn causes more fornication phobia.

A *generic infection* process is at work when a broad phobic attitude such as lust phobia motivates attacks on a specific type of sexual expression (like fornication), and that intolerance helps breed more lust phobia.

For example, anyone who believes that sex is in some way wrong *per se* would favor prohibitions on fornication because such rules limit the number of sexual partners and even the total amount of sex experienced in a lifetime. Even in a culture that allows divorce, the process of marriage and remarriage takes time. If marriage is a prerequisite to sexual partnership, few people will have more than one sexual partner, and lifelong sexual partnerships tend to be sexually minimalist. Sex researcher Seymour Fisher describes marriage as an "inhibited sexual state."[21] Sexual frequency and passion slumps in long-term relationships.[22] Allowing just one sexual partner is not conducive to an exciting sex life, and that will please anyone who believes that sex is somehow debased at its core. Lust phobia plays a role in the emphasis of the Bible's anti-fornication commandments by many modern conservative Christian leaders. They ignore many other clear non-sexual rules in the Bible, but assert the fornication prohibition because it accords with their own deep discomfort with sexuality.

Intolerance aimed specifically at fornication, in turn, helps breed lust phobia. If respected authorities rule that sex is permissible only within marriage, an inference is that sex must be illicit. Something intrinsically worthy would not need to be confined to matrimony and lifelong commitment. Fornication prohibitions thus help breed *delusions* about lust.

They also help imprint lust *aversions*. For example, the good Christian who gives in to carnal temptation and has sex out of wedlock will experience a stab of guilt. The more intense the fornicator's belief that this is sinful, the greater the negative feeling. This occurs precisely when the physical sensations of sex are prominent in the fornicator's mind, creating an aversion to the very feel of sex regardless of the type of sex performed. When a person who has fornicated guiltily for several years finally marries, the phobic aversion will still exist. Even though intercourse with the spouse will violate no spiritual or civil law, it will still provoke distress. "Because we still view sex, even in marriage, as not quite all right, we'd rather sneak our way into it—and call it spontaneity," says sexuality expert Bernie Zilbergeld.[23]

There are also opportunistic motives behind attacks on non-marital sex, and they act as a *catalyst* for these infection cycles. For example, stigmatizing non-marital sex provides important advantages for social elites, such as the hierarchy of the Catholic Church. Because the rule against non-marital sex is so unreasonable, many Catholics violate it. Their "sin" produces shame within them, and they relieve that shame through confession, a service that is a specialty of the Catholic Church. Attacking non-marital sex is thus good for the business of priests and popes. Such opportunistic antisexualism helps breed erotophobic attitudes and thus launches the infection cycle.

Contraception

Birth control techniques have been popular for thousands of years, and include herbs and pills, condoms, the rhythm method, external ejaculation, and even sterilization. Contraception is harmless. It simply allows the people who use it to avoid creating new life. Birth control obviously has enormous utility, such as in limiting the population of a desperately overcrowded world, empowering people to choose optimum times to reproduce, and avoiding risky genetic pairings.

Though contraception is highly valued by most people, and especially those of the gender who must bear children, it has been attacked throughout the ages. Negativity aimed at birth control is intolerant, and it is common in the history of western culture, thanks largely to the Catholic Church. Catholic moral doctrine requires that "each and every marriage act must remain open to the transmission of life,"[24] because "marriage and conjugal love are by their nature ordained toward the begetting and education of children."[25] Hence, artificial birth control is "illicit." Such attitudes led Cardinal Haime Sin of the Philippines, to say that condoms are "evil" and "fit only for animals."[26]

Such ideas make no sense. While the begetting of children is clearly a natural result of "conjugal love," no rational evidence suggests that procreation is the *only* natural purpose of such love. Evolution clearly designed sex to have other outcomes. For example, sex is relaxing; it reduces physical stress. Sexual intercourse also helps build emotional bonds between a couple, makes them more likely to stay together, and this will benefit any child of the union. Neither of these natural outcomes of sex require that intercourse "remain open to the transmission of life"; people will be less likely to engage in intercourse and obtain the relationship benefits of it if conception is possible. The idea that "nature" somehow opposes birth control is an obvious rationalization of some other motive. Indeed, the Church has made no rational attempt to justify its hostility to birth control, instead choosing to cite only its own long-standing position on the subject and its authority to impose moral rules.[27]

Secular laws in many jurisdictions have reinforced that type of antisexualism. For many years the state of Ireland banned the sale of birth control devices. Connecticut and Massachusetts prohibited contraceptives for decades until the courts struck down such laws in the 1960s and 1970s. Various American states have tried to restrict access to contraceptives by requiring that they be sold only by licensed pharmacists and by banning advertisements about them.[28]

Such action is primarily the result of *contraception phobia*, the vague idea that birth control is somehow illicit, and that preventing conception is somehow a moral wrong. Lust phobia plays an even more important role. Anyone who believes that sex is by nature depraved or anarchic will favor attacks on birth control because they want the fear of getting pregnant to inhibit sexual conduct. The greater your hostility to sex, the more you will favor policies that make sex dangerous and anxiety-ridden.

Opportunistic motives also inspire attacks on birth control. For example, the fact that the Catholic Church can influence governments to pass laws that reflect specifically Catholic sexual dogma is a sign to the community of the enormous authority of the Church. Further, this power is noticed every time members of the community must deal with their lack of access to birth control. Controlling private sexual acts is an important type of psychological domination that enhances the authority of the power elite. In 1968 the Pope rejected the right of Catholics to use artificial birth control for the reason that such devices would threaten "hierarchical authority."[29]

Many times in its history the medical profession has opposed contraception for the same reason. Personal control of one's own fertility is a form of medical self-help, and in the mid-1800s such individual autonomy threatened the attempt of the emerging medical profession to dominate the health system. In a bid to take control over life and limb, doctors of that era opposed condoms and diaphragms.[30] As late as the 1920s, medical organizations on both sides of the Atlantic attacked birth control as unsound "physiologically, psychologically and biologically."[31] The introduction in the 1960s of oral contraceptives and the IUD, both of which required medical intervention, finally gave doctors a central role in family planning, and their opposition to birth control disappeared.

Denying females the right to control their own fertility enormously undermines the social status of women. The greater control a woman has over her own body, the greater her freedom, and parity of power with men. Therefore, people who want women to have less social power than men will often oppose contraception. That is one reason overtly sexist social institutions such as the Roman Catholic Church and some fundamentalist religions attack birth control and information about it. Their policies help maintain male dominance.

Attacks on birth control have important phobigenic effects. They help generate contraceptive phobia. When respected social institutions prohibit birth control they communicate the message that contraception is somehow harmful or "bad." Birth control negativity also generates lust phobia. The message communicated by social authorities who say that sex is only legitimate when birth might result is that sex performed only for pleasure is immoral. The more sex is approved only for its non-physical outcomes, the more *sex per* se will become suspect, and that breeds lust phobia.

Further, denying sexually active people access to birth control is conducive to anxious sex and the worry of pregnancy. Women are more disposed to such fear because unwanted pregnancy obviously penalizes them far more heavily than men. Frequent juxtaposition of fear and sexual arousal is phobigenic. Such conditioning helps teach the emotional brain to associate arousal with fear, and acquire a lust aversion. Thereafter, sexual sensations will trigger fear, even when pregnancy is impossible.

Masturbation

Masturbation is probably the most frequently practiced sexual act, at least in modern western cultures. Kinsey found that, on average, men had more orgasms through masturbation than intercourse. Masturbation is usually our first sexual experience. Most of us have years of practice stroking our own erotic organs before we have sexual contact with other people.

Masturbation is harmless, and in fact has many benefits. Many people report that masturbation produces their most satisfying orgasms.[32] Solo sexual activity allows the complete focus of one's attention on erotic sensations without the distraction of engaging sexually and emotionally with another person.

Masturbation is also highly educational. It acquaints the autoeroticist with his or her own erotic organs, responses, and fantasies. Sexual arousal is partially a learned process; the greater experience we have in cultivating sexual heat on our own, the better we can respond with others. This is why masturbation is often a key part of the therapy for women who have never had an orgasm.[33] People who have no masturbation experience are more likely to have sexual problems in their relationships.[34]

Masturbation offers not only sexual pleasure, but also a powerful connection with the self. As Woody Allen says, "Don't knock masturbation: it's sex with someone I love." If not plagued by shame, masturbation can be a form of self-love, enhancing our self-esteem. Masturbation also facilitates independence. It allows us to have a sexual life even in the absence of sexual partners. In promoting both sexual self-sufficiency and self-love, we become more confident, both sexually and socially.

Yet in spite of these obvious benefits of masturbation, it attracts enormous negativity today as in the past, which is reflected even in the possible roots of the word "masturbation": *manu* "by hand" and *stuprare* "to defile."[35] But masturbation is harmless, and negativity aimed at it is intolerant.

Masturbation shame

In the largest survey ever conducted of human sexual behavior (in the U.S. in 1994), 37% of men reported that they did not masturbate at all in the last year; 58% of women reported the same.[36] Of course people may avoid masturbating not because they are uncomfortable, but simply because they are uninterested, perhaps because they prefer other sexual experiences. However, studies show that most women who discontinue masturbating do so due to their fear that it would lead to mental and physical deterioration.[37] Typical of these cases is a woman who began masturbating as part of a sexual therapy program and then developed a urinary tract infection. Her first thought was that the masturbation had caused it, an idea dismissed by medical authorities.[38]

Substantial numbers of people who do engage in the act feel guilty about it. A large American survey found that half the women and men who pleasure themselves are uncomfortable with the practice. Further, the surveys indicate that age is not necessarily related to such distress: "More guilt about masturbation is not necessarily found in older groups than in younger groups."[39] Large proportions of the American population—approximately 77% of women and 68.5% of men—either do not masturbate or feel guilty about it![40]

The male author of a recent article in *Cosmopolitan* expresses a classic and highly public example of this shame. The writer felt so guilty about his habit that he identified himself as "Anonymous." He begins the story thus: "I'm about to tell you something that I've never told anyone. Something my girlfriend will never, ever get me to admit. Something that hard-boiled cops in an interrogation room couldn't beat out of me. Look, here it is: I masturbate . . . . For a man, there's no worse disgrace in the world than to be outed as a masturbator."[41]

Even experienced sexuality researchers admit to such feelings. Lynn Ponton M.D., is an expert on youth psychology and the author of *The Sex Lives of Teenagers*.[42] In it she describes how she "froze" with embarrassment when an adolescent patient described the "jerking off" that occurred in his group home. She attributes some of her embarrassment to an education in Catholic schools where she learned that masturbation was unhealthy.

Sin and shame color these memories, and became fixedly woven into the fabric of my own attitudes despite years of education, therapy, and life experience that have contributed to many other, more positive feelings about masturbation. When I am tired, in a hurry, or taken by surprise, they [the negative attitudes] can still appear.[43]

A sign of the shame surrounding masturbation is the difficulty most people have in talking about it. That extends even to people who are professional interviewers. For example, the workers who conducted the large American sex survey mentioned above report that they had more difficulty asking questions about masturbation than any other subject. Those people had no problem inquiring about anal sex or homosexuality, yet were anxious talking about sexual self-pleasure.[44]

If you feel bad about masturbation but want the physical gratification, you will get the job over as fast as possible. Masturbation shame produces a quick race for an orgasm, focusing attention exclusively on the genitals and only on the fantasies and strokes that ensure quick release. The shameful masturbator fails to develop a slow, full-body autoerotic style.

The vast majority of boys in our culture engage in such furtive masturbation. Day after day they hurriedly stroke themselves to orgasm and feel shame about that act. Long before they ever have sex with a partner they have a well- practiced sexual sequence that gives scant attention to playful sensualism and is entirely devoted to quick release. No wonder that many women complain that so many men are bad lovers.

Masturbation shame has still more ill effects. Negativity aimed at the self is psychologically damaging. It impairs our sense of psychological wholeness and undermines our self-esteem. That, in turn, hinders our sense of independence and makes us more obedient to the control of others. As any politician or army general knows, internal conflict always assists external control, preventing united, confident action. Further, a person who feels "dirty" or "bad" is far more likely to seek the approval of others to compensate for the lack of self-esteem. Shame about masturbation calls into question the legitimacy of independence itself.[45] A leading sexual researcher, Seymour Fisher, says: "It is important to underscore that masturbation is more than a sexual act. It is also simultaneously a challenging statement of body ownership and therefore carries power implications."[46]

The more you feel shame about your autoerotic behavior, the more compliant you are likely to be. Masturbation shame grooms people for the political structure of dominance and submission. It is thus no coincidence that intolerance against masturbation reached its zenith in the Victorian era, precisely when western society was industrializing, requiring docile workers who would endure atrocious working conditions.[47] The greater the need of a parent, church, or other social institution to make a person compliant, the more likely they will attack masturbation for purely political ends. For example, in *Between Parent and Child*, Dr. Haim Ginott says: "Perhaps parents are not altogether wrong in not sanctioning masturbation. Self gratification may make the child less accessible to the influence of his parents and peers. When he takes the shortcut to gratification, he does not have to depend on pleasing anyone but himself . . . ."[48]

Social attacks on autoerotic sex play are common. Consider some examples.

Parental attacks

Studies indicate that approximately 60% of boys and 44% of girls in the two-to-five age group have been observed by one of their parents playing with their genitals.[49] Many parents intervene to prevent such behavior even when it is entirely private. Consider two examples reported by pediatrician Elaine Yates. Faith, a five-year-old girl, was caught by her mother rubbing her clitoris in the bathtub. The parent became upset and held the child's hands under very hot water, saying that she needed to cleanse them from dirty activity.[50] Morris, a two-year-old only child who is the center of his mother's life, was discovered playing with his penis. In an unusually sharp voice his mother said, "Don't do that. You go to sleep!" But he persisted. She then swatted him on the head.[51]

Even teenagers suffer the same parental abuse. Melanie, a fifteen-year-old contributor to the "I got caught" section of a website on teen sexuality reports: "I was lying in bed, stimulating my clitoris, and inserting my fingers for pleasure, and I started getting excited, and was breathing too, heaving and making too much noise. My mother heard it and walked in, and started yelling, calling me a sick little slut, and grounded me."[52]

In families that are not hostile to autoeroticism *per se*, masturbation is usually regarded as an activity that must be hidden. "Do that in the bedroom," the child is told. Because parents either fail to express their acceptance of self-pleasuring or overtly attack masturbation, most children who "play with themselves" do it covertly. Because few children have physical space that is secure from adult intervention, their covert masturbation will often occur while they are worried that they might be discovered and punished.

Ideological intolerance

Anti-masturbation ideology flows mainly from three sources: religious authorities, secular philosophers, and doctors. Most religions are uncomfortable with masturbation. Ancient Jewish authorities considered it the severest sin recorded in the Scriptures. The Talmud specifically forbids masturbation and any conduct that might encourage it. The Roman Catholic Church has also long regarded autoeroticism as a sin, and this view is still formal Church doctrine. The 1994 official *Catechism of the Catholic Church* calls masturbation "an intrinsically and gravely disordered action."[53] Conservative Protestant ideology holds the same view. According to best-selling Christian author Tim LaHaye, masturbation "is not an acceptable practice for Christians," and 83% of the pastors he surveyed agreed.[54]

Secular philosophers also condemn masturbation. Perhaps the most famous is Immanuel Kant (1724-1804), who on supposedly rational grounds opposed all sex outside marriage. Of masturbation he states: "The practice is contrary to the ends of humanity and even opposed to animal nature. By it man sets aside his person and degrades himself below the level of animals."[55] Such statements contain many unexamined assumptions, such as that masturbation is contrary to "animal nature" and contrary to the "ends" of humanity. Kant advances these assumptions as if they were fact, but tenders no evidence to support them. That is a serious error for anyone claiming a rationalist perspective. "Nature" is often the purported basis for the antisexual ideology of secular philosophers in exactly the same way that "God" or "papal infallibility" is used by religious leaders to support their attacks on sex. However, unlike God's will, nature is an objective reality that can be scientifically studied. Kant refers to "nature," yet summons no scientific evidence in support of his arguments.

Philosophers in the modern era also knock masturbation. Roger Scruton is an example. In his 1986 book *Sexual Desire*, he asserts that masturbation creates "a compliant world of desire, in which unreal objects become the focus of human emotions, and the emotions themselves are rendered incompetent to participate in the building of personal relations."[56] Like Kant, Scruton purports to be asserting fact, and like Kant he never offers confirming evidence. Masturbation is not in itself antithetical to building personal relations, indeed, many sex therapists assert that autoerotic experience is a key ingredient in the development of a fulfilling sexual partnership. Such evidence was available to Scruton when he wrote the book, but he ignored it in favor of sweeping anti-masturbation generalizations.

Since the eighteenth century, but not in the recent era, the medical establishment has been a prime force of anti-masturbation ideology. The most famous tract attacking autoeroticism was penned by the Swiss physician Tissot in 1760, entitled: *Onanism: A Treatise Upon The Disorders Produced By Masturbation*. The good doctor alleged that masturbation caused: cloudiness of ideas and sometimes even madness, a decay of bodily powers resulting in diseases like tuberculosis, pains in the head, pimples on the face, tumors in the bladders, and constipation. Benjamin Rush, who signed the Declaration of Independence, popularized Tissot's ideas in the United States. Famous health advocates in the 1800s, such as Sylvestor Graham, the originator of Graham crackers, and John Kellogg, inventor of the cereals that bear his name, worked tirelessly to warn people of what they thought were the terrible consequences of masturbation: ultimately, insanity.[57]

Because of these medical delusions, parents and others in that era tried to prevent children from engaging in "self abuse." In the nineteenth century, physicians recommended that the clitoris be cut out—with scissors, if necessary, while the penis be surrounded with a ring lined with spikes.

One nurse designed a steel and leather jacket that enclosed the lower torso; handcuffs were also prescribed.

Anti-masturbation ideas also spread into the twentieth century. For example, G. Stanley Hall, a leading American psychologist, contended that masturbation caused "one or more of the morbid forms of sex perversion." Such ideas would reach the minds of medical authorities in the modern era. The venerable Dr. Benjamin Spock, for example, was told by his mother that if a child touched himself he would ultimately produce deformed offspring.[58] Dr. Spock rejected such teaching, but cautions parents to be on the lookout for "excessive" masturbation, which he fails to define. Other learned doctors in the modern era advised parents to discourage masturbation because "it is not progressive; it does not result in social relationships or personal growth."[59]

The *Boy Scout Handbook* has denigrated masturbation to generations of American youth. Because approximately one-fifth of American boys are exposed to the book, its negative message has significant impact. Early editions indicated that masturbation violated the laws of nature and that a boy who practices it:

feels the foundations of his manhood undermined. He notes that his muscles are becoming more and more flabby; that his back is weak; his eyes after a time become sunken and 'fishy,' his hands clammy; he is unable to look anyone straight in the eye.[60]

By 1959 the *Handbook* editors had dropped such nonsense but still exhorted: "Any real boy knows that anything that causes him to worry should be avoided or overcome."[61]

In 1972 the editors printed the eighth edition of the *Handbook* with the information on masturbation revised. It sensibly advised Scouts that many young men like to masturbate and that people formerly thought this would cause problems. It added, "Doctors today agree that it doesn't cause any of these and is really a part of growing up sexually."[62] Religious sponsors of the Scout organization, such as the Roman Catholic and Mormon churches, objected to such information. Their opposition led to the destruction of 25,000 copies of that edition! The replacement edition simply advised boys to talk to their parents, spiritual advisor, or doctor about masturbation. The 1990 and 1998 editions of the *Handbook* ignore

masturbation and counsel boys to practice sexual abstinence until marriage.[63] The *Girl Scout Handbook* has never mentioned masturbation.[64]

While modern children are hearing less anti-masturbation ideology
than did generations of children in the past, they also grow up hearing
very little positive about solo eroticism. If anything, children today hear
very little about masturbation, good or bad, which is an advance on the
ideological intolerance of the past, but such silence is also a powerful
phobigenic force as well. Masturbation deserves lots of positive commen-
tary, but this does not exist, except on the social fringe. Only a few modern feminist sexual pioneers, such as Betty Dodson,[65] Loni Barbach,[66]
Joani Blank,[67] and a few others, offer an overtly pro-masturbation point of
view.

Giving children the benefit of such a positive perspective is still
highly controversial. President Clinton fired the nation's high-
est-ranking health officer, Surgeon General Joycelyn Elders, partially on
the basis that she advocated instruction about masturbation in public
schools.[68] Authorities in Britain have behaved with similar intolerance.
Consider the reaction to the sex-positive sex education book *A Kid's First
Book About Sex*, designed for children from five to nine years old. It describes how children often masturbate, such as touching themselves with
hands or fingers, or by squeezing a pillow or blanket between the legs,
and asks the reader, "Do you do it any of these ways?"[69] Because of such
statements the British Education Secretary ruled that even teachers
should not see it, and banned the publication from the library of research
materials for education professionals.[70]

Masturbation rarely receives positive reports in the mainstream media.
For example, the editors of *Cosmopolitan* headlined an article on masturbation in the following terms: "The Sex Sin He Won't Confess," and displayed
captions such as: "Here, the truth about your man's sinful solo sex life," and
"Masturbation is a habit, like smoking."[71] The editors of one of the most apparently sex-positive magazines in the western world are distressed about
simple self-pleasure, calling it a sin, and comparing it to smoking!

On mainstream television, masturbation is coming out of the closet,
but still only via whispers and allusions, as in the famous *Seinfeld* episode
on the subject. However, even that oblique attention from a mass-market

television show is a positive development. A producer of a documentary television series on sex says the *Seinfeld* episode had a revolutionary effect: "As soon as that show came out, suddenly everyone was talking about masturbation. It completely de-stigmatized it."[72] While that statement is obviously overblown, there is no doubt that as the media treats masturbation as normal and natural, phobic attitudes about it will decline.

Allusions to masturbation are a no-no in the advertising industry, at least in Britain. For example, the Gossard lingerie firm was ordered by the Advertising Standards Authority to remove posters referring to masturbation. One poster showed a woman in her bed, clothes strewn around the room, with the slogan: "If he's late, you can always start without him." Another message said: "Gossard. Find your G spot." The advertising censors felt that the poster was unacceptable because it "could cause offense to some people."[73]

Legal intolerance

As far as I am aware, masturbation is not a crime anywhere in the western world, unless one is a prison inmate. Stimulating your own genitals is an offence, according to federal Prison Regulations applying to over 100,000 prisoners in 100 prisons in the U.S.[74] Many American states also prohibit masturbating in prison, and courts have upheld these rules.[75]

The infection cycle

Attacks on masturbation are largely the product of *masturbation phobia*: irrational beliefs that autoeroticism *per se* is unmanly, unspiritual, or medically dangerous.

Such irrational attitudes are, in turn, caused by the many different types of intolerance aimed specifically at masturbation. For example, if you are punished for masturbating, or are exposed to the anti-masturbation ideology of the Catholic Church and Boy Scouts, or never hear anyone openly discuss the topic, or masturbate while anxious about being discovered, you will likely acquire some irrational attitudes about masturbation. Millions of people suffer such a fate: a specific phobia produces a negativity aimed at a specific sex act, which reproduces that same phobia in other minds.

Lust phobia also motivates attacks on masturbation. If I harbor an aversion to the experience of pleasure, or I falsely believe that all sexual hedonism is immoral or sinful, I will feel shame if I masturbate, and criticize others who do it. The lustful intent of masturbation is obvious and thus it is a natural target of people who fear lust.

Masturbation negativity also breeds lust phobia. Consider the effects of actual punishment or anticipated punishment involving masturbation. The average teenage boy engages in hundreds of masturbatory acts before having sexual intercourse. Often this autoerotic behavior takes place in an atmosphere of fear, as the child worries that he will be discovered. Such fear occurs precisely when the boy is aroused, and as we have already seen, arousal along with fear are conducive to phobigenic conditioning, leading to fear reflexes triggered by arousal.

Because actual punishment will occur far less often than anticipated punishment, the latter is the far more phobigenic force. That no overt punishment may occur helps conceal the fact that an aversion has been acquired. Sally Wendkos Olds in *The Eternal Garden: Seasons Of Our Sexuality*, says:

> Learning to masturbate is often a major sexual turning point in a person's life—his or her discovery of the pleasures the body can yield. If this discovery is followed by a sense that the pleasures are wrong, an ambivalence about sexuality arises that can dominate a person's entire life.[76]

Oral Sex

Moist lips and a skilled tongue can bring many erotic delights to a penis, vulva, or vagina. For many women, receiving such delicate stimulation on their genitals is more conducive to orgasm than intercourse. The sight of erotic organs, and the smell of their erotic scents, can also be powerfully stimulating to the person performing oral sex.

"Giving head" is harmless if the parties performing it are clean and healthy. Blanket negativity aimed at oral sex is intolerant.

Erotophobic inhibitions toward oral-genital contact are declining with each new generation, at least in the west. Kinsey reported that oral sex was popular in the 1940s and 1950s, especially among the educated classes, but that groups lower on the social ladder still regarded it as "perversion."[77] By the 1970s, oral sex was a common feature of the sex life of most couples, a change one sexologist called "an increase . . . of major and historic proportions."[78] It is even more popular in the modern day.

Yet several social institutions still attack oral sexuality. Consider first legal prohibitions against it. In many jurisdictions, including many American states, oral sex is a crime, even when performed in total privacy between married partners. For example, in Washington, D.C., the location of President Clinton's oral sex episodes with Monica Lewinsky, the penal code makes it an offense to "take the sexual organ of another person into one's mouth or anus or to place one's sexual organ in the mouth or anus of another or to have carnal copulation in an opening of the body other than the sexual parts with another person."[79] Some state courts have struck down similar laws on the basis that they violate constitutional rights to privacy. But, amazingly, courts in other states have upheld the same rules.

For example, in 2000 the Louisiana Supreme Court upheld the state's 1895 prohibition on oral sex. A man was accused of rape and having consensual oral sex. The evidence failed to sustain the rape charge, but the oral sex charge was proved. He appealed his conviction and the state's top court ruled that the legislature could lawfully regulate private consensual sexual conduct without breaching constitutional rights.[80] In a related case, the same court ruled that prostitutes who solicited oral sex could receive a more onerous prison term than those who solicited intercourse.[81]

Oral sex phobia is behind most intolerance aimed at that sexual behavior. The woman who thinks it is "not nice," or the man who feels it is "unsuitable for respectful women," or the judge who believes that oral sex is simply "immoral" or "an injury against the state" have all acquired delusions about this harmless sexual act. They will be loathe to engage in it and will attack others who do it. Other erotophobic attitudes also play a role. For example, homophobia will inspire attacks on oral sex involving homosexuals. Lust phobia also plays a role: the greater your aversion to genital pleasure, the less comfortable you will be with the passive hedonism of oral sex.[82]

Those attitudes played a key role in the legendary 1986 American

Supreme Court decision in *Bowers v. Hardwick*.[83] In that case, a man was charged with sodomy contrary to the penal code of Georgia after police observed him in his bedroom with another man performing oral sex. Police had gained entry to the home on an unrelated matter. The state dropped the charges, but the man attacked the statute as an unconstitutional invasion of his right to privacy. The U.S. Supreme Court split 5-4 against that argument. The majority rejected the idea that "any kind of private sexual conduct between consenting adults is constitutionally insulated from state proscription."

The *Bowers* case illustrates better than any other ruling in the modern era how supposedly rational decision-makers can support overtly intolerant sexual laws. In giving the state permission to intrude into the bedrooms of the nation to prohibit harmless adult oral sex, the majority of the court violated the deepest values of the American people: freedom and tolerance.

Fortunately the Supreme Court reversed the infamous Bowers decision in June 2003. In the landmark case *Lawrence v. Texas* the court set aside a Texas law that banned "homosexual conduct" including oral and anal sex.[84] As a result of that ruling, all laws in the nation prohibiting oral or anal sex in private are invalidated. The Texas decision is pivotal not only because it has de-criminalized oral and anal sex but also because the Court affirmed broad principles that could revolutionize the way governments regulate sexuality. The court ruled for the first time that adult, consensual sex in private is a constitutional right.

The case goes further than ever before in affirming the principle of tolerance in sexual cases. "The fact that the governing majority in a State has traditionally viewed a particular practice as immoral is not a sufficient reason for upholding a law prohibiting the practice," said the court. Before a government can intrude into "the personal and private life of the individual" it must show a "legitimate state interest," which it failed to do in the Texas case.

Rationality has finally trumped erotophobia in one of the most powerful institutions in the world. Time will tell how far this victory for democracy will extend. While the specific issue before the court involved sexual conduct between two men in a bedroom, the principles the court approved have much wider scope. The final words of the judgment suggest a more sexually tolerant future: "As the Constitution endures, persons in every generation can invoke its principles in their own search for greater freedom."

Anal Sex

The anus is rich in nerve endings. Stimulating it by fingers, lips, tongue, and penis can elicit powerful emotional and erotic feelings. When the anus is clean and healthy, and when the stimulation is gentle, lubricated, and relaxed, no harm results.[85] Blanket hostility toward anal sex *per se* is intolerant.

Such antisexualism is common in both the informal and institutional domains of life. The lowest orifice on our body is the target of the most intense of any inhibitions discussed in this book. While sexual surveys by Kinsey, Morton Hunt, and others indicate that a majority of Americans have had some experience with anal sexuality, very substantial numbers of the population completely avoid it, although such inhibitions are declining with each successive generation.[86] In fact, retailers of sex toys report that sales of "butt-plugs" have surged faster than any other product in recent years.[87]

The same laws that forbid oral sex usually include prohibitions against anal sexuality. Although laws in America no longer condemn anal sex practitioners to death, as they once did, many American states still make anal sex a crime under the anti-sodomy statutes discussed above.

Discourse about anal sex is also severely stunted. Prior to the last two decades there was almost no scientific research on the subject. Now there is a tiny literature exploring anal pleasure and health. The subject is still largely absent in the mainstream media. For example, while jokes about masturbation now occasionally appear on popular television sitcoms, any mention of anal sexuality is totally taboo.

The main cause of this type of antisexualism is *anus phobia*. It is technically not a type of erotophobia because it has nothing to do with sex. The anus emits the bulk of the body's wastes, and the odors of such waste are often innately aversive. Through a natural phobigenic conditioning process we learn to associate the organ, with the innately offensive material that comes out of it, and the result is an aversion to the orifice. Once this aversion is acquired, any form of anal stimuli including the sight, touch, or even the thought of it provokes intensely negative reactions. Much negativity aimed at anal *sex* is simply a subset of the more general intolerance aimed at the anus.

Many people also have an even more specific condition: *anal sex phobia*. They may have no strong aversion to the anus, but they do towards anal *sexuality*. Such attitudes are, in part, the product of social negativity directed at anal sex. Consider an example of this process. A teenage girl proposes that she touch her lover's anus during lovemaking, but her partner responds with disgust and contempt. The girl feels shame and humiliation. If the negative feelings are intense enough they may imprint in her mind negative associations with anal sex that she may never overcome. Such attitudes will be reinforced when she later learns that such conduct is considered by many to be "a crime against nature" or a "threat to the state." The intolerance toward anal sex transmits a phobia against that sexual act from mind to mind.

Lust phobia obviously also motivates the same antisexual action. Because anal sexuality involves sexual arousal and pleasure, anyone who believes that lust is wicked or illegitimate will see anal sex in the same light.

Homophobia also plays a role. Anal sex is an important part of gay male sexuality, and hostility toward homosexuality can transfer to the anal sex act. Further, homophobic heterosexual men inhibit their anal sexuality because they associate it with being gay. Because anal sexuality bears a rough similarity to vaginal receptivity, some men link it to a feminine sexual role, and men who harbor negative attitudes towards women will eschew anal sex for that reason as well.

Anal sex phobia can also result from painful anal sex experience, usually caused by inept or uncaring lovers. Successful anal sex play requires some skill, skill that is rare because of the lack of discourse on the subject and the lack of actual practice thanks in part to phobic attitudes towards the anus and anal sex. Because anal sex phobia has many causes independent of the infection cycle, it tends to be very common and very powerful.

Sex Toys

If you want a fast lesson about the extent of sexual fear in our culture, work a few shifts at a sex toy retailer. Consider my experience. In December 2002 my partner and I opened The Art of Loving (www.taol.ca), an erotic arts center in Vancouver, Canada. Even though I had spent twenty years studying erotophobia, I was amazed at the extent of social intolerance aimed at our tasteful shop.

My first discovery was the vast array of laws targeting vibrators, dildos, and other erotic toys. A local law in Vancouver, which is also common in many other municipalities in North America, requires that any store selling such products be more than 1000 feet from any school, park, day-care center or community center. The very few locations in the city that can meet that rule suffer from a lack of normal retail traffic, like ours. Fortunately, because our center involves a unique blend of art, educational seminars, pleasing decor, quality sex toys, and sex-positive activism, it has attracted significant media attention, and we survive despite our out-of-the-way location.

Civic officials cannot explain why a respectable, non-pornographic shop like ours must be segregated away from the mainstream. When I ask them to justify the rules, I hear the standard hollow chants: "protecting children," "morality," "community standards." I never get any real evidence that our shop actually harms children or offends community values.

The same dead phrases are mouthed in court to defend sex toys laws challenged as unconstitutional. Consider the litigation surrounding the infamous Alabama law that prohibits selling objects "for the stimulation of human genital organs." Defending the law, Alabama's Attorney General argued that a "ban on the sale of sexual devices and related orgasm stimulating paraphernalia is rationally related to a legitimate legislative interest in discouraging interests in autonomous sex." In other words, the government had a legitimate interest in preventing masturbation! The legal official also contended, "Commerce in the pursuit of orgasms by artificial means for their own sake is detrimental to the health and morality of the State."

Amazingly, a federal appeals court agreed with these specious arguments. In October 2000, the U.S. 11th Circuit Court of Appeals ruled that a statute banning the sale of sexual devices was rationally related to the state interest in "public morality."[88] As is typical of those who allege "immorality" to justify attacks on sex, the court failed to define that term. The judges assumed that simply by touting "immorality" they provided a rational reason for denying individuals the right to buy sex toys. Courts in totalitarian countries favor the same undemocratic ploy, asserting meaningless concepts to justify obvious infringements of basic liberties.

The judgment did not end the Alabama case. Another court ruled that the law violated the constitutional right to privacy. But state officials are appealing once more, and in April 2003 Alabama legislators voted to support the wacko law.[89]

Texas has a similar law, and enforces it. For example, in 2002 police conducting a driving investigation searched a car and found a box of sex toys. The female driver worked for a national firm that retails sex products at home parties. She was arrested on felony charges under the sex toy law and faces a two-year prison term.[90]

Laws are not the only source of intolerance against sex toys. Some banks are unwilling to deal with merchants who sell instruments of genital pleasure. Citibank, the largest financial organization in the world, refused our application for merchant credit card services simply because we sold products of a sexual nature.[91] Officials at the New York head offices of the banking behemoth could provide no coherent reason for the policy. Citibank has no problem working with people who sell things that kill, such as handguns or bombs; but selling instruments of erotic pleasure is totally taboo.

We encountered similar intolerance in advertising our store. For example, we wanted to reserve an ad in the program of a theater company that produces a major Shakespeare festival in our neighborhood. When arts administrators discovered that we sold sexual products, they shunned us, saying, "We are a family-focused event." The media featured our story when they learned that the festival's 2003 schedule included *Pericles*, which deals with incest, prostitution, and sexual violence.[92] Ironically, the fact that the theater company would expose families to such sex-negative material yet not a tasteful ad about our sex-positive store, garnered us more attention than any ad.

If governments, banks, or advertising outlets aimed prohibitions specifically at "Jewish products" or "homosexual products" most of us would quickly recognize that a prejudice against Jews or homosexuals was the real motive. Prohibitions aimed at a product simply because it provides erotic pleasure, involve an equivalent prejudice. Yet because phobias against sex toys and sex generally are not well recognized, lawmakers, bankers, and others have no idea that they are driven by irrational attitudes. By and large, the media lets them persist in that ignorance. Media vigilance is far more attuned to the easily recognized types of intolerance than the even more pervasive discrimination against sexuality.

When laws attempt to exclude sex toys out of the retail mainstream, when banks penalize sexual products, and when normal advertising channels are unavailable for respectable retailers, the implicit but powerful message is that sex toys and sex toys merchants are somehow worthy of their isolation, somehow dangerous to families and society. Spend the briefest time in the sex toy trade, and you will discover how prevalent that harmful message is. It in turn helps breed anxieties about sexual products in the minds of many otherwise intelligent people, and such fears prompt support for more discrimination against sexual products, and so churns another infection cycle.

7 / Attacking
Youthful Lust

CHILDREN ARE LUSTFUL CREATURES. Ultra-sound pictures show that the penises of male fetuses become erect in the womb. Most children begin playing sexually with their peers from an early age. Kinsey found that 48% of girls and 70% of boys engage in some sort of pre-adolescent sex play, usually exhibiting one's genitals or touching each other's erotic organs.[1]

Today teen sex is also common, ranging from necking and mutual masturbation to intercourse. According to a 2001 survey conducted by the Center for Disease Control, 60% of teens in twelfth-grade have engaged in sexual intercourse, and 22% have had four or more sexual partners.[2] Almost 70% of youths eighteen to nineteen have had intercourse, and the average youth in this group has sex relatively frequently, at least once per month for three-quarters of the months in the year.[3] Even children brought up in evangelical denominations and who attend church regularly are sexually active: 43% have had intercourse before their eighteenth birthday, while about the same number have engaged in some non-coital sex.[4]

Youth sex play attracts significant negativity from social institutions, parents, and even peers. Does all youthful sex cause harm such that it deserves blanket attack?

Three types of risks are involved in child and teen sex: the transmission of disease, unwanted pregnancy, and emotional trauma. The extent of these risks is a function of the maturity of the juveniles involved, and the type of sex performed. Kissing, necking, petting, and mutual masturbation provide no risk of disease transmission or pregnancy. The medical risks of penetrative sex are obviously much greater, and any type of intercourse involves significant emotional risks for girls. Many female teenagers are traumatized by sexual intercourse with partners with whom they have no emotional bond.[5]

Clearly large numbers of young people engage in unhealthy sexual interactions. Because the young are often impulsive and lack life experience and good judgment, their sexual contacts are less likely to be responsible and mature than those of adults. That is especially true of American youth. They are the most sexually irresponsible teenagers in the industrial world. Roughly 19% of non-virginal female teens in the U.S. become pregnant each year.[6]

Although many teens are sexually irresponsible, most are not. A majority of the teens that engage in sex never become pregnant. Further, 58% of U.S. teens used a condom the last time they had sex.[7]

We should encourage young people not to engage in penetrative sex until they are mature enough to prevent the harms it can cause. But negativity aimed at youthful sex play that avoids intercourse, or involves protected penetration between parties who are mature enough to handle the emotional intensity of such an experience, causes rather than prevents harm. The vast bulk of the opposition to youthful sex play is of that intolerant type. The target of attack is not harmful sex, but *all* sex, a categorical opposition to any form of erotic contact between young people.

The blanket attack on youthful sex has many ill effects. Besides producing erotophobia, such antisexualism helps generate the very harms it purportedly aims to prevent. When adults prohibit child sexual interactions, young people cannot acquire valuable sexual skills. Child sexuality experts report that most sex games between child peers are beneficial to a child's sexual development.[8] Although no experiments have yet been conducted testing the effect of denying children the opportunity to engage in sex play, tests on monkeys reveal that such deprivation radically interferes with adult sexual functioning. Sexologist John Money believes that the deprivation of normal sexual rehearsals in infancy and early childhood are responsible for an array of sexual disorders he calls "love sickness."[9] Sex researcher Sally Wendkos Olds says, "This repressive attitude towards childhood curiosity and sex play has been a prime suspect for the prevalence of sexual dysfunction in our society." She notes that cultures permissive toward childhood sex play are relatively free of sexual dysfunction and deviation.[10]

Blanket intolerance to youthful lust promotes unsafe sex. For example, when parents or institutions provide no secure place to have sex, youths must resort to the back seats of cars, dingy basements, or even parks and beaches. Because such places lack much comfort, and afford minimal protection from outside observation, the sex there is usually hurried and anxious. Unwanted pregnancies and sexual disease are much more likely to result from such rushed, impulsive sex.

Further, negativity towards all teen sex generates shame in the minds of young people about their sexual needs. Shame, in turn, helps cause irresponsible sex. For example, a major American study found that youths who break a formally pledged virginity vow are less likely than non-pledgers to use condoms. "It is hard to be contraceptively prepared and at the same time not intend to have sex," says the co-author of the study.[11] As I discuss further below, the best antidote to the dangers of youthful sex is comprehensive sex education that teaches not only about the pitfalls of sex, but also its intense physical and emotional rewards.

Informal Intolerance

Intolerance toward youthful sex first occurs in the home in our early years. Consider the following report told to the author of a study on childhood sexuality of an incident of mutual genital exposure involving two five-year-olds:

> We were caught in the act. Mother sent her home, told me not to
> do that again, gave me a good licking and sent me to my bedroom
> for the rest of the day. I couldn't understand why she was so mad;
> she never explained to me why I was punished. I was hurt and
> confused and, worse yet, my curiosity was still not appeased. This
> event is solidly implanted in my mind, for it was the first time I
> had encountered such fury from my mother.[12]

Such experience is very common in our culture, according to sex researcher Sally Wendkos Olds. She studied 250 sexual autobiographies from college students at the University of Puget Sound in Tacoma, Washington, and found a common theme, the memory of parental scoldings and punishments for childhood sexual play with peers, and the confusion such attacks produced. Over and over the students reported, "I couldn't understand what I had done wrong."[13]

Adult intolerance of child sexual play is well known to children and indeed is often incorporated into their games. For example, acting the part of an adult in such sex play, a child will say to his or her peers: "You bad kids, you get out of my house" or "I'm telling your mama."[14] Because children recognize adult hostility to their sex play they perform it secretly, where they hope they will not be discovered.

Most adults are equally hostile to *teen* sexual experimentation. One survey indicates that almost 70% of parents would not allow their teenagers to have sex in the home with a steady partner of the opposite gender. A parent commented, "It's easy to try to be open-minded, but I don't think it would be anything that I could allow." Another adult stated, "If you allow that then anything goes. Would you also allow them to smoke pot and get drunk?"[15] The parent equates teen sex with taking drugs or getting drunk!

Teenagers are also prone to act intolerantly toward their peers who enjoy sex. I experienced this in 1970 when I was eighteen. I told a close friend that I had "lost my virginity" with my girlfriend of two years. Coming of age during the rebellious days of the late 1960s, my friend had rejected most traditional values, especially those regarding drugs, religion, and career. He was as amazed as I was that he "lost respect" for me because I had "gone all the way" with my girlfriend. Though he acknowledged that these feelings made no sense to him, he could not hide the fact that they had arisen.

Such intolerance still seems to be alive and well. According to the National Campaign to Prevent Teen Pregnancy, 90% of teens think society should send young people stronger messages to abstain from sex at least until they are out of high school. Nearly 60% of the twelve to seventeen-year-old respondents believe it is unacceptable for high school students to have sex, even if they take precautions against pregnancy and sexual diseases.[16] A poll conducted by the *New York Times* and CBS News found that almost half of the over 1,000 teens surveyed said that premarital sex was "always wrong."[17]

Teen intolerance of teen sex is especially powerful against sexually active girls, and this has been true for generations. Growing up in the 1950's, a girl's "good name" was absolutely essential to social success. "Believe me, in those days a 'nice' girl didn't worry about things like pregnancy or diseases or anything like that; it was your reputation," says a woman who came of age in that era.[18]

Today a girl with a bad reputation is called a "slut." There is no equivalent term of disparagement for a sexually active male. Most girls shun "sluts" and so do most boys. Consider this statement from a seventeen-year-old boy:

> If you're looking for a girlfriend, not just some quick and dirty sex, you don't want to get involved with a slut, you know, one of those girls who goes out with more than one guy at a time, or a girl who goes for those one-nighters. You want her to be one of the nice girls, you know, the kind of girl who only has sex with her boyfriend, and she makes sure he's her boyfriend before she does it.[19]

The term "slut" thus does not disparage a girl because she has risky sex, but simply because she has sex outside a stable relationship. Primitive sexual fears prompt much of this intolerance. "Outlandish, archaic fears rise to the surface of the hormonal teenage mind—the fear of sexual disorientation, of a desire that could explode the family and wreck the home," says Emily White, author of *Fast Girls: Teenage Tribes and the Myth of the Slut*.[20]

Professor Mary Krueger expresses the sexual dilemma of female youths in these terms:

> Little permission exists for young women to explore and acknowledge the positive ways in which consensual erotic expression braids into the whole of their lives, and virtually *no* permission exists for them to explore eroticism as "[a] well of replenishing and provocative force...." [quoting Audre Lorde].[21]

Mary Piper in her book *Reviving Ophelia: Saving The Selves Of Adolescent Girls*, affirms that idea: "Girls need to be encouraged to be the sexual subjects of their own lives, not the objects of other's."[22]

School Intolerance

Sex education

Most school sex education programs are antisexual, sometimes overtly, sometimes subtly. Until the last twenty years, most schools in the west provided only minimal sex education. I graduated from high school in 1970 and had only two or three hours class instruction on the issue. More detailed sex education is now more common, but even today there are very important omissions in the instructional discourse about sex. Any comprehensive sex education program needs to examine four general sexual subjects: basic biology, the dangers of sex, pleasure skills, and erotophobia. Almost every program avoids the last two.

Every child needs to know the basics of sexual biology, and most children now receive some education in human sexual anatomy and reproduction. Imparting such purely biological information to children is relatively uncontroversial in the modern day. However, the majority of sex education curricula still do not identify the clitoris.[23] Typical is the student workbook *Sex Respect: The Option of True Sexual Freedom* used by thousands of schools and produced by a conservative sex education organization. It omits any mention of the clitoris in its anatomical drawings and text.[24]

Children also need to know about the dangers of sexual activity. Sexual contact can lead to deadly diseases, unwanted pregnancy, and interpersonal exploitation. Children need to be aware of the real threats posed by unprotected sexual contact, by sexual predators, and by uncaring sexual partners. Few people are opposed to giving children such negative sexual information. However, there is enormous controversy about how children should be counseled to protect themselves from the inherent dangers of sex.

A common policy of many schools throughout the world is to instruct children in only one defensive strategy: "No sex until marriage." Young people are given no information about other forms of protection, such as the use of condoms, or low risk sexual contact like mutual masturbation. This approach became the national rule in the U.S. in 1996 when Congress inserted into the Welfare Reform Act a provision requiring that federal funds used for sex education teach only "abstinence until marriage." The measure passed with virtually no public debate.[25] The average age of marriage in America is twenty-seven for males and twenty-five for females.[26]

The federal law has effected a revolution in sex education. Collectively the Clinton and Bush administrations have allocated over half a billion dollars under this program. President George Bush was a big fan of the abstinence message while Governor in Texas and as President has dramatically increased spending for it.[27] (His administration also has insisted that United Nations agreements relating to children approve only abstinence sex education policies, a position that only the Vatican and fundamentalist Islamic nations endorsed.[28])

One in three American schools now ignore lessons on birth control and teach that sexual abstinence is the only acceptable behavior. Over 900 abstinence programs preach the "no-sex" gospel with slogans such as: "Don't be a louse, wait for your spouse," or "Control your urgin, be a virgin." "Ten years ago abstinence was not even considered, it was laughed at," said a spokeswoman for the National Coalition of Abstinence Education. "A lot of avenues have opened up for kids to hear this message."[29]

The purported ground for such an absurdly narrow sex ed program is that educating children about alternatives to chastity promotes reckless sexual conduct, resulting in unwanted pregnancy, disease, and exploitation. But such an idea is empirically false.

Studies show that exposure to contraceptive education increases the chances that teens will use condoms when they begin having sex.[30] In the Netherlands, for example, which has a comprehensive sex education program, 76% of teens use contraceptives for their first sexual act.[31] The U.S. has the highest teen pregnancy rate in the western world, dramatically higher than other western countries that have much broader sex education programs. For example, the teen pregnancy rate in the United States is four times higher than in its northern neighbor, Canada, even though sexual activity rates are the same. As one expert wryly notes: "Vows of abstinence break far more easily than do condoms."[32] No rational educational system would deny children information about how to avoid the harms of sex.

Sex education experts rightly denounce the abstinence fetish. The National Campaign to Prevent Teen pregnancy points to the lack of evidence indicating that abstinence education delays the initiation of sex. AASECT, the American Association of Sex Educators, Counselors and Therapists, wants the American government to cease funding such programs.[33] The Sex Information and Education Council of the United States (SEICUS) and many other national organizations also oppose the current sex ed regime.[34]

Supporters of the "sex must wait" policy do not even try to justify their program on scientific grounds. In April 2002 Congress defeated proposed amendments to the legislation that would have required sex education policies to be "medically accurate" and "proven effective."[35] This decision shows an "abstinence from thinking" on the part of federal lawmakers, says one commentator.[36]

Avoiding sex is a sensible option for many youth, and especially young people who have had no real sex education. Sex is a risky activity no different than driving a car or handling a firearm. It requires some knowledge and maturity to prudently perform. Yet governments do not favor blanket prohibitions on young drivers or hunters. Legislators recognize that some youths can responsibly drive or hunt, and establish educational programs and licenses to encourage that result, although many teens are still involved in tragic car and gun mishaps. Politicians favor total abstinence in regard to teen sex and not teen driving or hunting, for cynical political reasons.

Sociology professor Janice Irvine shows in her book, *Talk About Sex: The Battles Over Sex Education in the United States*, how sex education policy has been key to the rise of the New Right.[37] For example, the abstinence program has delivered millions of dollars to conservative groups. It is "Pork for Prudes," says Christina Larson, editor of *Washington Monthly*.[38] "Federal grants have spurred the growth, not just of abstinence curricula in many public schools, but also of an entire industry of brochures, media campaigns, speakers, and novelty items to facilitate the new state programs . . . . The vast majority of companies developing and marketing abstinence material are, not surprisingly, politically conservative."[39]

Polls indicate that more than 80% of Americans think that young people should be given some birth control and safe sex information.[40] The abstinence agenda clearly does not enjoy popular support. It also violates basic democratic rights. After an exhaustive study of the abstinence education system in Texas, Human Rights Watch concludes that it offends international democratic standards in denying children information that could protect them from sexual disease.[41]

If abstinence-only education is downright harmful, instruction in safer sex is still inadequate to minimize risky teenage sexual behavior. Teens need a far broader sexual education than instruction in the use of condoms. As many commentators have observed, kids need to know but are not told even in most safer sex programs that sex is enhanced in both the short and long term by a deliberate program of sexual gradualism, whereby extensive sexual experience precedes the loss of virginity.[42] Virtually every other learning system involves a gradualist approach, and children naturally embrace it.

Instruction in sexual gradualism would teach a teen a way to explore the erotic responsiveness of his or her own body without contact with another person. As any sex therapist knows, such self-knowledge is essential for optimal partnered sex. Teens would also learn how to set the stage for healthy and satisfying sexual liaisons. They would learn, for example, that trust, emotional intimacy, relaxation, and verbal communication are all key to an optimal first sexual experience. As well, a course in sexual gradualism would teach young people about erotic massage and would emphasize the importance of non-coital erotic experimentation prior to intercourse.[43]

This step-by-step process also teaches a vital skill: sexual self-control. To supervise our primal itches, we must be familiar with them.[44] By celebrating rather than stigmatizing each sexual milestone (such as self-pleasuring, then necking, then petting, and so on) we encourage youths to linger in their sexual explorations, to become comfortable with each stage before moving on to the next, until finally they can "go all the way" when they are truly ready for it. The grave error of a system that demands that youths remain chaste is that they learn only the most primitive form of self-control, absolute repression of all sexual feeling. If that technique fails, as it usually does, youths have no skill in containing within safe boundaries their blooming lust. Their sexual impulses over-whelm them; unwanted pregnancies and disease are common results.

Further, teens who feel guilty about their lustful impulses often numb their shame with alcohol and drugs, or look for a sexual partner who will overpower them. Such responses usually lead to unsafe and unsatisfying sex. When we teach youths that sexual pleasure is wonderful and worthy, they have far less need for such self-destructive behaviors. Sharon Thompson's research into the sex lives of teenage girls reveals that girls with a positive attitude to sex and pleasure are sexually responsible:

> Because these teenage girls are looking forward to first sex, rather than grimly holding their breath until it's over, they usu-ally prepare for it, even carrying sponges and diaphragms and creams in their bags, even obtaining the pill, considerably before their boyfriends have imagined that sex might be imminent. They hold out for kisses, foreplay, oral sex, passion.[45]

Unfortunately, a sex-positive approach to formal sex education is un-known anywhere in America or even the world. President Bill Clinton fired his respected Surgeon General Joycelyn Elders for suggesting at an AIDS conference that masturbation was a natural part of human sexuality and that perhaps educators should say so.[46]

Another key omission in all school sex education programs is the lack of any information about the existence of erotophobia. Omitting a dis-cussion of the prevalence of irrational attitudes to sex and of the phobigenic system that generates those attitudes leaves a giant hole in any child's understanding of human sexuality. A sex education program that provides no information about erotophobia is as incomplete as a course in race relations that omits any mention of racism.

Condoms

Research indicates that easy access to condoms facilitates their use by stu-dents, and that school condom distribution programs are often supported by large majorities of parents and educators.[47] Yet many school officials disallow any form of condom distribution on school property.

Consider the situation in Long Island, New York. A *New York Times* report found that only one school on the island allows students access to condoms even though the region has the highest incidence of AIDS in any suburban area in the U.S. For example, at the health center of the Roosevelt High School in Nassau County students can obtain vaccinations, physical examinations, and even prenatal information, but not condoms. When the *Times* reporter questioned this policy, school officials refused comment. However, local religious leaders supported the condom ban. An official of the Roman Catholic Diocese in the area stated: "Schools should talk about the ideal and not send out negative messages to young people about their morality."[48]

In Tampa, Florida, the principal of Blake High School prevented the class president from giving her speech at graduation ceremonies after she included condoms in a gift bag for students attending the prom. Teachers refused to let students leave the prom until all condoms were collected. School Board officials supported the principal's decision, saying, "We can't be in a position to appear that we're endorsing underage sex or pre-marital sex. We promote abstinence."[49]

Teaching officials in Naples, Florida, summarily fired a ninth-grade teacher for giving a demonstration on condoms, using props including mood lighting, music, and a banana. The teacher said he intended to simulate situations his students might face, and believed that safe sex instruction was valuable. The country school board gave no reason for the dismissal except to say "The information is so clear: He doesn't belong in the classroom."[50]

Religious Intolerance

The official policy of most conservative churches is that a Christian must abstain from sex until marriage. For most conservative Christians, this antisexual rule applies to *all* pre-marital sexual activity, including non-penetrative genital conduct. For example, in a pamphlet produced by Focus on the Family, a highly vocal Christian lobby group, teens are told: "Some sex educators have tried to redefine abstinence to mean non-penetration, thus allowing for oral sex, mutual masturbation, etc. But this . . . misses the purpose of abstinence education, which is best defined as preserving sexual intimacy . . . for the commitment of marriage."[51]

At the organization's website kids are advised to avoid all sexual touch: "Petting leads to intercourse, plain and simple . . . . But until your hearts are bonded and the ring is securely placed on your left hand, don't play with fire or the forest will soon be ablaze, and your own home will be caught in the flames."[52]

Conservative Christian author Tim LaHaye, whose books have sold tens of millions of copies, draws the line against teen sex even further. His guidelines for dating require that all dates be approved by parents in advance, that the young people never go to a home or confined quarter without an adult in attendance, and that "all petting, caressing, or other physical expressions of affection that lead to sexual arousal" be avoided. God purportedly mandates this antisexualism: "If we are to live holy lives, we must discipline and control our sexual drive, confining it to the one human relationship God allows—marriage . . . . Because adultery is so consistently condemned by God, wise parents will teach their teenagers that foreplay or petting (which may well be the most exciting activity they have ever engaged in) only leads to frustration or adultery. In obedience to God it must be avoided."[53]

Religious antisexual groups also use non-biblical arguments to support their attempts to have youths abstain from all sex. They emphasize the real risks of sex, such as disease and pregnancy, but often exaggerate them. Abstinence advocates paint sex as an enormously dangerous experience, with the scepter of death looming close by.

Consider, for example, the pastoral statement of the Catholic Bishops of New York urging the teaching of abstinence in public schools. One reason the bishops give for their opposition to all sexual activity by school students is the "failure rate" of condoms, which the bishops contend is between 10% and 52% in preventing pregnancy and 17% for protecting against the HIV virus. "Can you imagine giving our children a cereal that caused death 17% of the time? Or buying them cars that were known to have a 17% rate of mechanical breakdown?"[54] New York Bishop John McGann told the *New York Times* that condoms fail "between 10 and 50 percent of the time."[55]

But such statements grossly misstate the real risks. Scientific studies show that the odds of a condom failure are low, although they vary significantly from person to person. Some people are highly disposed to condom failure, either through ignorance or sexual style, while others never break a rubber. "For most condom users, condom failure is rare," says the author of a study on the personal characteristics leading to the unsuccessful use of condoms.[56] The greater a user's knowledge about condom use and past experience with condoms, the less likely the condom will fail. Yet abstinence advocates seek to deny youths access to both information about the proper use of condoms, and free supplies of condoms as well.

James Dobson, founder of Focus on the Family, instructs teens to avoid pre-marital sex on another bogus ground: sex is addictive. "It is every bit as addictive as heroin or cocaine or any other drug. You get hooked on it, and you move further and further in that direction. I have seen lives absolutely destroyed by the addiction to a sexual kind of response that is irresponsible, especially for boys."[57]

The religious attack on all pre-marital sex is a major industry, and supported by the federal government. Organizations such as True Love Waits, Teen Aid, Sex Respect, Teen Choice, Focus on the Family, and many other organizations hold rallies, get teens to sign "chastity covenants," lobby politicians, place ads, and generally try to spread the message that all sex between unmarried youth is wrong.

Conservative Christian antisexualism is the most powerful ideological force behind the U.S. abstinence-only sex education regime. Yet lawmakers cannot acknowledge this overtly religious influence, because the American constitution requires the separation of church and state. Therefore, rare is the Senator or Congressman who justifies abstinence-only legislation by reference to Biblical prohibitions against fornication or lust. Religious dogma is translated into secular language – such as the baseless idea that such programs "protect children," and by this artifice Christian dogma is enshrined in secular law.

Ideological Intolerance

Much of the intellectual establishment is hostile to the idea that children are sexual beings. Consider the controversy that erupts when scholars challenge the myth that children are sexless or should be.

In July 1998 three academic researchers using meta-analysis techniques on existing studies published an article in the prestigious and peer-reviewed publication *Psychological Bulletin* challenging several assumptions about adult-child sexual contact. The first was the idea that such contact produces lasting, intense symptoms. In fact, the researchers discovered that such sexual experience correlated poorly with long-term maladjustment. The study also challenged the idea that children who had sexual contact with adults would not like it. In fact, 37% of boys reacted positively, 29% neutrally, and 33% negatively. Third, the researchers suggested that characterizing all adult-youth sexual contact as "abuse" was misleading, and proposed terms such as "adult-child sex" or "adult-adolescent sex."

These findings provoked a flap all over America. Overtly antisexual media pundits, such as Dr. Laura Schlessinger, misrepresented the study as an attempt to "normalize pedophilia". Churches, religious publications, and conservative organzations such as the Family Research Council attacked the scholarly paper. In an unprecedented move, the U.S. House of Representatives voted 355-0 to condemn the study. Under intense pressure, the American Psychological Association, which published the study, requested the American Association for the Advancement of Science (AAAS) to conduct an independent review of the article. The AAAS refused, saying there was no evidence of improper methodology or questionable practices, and lamenting the misrepresentation of the article by politicians and journalists.[58]

A second similar controversy greeted the publication in 2002 of the book *Harmful To Minors* by journalist Judith Levine.[59] Subtitled "the perils of protecting children from sex," she documents the harm done to children by laws and policies supposedly designed to protect young people. All commercial book publishers rejected the manuscript. The University of Minnesota eventually published it but the storm it generated prompted officials to review the university's publishing policy.[60] Her book begins: "In America today, it is nearly impossible to publish a book that says children and teenagers can have sexual pleasure and be safe too."

For spreading that sex-positive message Levine suffered heaps of abuse. The majority leader of the Minnesota House of Representatives denounced the book as promoting the "disgusting victimization of children."[61] Laura Schlessinger weighed in with similar predictable responses.

Church leaders called the book "evil". This froth in turn attracted national press attention, significantly boosting the book's readership.

Legal Intolerance

The laws governing the age of sexual consent are another type of intolerant restraint of youthful lust. Age of consent laws prohibit sexual contact between youths under a specified age with teens or adults above that age. For example, in California nobody of any age can have intercourse with anyone under eighteen, unless the parties are married. If the parties are three years or less apart in age, the offense is less serious than if the age gap is greater than three years.[62] In 1998 in a case involving sex between a sixteen-year-old boy and fourteen-year-old girl, the California Court of Appeal upheld the prohibition, ruling that although youths have a legal right to privacy in deciding whether to have an abortion, they have no legal right to privacy in respect of consensual sex.[63]

In Oregon a sixteen-year-old boy was convicted of "statutory rape" under a law that prohibited sexual relationships between youths under fourteen with partners more than three years older. The boy was three years and ten days older than his thirteen-year-old girlfriend. The court found that the girl had initiated the sexual activity. On two occasions she came to the house where the boy was staying, went into his bedroom, woke him up, joined him in bed, and engaged in sexual foreplay, which ultimately resulted in intercourse. At trial the girl said:

> Maybe what happened wasn't right legally, but we didn't know we were breaking any law. We just thought we were in love, and it happened because we both wanted it to. I know that everybody thinks we are too young to know what love is, but we don't think so. I still love Justin, and I know he still loves me.

The girl's mother, who originally reported the sexual contact between her daughter and the boy to the authorities, testified that although she did not condone the sexual activity, she did not consider "two young kids making love" to be rape.

Oregon law mandates a term of seventy-five months for such an offence. The trial court ruled that such a term was unconstitutional and sentenced the male youth to thirty-five months. The state appealed and in April 2000 the Oregon Court of Appeals imposed the mandatory term. Simply for having consensual sex with his girlfriend, a teenage boy was sentenced to over six years in jail![64]

In February 2001 police in Illinois arrested eighteen-year-old Brandon Parks after he appeared on *The Jerry Springer* show and admitted fathering the child of his fifteen-year-old girlfriend. Police told the media that the teen was charged because Illinois law prohibits even consensual sex with minors sixteen years and younger.[65]

Prohibitions on child pornography in many jurisdictions include sexually explicit images of teenagers under the age of sixteen or even eighteen and include images produced by teens themselves even for non-commercial purposes. Professor Philip Jenkins describes the effects of such prohibitions:

> This corpus of law has succeeded beyond the wildest dreams of decency campaigners in creating a perilous environment in which eroticism involving a person under eighteen is automatically criminal. A girl of sixteen may marry and bear children in many states, but if her husband takes a revealing photograph of her, he is creating child pornography.[66]

Media Antisexualism

The media has an enormous influence on young people. They spend hours in front of the television, on the internet, or reading youth magazines. Media intolerance toward teen sexual activity is expressed in two ways. The first is by ignoring the subject. As many women writers have noted, there are few coming of age stories of girls that include sexual details, unlike those for boys, such as Portnoy or Holden Caulfield.[67] Even the sexual details of *The Diary of Anne Frank* are censored in most published editions of the book.

The media is also intolerant of teen sexuality by portraying it only in negative terms, such as inherently dangerous or immoral. Consider, for example, how *Seventeen* magazine, read by millions of teenaged girls, deals with teen sex. An analysis conducted by Laura Carpenter of the University of Pennsylvania of 244 articles from 1974 to 1994 relating to sexuality and romance found that in 1974 and 1984, 62% of those articles portrayed sexuality as a form of victimization of women by men. The idea that a teen girl would have sexual desire appeared in only 15% of the stories in 1974, 19% in 1984, and 23% in 1994. Even when the subject of lust was raised, the common message of the editors was, "Don't give in to your desire." For example, one editor advised readers: "As time goes by, you will need to form your own set of values, your own reasons for saying no . . . ."

Similar moralizing continued in the magazine in the 1990s, but the idea that sex might be acceptable, that it might even involve "nothing more than a physical relationship" also begins to appear. Professor Carpenter concludes that the magazine is liberalizing its message yet still depicts sex-negative sexual scripts as preferable:

> Restricting sexual options may be a way of protecting the vulnerable—women, teens, or both—from danger . . . however, it may also constitute a maneuver to protect society from women's sexuality and power. Though perhaps unintentionally, the editors of *Seventeen* accomplish the latter.[68]

Any editorial position on teen sexuality other than the wary perspective expressed by *Seventeen* is dangerous for a publisher. The owners of *Sassy* magazine discovered exactly that when their editors took a non-judgmental stand on sex in their magazine for teen girls. Some of their articles had titles such as: "Sex for Absolute Beginners," "The Truth about Boys' Bodies," and "Getting Turned On." Several conservative Christian lobby groups, such as Women Aglow, threatened to boycott the magazine's major advertisers. The magazine owners instructed editors to remove all "controversial" content from the publication.[69]

Though the media reveals that many youths engage in sex and apparently enjoy themselves, rare is the further message that such youthful sex play can be healthy and beneficial, worthy of celebration and praise. Almost never do we hear of the countless happy youthful sexual relationships. This is partly because few youths in healthy sexual relationships seek attention, because of the intolerance it will attract. Still largely absent from the mainstream media is anything resembling a "discourse of desire," especially for teen girls. The dominant message of both advertising and entertainment is that girls are objects of male desire, rather than hot-blooded and lusty in their own right.

Antisexual Motives

Erotophobia

Much of the attack on youthful sexuality is the product of phobic delusions, such as the false belief that "playing doctor" is intrinsically exploitative or dangerous, or that teen sex must lead to pregnancy or sexual disease. Religious delusions about the immorality or "impurity" of non-marital sex also prompt attack on childhood sexuality.

A related fallacy holds that virginity is a gift to one's spouse. This idea assumes that virginity has intrinsic value, like food or clothing, which future mates will automatically value. But there is nothing inherently gratifying in taking another person's virginity. A virgin's lack of sexual experience is more likely than not to make him or her an unsatisfying sexual partner. Virgin men, for example, tend to ejaculate quickly during their first sexual episodes, long before the female is significantly aroused. Virgin women tend to experience pain, as their hymen tears during their first sexual congress, and this will distress most men. The greater our sexual experience, the more pleasure that we can provide our mates. In every other shared activity, such as cooking, cleaning, playing music, or dancing, more rather than less experience is considered a benefit for a mate. The idea that sexual inexperience is valuable is an absurd social construct. Many cultures encourage their youth to have sex before they are betrothed,[70] and some cultures do not even have a word for virginity.[71] Virgins are prized only in erotophobic societies.

Intolerance toward child and teen sexuality is also the product of lust phobia. If you harbor vague and inchoate delusions that sex is bad, then the thought of anyone engaging in sex, especially people in the formative years, will disturb you. The less anyone has sex the better you will feel.

Opportunism

Since the dawn of civilization, communities have used sexual prohibitions to draw social boundaries to define specific groups within the community. The classic example is the taboo against sexual contact between members of the same clan in many tribal societies. If you are a member of the "raven" clan, then you can copulate only with members of the "bear" clan. Who you can and cannot have sex with defines your membership in the clan in the same way that an emblem of a raven or bear defines your group.

Similarly, denying children sexual privileges is motivated in part by a need *some* people have to create an arbitrary social boundary between adults and childhood. The great sociologist of childhood, Philippe Aries, showed how this need to emphasize childhood status tends to vary from culture to culture, from generation to generation. For example, prior to the 1600s, explicit sexual jokes were commonly told in front of children. But over the next century children came to be perceived as "innocent" and in need of protection, especially from any exposure to sexual information.[72] Rousseau would have shielded Emile from any knowledge of sex until age twenty. Classic works of literature were expurgated to make a childhood edition. Erotic censorship aimed specifically at children became a tool of generational segregation, of emphasizing differences based on age. A common synonym for porn, "adult" material, draws attention to the age boundary.

Why would anyone want to exaggerate the natural differences between adults and children? There are several motives. The first is mere habit. If we grow up with a sense of a wide "generation gap," we will tend to favor the same distance in our relationships with children. A deeper motive is to solidify the adult ego. For reasons too complex to explore here, many people have a strong need to identify themselves not just as individuals, but also as members of specific social groups. The stronger you identify yourself as "adult" or "male" or "lawyer" or "Yankees fan," the greater your incentive to keep the boundaries of these social groups defined. The dissolution of such boundaries will impair your sense of identity. A person who identifies strongly as an "adult" will want to segregate as clearly as possible social boundaries between adults and children. Allowing children adult privileges diminishes such segregation.

Another motive for creating and exaggerating social boundaries is to formalize relationships between members of different groups so that they can interact through social roles rather than as individuals, thus avoiding the spontaneity and uncertainty of intimacy. Adults frightened of intimate, non-roled relationships with children will thus favor boundary-creating rules, such as those denying children the right to engage in sex.

Sexual prohibitions also help adults dominate children. Denying children sexual rights powerfully symbolizes adult control over them. Conservative Christian author Tim LaHaye recommends that children be prevented from engaging in sex play even to satisfy their curiosity about the anatomy of the opposite gender. "We should let the child know that he should learn about male and female differences from us, not from personal investigation."[73] Further, he urges parents to advise children: "Your body belongs to God, not to you."[74]

Sex play is itself highly conducive to a sense of self-control and power. As pediatrician Elaine Yates explains: "Both boys and girls feel potent. They're doing something new, daring, and entirely of their own design. Each other's genitals are exciting and powerful. The girl realizes that her body is desirable. The boy feels proud; his penis elicits awe."[75] The attack on childhood sex interferes with this opportunity to cultivate independence and sense of attractiveness.

Another more emotional type of generational opportunism also promotes intolerance toward youthful lust. A person gripped with a phobic attitude (of any type) has a selfish interest to ensure that the next generation shares it. Phobic individuals seek company. The prevalence of the fear helps rationalize it. A person who has a fear that few others share naturally feels unusual and irrational. If all sex causes you alarm then you will feel better if you know that other people react the same way.

Childhood is the time of life when important beliefs are acquired. Sadly, but perhaps naturally, our desire to educate our children sometimes flows not only from our belief that what we teach them is right, but also from our selfish desire to make them think like us. Much of the adult negativity aimed at childhood sexuality is designed to make them fear sex and thus be like their elders.

Further, many adults favor prohibitions on youthful sex play simply to deny young people what their elders were denied in their youth. Some adults feel jealous that young people today might be able to avoid that antisexualism that victimized previous generations. Demanding that the young remain chaste makes repressed adults feel less deprived.

Phobigenic Effects

Whether motivated by phobia or opportunism, intolerance aimed at youthful sex play helps cause several erotophobic attitudes. When youths are indoctrinated in the delusions that teen sexuality is "immoral," "impure," or "deadly," many youths will accept such false ideas. Ideological antisexualism breeds more erotophobia.

False ideas about juvenile sexual expression are also the product of rationalizing the enormous social negativity aimed at youth sexuality. If as a teenager you observe every trusted adult you know react with alarm to the idea that you might have sex with your sweetheart, the chances are high that you will make sense of their fear by concluding that teens can do nothing but harm when they have sex. Adults never have to say why teen sex is wrong, they only have to oppose it, and many youths will acquire hazy ideas that indeed it is wrong.

For example, the self-loathing evident in the following statements of girls from religious families who confess to having sex clearly shows that they have internalized powerful antisexual messages. "Mary," a correspondent at the True Love Waits website, says:

> I am 16 years old right now, and I lost my virginity when I was 13. It was the biggest mistake of my life, but at the same time, it was also the best lesson I ever learned. For two years I totally hated myself for what I did. Not only did I take away practically the one most important thing I could have given my husband, I let God down. That was probably the worst part. For two years I pleaded with God to forgive me. I would have even cried myself to sleep. It is very painful knowing you lost something you can never have back.[76]

"Christine," another correspondent at the same site, reports:

> I lost my virginity at age 18 to a man that I thought I was in love with. If you think final exams, SAT's, driving, or saying no to sex are stressful, then you aren't sexually active. Sex before marriage is more stress and guilt than it is worth . . . I gave my virginity away after much consideration and I truly thought I was ready. I wasn't and I lost respect for myself and felt like a piece of meat . . . it really lowered my self-esteem!!!

Sharon Lamb discloses in the preface to her book *The Secret Lives of Girls*, that as a child she played erotically with other girls but suffered intense shame because of it.

> The games I played were delightful games of heterosexual romance where a handsome young "man" would seduce or trap a young "woman" into sharing his bed and rubbing up against him. But I felt so terribly guilty for years about these games that I sought out therapists and social workers in high school to tell me if there was something wrong with me.[77]

This shame can be so strong and lasting that even decades after their teen years some people feel the need to hide their youthful sexual experimentation. Consider the following story related to psychologist Lillian Rubin. A woman in her forties told a friend how she lost her virginity when she was in high school. Her friend replied: "You mean you actually fucked in high school?" The woman instantly answered, "No, of course we didn't." That was a lie. She later explained to the therapist: "I was so surprised at myself; I answered her as if I were still that teenager whose life depended on people understanding that I was one of the good girls. It was really crazy; it threw me right back to those years and all the feelings I had then."[78]

Attacking child and teen sexual play also helps produce lust phobia. Consider the conditioning effect on pre-teen children of being "caught in the act" during an episode of sexual touching, and then shamed or punished. That occurs precisely when they are aroused, when they are in their first stages of sexual intimacy with another party. The result can be a permanent erotic wound. Pediatrician Elaine Yates notes:

> Children who are caught pay an enormous price which can cripple their eroticism for life. The price is humiliatio —a dramatic increase in shame . . . . An excruciating sensation that reddens the face and is impossible to forget. Most youngsters are ashamed about sex anyway, and are thus prone to humiliation. Once children are humiliated they may never again participate freely.[79]

These phobigenic effects can be achieved not just through actual adult intervention, but also merely through the threat of discovery. A child who engages in sex play furtively and with fear of discovery, as most of us did, experiences anxiety and arousal at the same time—a phobigenic combination.

Imagine the long-term effects of intense self-loathing in the teen years of people like the girls mentioned above who engaged in pre-marital sex contrary to the intolerant teachings of their religion. People who suffer years of torment simply for having sex before marriage cannot help but view their sexual impulses as inherently dangerous. Their first major lesson about their own sexuality is that it is the cause of enormous suffering. They have no idea their pain is entirely the creation of antisexualism. Whenever their sexual appetite arises again, prior to marriage, they must suppress it, to spare themselves more guilt and possibly social penalty. All such experience helps breed the attitude that sexuality is dangerous and worthy of the strictest control. No wonder then that when such people marry, their sexuality is often enormously inhibited. As sexologist Seymour Fisher puts it:

> The power of early inculcated sex guilt and early directives about shutting out the sexuality of one's body may chronically restrict spontaneous sexual action. There may be long-lasting inhibitory attitudes that keep clamping down, despite periodic loosening up resulting from exciting novelty or the demands characteristic of certain life situations (e.g., honeymoon). In other words, persons may for extended periods find they are most comfortable if they restrict the quantity of their sexual intimacy.[80]

A rational society would not attack all youthful sexual play, but only conduct that caused demonstrable harm. Unfortunately, however, our society is not rational when the sexuality of youths is an issue. Phobic attitudes toward the sexuality of children and teens are deeply entrenched and will not soon disappear.

8 / Mandatory Monogamy

IN EVERY AREA OF LIFE, the new and fresh has innate appeal to our senses. That is why we seek variety in food, friends, music, recreation, and travel. Most of us have an appetite for sexual variety too. Though we prefer a single committed relationship, we also have a roving eye and fantasize about having sex with other people. Some of us actualize those desires, jumping into bed with one-night dates or prostitutes. Others have affairs with colleagues or friends, and some couples embrace the formalized sexual variety of "swinging" and "polyamory."

This chapter examines the various alternatives to monogamy common in the modern era, and the negativity directed at such erotic expression. I use the terms "sex fantasy" to refer to purely mental non-monogamy, involving only thoughts and daydreams. "Sex variety" (or "non-exclusivity") refers to actual sexual behavior with someone other than a primary partner.

Is Sex Fantasy Harmful?

Large proportions of men and women regularly fantasize about sex with people other than their partner. Surveys indicate that most people indulge in such fantasy at least once a month. Over 50% of men fantasize about sex several times *each day*; 15% to 20% of women do the same.[1] In a study of college students, 32% of males and 8% of females reported that they had over one thousand imaginary partners.[2] Another study of men and women age eighteen to seventy found that 87% of the participants currently in a relationship fantasized about other people in the past two months.[3]

Some people have sexual fantasies that are so strong or obsessive that they undermine intimacy with their partner. People who have addictions to pornography or other forms of sexual entertainment, or who constantly "rubber-neck" every attractive person they see, or who flirt compulsively, have a real problem. So do those who cannot make love to a partner without escaping into the fantasy realm. Such disruptive fantasizing is unhealthy.

But relatively few people are so consumed by their fantasies. Less than 10% of the population are sex addicts. Most people indulge in erotic daydreams without any harm. We fantasize about having sex with others because of the fleeting pleasure such thoughts bring. Similar pleasure also naturally arises when we imagine other desirable experiences such as a eating a tasty meal, lying on a tropical beach, or skiing down a mountain. Sex fantasies arise more or less spontaneously, usually triggered by the random sight of an attractive person. They can also pop into the mind during masturbation or sex with a partner. Most fantasies last just a few seconds, and vanish as fast as they appear.

The bulk of our sex fantasies have no real impact on our love and affection for our partner. Indeed, sexual fantasies can increase the desire for our spouse. Years of sex with the same person can become boring. Getting aroused by watching strippers or sex films can kindle desire that we can bring to our relationship.[4] As an old saying puts it, "I don't worry where my man gets his appetite as long as he comes home to eat." People with active sex imaginations are more likely to stay sexually active with their partners. Further, brief erotic thoughts about other people that occur while having sex with our partner can keep us sexually aroused, allowing a continued high level of charge that our partner can enjoy.

Dr. William Fitzgerald, who specializes in marital and sexual therapy in San Jose, California, and is the author of SEX: What Every Young Woman Needs to Know,[5] recommends that if either partner enjoys sexual fantasy the couple include it in their sex play. He tells a wife whose husband occasionally likes to imagine having sex with centerfold models, to "Tie him up and tell him that you're this month's Playmate, sent by his wife, and that you're going to fuck his brains out . . . . Ask him what turns him on about the picture and incorporate it into your lovemaking. If it's 'the red-head's big tits,' tell him to close his eyes, imagine he's in bed with her, and put your breast in his mouth!"[6] By incorporating some sexual fantasy into their sex life, couples can have some of the pleasure of sexual variety without the complication of actual external sexual contacts.

David Snarch, author of *Passionate Marriage*, also believes that sexual fantasy has a place in committed relationships. Snarch is the main advocate of the idea that a mature partnership requires not only a high level of commitment, but also a high level of independence and "differentiation." He argues that blanket hostility towards sexual fantasy is typical of undifferentiated couples, people who depend heavily on the validation of their partner to feel good about themselves. Moreover, his twenty years of clinical practice reveals that such people are themselves predisposed to fantasizing. "People wounded by the discovery that they are not their partner's 'one and only' are likely to be fantasizing about someone else. Being dependent on validation from others, they have to lie about it even while they are complaining about their partner."[7] While undifferentiated couples use fantasy to *tune out* intimacy, highly differentiated couples use fantasies to *tune in*—"creating new psychological links in bed (and out)."[8]

Telling the "microscopic truth" in a committed relationship is an intimacy-building strategy of Gay and Kathlyn Hendricks, authors of *The Conscious Heart* and many other books on communication and intimacy. They advise lovers to "commit to full expression, to holding back nothing. This means telling the truth about everything, including my feelings, my fantasies and my actions."[9] The Hendricks walk their talk. Their book describes how they dealt with Gay's sexual attraction to another woman that he fully disclosed to Kathlyn. They show how openness and honesty about sexual attractions, even those directed outside the relationship, can enhance a couple's intimacy and creativity.

While not all sexual fantasy causes harm, blanket negativity toward it does cause harm. Couples who must conceal their fantasy life from each other weaken their intimacy bond. Without such disclosures each partner remains ignorant of what is going on within the mind of the other. Further, such concealment can increase the power of the fantasies. By openly revealing them we vent the sexual energy they produce. Also, when all outside sexual attractions are concealed, the fantasies that do come to light are more likely to be interpreted as more important than they actually are. When partners see that their mate's outside sexual attractions are fleeting and insignificant, then sexual fantasies *per se* will elicit little fear when disclosed.

Sexual Fantasy Attacked

The Bible reports that two thousand years ago Jesus said: "If a man look on a woman with a lustful eye, he has already committed adultery with her in his heart."[10] Merely thinking about sex is equivalent to performing it. Pope John Paul II elaborates on that draconian idea: "Adultery in the heart is committed not only because a man looks in a certain way at a woman who is not his wife, but precisely because he is looking at a woman that way. Even if he were to look that way at a woman who is his wife, he would be committing the same adultery in the heart."[11]

Hostility to sexual fantasy is still popular. Consider, for example, the position of one of the most popular relationship commentators in America, Barbara De Angelis. She hosts radio and television programs and has written several books, a few of which have reached the bestseller lists. Her *Are You The One For Me?* provides valuable insight into the difficult process of choosing a suitable mate. But she expresses highly intolerant views on sexual fantasy. She states (in bold letters): "Indulging in sexual fantasy about other people, in your mind, through reading magazines or watching films, is a form of infidelity. You've made a commitment to be sexually monogamous with your partner, and you're breaking it by deliberately focusing your sexual attention on someone else."[12]

She then quotes an unnamed man who questions her anti-fantasy assertion. He says, "How can you make such a broad statement? There's nothing wrong with fantasizing or looking at naked women as long as you don't do anything about it. It's harmless." De Angelis responds: "Harmless? Tell that to the thousands of women who've called me in tears because they found out their husband watches porno movies each night after their wives go to bed alone . . . . Tell that to the man who feels sexually inadequate because his girlfriend can get turned on only when she fantasizes about her ex-husband."

De Angelis attacks the broad category of sexual fantasy yet gives examples only where such fantasy is obsessive. A man who uses porn *every* night, or a woman who is sexually excited *only* by an ex-partner, clearly has problems. Most people can attend a male or female strip show, or have an erotic daydream about an attractive colleague, and later go home and focus their sexual passion on their partner. De Angelis makes the common mistake of stereotyping an entire category on the basis of negative subsets of it.

De Angelis continues in the same intolerant vein when she labels as a "sexual fatal flaw" the process of "leaking" sexual energy "in someone else's direction" which includes: "flirting with other people," "making sexual comments about your friend, strangers, etc.," and "making sexual comments to your friends, strangers, etc." All of this, according to De Angelis, "doesn't honor the sanctity of your monogamous relationship." It amounts to a "lack of sexual integrity."[13]

To justify her hostility towards *any* externalizing of sexual energy, De Angelis gives an example of a woman who married an obviously troubled man who ogled every woman he met. Ultimately he had a secret affair. She assumes that any diversion of sexual energy in any context causes such problems. She again recklessly over-generalizes. While the link between compulsive fantasizing and cheating may well be strong, the idea that all or even most fantasies about sex with others leads to actual sex is clearly wrong. A large part of the excitement of fantasies, sexual and non-sexual, is the fact that they are unreal. Only when such externalizing becomes compulsive does it threaten the relationship, but De Angelis does not confine her attack to just that category of conduct.

Oprah Winfrey's pop psychologist "Dr. Phil" McGraw casts the same unreasonably wide net in attacking men who are in relationships and who watch porn. In a February 2002 *Oprah* show he says that viewing internet porn is equivalent to cheating. To women who for any reason object to their man viewing such imagery, he counsels:

> You have good reason to be upset! That sort of behavior is disrespectful to the relationship that the two of you created. Talk to your partner. Explain that the pornography has to go—no ifs, ands or buts. Don't accept excuses like, "Everyone looks at porn," or "It's just the internet." That attitude speaks volumes about the health of your relationship. Your partner has to choose what's more important: pornography or the relationship.[14]

Anne Stirling Hastings, author of several books on human sexuality, presents another antisexual perspective on fantasy. She contends: "The automatic sexual 'hits' we get while watching television, and even walking down the street, are accepted as natural [in our culture]. They are not. Rather, they are examples of cross-wiring that almost everyone experiences. They interfere with you and your mate finding out what is possible sexually."[15] No evidence is given to support such a sweeping statement, and it violates common sense. The instant tingle of lust in our loins that sometimes spontaneously arises on a normal day has no greater impact on our relationship with our mate than the hungry tingle of our taste-buds. The vast majority of such feelings disappear moments after they arise and have no lasting effects. To condemn them all as "cross-wired" is nonsense.

Similar antisexualism is also very common in the interactions of sexual partners. Many people attack their partners merely for disclosing fleeting sexual interest in someone else, such as when a woman glares at her boyfriend when he admires the shapely figure of a woman walking across the street, or when a husband gets angry with a wife who comments on the build of a muscular tradesman. The trigger for the negativity is sexual attraction or fantasy, and not rational evidence that the sexual interest poses any real threat to the partnership.

Is Sexual Variety Harmful?

Some externally directed sexual energy goes beyond mere thoughts and feelings and involves actual sexual conduct with third parties, ranging from kissing, to sexual touch, to sexual intercourse. Such sexual variety seems inherently attractive to our species.[16] Sexual non-exclusivity occurs even in cultures where it is punishable by death. Anthropologist Helen Fisher, author of *Anatomy of Love*, says that only 16% of cultures on record actually mandate monogamy. The vast majority of societies allow for some form of sexual variety, although usually only for men. Fisher also studied divorce in sixty-two societies, and discovered that couples have a consistent tendency to separate after just four years—long enough to raise a child past infancy.[17] Further, studies of blood types indicate that worldwide at least ten percent of children are fathered by someone other than the man who believes he is the father.[18]

Recent discoveries about human sperm also suggest that we are innately promiscuous. Only one per cent of the millions of sperm cells that a man ejaculates into a woman's vagina are designed to impregnate her. The rest are "fighters" and "blockers" that nature created to prevent the sperm of *other men* from inseminating the woman. As Robin Baker, one of the co-discoverers of these remarkable facts, discusses in his book *Sperm Wars: The Science Of Sex*, the message of human biology is that humans are not naturally chaste. Males need "fighter" and "blocker" sperm because their women, at times, innately favor many partners. He says: "Both sexes have been programmed to shift between fidelity and infidelity as and when their circumstances dictate."[19]

Surveys indicate that the need for sexual variety is one of the key motives prompting married people to have affairs and single people to have casual "one-night" sex. "I just needed to feel like I could explore sexually, without any ties and obligations," one woman explained to researchers studying casual sex. A male participant in the study explained that he indulges in causal sex to "sexually experiment and satisfy my curiosity about what it's like to be with different people."[20]

Although many people have a powerful interest in sexual variety, modern western culture is tolerant of it only in the form of "serial monogamy." The most permissive of the prevailing ethics holds that sexual variety is acceptable as long as sexual relationships do not overlap in time. Yet concurrent sexual conduct is enormously popular in the west. Various sexual surveys estimate that from 25% to 50% of married men or women have had sexual contacts outside their primary relationship.[21] Clearly, many people have strong needs to both maintain a committed partnership and have some other erotic interaction. Is acting on this desire harmful?

Yes, if the outside sex is clandestine and if the primary partners have an agreement to remain sexually exclusive. Such "cheating" involves a violation of trust and often much dishonesty to conceal the outside contact. Many sexual excursions are not disclosed for unethical reasons: such as not wanting to grant a partner the same sexual privileges the cheater is taking, or because the cheater knows his or her sexual excursions pose serious health or emotional risks. Further, sexual non-exclusivity often occurs when the primary relationship is crumbling; the motive for the sexual variety is to find a replacement for the existing partner. Even if both parties consent to the sexual contact, it would still be harmful if it spread disease or caused emotional entanglements with the third party, or drained sexual energy from the primary partnership, or simply used up the time the partners need to spend together.

But not all non-monogamous sexual conduct need have those effects. Consider, for example, professional erotic massage. In a typical erotic massage session a client meets the erotic massage practitioner, undresses, showers, and then receives a full-body massage, with attention specially focused on the genitals. Erotic massage workers do not engage in oral sex or intercourse. Health risks are minimal. The client and practitioner are usually strangers to each other and have no contact outside the professional context. Although these sessions can be emotionally intimate, there is no real risk of emotional attachments that would threaten a healthy committed partnership. The session lasts from sixty to ninety minutes. It is very similar to that offered by traditional masseurs except that it involves genital touch and usually orgasm. Men are the main market for this service and women are the main practitioners, although there is a small market for male homosexual erotic massage, and a tiny demand from women.

Some women training to do this work seek to practice erotic massage techniques on volunteer men. I have assisted several women in recruiting the necessary male bodies. My experience was instructive. Every *married* man who was interested in the job had to reject the offer due to objections from his wife. Sometimes her complaints were reasonable because their partnership was in crisis or because the woman was dissatisfied with the small amount of sexual energy she was getting from her partner. But far more often the wives had no such complaint. They still adamantly opposed their husbands having *any* outside sexual contact, even though the men were willing to allow the women the same experience. While the wives could accept their partner having *non-genital* pleasure in a traditional massage and could tolerate their partner disclosing deeply intimate feelings with a professional talk therapist, they could not bear even the thought of their man getting a few minutes of erotic delight from a stranger he would never see again.

Several of the wives contended that the erotic massage would cause harm to the relationship simply by making the wives feel uncomfortable. But such an allegation offends any rational conception of harm. Not all fear is sensible; often it is phobic. In such cases the phobia is the real cause of harm, not the person who triggers it.

In no other type of conflict is one partner's emotional response to the other's behavior the sole test of whether the behavior causes harm. For example, consider a woman who objects to her husband eating Chinese food or wearing the color red. Nobody would say her husband is causing harm to the relationship by eating Chinese food or wearing red clothes; rather, every rational person would say that the woman's attitudes are the real source of the problem. We recognize her attitudes as senseless because we know that eating Chinese food and wearing the color red are harmless. We are helped in that perception by the fact that there is no mass social intolerance aimed at eating Chinese food or wearing red clothes.

An occasional professional erotic massage is equally harmless to any committed, healthy relationship. Indeed it can be beneficial, not only to the individual engaging in it, but also the partnership. In the same way that French cooking benefits from exposure to Oriental cooking (and vice versa), some outside sexual exchanges can benefit the sexual intimacy of the committed couple. It acquaints the partner with new sexual styles and techniques. It can put the spark back into a flagging sexual drive. The aphrodisiac effect on couples that have some disclosed outside sexual contacts has been well documented.[22]

The blanket demand that a partner give up *all* sexual conduct with third parties is little different than the demand that a mate not eat Chinese food or wear the color red. We have difficulty recognizing the parallel because of the mass intolerance we observe aimed at sexual variety.

Some evolutionists argue that humans are genetically programmed to react negatively to *any* sexual excursion by their mate. The leading theorist in this area is David Buss, author of *The Dangerous Passion: Why Jealousy Is As Necessary As Love And Sex.*[23] One need not be an evolutionary psychologist to accept that humans are innately disposed to react negatively to a real threat of losing something valuable, such as the on-going affections of a mate or the certainty of paternity. If the sexual conduct of our partners actually threatens these interests, our jealousy is natural, and rational too. But Buss goes further and argues that *any* sexual excursion, even sexual conduct that poses no real risk to the partnership and may even enhance the primary relationship, is likely to provoke a jealousy gene. The evidence to support the existence of such a non-rational genetic mandate is far from convincing and offends common sense because irrational jealousy is likely to interfere with reproductive success. For example, irrational jealousy and the excessive control it fosters are not conducive to a happy primary relationship, and thus impede the chances of pregnancy.

Although positing the existence of a jealousy gene offers a convenient explanation for the large amount of non-rational sexual jealousy observed in most cultures, it is too simplistic. Such biological reductionism has appeal in the absence of any understanding of the complex machinations of phobigenic systems.

Blanket opposition to all sexual variety is intolerant. It forces a partner who has a great need for some sexual variety to put an end to the existing relationship. A total ban on sexual non-exclusivity promotes serial monogamy rather than an enduring relationship. It is also conducive to cheating. When partners allow some room to engage in sexual non-exclusivity, they can negotiate healthy limits and restraints upon it. Key to the unhealthiness of much sexual non-exclusivity is the fact that it must be hidden.

Attacking Sexual Variety

While many counselors approve sexual fantasy in a relationship, actual sexual variety of any type is almost universally assumed to be a no-no. The reasons are supposedly so self-evident that traditional marital therapists never discuss them.

Even David Snarch, author of the ground-breaking *Passionate Marriage*, assumes that highly mature couples will embrace monogamy. He argues that while undifferentiated couples approach monogamy as a "mutual deprivation pact," more mature couples choose monogamy as a "commitment to *oneself*." Monogamy is then "driven more by personal integrity and mutual respect than by reciprocal deprivation or bludgeoning."[24]

But there is nothing disrespectful or lacking in integrity about satisfying the natural need for some type of sexual variety. Whether purely voluntary or coerced by a needy spouse, monogamy deprives partners of the variety they may need. In the same way that mature couples can use sex fantasies about others as a pathway to greater intimacy, they can do the same with carefully planned sexual contacts with others. Such a policy allows them both sexual variety *and* relationship commitment, rather than "either-or." But Snarch ignores that optimizing alternative. He assumes that mature couples would naturally favor absolute monogamy, yet never explains why. Only the emerging literature of swingers and the polyamory movement, discussed further below, recognizes that some types of sexual variety can be a healthy choice for committed, mature partners.

Religion is an important source of institutional intolerance against sexual variety. Most religions prohibit "adultery": any sexual conduct involving anyone other than one's spouse. Patriarchal religions condemn adultery only when married women practice it. For example, ancient rabbinic interpretation of the Torah held that the commandment against adultery (for which violators could face the death penalty!) applied only to women. A husband having sex with an unattached woman committed no sin. Jesus radically re-interpreted the anti-adultery provision, applying it to both men and women.[25] To Christ, even sex after divorce and with a new spouse, constitutes adultery: "A man who divorces his wife and marries another commits adultery; and anyone who marries a woman divorced from her husband commits adultery."[26] The anti-adultery provisions in the Bible afford obedient Christians no opportunity to engage in sexual variety of any type, regardless of whether it causes any real harm, or whether the spouses agree to it.

The media can also be intolerant of people who reject the notion that all sexual conduct with third parties is incompatible with a healthy, committed relationship. Consider the media's treatment of "swinging," a non-exclusive sexual pastime that several million Americans favor. Swingers allow their partners sexual contact with third parties, usually at clubs and organized events. Swingers follow protocols that are designed to protect the primary relationship. For example, many swingers' clubs insist that only stable, established couples participate in the fun, and that both partners approve. Academic studies reveal that swingers tend to be politically conservative, white-collar suburbanites who hold mainstream values in every respect except for their sexuality. Yet despite their protocols and conservatism, the media disparages their lifestyle.

Consider, for example, *Cosmopolitan* magazine, a publication that unabashedly celebrates sex. In reply to a letter from a woman expressing interest in group sex, columnist Irma Kurtz says, "Sex, by the way, is meant for *couples*. We are not group sex animals. So forget about the exploits of a few free spirits." To another woman curious about swinging, the columnist responds:

I think swinging is detrimental, dangerous and just plain tacky. You say you want something more. It seems to me that when two people who love each other and have good sex decide to include strangers, they are settling for something a lot less than what they already have: true intimacy that commitment creates.[27]

Such a statement is another example of a false generalization. It incorrectly assumes that *all* sex with an intimate, committed partner is always superior to sex with somebody new. While sex with committed partners is usually the best type of sex, sexual variety is sometimes preferable to some people because it offers what sex with a partner cannot: newness. Kurtz clearly would not enjoy swinging. But her own subjective dislikes are no basis for the sweeping conclusions that swinging sex must always be inferior to sex with a partner.

Similar negativity toward swinging can be found in almost every journalistic treatment of the subject. *GQ, Marie Claire, Details*, and *Penthouse* have all published sanctimonious, anti-swinging articles, and the title of an *Esquire* article on the subject reveals the common perception: "Deviates in Love."[28] That was also the perspective of journalist Terry Gould when he wrote a 1989 article on swinging. But his attitudes changed dramatically after detailed research, leading to his 1999 book *The Lifestyle.*[29] Taking the time to talk to swingers and really understand their lifestyle, he dropped his prejudices. Yet he encountered the same antisexual attitudes at every stage of his project: "From the very first time I started sounding out the reaction to a book on the lifestyle it became apparent to me that trying to discuss swingers without condemning them the way I had in 1989 made most editors and journalists suspect I was working on a profoundly immoral project."[30]

The mainstream media is less judgmental about "polyamory": sex in committed relationships involving more than two people. Because polyamory confines sex to serious relationships, it is less threatening to those hostile to all casual sex. *Time* magazine and many other mainstream print publications have reported on polyamory and largely avoided the overt prejudices evident in most media investigations of swinging.[31]

Legal Intolerance

The law in many places prohibits sexual variety for married people. Most American states make adultery a crime. In New York, for example, the penal code defines adultery as "sexual intercourse between two persons, one of whom has a living spouse," and is prohibited as a misdemeanor. Adultery charges are rare, but do occur.[32]

Laws controlling the behavior of public employees also attack adultery. For example, many police departments prohibit "conduct unbecoming an officer." Some police officers have lost jobs or promotions because they had an adulterous liaison. American courts are divided over the constitutionality of such action. Some judges have upheld the prohibition while others have struck it down as a violation of a constitutional right to privacy.[33]

The military also enforces draconian laws against adultery. A celebrated British case in 1994 involved the nation's top military officer who issued a code of conduct that prohibited soldiers from committing adultery. Married for thrity-nine years, the hypocrisy of the chief of staff was revealed when a sexy socialite sold the story of her affair with the man to a tabloid weekly. American military personnel have also been caught in the net of such laws. Perhaps the most famous case involved Kelly Flinn, the first female bomber pilot in the U.S. Air Force. She lost her "wings" for an adulterous relationship with a separated but married man.[34] Several enlisted personnel charged with adultery have committed suicide rather than be imprisoned or expelled from the forces.[35] Even employees in the private sector sometimes face anti-adultery intolerance from their bosses.

For example, until 1994 when the company lost a court fight on the matter, the Wal-Mart organization fired any employee who acknowledged
committing adultery.[36]

Swingers are a common target of antisexual police officers and prosecutors. Every year in North America, police use vague laws aimed at
"lewdness" or "indecency" to raid swingers' clubs. The gross invasions of
privacy arising from police action against swingers rarely attract much
controversy because the press and the public share the police antipathy to
sex variety. The prevalence of such phobic attitudes keeps most swingers
mum about their lifestyle. While millions of homosexuals feel comfortable "coming out" of the closet, rare is the swinger who feels the same. So
great is the social stigma against swinging that the law regards a false allegation that an individual is a swinger, as defamation. For example, a
newspaper columnist wrote that two lawyers had been "cementing their
connections through the lawn tennis circuits and wife-swapping bri-
gades." The columnist contended his article was intended to be humor-
ous and an exaggeration, but the lawyers successfully sued for libel. The
judge ruled that to insinuate that the lawyers and their wives "were capable of such immorality" was impermissible.[37]

Child custody laws provide another opportunity for legal officials to
attack sexual variety. Such laws allow judges and child welfare officials to
examine the appropriateness of parental behavior, and sometimes highly
erotophobic standards are imposed. Gays, prostitutes, and other social
minorities have battled this form of sex antisexualism for years. Now
polyamorists are suffering the same fate.

Consider, for example, the case of April Divilbliss of Memphis, Tennessee. She had a daughter by a man who left town with no forwarding
address a week after he was told of the pregnancy. Divilbliss later married
and in addition cohabited with another man in a polyamorous relationship. Both men were father-figures in her daughter's life, and they referred to her as their daughter. In November 1998, MTV aired a
documentary about polyamory that featured Divilbliss and her family.

Immediately after the broadcast the child's paternal grandparents applied to the state of Tennessee for emergency protective custody of the
child—on the basis that the mother's relationships amounted to "depravity"

that could "endanger the morals or health" of the little girl. A judge agreed and ruled that one of the men had to move out before he would consider returning the child.[38] The mother and grandparents ultimately found a mutually agreeable solution for the care of the child. But the court judgment shocked the polyamory movement, and its support groups warned their members not to "go public" with their unconventional family arrangements. *Time* magazine called the case a "tale of injustice."[39]

The Infection Cycle

Intolerance aimed at sexual fantasy and actual sexual variety flows from several types of erotophobic attitudes, and helps cause such attitudes, as this section discusses.

Sexual fantasy

Blanket attacks on sexual fantasy are motivated in part by a *sexual fantasy phobia*. Jesus, Barbara De Angelis, and Anne Stirling Hastings are afflicted with this condition. They believe *all* sexual fantasy, without exception, is bad or a threat to the primary relationship. Such an attitude is clearly an invalid overgeneralization.

Beneath that delusion often lays a more primitive aversion. The distress many people feel when they detect their partner having *any* external sexual interest is highly reflexive. It arises suddenly and without conscious control. Consider how phobigenic conditioning could imprint an aversion to any sign of externally directed sexual desire by our mate.

From a young age we may observe one of our parents chide the other simply for sexually admiring a third party. We see characters in a television sitcom berate their partners for similar conduct. We never see positive reactions to such disclosed sexual interest. Constant negative experience like that helps breed aversions to our partner's attractions. Thereafter we will automatically get upset when we hear our partners reveal their lusts. Our distress is entirely non-rational, the product of a conditioned emotional program in our brain. The real threat to the relationship is not the transitory attraction, but the fearful response. Yet such a knee-jerk response is so common in our culture that it appears to be natural and even reasonable.

To make sense of the attacks on sex fantasy we invent nonsensical delusions that all such fantasies will lead to affairs, or that they amount to "cross-wiring" in the mind, or a lack of "sexual integrity," or that any interest in a third party means our partner has lost interest in us.

Hostility to sexual fantasizing also engenders lust phobia. Picture a devout Christian husband who sees an attractive colleague, and in a few seconds of fantasy, undresses her and has sex. In the eyes of Jesus, he will have committed a sin. The Christian or anyone who has moral qualms about adulterous thoughts will experience the rush of lust and then shame. When the pairing of arousal and shame occurs repeatedly, conditioning will produce a negative association with arousal *per se*. Negativity aimed at fantasy helps breed an aversion to lust. A man or woman who for ten years or more experiences adulterous thoughts and simultaneously experiences shame, will acquire some aversion to his or her own sexual impulses. Such phobic feelings cannot be turned off easily, even when the person is having sex with a spouse. To the person's emotional mind, all desire is aversive, even when it is directed at the spouse. Sexual inhibition within marriage is one result.

Actual sexual variety

When Jesus condemns adultery in real or imaginary form, when laws outlaw it, when journalists attack consensual swinging, when nobody is ever heard to say anything positive about those who engage in sex with third parties, delusions about sexual non-exclusivity are likely to form in many minds.

Because much sexual variety *is* unhealthy, we rarely hear of any other type. Such a situation is highly conducive to *stereotyping*. I pause to discuss the psychology of this delusional process.

A child in apartheid South Africa sees police posters of fugitive criminals, notes that all of them have black racial features, and concludes that all black people are criminals; a child in pre-Nazi Germany observes a parent borrow money at usurious rates from a lender known to be Jewish, and infers that Jews are a greedy group. The child may never have been expressly told that blacks are dangerous or Jews greedy, but unilaterally jumps to such conclusions. Such self-deception can occur without any input from others, and entirely as a result of cognitive errors. In the early 1950s, Gordon Allport in a classic text, *The Nature of Prejudice*, revealed how commonly the mind plays such generalizing tricks, and especially so in regard to social minorities.

Because healthy non-monogamy is concealed in our culture, the non-monogamy that gets all the attention is the unsavory variety. The result is that most people stereotype *all* non-monogamy by its negative subsets. For example, when I was helping erotic massage trainees find male volunteers I often heard wives justify their opposition to their husband having an erotic massage by the statement that they had been with "cheaters" in the past and did not want to re-live the experience. The thought of their partner having a disclosed erotic massage by a professional provoked the same feelings of anger and distress that surfaced when the clandestine affair was uncovered. Swingers and polyamorists are often stereotyped in the same way.

To overcome this stereotyping process our culture needs to develop examples of sexual non-exclusivity that are ethical, respectful, and healthy, and to make them more visible. The Body Electric School in Oakland, California, which uses erotic massage in group sessions as a tool of personal and spiritual growth, provides an alternative perspective on sexual variety. So does the growing literature and community of the polyamory movement. Through magazines such as *Loving More*,[40] books such as *Polyamory: The New Love Without Limits*,[41] and *The Ethical Slut*,[42] and annual conferences, the polyamorist community is refining the formula by which sexual activity outside a committed partnership can be a growthful and healthy experience for all the parties involved. The more these alternative forms of sexual variety gain attention, the less likely that automatic negative stereotyping of all forms of non-exclusivity will occur.

Hostility toward sexual variety generates lust phobia: the generic infection cycle again. Imagine that you are an undercover police officer gathering evidence at a swingers' party. To prove an offense under adultery prohibitions or other laws that prohibit "indecency," you need evidence that the swingers actually had sex. If they gathered and just talked, or knitted sexy outfits, they would offend no law. Even if they gathered and simply massaged each other's backs and legs and feet, they would commit no crime. You need to see genital stimulation. Unless some penis is erect, some vagina penetrated, you can lay no charge. You must look for exactly the same evidence of genital arousal in enforcing laws against prostitution, public sex, fornication, and adultery.

The law has a curious fascination with genital arousal. The mere fact that a penis is aroused turns a lawful event into a crime. Such institutional action aimed specifically at genital arousal cannot help but stimulate rationalizing in your mind: something must be wrong with genital arousal if the laws attack genital arousal in so many contexts. The special exposure of legal officials to the bizarre antisexualism of the law makes them especially susceptible to lust phobia, which, in turn, promotes their antisexual enforcement of the law.

Sexual Exclusivity as a Symbol

Phobia is not the only cause of blanket negativity toward all sexual non-exclusivity. A complex symbol system also plays a key role, and it is an important catalyst of the infection cycle.

Most of the cultures of the world have used sexual renunciation to make non-sexual statements. For example, elites in several religious traditions take vows of celibacy to show their "purity," or simply to distinguish their group from the carnal hordes. The incest taboo similarly helps define the boundaries of a family. Lovers often express their commitment to each other by renouncing sex with anyone else.

Sexual exclusivity makes some sense as a symbol of love and honor for two reasons. First, giving up something of value is a time-honored way to express positive feelings. Religious rites pay homage to the gods by sacrificing a valued animal or even a human being. Giving up all sexual contact outside the relationship powerfully expresses valuation of the primary partner. Of course, to renounce anything could express the same message. Lovers could symbolize their relationship by giving up their hair—shaving their heads—as some religious devotees do; or they could give up wearing any color but green; or give up wearing regular shoes in favor of "lover's shoes." All such symbols could express the same commitment-affirming message as sexual exclusivity.

Sexual exclusivity has some practical advantages as a symbol of a committed relationship. It ensures no offspring will be born outside the relationship and protects the couple against sexual disease. It also prevents the emotional complications that often result from intimate relations with a third party. But not all sexual interaction involves such risks.

Symbolizing commitment and love through sexual exclusivity is enormously popular in modern western culture. But it has two serious problems: it is highly phobigenic, and it motivates intolerant attacks on people who express commitment in other ways.

The sexual exclusivity symbol system has these effects by producing an attachment to sexual renunciation. Many other symbol systems produce similar attachments to their symbols. Consider, for example, the attachment many folks have towards their nation's flag. Through a complex conditioning process many people learn to respect their flag as something intrinsically valuable. The sight of the Stars and Stripes stirs pride and respect in many Americans, as revealed by the events following the September 11 terror. Wedding rings have similar emotional significance for many people. Through long tradition and the advertising campaigns of jewelers and diamond companies, many couples learn to associate the good feelings of commitment and love that their wedding band signifies with the band itself. They develop a powerful sentimental attachment to the piece of metal on their finger and can get profoundly distressed if they lose it.

Like a wedding ring, sexual exclusivity can acquire intrinsic value. The loss of sexual exclusivity, like the loss of a wedding ring, provokes very negative feelings, even though the relationship may not actually be threatened. The mere thought of a partner's sexual attraction to others provokes automatic distress. In this way the symbol system helps imprint an aversion to *all* sexual variety.

Further, people who adhere to the sexual exclusivity symbol system must constantly police their own sexuality and this too has phobigenic effects. Stephen Levine, who has written several brilliant books on death, meditation, and relationship, provides an example. He embraces an extreme form of sexual exclusivity with his wife Ondrea:

> To enhance our commitment, one of our practices is 'the withdrawal of the senses.' If my attention falls on any object that

could engender lust, awareness mindfully diverts . . . . I do not allow my attention to rest on any object that could lead to a mind-moment of sexual desire. Even in my dreams, if a sexually motivated person approaches, I watch myself turn away, saying that I'm in a committed relationship . . . . The withdrawal of the senses is not suppression, it's commitment.[43]

The problem with a practice of constantly controlling every "mind-moment of sexual desire" is that such restraint is phobigenic. Humans are sexual beings, and our lust often arises spontaneously. A person who must constantly shut down those feelings and repeatedly avoid all sexual stimuli beyond their spouse engages in a potent form of phobigenic conditioning and is likely to acquire phobic aversions not just to externally directed lust, but all lust. Recall that conditioned sex aversions tend to be generic. That is why women who have been raped can acquire aversions to *any* sexual interaction, not just an abusive one. Similarly, people who have been schooled in the evils of pre-marital sex and who righteously delay sex until they are married, often remain inhibited even in bed with their spouse.[44] If every feeling of lust for a third party is constantly inhibited as Levine describes, rather than mindfully allowed to naturally arise and then subside, the emotional mind is likely to regard all lust with suspicion.

Symbol systems only work effectively when large numbers of people adopt them. People who are attached to a specific meaning of a symbol take comfort in seeing everyone interpret it in the same way and get upset when some people reject the symbol. A person who holds sexual exclusivity as the major sign of love and commitment will naturally feel uncomfortable observing the rites of swingers, who enjoy committed relationships that flout that rule.

Further, renouncing sexual interest in anyone other than one's partner takes energy and discipline, and reduces the amount of sexual pleasure available. This burden is more bearable when it is shared. Non-monogamous couples such as swingers who enjoy both committed relationships and sexual variety, naturally raise the ire of people who chose to signify love through mutual self-denial. Such anger ultimately breeds social discrimination against swingers and other non-monogamous groups.

Healthy symbol systems require appropriate symbols of membership. The sexual exclusivity symbol system is dysfunctional because it promotes blanket negativity toward all sexual non-exclusivity, even that which involves no diminution of love and commitment in the relationship. A rational society would find symbols other than sexual exclusivity to signify romantic relationships. A healthy couple would not automatically expect that their partner would avoid every opportunity for sexual variety. Their anti-exclusivity rules would take aim only at fantasies or conduct that truly threatened their partnership. They would forbid unsafe sexual practices, or those involving emotional entanglements or dishonesty. But they would not automatically interpret sexual contact with a third party as a threat.

9 / The Sexual Hush

WE ACQUIRE LANGUAGE in our first year of life. Through the spoken and written word we will gain much of our knowledge of the world and ourselves. Our parents, teachers, employers, and society at large will reward us for being articulate and expressive.

Except in regard to sex.

From our earliest days we observe constant and often subtle negativity aimed at discourse about genitals and lust. We learn that in the realm of sex, sealing our lips is the best policy. As a result, we communicate little about the subject to our parents, children, and friends. Even most lovers share few words about sex. Negativity toward sexual communication is more common than any other type of antisexual behavior; hence it has the greatest phobigenic effect, helping breed phobic attitudes towards not only sexual communication but also sex itself.

Yet a common myth is that ours is a sexually verbose culture and that we have cast off the verbal taboos of former generations. One sexual historian even claims that the repression of sexual discourse is now "nonexistent."[1] The pervasive sexual hush in our culture is not well recognized largely because the media gives prominent attention to the few individuals who will talk openly about things erotic. A television show or newspaper article that features the rare individual who is comfortable communicating about sex is far more likely to attract an audience and improve ratings than one that features the more average individual who is sexually tongue-tied. Open sex discourse is interesting; sexual muteness is not. The media helps us overestimate the prevalence of sex discourse.

Some types of sex discourse are dangerous and deserve disapproval. A statement such as, "Oral sex poses no risk of transmitting AIDS," could induce those who hear it to engage in unsafe sexual behavior. Similarly, a child's false statement that "My father raped me," could enormously harm the parent. Bigoted statements such as "All homosexuals are pedophiles," or "Women like to be taken by force," are also harmful if believed. Negativity aimed at such misinformation is not intolerant.

Fictional sex discourse in books, poems, plays and movies, that portray nasty sexuality such as violence or child sexual exploitation, may in rare circumstances have unhealthy effects like the violent or child pornography discussed in the next chapter. Negativity aimed precisely at such nasty sex content is not antisexual, although censorship is probably not the best strategy, because it often causes more problems than it solves.

Most negativity aimed at sex discourse does not target misinformation or nastiness. A hush occurs merely because the subject is sex, any type of sex. This helps breed the range of erotophobic attitudes discussed below, but it also has another unhappy outcome: sexual ignorance in both children and adults. Inhibitions in communicating about sex make people sexually stupid.

American children are especially prone to what some researchers call "sexual retardation." A majority of children in each of several age cohorts, from age five to nine in one major study, failed to conceptualize gender differences in genital terms. Responding to the question: "How can anyone know that a newborn baby is a boy or a girl?" most children failed to specify genital differentiation. Even young teens, although aware of the genital criteria, were largely unable to use a vocabulary accurately labeling sex organs.[2] Many British children suffer the same ignorance. A survey of almost 10,500 children revealed that more than a quarter of pupils fourteen to sixteen years falsely believe that taking birth control pills would prevent sexually transmitted diseases.[3]

Large numbers of adults suffer the same ignorance. In surveys conducted by the Kinsey Institute only 20% of the American public could give correct answers to twelve of eighteen questions about sexuality, such as: normal penis size, how AIDS is contracted, and when females can get pregnant.[4]

Lack of sexual knowledge makes the ignorant individual more likely to engage in unsafe sexual conduct. Lacking knowledge about the transmission of sexual diseases, and ways to prevent it, millions of people engage in risky sex. The result is an epidemic of unwanted teen pregnancies and sexually transmitted diseases.

Sexual ignorance also stunts erotic pleasure. Good sex is enhanced by a broad sexual knowledge base and by the ability to communicate openly and honestly.[5] Intolerance toward sex discourse helps make sex dull and routine, because it makes people reluctant to talk about sex and make it better.

Sexual ignorance also undermines the ability to recognize erotophobia and overcome it. Accurate information about sexuality is a potent antidote to erotophobia. For example, only when your rational mind learns that masturbation causes no disease and that homosexuals are not pedophiles, can you begin to control erotophobic attitudes towards masturbation and gays. A reluctance to communicate about sex frustrates that counter-phobigenic process. As American judge and scholar Richard Posner says in his book *Sex and Reason*, "Much of the revulsion we feel about sexual behavior different from our own reflects an ignorance about sex and its consequences...."[6]

Finally, another indirect effect of the sexual hush is sexual assault. Many victims of sexual abuse never report the attack simply because they are too shamed to utter the words to describe it. Some sexual predators deliberately seek out children who are especially inhibited in talking about sex, for such muteness ensures the crime will not be reported or prosecuted.[7]

Negativity towards sexual discourse displays a pattern, and all of us have observed it at least unconsciously: the more the communication concerns the dangers of sex, the more tolerated it is; the more it concerns the benefits of sex, the more negativity it attracts. Sex discourse focusing on the physical pleasure of sex, and how to enhance it, attracts the most negativity of all. Parents, sex educators, the media, and other social institutions are far more likely to talk about sexual danger than about sexual desire and gratification. Children grow up learning that they can discuss sex only if they are reporting a problem, and many do not even feel they have permission to do that.

Intolerance towards sex discourse occurs both in the informal domain of family and friends and in social institutions. Consider examples of this type of irrational negativity in the home.

The Informal Hush

A key part of the parenting process is to educate children about their bodies. Some of the first words a child learns are the names of body parts. Most parents are able to pronounce for their children the names for the nose, hands, legs, and other external organs. But the names of genitals, especially female genitals, are often ignored. In a study of three-to-six-year-old children, only 14% of the girls could offer any word for female genitals; over 50% of the boys could name the penis.[8] In another study of eighty parents, all the caregivers reported that they named their sons' genitals, but only 27% used the name "vagina" or a derivative, 29% referred to the vagina as "bottom" or "front bottom," and 39% used no particular word at all.[9]

Even many adult women have trouble using the words that describe their genitals. The actress Jane Fonda recently admitted that she was one of these women. "I was afraid to say the word vagina. I was afraid to say the word for my most intimate, core, feminine part. I have that fear in common with most women."[10] Some viewers say Oprah Winfrey has the same problem, stumbling over the words "vagina" and "clitoris" on her show.[11]

Virtually never do parents provide names for the clitoris and labia. I know of not a single adult woman who learned these names in her childhood. Indeed our vernacular almost completely lacked the word "clitoris" until the late 1960s. Then it started to appear in a new genre of scientific and popular books focusing specifically on sexual pleasure, such as the works of Masters and Johnson and *The Joy of Sex* by Alex Comfort. The word also became more popular as the emerging feminist movement gave special attention to female sexuality. But even today, a full generation after the term "clitoris" entered the social consciousness of large numbers of women, modern mothers omit it when identifying the body parts of their daughters. My own informal poll of scores of women reveals only a couple of mothers who have named that organ for their daughters. Other commentators report a similar trend.[12]

If parents are loath to provide the names for sexual body parts, they are even more inhibited in communicating about sexual functions. "My mother's sex talk consisted of telling me, 'If you get pregnant, don't come home,'" says the mother of two girls age nine and ten. "I know I should have talked to the girls about sex by now, but I've been putting it off and putting it off. I just don't know what to say."[13]

That mother is not unusual. Sex education in the family is minimal. Peers and the media are the primary sources of sexual information for most children.[14] In a study of university students and their parents, more than half the students reported that they had never had a meaningful discussion about sex with their parents. Interestingly, 60% of those parents claimed to have communicated meaningfully with their children about sex. The researchers concluded that many parents greatly underestimate the amount of sexual information their children need.[15]

Parents also inhibit adult discussion of sexual issues if children are within earshot. When sex is the topic, adults will lower their voices and speak in hushed tones or double entendres, or say things like "I can't speak of this in front of the children." Children recognize this inhibition. They learn that adults do not like to communicate about sex, and especially when children are near.

Children sometimes initiate sexual conversations with adults, asking questions and making sexual statements. Adults often react negatively to such statements. The red-faced flush of embarrassment or stammering for words powerfully conveys to children the adult discomfort with sexual dialogue. Sometimes the adult's response is worse. In many families a child's statement such as "my penis is hard" or "I think my vagina is pretty" will provoke overt adult hostility. Children have been slapped, had their mouths washed out with soap, or been verbally abused for making sexual comments.

Most children grow up entirely ignorant of their parent's sexual lives. "We didn't have sex in our house. There was no such thing! My parents never talked about it, and I never thought of them as having sex," is a typical comment when someone is asked their impression of their parents' sexual life.[16] Family therapists Miriam and Otto Ehrenberg call this desexualization of parents "The Myth of the Virgin Couple."[17] Children perceive as sexless the people who should be their most important sexual role models.

Many parents are equally ignorant of the sex life of their youth. According to researchers at the University of Minnesota, half of all mothers of sexually active teens falsely believe that their children are still virgins.[18]

The family infection cycle

A variety of erotophobic motives inspire intolerance toward parent-child communication: aversions to the sound of sexual words, discomfort with speaking about sex to anyone, and a more specific phobia about talking to children about sex.

Consider the first of these: *sex word phobia*. Specific sexual words such as "fuck," "cock," or "cunt"—the common Anglo-Saxon terms for genitals and sex acts—prompt powerful offense in many English-speaking people, even when such terms are not used in a threatening manner. The mere sound of such words when spoken, or their sight when written, elicits discomfort.

Parental negativity aimed very specifically at such words helps transmit that very specific phobia to children. For example, a child is more likely to be punished for yelling "Fuck you," at a parent than "I hate you." Similarly, the average child discovers that parents will more often deny access to television programs where words like "fuck" are heard than shows free of slang. The child will also hear parents utter such terms in a hush when children might hear them. Parental negativity is reinforced by media intolerance toward the same terms, as discussed later in this chapter. Even children of a tender age learn that specific sexual words attract a powerful negative charge, and in time the same words will elicit similar feelings in them.

The failure to communicate about sex prompts children to draw negative conclusions about sex itself. Children recognize that people usually are uncomfortable talking about terrible things, like illness and death. The fact that virtually everyone avoids sex talk suggests that the things the words designate are worthy of avoidance. The mother who never tells her daughter the name for the clitoris, and the father who never mentions to his son the pleasure of masturbation, will leave the child with vague ideas that there is something wrong with the clitoris and masturbation.[19]

Avoiding communicating with children about sex is also a function of the desire of some adults to maintain arbitrary social roles. For example, some parents deny their children access to sexual information because they view sexual ignorance as the very basis of childhood "innocence." Further, denying children sexual information is a symbol of their inferiority, and some adults need that sense of superiority to feel comfortable relating to children, as discussed in Chapter 7.[20]

Age Peers

Children usually feel more comfortable talking about sex with age peers than with adults. But most children are ignorant about sexuality and give each other much false information. As children mature and become sexually active they acquire sexual data and experience, but as they age their dialogue will focus on the non-erotic significance of the sexual act, especially its positive or negative impact on social status. Thus to boys a greater thrill than actually losing their virginity is bragging about their "score" with their male friends. For many girls, today as in the past, disclosing sexual activity risks diminishing their social status, attracting epithets like "slut," and so most girls are far more inhibited than boys in their sex talk. Even when girls do talk about sex, the focus is more likely to be on its emotional, moral, medical, and relational aspects, rather than its sensual dimension.

Similar inhibitions affect most adult peer discussions of sex. The result is that most friends know little about each other's sexuality. We have no idea what sexually excites our pals, whether they have a strong sexual appetite, whether they suffer from sexual dysfunctions. Though the media often reports sensational details of the intimate sex lives of celebrities, most average folk have enormous difficulty talking openly about the subject.

Even therapists have trouble communicating about sex with their clients. Professor Lillian Rubin reports: "For even in the consulting rooms of psychotherapists of all persuasions, sex is, at best, a topic that makes both therapist and patient uneasy."[21] Author Stephanie Covington notes that the sexual hush extends to recovery counselors and Twelve-Step groups. She says, "The saddest part was that during my early recovery no one told me that I would need to explore my sexuality. No one pointed to the sexual problems that I might encounter in sobriety, and no one reassured me that most women had similar experiences."[22]

Surveys conducted by the American Medical Association indicate that most people are reluctant to talk about sexual problems even with their physician. Sixty-eight per cent of the respondents in the poll said they believed their doctors would be too embarrassed to discuss the subject. Commenting on the survey, sexuality specialist Dr. Marianne Legato says: "Clearly, sexual relations are of tremendous importance to the vast majority of the population, yet there remain inherent fears, misperceptions, and stigmas about such issues."[23]

Sexual partners

The inhibition of sex discourse is also common between sexual partners. As every sex therapist knows, and as women's magazines frequently proclaim, the most pervasive problem in the bedroom is the inability of most partners to communicate clearly about sex. In their study of 1000 sexual relationships, the authors of *What Really Happens in Bed* found that the most common complaint of sexual partners is their mutual sexual silence. "Everyone we spoke to wanted to be more capable of opening up to their partners and talking honestly and openly about sex, but they didn't know how to go about doing it."[24] Further, "many were painfully aware that within their relationships, sexual patterns and sexual futures were being shaped not so much by what *was* being said as by what was *not* being said."[25]

In a survey conducted by a sexology institute, 89% of the male respondents said that it was hard to talk about sex with their female partners. Fifty per cent of women had the same problem talking about sex with their men.[26] Many people feel more comfortable sharing body fluids than words about the event.

Generally, three different types of disclosures are absent from our sexual communication with our mates. The first, and perhaps most important, involves our failure to express our idiosyncratic sexual needs and desires. Couples can act out sexual routines for years that are unfulfilling to one or both partners simply because they lack the ability to express what turns them on or off in bed.

This erotic muteness is evident even in porn films. The typical plot of an adult movie shows strangers meeting, briefly interacting verbally, and then stripping off their clothes and having sex. Few words are spoken. The characters almost never ask each other what type of sex they like, or disclose their special needs; they go directly to physical sexual acts. On-screen sex talk can be as hot to both viewer and performer as the most explicit physical acts, but only grunts and groans are heard; verbal sexual inhibitions prevail in sex films as commonly as they do in real life.

Partners also conceal their sexual histories. Mates disclose their sexual background only in "whispers and fragments," as the authors of *What Really Happens in Bed* put it.[27] We lack an understanding of the experiences that have shaped our partner's sexuality. The part of their background that directly influences their current relationship with us remains a mystery.

The third, and by far most commonly omitted topic of discourse, is disclosure of sexual desires outside the primary relationship. For example, many sexual partners have some measure of an independent sexual life in their autoerotic behavior. Yet rare is the partner who shares any details about that private world of desire. Masturbation is a taboo subject, even between sexual partners. The authors of *What Really Happens in Bed* report: "Most of the people we spoke to were masturbating alone and not telling their partners."[28] Sexual fantasies about other people, such as friends and colleagues, or untouchable movie stars, are also rarely disclosed. Most of us have imaginary sex lives that our partners have no inkling of. Many partners actualize their fantasies and have sexual relations with people outside the relationship. These too are rarely disclosed, and are concealed through dishonesty and lies, as discussed in the previous chapter.

Most of this inhibition is the result of erotophobia. Partners cannot talk freely with their lovers about sex for the same reason that they cannot talk freely with peers, parents, or children about it. The very sound of sexual words triggers their auditory aversions. Vague delusions that sexual discourse is somehow dangerous and illicit also freezes their tongue. Specific phobic anxieties about masturbation, sexual fantasy and pleasure, and extra-relationship sexual interests also inhibit talking about those subjects.

Of course, very pragmatic interests can also motivate the same silence. We often rightly surmise that our partners will be uncomfortable if we talk about our sexuality, and we spare them that discomfort by curbing our disclosures. Further, we fear that they will judge us negatively if we do reveal the truth. Many women know that appearing too sexually experienced will threaten their mates, while many men are embarrassed about their lack of sexual experience.

Regardless of the motive behind the inhibition, the failure to communicate about sex is phobigenic. It reinforces the sex discourse taboo. It teaches that even in the supposed intimacy of the sexual relationship, silence is preferable to disclosure. And it buttresses erotophobic fears about the undisclosed sex acts, fantasies, and pleasures. For example, when partners never talk about their autoerotic life, their secrecy enhances the shame they are likely to feel about masturbation.

Schools

Chapter 7 examined the deficiencies of school sex education classes. Most schools also restrict communicating about sex in any other class. For example, the subject of human sexuality is taboo in literature courses. Consider the case of a Manhattan high school teacher who was disciplined for distributing a sexually explicit poem to a tenth-grade English class. The poem "Climaxin" was written by a former student and graphically described a sexual fantasy. The teacher hoped that the exercise would inspire his students to write poetry. But his decision attracted a storm of controversy. School officials formally reprimanded him. An angry parent transferred her daughter from the school. Even New York Governor George Pataki got involved. "The teacher's actions were unconscionable in my view," he told the media.[29]

In a similar case, a drama teacher in North Carolina coached four student-actresses in a state acting competition. They performed a play about a divorced mother and three daughters, one a lesbian, another pregnant with an illegitimate child. Their performance earned several awards. A parent complained about the sexual content in the play after it was presented in a high school English class. A public controversy erupted and the School Board demoted the teacher to a junior position in another school.[30]

When sexual discourse does occur in adult educational institutions, it often attracts attack, as occurred when the Women's Studies Program at the State University of New York in New Paltz selected female sexuality as the theme for its 21st annual conference. Workshops involved HIV education, marriage and sexuality in Africa, and other mainstream academic subjects. There were also presentations on lesbian sexuality, sex toys, and consensual s/m, and those events later prompted a range of hysterical responses. A SUNY trustee called for the dismissal of the college president. A writer in the *Wall Street Journal* said the event was a "Syllabus For Sickos." Governor George Pataki called it "outrageous." But students supported the decision to hold the workshop. As a design student put it, "How are we going to develop our own opinions if we can't hear all the sides?"[31]

The Pennsylvania House of Representatives officially censured Penn State University when a women's group hosted a Sex Faire on campus that aimed to promote healthy sexual relations and gender equality through innovative interactive games such as "Pin the Clitoris on the Vulva" and "Orgasm Bingo." State Representative John Lawless called the event "trash," and sponsored the legislation reducing the university's public financing as a gesture of disapproval.[32]

In Durango, Colorado officials of Fort Lewis College dropped from the community college's curriculum a scheduled course called the "Poetics of Porn" that would have examined the evolution and significance of pornography in modern culture.[33] Congressman Scott McInnis supported the move: "Any kind of pornography class has no academic valor. There is nothing to be gained by holding a pornography class at the college."[34]

In March 2003 the Kansas state Senate voted to prohibit explicit materials used in university sexuality courses, such as the one taught at the University of Kansas for twenty years by an award-winning professor in the School of Social Welfare. "I think what is going on in this undergraduate class is obscene and I want to make this type of activity not funded by the taxpayer," said a senator who voted for the measure.[35]

Harmless sexual communication is attacked even in bohemian adult educational institutions. Consider, for example, drama colleges. Actors are regularly trained how to fight or die, use foreign accents, or make audiences laugh. But they never learn how to act sex scenes. As English actress Imogen Stubbs has written, actors get no guidance on how to stage sexual desire and connection. Generations of actors imitate the stereotyped sexual performances they see in other plays. Thespian educators and performers are as sexually mute as everyone else.[36]

Most family physicians receive very little training in human sexuality. Only a handful of universities have degree programs in sexology.[37] Courses on human sexuality are also rare in the private education sector. A tiny number of private agencies offer programs on personal sexual development. In the average large city you can find a variety of public and private courses for amateur cooks, gardeners, carpenters, athletes, computer users, and every other special interest, but almost nothing for people with a special interest in sex.

Print Media

Sexual discourse is more frequently heard in the media than in private life. Many professional entertainers and journalists have special economic incentives to communicate about sex. But when they do they often attract the hostility of media executives, legal officials, and pressure groups. Consider some examples, beginning with the print media.

Books, newspapers, and magazines

From the mid-1800s until the 1950s the publication of almost any type of sexual communication, except antisexual dogma, was legally suspect under obscenity laws around the world. During that period police seized informative books on abortion, homosexuality, birth control, sex education, prostitution, and many other sexual subjects, and imprisoned the individuals who wrote, published, and distributed them.

Many great works of literature were also caught in this attack on sex discourse. I first learned of such censorship in 1962 when I was ten. My parents were avid readers, and I grew up surrounded by books. My mother brought home a controversial novel, *Lady Chatterley's Lover*. For over thirty years law enforcement officials had banned the book, but thanks to a series of court rulings between 1959 and 1962 in the United States, Britain, and Canada, the ban was lifted and D. H. Lawrence's last book finally had a mass audience. I briefly examined the novel, saw the word "penis" and sexual descriptions, but was amazed that governments would ban it.

Though the criminalization of sexual writing is less common today than forty years ago, the censorship of written information about sex is still prevalent enough that rarely does a week go by without a news story chronicling an attack by police officers, school boards, or religious groups on printed sex words. Several organizations keep tabs on such censorship attempts. To see how common such antisexualism is, visit the websites of the leading anti-censorship organizations, such as the Free Expression Network or the Index on Censorship.[38]

One of the most bizarre official attacks on sex words in the modern era was carried out by the Canadian government for over ten years from the mid 1980s on. Senior bureaucrats unilaterally decided, without any specific legislative backing, to confiscate at the border any reference to anal sexuality in printed material. A statement in a novel such as "She slipped his cock into her pussy and then her asshole," could be legally imported into Canada only if the term "asshole" was blanked out. Thousands of books were turned away at the border simply because they referred to anal sex. A tiny group of erotophobic decision-makers made the country the laughing-stock of the literate world for a decade.

Simple opportunism also played a role; the policy emerged soon after a court decision had radically reduced the power of customs officials to exclude sexual media at the border. Customs officials responded by creating new rules that allowed written depictions of vaginal and oral sex, but not anal sex, thereby ensuring their job security in the sex censorship business. The bureaucratic policy was reversed only after another court challenge that lasted ten years.

The print media is an effective self-censor. For example, no media examines sexuality from a child's perspective: no television cartoons, no movies, no novels about sex that a child would find interesting. With a few exceptions, such as *A Kid's First Book About Sex*,[39] the only information about sex for children is clothed in the dry language of sex education literature, and skims over the subject of pleasure.

For adults the mainstream media is full of discourse about sex, but largely about its dangers or status-enhancing aspects. In the daily newspaper we read about AIDS, rape, sexual dishonesty, and the sex life of celebrities, but very little about the sensual dimension of sex. The daily newspaper rarely says much about sex toys, mutual masturbation, or anal sex. While modern newspapers have reporters who cover "beats" such as crime, politics, community planning, the environment, business, computers, cars, wine, and most other special interests, very few general publications have a reporter assigned to the "sex beat." But even in seemingly sex-positive media, such as magazines directed at youthful women, the discussion of sex is largely directed at performance, not pleasure. Dr. Petra Boynton, author of a study of the sexual content of publications such as *Cosmopolitan* and *Marie Clare*, says:

> These articles are not empowering. They don't talk to you about desire, pleasure and enjoyment, and they don't allow people any room to ask if they have a problem. Sex is seen as a serious activity to perform alongside all the other activities in a busy woman's day.[40]

Most modern newspapers have erotophobic policies aimed at sex words such as "fuck" or "cock," even when such words are an integral part of a news story, like when they are uttered by a politician or professional athlete. The words are censored with hyphens as in "f——." Such censorship, like the digital blurring or black bars defacing the genital portion of newspaper photos, violates elementary journalistic ethics, for the reasons discussed in Chapter 4. Further, such censorship reinforces sex word phobias acquired during childhood. The daily newspapers that overtly censor such terms, often asserting high-minded ideals as they do so, are actually helping generate and perpetuate primitive dysfunctional aversions. "It is especially curious that 'respectable' members of society, when they inculcate and enforce the word taboos, are insuring that the unhealthy attitudes will continue," says one expert on the psychology of "dirty words."[41]

The popular press is also constrained by antisexual forces outside its ranks. For example, advertisers sometimes take umbrage at controversial sexual content in the publications in which their advertisements appear. Chrysler Corporation, the fourth-largest advertiser in the U.S., formally required publishers to give advance notice of major themes and articles in upcoming issues so that it could reschedule its advertising if desired. That policy came to light when *Esquire* dropped a sexually explicit short story in an issue in which Chrysler had four full pages of ads. The magazine's literary editor quit in protest.[42]

The sex content of mainstream magazines causes problems not only with advertisers, but also with retailers. For example, the Kroger Company, one of the largest supermarket chains in America, uses "blinders" on newsstand racks to conceal the covers of mainstream magazines such as *Cosmopolitan* that often display sexual words in cover headlines. That policy followed a lobbying effort by the erotophobic pressure group, Morality in Media Inc. It attacked as indecent and a threat to children, headlines such as "10 make-him-throb moves so hot you'll need a fire hose to cool down the bed" on the cover of *Cosmopolitan*.[43] Under similar pressure, in May 2003 the retail behemoth Wal-Mart halted sales of men's magazines *Maxim*, *Stuff*, and *FHM*.[44]

Advertising standards are also aimed at written or spoken sexual content. For example, section 5.1 of the British Advertising Code says that ads "should contain nothing that is likely to cause serious or widespread offence." The advertising ayatollahs who enforce the code regularly censure ads merely because of harmless sexual content. For example, an ad for a film magazine that appeared in a computer magazine pictured the actress Cameron Diaz with her hand inside her pants, and said: "Cameron 'The Pleasure's All Mine' Diaz Interview And Poster." Thousands of people saw the ad; three complained. The censors concluded that the ad violated the Code because the reference to masturbation "was likely to cause serious or widespread offence."[45]

Connecticut state senator Winthrop Smith believes that genital words should be banned from roadside billboards, and introduced legislation to that end. He objected to a huge sign advertising the play *The Vagina Monologues*. "There are some words that should not be up on a 20-foot billboard, like penis. I can turn off television. I can turn off radio. I can't stop a 20 foot billboard from screaming at my children."[46]

Sex Research

For over one hundred years, small numbers of researchers have devoted themselves to the study of the medical, psychological, and sociological aspects of sex. Yet their work often earns them more pain than gain. Sex researchers have been investigated by the police, thrown out of their laboratories, ridiculed by professional associations, and disparaged in the press.

Consider the experience of Alfred Kinsey, the American professor who conducted the first mass survey of sexual behavior in the United States in the late 1940s and 1950s. His work revealed that tens of millions of Americans regularly engaged in sexual activities like masturbation and pre-marital sex that religious and other social institutions opposed. For simply revealing such facts he was widely attacked by erotophobic moralists all over the world. The *New York Times* refused to accept advertisements for his books. Other sexual research pioneers, such as Masters and Johnson, the first scientists to investigate actual human sexual responses in the laboratory, suffered similar abuse.[47]

Likewise, the largest survey of sexual behaviors in America, conducted by the University of Chicago in the early 1990s, was denied federal government funding after a majority of members of the U.S. Senate concluded that such surveys supported "homosexuality and sexual decadence." The survey was completed with money from private foundations.[48] Similar state-funded attempts to study sex habits in the United Kingdom have also met the wrath of erotophobic politicians.[49]

Under the administration of President George Bush scientists seeking federal money to investigate sexual diseases have to be careful not to use language that provokes the language phobias of public officials. The *New York Times* reports that applicants for funding have been informally advised not to use words such as "sex workers," "men who sleep with men," and "anal sex." A scientist at Johns Hopkins University said that the idea that grants might be subject to political review has created "a pernicious sense of insecurity" among researchers.[50]

Research into childhood sexuality attracts the most pronounced antisexualism today. That is why no textbook of pediatrics contains a chapter on childrens' sexual health, and why there is no clinic anywhere that treats childhood sexological problems. Applications for research grants into the subject of childhood sexuality are, in the words of one prominent sex researcher, "dropped like a hot potato."[51]

Funding is unavailable even for studies of the impact of the media on children's sexual behavior. Pediatric specialists from the University of New Mexico School of Medicine could not get school boards, the state Department of Education, or private foundations to support such research.

Questioning youth about sex was simply too controversial for funding agencies that are supposed to have the welfare of children at heart.[52]

Erotophobia prompts this hostility to sexual research. For example, a person who believes that pre-marital sex is inherently sinful does not want to know and does not want others to know that vast numbers of people are fornicators. The fact that many people have pre-marital sex suggests that such conduct might not be sinful, but rather normal and healthy. Similarly, a person who believes that children are by nature non-sexual, or should be non-sexual, will oppose information showing that children do have a sexual life. The truth is threatening to the erotophobic mind.

Further, erotophobic people attack sex research not only because of the truth it reveals, but also because it helps dispel erotophobia. Julia A. Ericksen, author of the only major study of sexual surveys, *Kiss And Tell: Surveying Sex In The Twentieth Century*, makes this point in the concluding chapter of her study:

> Talking about sex, thinking about it, and asking questions about it make people more comfortable with sex and its variety. Those whose political agendas are served by public discomfort over such topics as homosexuality, teenage sexuality, and sex outside of marriage will continue to see sex surveys as a political strategy of the enemy.[53]

Verbal Media

The spoken word is obviously a vital part of much media content. When media speech focuses on sex and genitals it often attracts negativity, both from within the media and outside.

Television and radio

Television is the most important media format today. Sex is a frequent issue in mainstream television entertainment, but the discourse about actual sexual acts is rarely open and honest. Sex discourse is usually the subject of innuendo and double entendre. For example, masturbation was a theme of the famous *Seinfeld* episode, "Master of Your Domain," yet the word itself was never used and the subject never openly discussed. Indeed the episode is an ironic parody of the media conventions that constrained it. Yet the sitcom still broke new ground in making autoeroticism the focus of a prime time network show.

Some cable broadcasters are pushing the envelope further, in the form of more thoughtful and explicit discussions of sexuality in shows such as *Sex in the City* (HBO) or *Sex Files* (Discovery). Those shows even explore the somatic dimension of sex, as in the *Sex in the City* episode that discussed the taste of semen. However, such real sexual discourse may be too much for the advertisers that finance the television industry. Media trade magazine *Variety* says of *Sex in the City*, "Many of the episodes are so suffused with boundary-stretching sexual themes that advertisers may shrivel up at the prospect of associating their brand with such a program."[54]

Outside those more adventurous shows, when television deals with sex the focus is always on the consequences of sex, such as its status-enhancing effects, or impact on a cheating spouse. The hedonic aspects of sex are still too controversial for television discourse. A typical example of such self-censorship is the decision of executives of the FOX network to pull a scene in the show *Manchester Prep* that shows one teenage girl being coached by another girl on how to reach orgasm while riding on horseback.[55]

Banning sexual discourse on popular television is the express aim of the Parent's Television Council, a group that boasts a host of celebrities as advisors and 625,000 members. The organization lobbies politicians and media executives, prepares reports, and takes out full-page ads in an attempt to "clean up" television. The group objects to virtually all sex discourse in entertainment shows. For example, it describes the horseback/orgasm scene in the *Manchester Prep* show mentioned above as "filthy" and "disgusting," and says that "ABC polluted the 8:00 hour with raunchy adult-oriented programs such as the constantly vulgar *Spin City*, which this season had the mayor playing with a phallic paperweight, rubbing it on his chin and face, and holding it just below his mouth while asking an assistant if anything about him suggested he was gay."[56]

The broadcast *news* media also censors specific genital words and sex words, much the same as it does images of genitals and sex. Entercom Communications, a national radio conglomerate, ordered its five New

Orleans stations not to mention *The Vagina Monologues* in newscasts or air ads for it because executives believed the word "vagina" would elicit a negative response from their audience.[57] Similar censorship occurred on an almost daily basis during the Clinton sex scandals. For example in a *60 Minutes* television interview, Mike Wallace uttered the word "pussy," but the producers "beeped" it out of the soundtrack. That is the audio equivalent of the black dot: overt and obvious censorship targeting specifically erotic stimuli. Hateful and offensive terms and expressions are often uttered in newscasts and documentaries, but rarely overtly censored. Yet a common term for normal human body parts spoken in the normal course of an interview by a respected journalist is deemed worthy of the beep.

Mainstream television executives, in the U.S. at least, are also uncomfortable with revenue-producing advertisements involving sexual products. Consider the decision of FOX television executives in February 2001 who refused to allow an ad for a spermicide contraceptive to be aired on the series *Temptation Island*. The show takes four unmarried couples to an idyllic island to test their relationships by having them date attractive singles. The show was widely attacked as promoting promiscuity. Yet even with such a controversial theme, the network refused the ad. Only if a sexual product is advertised for "disease protection" will the network take it, and a spermicide did not qualify.[58]

Or consider condom advertising. All the major American networks banned such ads for decades, and many still do, claiming that such content would offend audiences and advertisers. Yet surveys indicate that over 70% of Americans say the networks should accept condom commercials.[59]

Such "condomphobia," as one commentator put it, even extends to public service announcements (PSAs).[60] Networks occasionally allow condom PSAs, but only as long as they stress birth control or disease prevention and not pleasure. But even then the message is often bizarrely cryptic. Consider the following PSA prepared by the U.S. Center for Disease Control, designed to encourage the use of condoms without ever explicitly referring to them. The segment depicts a barefoot man saying, "If I told you that I could save my life just by putting on my socks, you wouldn't take me seriously because life is never that simple . . . . But there is something just as simple that could." That ad is a good example of what sexual historian Michel Foucault has identified as discourse "that speaks verbosely of its own silence."[61] While television networks have donated $2 *billion* worth of airtime for aggressive antidrug PSAs, a tiny fraction of that amount has been donated for PSAs with a sexual health message.

Condom phobia is not unique to America. In the Philippines, where the maternal mortality rate is one in seventy-five, religious leaders from Catholic and Episcopal churches expressed outrage when condom ads began appearing on TV and radio.[62] In China, the first condom television commercial was quickly pulled from the airwaves because it was "contrary to national conventions and moral concepts" and possibly an offence under laws banning advertising for sex products. The ad showed a condom image and displayed the phrase: "Condoms, no worries."[63]

The Federal Communications Commission ban on "indecent" material broadcast between 6 a.m. and 10 p.m., discussed in Chapter 4 in relation to nudity images, also applies to sexual words such as "fuck" or "cunt," or any other type of raunchy sexual talk. The most famous target of such laws is radio talk show host Howard Stern who has pioneered a new and banal format sometimes called "extreme talk," featuring discourse about excretory functions, sex, and anything bizarre and outrageous. The F.C.C. fined him for saying things such as: "The closest I ever came to making love to a black woman was masturbating to a picture of Aunt Jemima on a pancake box," and for telling a story about a man who played piano with his penis.[64]

Even more serious discussions of sexuality run afoul of the prohibitions on indecent speech. For example, in a case involving KLOL-FM in Houston, Texas, the F.C.C. found that a call-in sex survey violated the rule. A DJ and a doctor discussed issues such as a medical procedure to enhance penis size, and some callers made statements such as "he was so large that it was ruining his marriages." The Commission found that the news content of the show was minimal and that its predominant characteristic was a "pandering and titillating exchange of sexual banter about penis size and shape." The radio station was fined $33,750 for broadcasting such sex talk![65]

In April 2001 the F.C.C. fined a Chicago station for discussing "in explicit detail a sexual technique familiar to a female porn star" and "specific aspects of fellatio" that "included the sounds of women moaning in the background."[66] No wonder that radio executives are squeamish about such discourse even when interviewing sex journalists such as Susie Bright. She describes how prior to a broadcast a Los Angeles radio manager handed her a note saying, "Please do not use the word *clitoris*."[67]

The common myth that the media is filled with sexual content results largely from high-profile exceptions to the media's normal antipathy toward meaningful sexual dialogue and disclosure. The most bizarre examples of such open discourse occur on sensationalist daytime television interview shows hosted by celebrities such as Jerry Springer. Induced by the rewards of instant and transitory fame, ordinary folk who would otherwise remain silent about their sexuality confess the most intimate details of their sex life to a national television audience. But their dialogue is almost always negative, focusing on cheating, abuse, disease, and dysfunction, and their statements are rarely more than insults and accusations. Even these verbal exhibitionists are as incompetent in communicating about sex as everyone else.

Movies

The rating system used by the Motion Picture Association of America, discussed in earlier chapters in relation to images, also targets sexual words. For example, the "automatic language rule" requires that if the word "fuck" is used only once, and as an expletive, the movie must get at least the PG-13 or a more restrictive rating. When that word is uttered as a verb, as in "I want to fuck you," the film is automatically given an R rating, meaning children under seventeen cannot attend without an adult.[68] Thanks to the rating system, the utterance of a single word has extraordinary negative significance for movie producers, as well as the parents and youths who want to view their films.

The music industry has a similar rating system targeting sexual language and other themes, a process that started in 1985 when Tipper Gore, the wife of the former U.S. vice-president, bought the album *Purple Rain* for her eleven-year-old daughter. Ms Gore listened to the song "Darling Nikki," which mentions a woman masturbating with a magazine, and her reaction prompted Senate hearings and the formation of a private lobby group, the Parents Musical Resource Center. No legislation was ever enacted, but in 1990 the Recording Industry Association of America (RIAA) introduced a labeling system using the warning, "Parental Advisory—Explicit Lyrics." The RIAA failed to provide any definition as to what constituted "explicit lyrics," leaving that decision exclusively to record companies.

Because that system is both voluntary and erratic, legislators in various jurisdictions have proposed bills that would impose mandatory warnings on music labels. For example, a State of Washington law required retailers to place "adults only" stickers on recordings with "erotic" material, and criminalized the sale of such material to minors. A state court later declared the law unconstitutional, but Washington legislators then proposed new legislation,[69] and many other states have proposed related laws.[70]

Obscenity laws have also been used to attack sexual discourse in music. The most famous example is the case of the rap group 2LiveCrew. Their multi-million selling album *As Nasty as They Wanna Be* contained songs like "Me So Horny" that Christian fundamentalists attacked because of "87 descriptions of oral sex, 116 mentions of male and female genitalia and other lyrical passages referring to male ejaculation." A judge in Florida found the album obscene because it appealed to "dirty thoughts and the loins, not to the intellect and the mind."[71]

Telephone

The 1980s saw a new type of sex discourse: commercial telephone sex. For a fee a customer could dial a number and hear a recorded sex fantasy, or talk with a telephone sex worker. That type of private discourse provoked many antisexual responses. Some police attacked such aural sex as obscene and illegal.[72] Municipal officials refused to grant local business licenses to phone fantasy firms. Credit card companies rejected the business too. Telephone companies blocked access to sex talk firms that used the 900 service. The federal government even passed a law prohibiting all commercial telephone sex conversations regardless of age, although the U.S. Supreme Court later struck it down.[73]

Such negativity is motivated in part by the concern that children might access telephone sex lines. For many parents, the thought of their children talking explicitly about sex provokes extreme anxiety. Other parents have more rational worries about children running up huge phone bills. But aside from the issue of child access, much of the attack on phone sex lines flowed simply from phobic attitudes toward all sex discourse and sex. The mere fact that adults were getting aroused while privately talking about sex was enough to prompt a censorious response from many social officials. Fortunately, such institutional antisexualism has greatly diminished since the early 1990s and phone fantasy firms now rarely attract negative notice.

Employers

Employees who write or talk about sex, on or off the job, often run afoul of erotophobic employers. Consider some diverse examples. Many academics report that studying human sexuality has harmed their university career.[74] That was the experience of Rachael Maines, historian and author of *The Technology of Orgasm: "Hysteria," the Vibrator, and Women's Sexual Satisfaction*. The book tells the fascinating story of how a century ago doctors used vibrators to give women orgasms to relieve "hysteria," and how nobody perceived the treatment as sexual. But administrators at Clarkson University in New York failed to renew her teaching contract, in part because they feared that alumni would stop supporting the university if they found out about her work.[75]

Or consider the tale of Christian poet Scott Cairns. He was hired as an English professor by Seattle Pacific University, a Free Methodist liberal arts college in Washington State. College administrators discovered that one of his poems, "Interval with Erato," written three years earlier and published in *The Paris Review*, depicts a poet making love to his muse. Fellow academics saw the poem as an attempt to reclaim the body for Christian art and theology. But the college president had trouble with graphic lines such as "I sucked her belly, cupped her sopping vulva with my hand," and fired the newly appointed professor.[76]

Many employees have also been fired for using company computers to send or receive private e-mail messages that contain sex words, such as jokes. In perhaps the most famous case, the *New York Times* terminated twenty workers because they sent or received e-mail messages with sexual content. "Our policy essentially says e-mail is primarily a tool for business communication and, like any other communication here, [e-mail messages] must be consistent with conventional standards of ethical and proper conduct, behavior, and manners," says *New York Times* spokeswoman Nancy Nielsen.[77] She refused to describe the e-mails in question, but press reports indicate that they were "X-rated": a mix of jokes and photos. Many other companies have similar policies. Employment experts now counsel workers to avoid any reference to sex in corporate e-mail communications. "Keep your work account so clean that it squeaks," advises a writer in the *Seattle Times*, who adds, "Don't send any joke that could be offensive to anyone."[78]

Some employers are paranoid about their employees communicating about sex because they fear sexual harassment suits. Courts have ruled that such harassment can flow from talk alone. Fear of sexual talk prompted the University of New Hampshire to suspend a professor of technical writing because in a class he compared writing to sex, and made statements such as: "Belly dancing is like jello on a plate with a vibrator under the plate." The university ruled that such talk harassed his listeners, but a court overturned that decision.[79]

Perhaps the most famous attack on sexual talk on the job involved a brewery executive who was fired when a co-worker accused him of sexual harassment for recounting to her an episode of *Seinfeld*, in which a character tries to recall the name of a woman (later revealed to be "Delores"), and remembers that it rhymes with a female body part, an indirect reference to "clitoris." The employer found that the brewery executive harassed the employee by showing her the word "clitoris" in a dictionary. A jury disagreed and awarded the executive almost $27 million in damages for wrongful dismissal.[80] Sexual harassment consultants advise both employers and employees: "If what you are thinking even vaguely involves sex, keep it to yourself."[81] Sadly, that injunction could describe how most people deal with sex discourse not only on the job, but everywhere else; they remain silent.

10 / Porn War

SINCE TIME IMMEMORIAL humans have crafted images of sex designed to arouse the lust of the viewer. *Pornography* is the most commonly used generic label for such material. Unfortunately that term has a different meaning to different people. Some people use it to refer not to the whole genre of lust-arousing material, but rather specific types of it, namely that which depicts children, violence, degradation, or the subordination of women. They recognize that not all sexually explicit and lust-generating material is of that type.

The lack of consensus on the definition of "pornography" has led to enormous confusion in discussions of lust-arousing sex images. I am tempted to use a new term such as "explicita" or "erogenica" to refer to the whole genre. In the end I am sticking with *pornography* (or "porn"), as it is the one most people use to describe the entire genre. I use three different labels to refer to the main types of the porn genre: "child porn" depicting children performing sexual acts; "nasty porn" depicting adult sexuality in a context of violence, degradation, or subordination; and "friendly porn" depicting adult, mutualistic sexuality.

People who attack the whole genre do so simply because it is sexually explicit and sexually arousing. Rational motives would account for such category-wide negativity if all porn causes harm. Does it?

Child pornography is obviously harmful. Creating such material violates the sexual autonomy of children. The market for child porn encourages child abuse. Nasty porn is probably harmful too. Such material teaches negative attitudes about women, men, and sexuality and may also encourage people who view it to engage in the anti-social behaviors depicted. Recall that our emotional brain is susceptible to erotic conditioning. Constant exposure to sexually titillating images of, say, men dominating women, could well imprint an erotic program in a man's brain that associates sexual arousal with sexual dominance. A man sexually excited by scenes of sexual domination might seek out not only images of domination, but actual experiences in which he sexually overpowers women. A variety of clinical studies indicate that nasty porn may indeed have anti-social effects.[1] Whether these unhappy outcomes justify the censorship of violent porn is a difficult question because censorship often creates more problems than it solves, but the fact remains that such material is unhealthy. Negativity aimed specifically at child porn and violent porn is not intolerant.

Is All Porn Harmful?

But many people oppose all porn, even the friendly variety, because they claim that any material that is explicit and arousing causes a variety of harms.[2]

Undefined harm

The attack on porn began in earnest in the late nineteenth century, when technology enabled the production of mass copies of photographs and drawings. The early censors of sexually titillating material believed that it would "deprave and corrupt" its viewers.[3] But they never bothered to define those terms. What they probably meant was that the material would sexually excite those who viewed it, and that such excitement was, somehow, inherently vile. On the basis of such vague notions, hundreds of thousands of sexually explicit photos and magazines were destroyed every year in America, from the 1870s through to the First World War.[4]

Opponents of porn in the modern era have also embraced absurdly vague notions of harm. As examples later in this chapter reveal, judges, church leaders, school officials, and others condemn an image as "immoral," "indecent," "obscene" or "inappropriate" simply because it is sexually explicit and designed to prompt lust. No rational mind would accept such flimsy ideas as any justification for such attacks.

The intellectual primitivism of these allegations is undoubtedly the result of erotophobic aversions. For example, anyone who has acquired a *visual* aversion triggered by the sight of genitals will react negatively to the porn genre simply because it makes genitals visible. Further, anyone who has acquired an aversion to lustful *sensations* will also react negatively to porn, as it usually does prompt such feelings. Because sex aversions are often unconscious, and because their phobic nature is not understood, the negative feelings that porn prompts are rationalized with ridiculously vague ideas, like the notion that all porn is somehow intrinsically "immoral."

Porn and anti-social behavior

A more precise allegation against porn is that it causes its viewers to lose control and commit anti-social acts. Consider, for example, the following statement by an activist in Philadelphia in the 1950s on the effects of explicit material: "Girls run away from their homes and become entangled in prostitution. Boys and young men who have difficulty resisting the undue sexual stimulation become sexually aggressive and generally incorrigible. The more vicious . . . may become an exhibitionist, a rapist, a sadist, a fetishist. He may commit such antisocial acts as arson, pyromania, and kleptomania which are often symbolic sexual acts."[5]

Such arguments are still heard in the modern day. For example, the 7-Eleven convenience store chain stopped selling all sexually explicit magazines at its 4,500 corporate-owned outlets because of a "possible connection between adult magazines and crime, violence, and child abuse."[6] The firm designates a magazine as "adult" simply because it is erotically explicit and not because it depicts children or violence.

The idea that a publication prompts crime or violence merely because it is explicitly titillating lacks any empirical support. Since the 1950s, the effects of the porn genre have been investigated by many academics and several government inquiries. Public inquiries in the United States in 1970 and 1986, in the United Kingdom in 1979, and in Canada in 1986 studied in detail the hypothesis that explicit imagery causes crime.[7] The authorities uniformly rejected such a proposition. Dozens of subsequent scientific studies support the same conclusion. Erotic explicitness *per se* has no anti-social effect. Allegations that all porn causes crime or violence are false.

Objectification

Porn is also said to "objectify" people, usually women. "Objectification" is another vague term, used differently by different individuals, but it is usually meant to refer to the unhealthy message that women (or men) are just sex objects, devoid of the full spectrum of human personality.

While some porn does depict some people as one-dimensional, sex-crazed creatures, and some porn may even communicate the message that all men and women are of that type, the idea that *all* porn expresses that message is false. In fact, some types of porn features amateur models precisely because they are so ordinary. They are depicted as the real persons they are, with a job, often a spouse and children, and hobbies, feelings, and thoughts.

The notion that simply because the porn genre emphasizes the sexual assets of the models, viewers will thereby automatically assume that they are mere objects, and assume further that everyone with the same gender as the model is a mere object, lacks all credibility. While the sexual display of the model obviously highlights his or her sexuality, it does not exclude other personality features, any more than a model shown performing tasks such as cooking, working on a car, caring for children, or playing sports suggests that such activities define the full measure of that person. Further, millions of people, especially women, enjoy being objects of lust. They relish the attention they get by being sexually attractive. "We like to see men do the neck swivel," say the editors of *Glamour* magazine.[8]

Lustful effect

If sexual arousal is harmful, then the lust effect of the porn genre would be harmful too. But sexual arousal is not harmful. Beliefs to the contrary, though widespread, are false. Other fallacies hold that sexual arousal prompted by persons other than one's lawfully wedded spouse is harmful. These too are false. Porn commonly leads to masturbation. The false idea that masturbation is somehow unhealthy or sinful is still popular in many religious groups. People gripped with anti-masturbation phobias will naturally oppose all porn.

Porn can also prompt lustful feelings in children and teenagers. Is such youth arousal harmful? A very popular fallacy holds that sexual interest and experience is somehow harmful to children because it destroys their "innocence." Yet no evidence has ever been tendered to show that sexual feelings in children are harmful to them. Erotic arousal in a young person, like in an adult, is a normal experience. There is nothing unhealthy about the rise and fall of sexual desire, even in a youth.

However, repeated exposure to the porn genre can prompt erotic conditioning, especially in a young person with minimal previous erotic experience. Recall that this occurs when a person is repeatedly sexually aroused while exposed to the same neutral stimuli, such as a yellow raincoat, high heels, lingerie, blonde hair, slim waistlines, or any other stimuli. The result is that future exposures to such stimuli will elicit a sexual charge. Because the porn genre arouses lust it helps eroticize the stimuli commonly displayed in the porn genre. Is this a problem?

Only if it unduly narrows the individual's erotic reflexes, so that they are triggered only by a slim range of erotic stimuli that do not reflect sexuality in the real world. Such harm would occur, for example, if the only porn available to a young person depicted a narrow range of sexual acts, such as intercourse in the missionary position, or a narrow range of body-types, such as only slim women with big breasts and no stretch marks, pimples, or cellulite, or only muscular men with large penises but no beer bellies or bald heads. Constant exposure to such a narrow range of porn could produce a sexual appetite only for a few sexual positions and body-types.

The culprit here is not the porn genre, only its narrow range. When most baby-boomers were masturbating teenagers the scope of porn was very limited. Today, the porn genre has a much wider compass. Magazines and videos that feature amateur models with normal proportions and the occasional pimple and wart are very popular. Specialty publications feature models in all age groups, even grandparents. The greater the diversity of porn in terms of the age, race, physical characteristics, and even personality of the people depicted, the less likely that such material will narrow the sexuality of those who use it. As long as children are exposed to a range of sexual imagery, and as long as it depicts healthy, ethical sexual behavior, they can avoid the "centerfold syndrome" or any other narrowing effect.

Offensiveness

So far I have discussed whether the porn genre is harmful when exposed to people who want it. Does the porn genre cause harm if it offends people who are involuntarily exposed to it? Recall that only a stimulus that provokes *innate* offense causes real harm. Some porn is innately offensive. For example, porn that shows a violent rape, where the victim's agony and humiliation are clearly evident, could well provoke innate aversions to the sight of human distress. Child porn would prompt similar natural aversions to the sight of the abuse of children. But not all porn contains such innately offensive content.

Many people contend that the sight of sexual conduct is innately offensive, that images of explicit sex trigger in-born disgust reflexes. But there is no evidence to support such an idea. We are born with a powerful curiosity and it extends to an interest in sexual acts. While we may have an innate aversion to seeing other people in pain, observing their pleasure is probably an innately positive experience. The fact that millions of people in many different cultures enjoy seeing sex indicates that such sights do not frighten our genes. However, the explicitness of porn will offend anyone who has acquired lust phobia, genital phobia, or more specific delusions that all porn causes harm.

Community standards

Sexual media is often attacked because it offends "community standards." But such standards are usually the product of phobia and thus provide no valid basis for democratic action. Community standards are touted even when there is no evidence to support the contention that the community opposes the sexual media. Perceptions of community standards are often distorted.

Consider, for example, the study of the attitudes of a cross-section of residents of a county in North Carolina toward sexually explicit media involved in a criminal obscenity prosecution. After viewing the material, most of the residents found it not to be obscene, but most thought that the community at large would not tolerate the material. The respondents' personal judgments of the sexual media were much more tolerant than their perception of the attitudes of most others in their community. Why the discrepancy?

The researchers believe that rationalizing is to blame. The very fact that legal authorities prosecuted the material in question suggested to the respondents that the community opposes such material: "The legal system may be an unwitting but critical contributor to the very standard it is trying to discover through the fact-finding process," say the researchers.[9] hey also noted: "The erroneous belief in lack of tolerance for sexually explicit material in the community may lead people to be hesitant to speak out honestly about their own opinions for fear they are deviant." This leads toward a "spiral of silence" where a majority says nothing and allows a minority opinion to prevail, thus reinforcing the false belief that the minority represents the majority.[10] A senior sex researcher, Don Mosher, holds that most Americans are in favor of adult access to sexual materials but refrain from defending others' rights to view the material or from acknowledging that they personally use it.[11]

Benefits of friendly porn

Friendly porn is educational. Aside from teaching about sexual styles and techniques, friendly porn conveys a very powerful message about the legitimacy of human sexuality. Friendly porn is an advertisement for lust and pleasure. The open circulation of such material teaches that sex is inherently good and normal. "Porn is essentially an ideology, a statement of naturalism documenting the existence of animal energy as a positive force in man's life," notes Professor William Brigman.[12] Porn depicting happy people is powerfully counter-phobigenic, helping defuse lust delusions. The positive, liberating message of friendly porn is one reason why erotophobic people are opposed to it.

In a culture where antisexualism is prevalent, few people will come forward to defend images that have no purpose other than to arouse lust. While false allegations such as that sexual explicitness is "immoral," "sexist," "degrading," or "harmful to children" are frequently heard in the media, the idea that such imagery is good and beneficial is rarely pronounced. The only people the media can find to support the porn genre are those who produce and distribute it, but their credibility is suspect because they have an obvious financial interest in their position. The public rarely hears any independent authority celebrate lustful imagery.

Because decision-makers never encounter organized campaigns in favor of sex media by the millions of consumers of such material, and observe only anti-explicit public protests, meetings and letter-writing campaigns, they are apt to over-emphasize the extent of public hostility to erotic imagery. When no numerically significant grass-roots pressure group promotes porn, and many attack it, politicians and media managers are more likely to capitulate to the latter.

Attacking all porn breeds nasty porn

When the social mainstream stigmatizes a business, especially one that caters to an enormous demand, the relatively few people doing such work can make large profits. Underground commerce naturally attracts greedy outcasts who have little reputation to lose and are not frightened by social isolation or even jail. Macho males, typified by the average mafia godfather or leader of an outlaw motorcycle gang, are commonly found running such operations. The indiscriminate attack on all porn by legal officials, religious leaders, media managers, and a significant proportion of the population simply delivers the production of sexually arousing media into the hands of unsavory characters.

For example, consider Chuck Trainor, the former husband and manager of the most famous pornographic performer in history, the late Linda Lovelace, star of *Deep Throat*. Trainor regularly beat and abused his wife. At the height of her fame in 1972, she was so dominated by her husband that she agreed to perform degrading sexual acts at his command, such as a legendary attempt at having sex with a dog in front of the *Playboy* publisher, Hugh Hefner, at his mansion in Los Angeles.[13]

Porn reflects the values of those who produce it. When the only people involved in the business are greedy, sexist males, nasty porn is the inevitable result. Pushed into a stigmatized social ghetto, porn gets ugly. The proliferation of this type of porn helps to negatively stereotype the genre, leading people to falsely conclude that the porn genre is intrinsically unaesthetic and misogynist, a circular process.

But the nastiness of so much porn is largely a consequence of the social stigmatization of the entire genre. When such blanket negativity diminishes, more socially conscious producers and performers enter the business, and the result is more aesthetic, mutualistic porn, as the recent history of the porn genre reveals. For example, a fast-growing segment of the current porn industry is material designed for couples, and produced largely by women, such as Candide Royalle. No outlaw underground business could ever create such material.

Though porn intolerance is not nearly so intense today as in the past, much of it still exists, as the next sections show.

Self-Censorship

The sight of an explicit image of sex is so repugnant to some people that they deliberately avoid exposure to it. I am always surprised how many people decline my invitation to look at porn images that I regard as innovative or interesting, even when I describe the material as friendly. Some people take me up on the offer, but many do not. They know that the sight of naked copulating bodies is too much for them, hence deny themselves exposure to it.

Because large numbers of people are averse to images that are sexually graphic, porn enthusiasts are usually covert about possessing such material. Hence porn leaves retail shops stuffed in brown paper bags or hidden in briefcases and then gets stashed in secret places at home.

Paul Henderson, a retired hockey star who also leads sexual seminars for couples, is so fearful of encountering stimulating images that he will not turn on the television when traveling alone. "As long as there is blood in my veins, I'm going to be tempted. So what you learn to do is put up some roadblocks," he says.[14]

Such self-censorship has a phobigenic effect when observed by others. Consider, for example, the negative inferences a boy is likely to make about porn and sexuality when he learns that his father will not even turn on the television for fear of seeing sexual images. The father's inhibition teaches that sex images and sex itself are dangerous.

Consider also the phobigenic effects of an interaction that occurred when I was a teenager. When my friend and I sat down on a bench at a bus stop a sex magazine slid out onto the ground from my friend's gym bag, in plain view of a girl and her mother. The parent gasped, as if she had just witnessed a car accident, and put her hands over her eyes. She then yanked the girl away from the bench, snorting out the word "disgusting," as they walked away. I still remember the look of alarm on the child's face as she looked back and forth at her mother and the magazine. This was likely her first exposure to explicit imagery, and her mother's aversive reaction helps plant the seeds of porn phobia in her mind.

Parental Censors

Porn enters the home in two ways, through the door in magazines and videos, and through a wire via television and the internet. Parents have only limited control over their children's access to media. Some parents use censorship devices in their televisions and computers to filter out explicit sexual content. Internet blocking technology is still primitive and any child who really wants pornographic images can get them. But children nevertheless understand that their parents are hostile to such material.

For example, I first came into possession of a porn magazine in the early 1960s, when I was fourteen. No adult had ever mentioned the existence of such material, let alone tried to steer me away from it. But I nevertheless knew that I had to smuggle it into my home because my parents would not want me to have it. To reveal that I had such material would end in its seizure, and perhaps an angry lecture as well. The magazine circulated amongst several of my friends, and they also knew that their parents would take it away if it were discovered. So we possessed it covertly, like we later would do with alcohol and tobacco. We also knew that parental opposition was focused directly on its explicit sexual content, and not its poor photographic quality or negative messages about women.

Though the porn genre is less stigmatized in the modern day, rare is the parent who discusses pornography, except negatively, and almost non-existent is the parent who introduces their children to the friendly varieties of porn, and uses the occasion to provide an extremely valuable lesson about both sex and sex media.

Intolerance aimed specifically at the access of minors to sex imagery helps generate the false idea that porn harms them. From an early age children recognize that adults are powerfully opposed to children seeing explicit sexual imagery. Children recognize that almost no other type of image attracts the same negative response. Children know that most of them are allowed to see images of death, war, crime, disease, and everything else that occurs in life, but not explicit images of sexual behavior. Kids come to understand that the dividing line between what they can and cannot see is the very specific visual stimuli of sex.

The knowledge that adults are powerfully opposed to children seeing explicit genital imagery, but virtually nothing else, helps breed the phobic idea in their young minds that sexual imagery is harmful to children. Before a child knows about the differences between nasty porn and friendly porn, or artistic porn and unaesthetic porn, he or she will have formed phobic delusions about the more general category of sex imagery, and will have acquired the more specific idea that children should not see such material. When the child becomes an adult he or she will attempt in turn to shield kids from such material: and so the infection cycle spins again.

Legal Censors

During the first years of my law practice in the early 1980s I became aware of the irrational distress that explicit images provoke in the minds of bureaucrats. A client had purchased a porn magazine, of the friendly variety, at a store in a small town north of Seattle, Washington. The magazine tells a story in pictures of a male airline passenger meeting a female flight attendant and the two going back to a hotel for oral sex and intercourse. Both models are shown as horny and happy; there is no hint of violence, domination, or degradation. My client drove north to the Canadian border, where Canadian customs officials asked him the usual questions about whether he had purchased gifts or alcohol or anything else that he intended to bring into Canada. He told them he had purchased a porn magazine. The guards seized it, saying that porn was prohibited under Canadian customs law. My client hired me to sue the Canadian government, alleging that it had violated basic democratic rights.

Canadian government lawyers claimed the seizure was valid on the basis of an 1867 law, which prohibited "immoral or indecent" material.

During the lawsuit I questioned customs inspectors to determine exactly how they defined "immoral" and thus distinguished between allowable and prohibited sexual imagery. I presented to the officers images of overtly anti-female images, such as a naked woman bound and gagged and hung by a meat hook on a conveyer belt with slabs of beef. The officials informed me that such images were not immoral because "only butts are visible." When I asked what was "immoral" about the images in the magazine seized from my client, the officials directed me to the images of sexual penetration and ejaculation in the magazine.

The censors guarding the Canadian border were concerned only about the explicitness of a sex image, and nothing else. They allowed overtly anti-female images into the country without interference, but seized images of erotic body fluids and normal sexual acts as they would heroin or automatic guns.

When I researched the effects of mere explicitness, I discovered that the social scientists who had studied the issue had determined that explicitness *per se* caused no harm. Prohibitions aimed at the private use of images of friendly porn lacked rational support. Canadian law was clearly antisexual. Yet I soon discovered that Canadian policy in this area was not unusual and that similar intolerance was evident in the anti-porn laws of almost every jurisdiction of the world. My quest to understand why intelligent decision-makers could craft rules so obviously foolish ultimately led me to the concept of erotophobia, and the phobigenic system that produces it.[15]

Obscenity laws

Obscenity law is important because it blocks both the public and private use of material that meets the obscenity definition. Unlike laws aimed at public nudity, obscenity law reaches into the private domain, forbidding people from producing and consuming material that will never be exposed to people who do not want to see it. Such controls are valid if the obscenity at issue causes harm, as does child pornography. But much obscenity law fails to discriminate between the different types of porn, and targets the whole genre.

Prior to the modern era, obscenity law never specifically identified erotic explicitness as the target. Vague prohibitions against "immoral" material, like those contained in Canadian customs law, were understood by everyone involved with the law to include not only explicitness in the porn genre, but also explicit images in birth control manuals and classic art. By the 1950s, lawmakers all over the world began to narrow the scope of obscenity law, aiming it exclusively at porn explicitness.

Consider, for example, the modern history of obscenity law in the United States. From the late 1950s to the early 1970s, a series of decisions by the United States Supreme Court refined obscenity law to specifically target porn and not educational or scientific sex imagery. In its famous 1973 decision *Miller* v. *California*,[16] still in force today, the court provided several criteria to determine whether a work was obscene. The first of those contained the anti-explicitness rule. An image had to show "hard-core" sex, defined as: "ultimate sexual acts, normal or perverted, actual or simulated, . . . masturbation, excretory functions, and lewd exhibition of the genitals."[17] If an image had no explicit sexual content, obscenity law would no longer touch it, no matter how disgusting or repulsive the image might be, even to a majority of the community.

Secondly, the court ruled that the "hardcore" content must "appeal to the prurient interest." In a previous case the court had defined "prurient" as "material having a tendency to excite lustful thoughts."[18] The porn genre, of course, is designed to have precisely that effect. The court further ruled that even material appealing to the prurient interest was not obscene if it had "serious literary, artistic, political or scientific value."[19] Most porn has no such pretensions.

Finally, the court ruled that material was still not obscene, no matter how pornographic, if it did not offend local "community standards." That concept was the loophole by which porn legally entered tolerant local communities, such as the small town north of Seattle where my client bought his porn magazine in the early 1980s. In short, under American law porn is obscene unless the local community tolerates it.

The only really clear part of the obscenity definition is the anti-explicitness rule. Whether an erect penis is visible or not, or whether a finger is visibly inside a vagina or not, can be readily assessed. Individuals and companies that distribute porn to every region of the country need to be sure that they will not face a charge of obscenity in any antisexual local community. To ensure no conviction, their material must avoid depicting actual sexual acts.

That is a key reason friendly porn is still largely unavailable in the mainstream media, even in twenty-first century America. To show an image of an ejaculating penis or a tongue entering a vagina in a mass distribution magazine or television program is to risk criminal prosecution somewhere in the country. Concealing sexually aroused genitals ensures that the material is legal; hence some mainstream porn producers deface the genital portion of their material with a "black dot" or digital blur. The black dot was very common in porn produced in the 1970s and 1980s, and is still visible in some publications. Two generations of North American men were regularly exposed to this dot while they masturbated using sex magazines.

Consider the phobigenic effects of such censorship. Holding an erect penis in his hand, a masturbating youth gazes at sexual images defaced by black dots concealing erect penises. Images of flaccid penises are not defaced by black dots, only erect or ejaculating phalluses are hidden. That censorship pattern expresses powerful negative messages about erect penises and ejaculation. That negative message is received precisely at the time that the male masturbator is aroused. The paired experience of negative feeling plus sexual arousal is phobigenic. Exposed over and over to the black dot while masturbating, millions of men cannot help but have acquired some aversion to lust. A rational society would prohibit the black dot, not the imagery it conceals.

In all of its obscenity cases, the United States Supreme Court dealt with the issue of harm only once, in a never overruled decision issued along with the famous *Miller* ruling, *Paris Adult Theater I v. Slaton*[20]. In that case, the U.S. Supreme Court considered the constitutional validity of a Georgia law that criminalized two porn films, *Magic Mirror* and *It All Comes Out in the End*, because they were sexually explicit. The theater owner argued that the films deserved constitutional protection because they were exhibited for consenting adults and because there was no evidence that mere explicitness had any anti-social effect. America's highest court rejected that argument.

The court found that the films "possibly" compromised public safety and referred to the first major study of the porn genre, the 1970 Commission on Obscenity and Pornography. But the court cited the *minority* report, written by a few religious members of the 1970 commission, who concluded that there is an "arguable correlation" between explicit material and crime. The court ignored the findings of the majority of the Commission that no evidence establishes such a correlation! The court stated: "Although there is no conclusive proof of a connection between anti-social behavior and obscene material, the legislature of Georgia could quite reasonably determine that such a connection does or might exist." The court even went so far to say that obscenity prohibitions are valid even if based on an "unprovable assumption."

But if courts will allow the censorship of the media on the basis of "unprovable assumptions" and "arguable correlations," then the cherished constitutional right to freedom of expression has no substance. Throughout history dictators have justified their control of the media on exactly the same type of "possible harm" allegations. For the Supreme Court to justify the censorship of porn on the same basis betrays a remarkable intellectual lapse.

The judicial attack specifically on erotic explicitness, and the failure to seek conclusive evidence that all porn images cause harm, is evidence of minds plagued by erotophobic aversions. Recall that a key outcome of erotophobic aversions is to prevent the rational mind from thinking clearly about the thing that triggers alarm. Anyone afflicted with a potent aversion to the sight of sexual stimuli or the erotic sensations such stimuli elicits, will react emotionally when exposed to such material, or even when they imagine it. The mental static arising from such distress undermines rational analysis and prompts generalizing.

People who produce friendly porn today are still subject to obscenity charges. Consider, for example, the experience of Tammy Robinson of Lakeland, Florida, a suburban housewife and mother of three. She posted 400 nude pictures of herself on the web. Somebody sent her an e-mail promising to rape and kill her children and make her watch. She called the police. They looked at her site and then raided her house and charged her with promoting obscene material. "When they put their bedroom on the internet, they opened it up to the world," said the chief of investigations for the local Sheriff's Office. He added, "We know what we are doing is right." Police arrested a couple in the same town the same day for filming themselves in their home for a similar website. After their arrest the two lost their jobs, broke off their engagement, and moved out of town. The police dropped the charges when they closed their website.[21] Such attacks on friendly porn occur every year in many different American jurisdictions.

Age-based laws

Even in communities where all porn is not considered "obscene" (because community standards are believed to tolerate it), a variety of laws still target the genre. Many of these laws are aimed at preventing children from having access to any type of porn, regardless of its content. Perhaps the most important of such restrictions in most countries are rules that prohibit porn on television broadcasts except late at night. For example, American regulations forbid "indecent" material on radio or television airwaves from 6 a.m. to 10 p.m., and this excludes sexual material that is "patently offensive as measured by contemporary community standards for the broadcast medium."[22] All types of porn, even the friendly variety, are caught by this ban. The result is that no adult can watch the porn genre on television (except by cable or satellite) during most of the day.

The ostensible purpose of the ban is to protect children. Yet regulators have never been able to show that all porn harms children and American courts have never required that they do. In a series of decisions starting in the 1970s and continuing to the present time, courts have ruled that the government need not scientifically demonstrate harm to children to support the television ban. In these cases, the courts cite "compelling interests" in favor of the censorship, but do not define what that interest is.[23]

Consider also the spate of new laws aimed at preventing "minors" (under age seventeen) from viewing explicit sexual images on the internet. Many jurisdictions have enacted legislation that defines all porn as "harmful to minors." For example, the federal Child Online Protection Act defines such "harmful" material as any image designed to pander to the prurient interest and that depicts "an actual or simulated normal or perverted sex act, or a lewd exhibition of the genitals or post-pubescent female breast."[24] A Michigan law defines as "harmful to minors" internet material which depicts "nudity, sexual excitement, erotic fondling, sexual intercourse."[25]

In all of these examples, intelligent officials have simply jumped to the conclusion that all porn harms kids, when, in fact, no evidence justifies such a sweeping conclusion. While some porn is undoubtedly harmful to minors, friendly porn that accurately depicts happy people engaging in normal sexual conduct could not harm a child. Children are daily exposed to images showing the harsh reality of life in a troubled world. Few people advocate censorship of such non-sexual material "for the protection of children." Yet the mere fact that images contain *any* explicit sexual content is said to harm children, even those millions of teenagers who have already started having sex.

Consider the hysteria caused when a satellite firm broadcasting a World Wrestling Federation (WWF) show at movie theaters attended by adults and children accidentally included thirty seconds of an oral sex scene from a porn movie. "It was totally the most terrible thing we could have done," atoned an executive of the satellite firm. "My eleven-year old was devastated," said a mother, "Little girls were coming out crying."[26]

WWF events glorify violence and humiliation. They celebrate extreme stereotypes of masculinity and femininity. Such entertainment is "the first pornography to be openly marketed to children," says journalist David Kamp.[27] The fact that media executives and countless parents eagerly expose children to the toxic garbage of the WWF yet react with alarm when children observe a normal human sexual act is a powerful example of the force of irrationality in our culture.

Municipal laws

Municipal governments are avid porn censors. Most towns and cities in the western world have a variety of laws aimed at isolating the retail sale of porn out of the social mainstream. Here again, the laws target material solely because of its erotic explicitness.

Perhaps the most famous such municipal law was passed in 1995 in

New York City under the leadership of Mayor Giuliani, and is still the subject of litigation. The laws are aimed at material showing "specified sexual activities" or "specified anatomical areas." Whether such media depicts mutualistic loving sex or violent degrading sex is irrelevant. The new law confines retailers to specified manufacturing and commercial zones and requires that even there they not locate within 500 feet of schools, day-care centers, churches, or each other. Yet to escape the law a retailer has only to reduce the amount of porn to less that 40% of the store's inventory. For example, a previous all-porn video retailer can stay put if it replaces 60% of its porn with movies rated "G" or "R."

New York authorities contend that the laws are not aimed at sexual explicitness *per se*. They say they are really trying to protect the community from crime and reduced property values in the area surrounding the stores.

Consider first their crime hypothesis. There is evidence that areas with high concentrations of porn shops tend to have higher crime rates than areas lacking them. Yet the city admits that its studies cannot prove that porn retailers or their customers cause crime. In its "Adult Entertainment Study," the Department of City Planning states that its survey "did not yield conclusive evidence of a direct relationship between the adult use and the urban ills affecting the community. This reflects the fact that, in a city as dense and diverse as New York, it is difficult to isolate specific impacts attributable to a particular land use. Other cities [such as Los Angeles] that have conducted similar studies have acknowledged this same difficulty."[28]

The idea that porn retailers are a cause of crime is bogus. Porn stores attract people, and some people may commit crimes on their way to or from a porn shop. But some customers of restaurants, convenience stores, banks, and gun shops also commit crimes enroute. Sporting events, music concerts, and business conventions attract large numbers of people to specific locations as well, and some of these individuals will engage in criminal conduct. Simply because a store or event attracts people, it will increase the likelihood of crime. Absent evidence that the patrons of a store are somehow specially disposed to crime, there is no basis to conclude that the store is in any way responsible for crime, and thus no

basis to treat it any differently than any other store. There is no evidence
that the customers of porn shops are specifically disposed to crime. The
hypothesis that porn stores are responsible for increased crime rates is as
faulty as the idea that all porn harms minors.

Nor is there convincing evidence that porn shops have a negative affect on property values in the surrounding area. For example, in a major
study conducted by the Times Square Business Investment District, researchers found that property values in areas with high concentrations of
sex shops tended to increase more slowly than areas without such density.
The study concluded:

> While it may well be that the concentration of adult use estab-
> lishments has a generally depressive effect on the adjoining prop-
> erties, as a statistical matter we do not have sufficient data to
> prove or disprove this thesis. It may also be that simply the pres-
> ence of adult use establishments is subjectively viewed by asses-
> sors as a factor that necessarily reduces the value of a property. In
> short, assumptions may influence assessment.[29]

Let's assume that sex shops do help deflate property values. If sex
shops in fact cause no real harm, such as crime or nuisance, then diminished property values are the product of "subjective assumptions," as the
Times Square report states. There is no doubt that many people are opposed to porn shops simply because of the explicit content of the material
sold there. If in any community many people hold such erotophobic attitudes, then property values near porn shops will be adversely affected.
Phobic attitudes can indeed affect property values. That is why property
values in a racist neighborhood have been known to fall simply because a
member of a hated minority moves in. The saying, "There goes the
neighborhood!" reflects this phobic response. Generations ago racist
communities dealt with that problem by enacting segregation laws.

The real "property values" problem is not porn shops, but rather
phobic community attitudes toward them. The solution is to change
phobic attitudes. But the isolation of porn shops only enhances the phobia against them. No ethical democrat approves of social policy that both
panders to and increases mass irrationality. The New York response to
porn shops is a classic example of the phobigenic infection cycle at work.

The courts are the final defense against such irrationality. But they upheld the New York laws, without one word of analysis as to whether phobic attitudes to the porn genre and sex could be the root of the problem.[30]

Media Censors

While images of genitals are a rare sight in the mainstream media, images of sexually functioning genitals are completely absent. Porn is unavailable on mainstream television or in mainstream theaters.

Consider, for example, how Hollywood deals with sexual explicitness. Recall that the film industry has a ratings system that classifies most movies. Any film showing more than fleeting erotic explicitness receives the most restrictive classification, NC-17. Theaters showing such films must exclude everyone under seventeen, even if accompanied by a parent. Solely because the film is erotically explicit, and without regard to the message of the material, minors are denied access.

Such a rating has several other negative effects on the distribution of the film. Some theater landlords prohibit the screening of any unrated or NC-17 movie, even for an adult audience. Some newspapers will not accept advertising for such films. Some national video retailers will not stock them. Because this "scarlet letter" reduces the profitability of a film, Hollywood producers try to avoid such a rating. Indeed they will go to extraordinary lengths to conceal the erotic imagery that bothers film classifiers. For example, the producers of the late Stanley Kubrick film *Eyes Wide Shut* released it only after it was digitally altered to conceal a sex scene. The censorship outraged film critics. A letter signed by twenty-eight members of New York Film Critics Circle stated, "The fundamental issue underlying this controversy is that the classification and ratings administration of the Motion Picture Assn of America (MPAA) is out of control. It has become a punitive and restrictive force, effectively trampling the freedom of American filmmakers."[31]

The internet entertainment industry also has a ratings system that includes "explicit sexual acts."[32] The system includes violence or hate crimes in its censorship criteria. Such classifying systems send the message that sex images or sex itself are somehow worthy of being equated with gratuitous violence or bigotry that actually do cause harm. Linking porn and harm in this way is phobigenic, helping generate hazy attitudes that indeed porn causes harm and thus is worthy of censorship.

Employer Censors

A fast-growing segment of the porn industry consists of explicit material depicting non-professional models. Such "amateur porn" in magazines, videos, and websites depicts people from all walks of life displaying provocative poses or performing sex acts. They do it mostly for fun, but sometimes also for prizes or a second income. The vast majority of those people have jobs outside the porn industry, and every year some of them have to deal with the antisexual reactions of their employers to their porn fling.

Consider, for example, the experience of Wendy Gesellschap, a counselor at a private firm in Florida, who posted sexy pictures of herself on her website. Only paying customers could access the material. Her employer summarily fired her, saying, "This behavior portrays an image that is unacceptable for our employees."[33] In Arizona, two critical-care workers at a Scottsdale health care facility experienced similar intolerance when they were terminated because they posted images of themselves having sex on a commercial internet site. The nurses opposed their suspensions as an unwarranted intrusion into their private lives.[34]

Many additional examples of such employer antisexualism could be cited, but I will discuss just one more here because it caught the attention of the international press and involved extensive litigation where the issues involved were fully examined. A female teacher was suspended from her job by the school board in a town near Vancouver, British Columbia. She sent a photo of herself to the "Girl Next Door" feature in a sexually explicit magazine. The image shows her lying on her back, smiling toward the cameras, wearing a garter belt, stockings, and high-heeled shoes. A breast is visible. The caption below the photo gives her first name and the first initial of her last name, and says she is a teacher in a named small town.

A reporter informed the school board of the image. The superintendent was "shocked and sickened" by it. The board suspended the thirty-four-year-old junior high teacher for "misconduct." Her husband who took the photo, a teacher too, was also suspended. When news of her suspension reached the school, thirty of her students walked out in protest. "If she wants to pose nude, that's her personal right," a tenth-grade student told the press.[35]

The teachers challenged their suspension and the matter ultimately reached the courts. The law allowed school boards to fire teachers for "misconduct," but did not specify what that was. The court ruled that because the image in question offended community standards, the teachers were guilty of misconduct and thus upheld the suspension.[36] The court did not inquire as to whether the community standards were rational or not, but accepted them as a legitimate basis for the control of the private lives of the teachers. Nobody suggested that the teachers' action constituted real harm.

Employers also have the power to censor sexual material as a result of their control of retail space on their premises. The American government uses that power to prohibit the sale of all porn on military bases. Congress passed the Military Honor and Decency Act in 1996 forbidding the sale of visual material "the dominant theme of which depicts or describes nudity, including sexual or excretory activities or organs, in a lascivious way."[37] The government defended the prohibition on the basis that the sale of explicit material tarnishes "the military's image of honor, professionalism, and proper decorum." The government also argued that the sale of the material sends a message that the military approves of it and this frustrates the military policy that "encourages its personnel to 'lead by example' and display the highest form of personal and professional conduct."[38] In litigation attacking the law, the courts accepted this argument as valid evidence of a legitimate governmental concern.[39]

What nonsense! At the heart of the government's position is the unstated idea that there is something wrong with all porn. Because the entire genre is assumed to be, somehow, "bad," selling it tarnishes the military's reputation and prevents it from "leading by example." The assumption that all porn is unworthy is invalid. Only an erotophobic mind would draw such a conclusion. While much porn is unsavory, not all is. To exclude material just because it is explicit suggests irrationality, and that discredits the military.

Many employees work with a computer and can use it to view the internet and send e-mail. Employers, of course, do not want their workers to use computers or any other equipment for personal reasons during job hours. But some employers have issued rules designed specifically to prevent workers from using employer computers to access sex images at any time. For example, the State of Virginia passed a law prohibiting state employees from using state equipment to "access, download, print, or store" any information having "sexually explicit content."[40] This prohibition includes the use of the computer on the employee's own time. No similar prohibition is aimed at private e-mail, stock quotes, sports scores, or any other type of information. Six Virginia university professors challenged the prohibition, but an appeal court upheld it.[41]

Many private employers have similar rules. Perhaps the most famous case of an employee running afoul of such intolerance was the firing of Harvard Divinity School dean Ronald Thiemann, an internationally respected scholar. Harvard University forbids the use of its computers for material that is "inappropriate, obscene, bigoted, or abusive." When university technicians replaced the hard drive on the dean's university owned *home* computer, they found some legal porn, not illegal material such as child porn. The president of Harvard sacked the esteemed dean.[42]

Had the scholar done wrong? If the dean had been viewing child porn, the firing would have been appropriate because the professor would have been using university property to commit a crime. But no such material was involved. The administration dismissed him simply because images of sex were involved. Had the technicians found photos of sailboats or racing cars, the private use of the computer would have been completely ignored. But the dean lost his position because some people have a phobic fear of anything that is sexually explicit. The administrators of Harvard allowed phobic attitudes to govern its action. If such irrationalism can prevail at an institution dedicated to reason and tolerance, imagine how rife it is elsewhere.

Religious Censors

A vast number of pressure groups feed the attack on all manner of porn. Most of these are Christian organizations. Consider, for example, one of the oldest of such groups, Morality in Media Inc. Founded in 1962 by a Jesuit cleric, Father Morton Hill, this "interfaith" professional lobby group is still going strong. Hill was one of the authors of the minority report of the 1970 Presidential Commission on Obscenity and Pornography, cited by the U.S. Supreme Court in the *Miller* case mentioned above. He concluded that mere sexual explicitness caused social harm, a proposition rejected by the majority of the Commission and almost every social scientist who has investigated the issue.

Morality in Media considers all porn, regardless of its type, to be either "obscene" or "indecent." In the last few years it has successfully lobbied the American Congress to pass a variety of anti-porn laws, and has fought against any relaxation of the Federal Communications Commission rule prohibiting "indecent" television broadcasts between 6 a.m. and 10 p.m. It operates the National Obscenity Law Center, a clearinghouse of information on the law regulating porn, and offers its services to groups and municipalities who want to fight sexual explicitness in the media.

Another powerful anti-porn group is the American Family Association, headed by longtime erotophobic workhorse Donald Wildmon, who operated the Citizens for Decency through Law organization for many years until it was absorbed by the AFA. It bases its anti-porn campaign (and many other programs) on the philosophy "that God has communicated absolute truth to man, and that all men are subject to the authority of God's Word at all times." It sells billboards with simplistic overgeneralized statements such as: "Pornography is a web of deception" and "Pornography pollutes body, mind and soul." It organizes boycotts of private companies involved in the sale or distribution of any type of porn or other "immoral" pursuits. It claims to have an army of volunteers fighting the anti-porn battle in every American state.

Other Christian groups opposed to all porn include the Family Research Council, Concerned Women For America, Focus on the Family, the American Decency Association, and the Christian Family Network. Nobody within such organizations recognizes any worth in any type of erotic explicitness, as far as I can tell.

While Christian pressure groups are the shock troops of anti-porn action, ordinary churches in every community play an important role too.

Most Christian pastors or priests have an anti-porn sermon on their roster, and they preach that all porn is bad. Consider, for example, the sermon given by a pastor at a Pentecostal church in Lincoln, Nebraska, and published in a church journal.[43] According to him, pornography is "anything that represents illicit, immoral expression and is intended to arouse in a person illicit or immoral sexual feelings or responses." That includes porn magazines, videos, and movies, as well as *Victoria's Secret* catalogs, the "sensual covers" of paperback novels, and the nudity in moves such as *Titanic*. He recommends that Christians have nothing to do with any type of porn, and goes so far as to recommend that people get rid of their television set, and when they go to hotel rooms to "unplug the TV" so as not to be tempted.

Such messages cannot help but influence the faithful folk who look to their religious leaders for guidance. Because conservative religions are tireless in their intolerance towards explicit media, porn phobia is rife in such communities.

Feminist Censors

In the last twenty years porn has been attacked from a new quarter: a segment of the feminist movement. While nasty porn deserves the wrath of women, or any nonsexist person, not all porn is of that type. Indeed some of it is produced by feminists. Some women's activists, such as Gloria Steinem,[44] recognize the distinction between nasty porn and material they call "erotica," but many others do not. The most famous of these are Andrea Dworkin and Katherine MacKinnon. For example, Dworkin in her book *Letters From a War Zone* says that porn consists of "the artsy-fartsy pornography that the intellectuals call erotica, to the under-the-counter kiddie porn, to the slick glossy men's 'entertainment' magazines." She adds: "The one message that is carried in all pornography all the time is this: she wants it; she wants to be beaten; she wants to be forced; she wants to be raped; she wants to be brutalized; she wants to be hurt. This is the premise, the first principle, of all pornography."[45]

That is, of course, a ridiculous overstatement. No reasonable person could conclude that the message of all porn, including erotica or men's magazines, is that women want to be beaten and raped. Yet that is what that feminist believes. She is a leading advocate of a radical system of censorship that would give individuals the right to sue anyone who felt themselves aggrieved by porn. Dworkin and MacKinnon convinced the City of Indianapolis to pass such a law.

While the usual erotophobic attitudes undoubtedly play a role in the intense fear of all porn exhibited by such feminists, an interesting type of sexist erotophobia must also be involved. Some feminists view male sexuality the way many erotophobic Christians see human sexuality: as something inherently dangerous and demonic. Dworkin is one of the leading proponents of this false idea. She says: "Men love death . . . slow murder is the heart of eros."[46] Also:

> Each man, knowing his deep-rooted impulse to savagery, can presuppose this same impulse in other men and seeks to protect himself from it. The rituals of male sexual sadism over and against the bodies of women are the means by which male aggression is socialized so that a man can associate with other men without the imminent danger of male aggression against his own person.[47]

Possessed of such delusions, a person would naturally be uncomfortable with any sort of material that was designed to stimulate the monster of male lust.

Opportunistic Censors

Porn censorship is an industry in every country of the world, and involves the work of vice squad officers, by-law inspectors, postal officials, customs agents, film classifiers, and others. The greater the scope of porn censorship, the better their job security. They have a direct and special economic interest in perpetuating attacks on all porn. That is one reason censors virtually never advocate or initiate changes to the sexual censorship system. Reform tends to occur when it is forced upon censors by courts, politicians, or community pressure.

In any phobic culture, political advantages always accrue to those who attack the object of phobia. In a culture where delusions about porn are rampant, attacking porn will make an erotophobic community feel more secure. An ambitious district attorney or politician can garner enormous public attention with a campaign against "smut." They get their names in the news; they express their concerns for the social welfare; they are perceived as decisive and strong.

People outside the legal and political community also exploit censorship to advance their own interests. Consider, for example, how an attack on all porn would be politically beneficial to a group of like-minded feminists, even if the images posed no harm to women. First, such an attack is a way to deny men something they value. The porn genre has been produced largely for men, although ever-increasing numbers of women are discovering an interest in it. In the same way that denying women the right to abortion is a powerful symbol of male dominance over women, prohibiting all porn is a powerful symbol of female power over men. Men have done exactly that for eons. An attack on a male prerogative evens the score, and appeals to many feminists for that reason alone.

Secondly, attacking porn provides a specific issue around which women can rally, helping cultivate political skills. Anti-porn campaigners learn how to speak in public, manage the press, lobby legislators and law enforcers, and organize a focused campaign. The feminist attack on erotic media has given many feminists a national stage to advance their agenda. Such a campaign can gain the movement sympathizers, and sometimes even patrons. For example, the Indianapolis bylaw sponsored by Andrea Dworkin, mentioned above, attracted the support of constituencies traditionally hostile to feminist concerns, such as religious, law enforcement, and conservative political groups. The passage of the law marked the first time feminists had cooperated with fundamentalists and conservative Republicans to attack erotic material.

Opportunistic porn intolerance is an important catalyst of the infection cycle. When government officials, religious groups, or feminists fight porn for purely selfish motives their action helps breed senseless fears about explicit media in the minds of many people who observe such attacks. What begins as opportunism in some people ends up as phobia in others, spinning the phobic system for another loop.

11 / Secluding Sex

MOST OF US SEEK PRIVACY in our sexual life. We feel uncomfortable expressing our erotic passion around anyone other than our lover. But not everyone values sexual privacy all the time. Many young children feel no shame masturbating in the presence of family and friends, until they learn of the almost universal intolerance to such behavior. Some teens delight in gatherings where they openly engage in sex. Men and women who attend homosexual bathhouses get a thrill out of explicit sexual display. So do the millions of people who call themselves "swingers" and engage in organized group sexual activities. Thousands of strippers and other sexual entertainers also shed their sexual publicity inhibitions to obtain the cash rewards for an on-stage sexual performance.

Negativity is aimed at live sex in four situations. The first two consist of involuntary exposures to sex. This commonly occurs when parents or other family members see a child openly and shamelessly masturbating in a living room or other common area. It also happens when members of the public encounter people having sex in parked cars, public washrooms, public parks or beaches. Live sex is also attacked even though only willing eyes can see it, such as private parties where group sex takes place, and commercial on-stage sexual performances, such as exotic dancing.

If visible sex is unhygienic then it properly attracts wrath. For example a child who masturbates in common areas of the home poses sanitary problems. Fingers should be cleaned before and after they fondle a penis or clitoris. Similarly adult public sex can be unhygienic. Semen and other erotic fluids can carry deadly diseases. Any sexual behavior that deposits erotic fluids on toilet seats, urinals, park benches or any other space the public is likely to contact, risks harm and is irresponsible.

Similarly, if the sex is deliberately performed to shock or frighten bystanders, then it also deserves attack. We are naturally averse to the sight of overt malice. A man who approaches strangers on the street and then opens his coat and exposes himself masturbating commits a form of assault. Laws and social negativity aimed at such behavior are not intolerant.

Erotophobic motives, however, prompt most attacks on visible sex. A person with genital phobia will react negatively upon involuntarily observing sexual acts, if erotic organs can be seen. While many adults learn to enjoy the sight of aroused genitals in certain contexts (such as during sex with their spouse), genital anxieties will surface when masturbating children or strangers performing sex are discovered.

Lust phobia also motivates intolerance toward visible sex. Unlike nudity, which is not innately arousing, visible sex often is, for the same reasons that porn is too. A person suffering lust phobia will not enjoy visually stimulated arousal, and will favor social restrictions that seclude sex.

Visible sex helps legitimate lust. Openly exposing sex endorses it. If people are allowed to perform sex in public, or even if they can privately gather and watch each other perform sexual acts or pay entertainers to do the same on a private stage, they help normalize sexuality, bring it into the routine of life. People who believe that lust is inherently dangerous do not want such messages to be expressed.

Visible Masturbation

Many children begin autoerotic play very early in life. Even infants enjoy pleasuring themselves, sometimes to climax. Baby girls clench their thighs together and coo with erotic delight; baby boys thrust themselves erect. In their first or second year many children begin fondling their erotic organs regularly. Some will rub their crotches on beds, sofas, dolls, and even people. Toddlers do this without concern that other people can see them. Greater numbers of nursery school kids, especially boys, begin autoerotic exploration and sometimes within sight of adults. Around this age children discover that touching or otherwise stimulating the place between their legs causes adults to react with alarm.

Most modern parents oppose not masturbation *per se* but only its visibility. Parents tell their children that masturbation must be confined to places where nobody can see it. Mainstream family "experts" agree with that response. For example, Dr. B.D. Schmitt, author of *Your Child's Health*, says:

> You want your child to feel good about masturbation. The only thing you can control is where he does it. A reasonable goal is to perform masturbation only in the bedroom and bathroom. You might say to your child, "It's OK to do that in your bedroom or the bathroom." If you completely ignore masturbation, no matter where you child does it, he will think he can do it freely in any setting.[1]

Erica Neuman, the "Sex Ed Mom" who writes for the popular Oxygen website for women, counsels parents to tell kids, "Honey, that is something we do in the privacy of our bedrooms." She advises parents to be prepared for kids to ask "Why?" She answers, "At this point you can compare it to using the restroom. 'It's just one of those things we do in private.'"[2] But that answer is purely circular and does not explain why childhood masturbation must be invisible.

Adults compel children to masturbate in private for a simple reason: the sight of such youthful sexual activity offends them. Most adults feel very uncomfortable observing an open, innocent sexual act of a child. Yet few adults can make sense of their stress. A child needs to know that most adults find open masturbation offensive; but children also need to know that such offense is not rational. A parent should tell a child who is openly masturbating that such an activity is healthy and fun, but also that it triggers foolish fears in the minds of many people, and that if the child wants to avoid such responses then they child should do it in private. Such information locates the source of the problem where it belongs, not in the child's conduct, but rather in the head of the antisexual person.

Intolerance aimed at the mere sight of childhood masturbation helps produce several erotophobic attitudes. Sex therapist Helen Singer Kaplan says, "A youngster's sex education begins when he senses his mother's voice assuming a slightly harsher note and her movements becoming tense as she notices his erection in the tub. It becomes crystal clear to the perceptive child his sexual feelings are definitely not okay."[3] Attacking the visibility of masturbation not only impugns autoeroticism and the visibility of such self-pleasure, but also lust itself.

The delusion acquired in childhood that masturbation is inherently private and must always be hidden is very common and is often never defused. It can appear in adult sexual relationships. For example, while some adult sex partners enjoy watching each other masturbate, many people avoid the sight of their partner's autoerotic play and hide their own. Sometimes such avoidance is the result of phobic attitudes that masturbation is sinful or improper at any time, but often people who feel entirely comfortable with performing the act alone feel distressed sharing the experience with their lover. I have questioned many people about the matter and am always amazed how many report such discomfort (over 50%). Some people tell me they are uneasy because they believe that their partner would be uncomfortable watching them, but most people report that regardless of the anticipated response of their lover, they feel anxious about being seen while masturbating.

Public Sex

Some couples, especially adolescents, must resort to semi-public places to have sex because they have no private area where parents, siblings, and police won't intrude. Even people who do have secure boudoirs occasionally find themselves in the throes of erotic passion in cars, parks, beaches, or other public spaces and choose not to delay their pleasure. Gay men often have sex with strangers in public places because they get a sexual thrill from the threat of being discovered, or because such quick, spontaneous interactions allow them anonymity.

Public sex attracts enormous negativity. The most important institutional example is the law that regulates the publicity of sexual affection. The law intervenes the moment any sort of genital contact is visible. For example, Ohio legislation provides: "No person shall recklessly do any of the following if it is likely to be viewed by and affront others who are not members of the offender's household: expose his or her private parts or engage in masturbation; engage in sexual conduct; or engage in conduct which to an ordinary observer would appear to be sexual conduct or masturbation."[4]

Some lawmakers oppose even covered male genitals that are visibly erect. A Republican state senator in Mississippi introduced a bill that prohibits obviously aroused men from appearing anywhere in public. The

"Boner Ban" would make it illegal to display "covered male genitals in a discernibly turgid state."[5] Most laws prohibiting such public conduct are framed in far more vague terms such as "indecency," "immorality," or "lewdness." For example, the California Penal Code prohibits any act that is "offensive to decency, or is adopted to excite vicious or lewd thoughts or acts."

Every year these prohibitions are frequently enforced in America. Consider the experience of a judge from Pennsylvania vacationing in Cleveland, Ohio. He met a woman in a bar one evening and later police observed the two engaged in oral sex in a car parked beside a Holiday Inn. Both were charged with "public indecency." As a result of the charge, the judge was temporarily stripped of his duties. The Constitution of Pennsylvania says that a judge can be removed from office for "conduct which prejudices the proper administration of justice or brings the judicial office into disrepute."[6] Here again, antisexual law helps tarnish another professional career.

Teens often have sex in public areas and when discovered can be victimized by prohibitions against public sex. For example, the Police Department in Windcrest, Texas, responded to a report from office workers that two people were having sex behind a carwash operation. The cops arrested two teens and charged them with "public lewdness."[7]

Though such antisexual laws sometimes snare heterosexuals, homosexuals are by far the most common targets. Most prosecutions for public sex are the result of "sting" operations during which undercover officers attend public parks and washrooms where homosexuals cruise for sex. The officer then solicits a sexual interaction or waits for somebody to make that offer. One of the most famous such cases involved the British pop star George Michael. He entered a washroom in a quiet park in the middle of Beverly Hills, California. The premises were empty except for a good-looking man whom George said was "basically masturbating." The pop star decided to "return the favor in kind" from about eight feet away. The man was a police decoy and Michael was arrested.[8] Such sting operations are exclusively aimed at gays. Police never send out female decoys enticing heterosexual men to have public sex.

Employers can be guilty of the same type of intolerance. For example, a bank fired a worker when he was charged with committing an "indecency" offense in a public washroom. The employer considered his conduct "inappropriate" and thought it would tarnish the bank's reputation. The employee sued for wrongful dismissal. The court found that customers or co-workers did not complain about the worker, that nobody other than the employer would have known of the charges, that the incident did not cause a loss of business for the bank, and did not affect the worker's ability to do the job. The court ordered the employer to pay damages for unjustly firing the worker.[9]

Some jurisdictions have wisely decided not to waste scarce law enforcement resources fighting public sex. For example, if George Michael had been caught fondling himself in a lavatory in London, England, he would have been cautioned by police, but not charged. Police no longer conduct surveillance of popular gay cruising areas there.[10]

But erotophobic members of the community oppose any letup in the attack on public sex. Writing in the *Sunday Times* (London), Melanie Phillips states: "All public sex is an affront to human dignity. If such encounters are an integral part of the homosexual lifestyle, they remain such an affront. To say so is not to display prejudice. On the contrary, those who endorse such behavior are pushing something quite vile and pernicious with damage that is potentially incalculable."[11] Note the vague generality of the harms attributed to public sex. Clearly that writer is hostile to the mere visibility of a normal human act. But she cannot articulate a cogent reason why people who want to play sexually in public should be treated like criminals. She harbors *public sex phobia*, very similar to porn phobia, consisting of vague delusions that somehow the mere visibility of sex causes harm.

As the last chapter argued, there is nothing innately offensive about seeing sex, and the idea that a child is harmed merely by the sight of any type of lustful conduct is also false. In Mangaia in the Cook Islands, for example, families live in single rooms and children learn that sexual intercourse "is not mortal combat but an enjoyable, mutual transaction."[12]

Obviously, not every type of sex is appropriate for children to see. In the same way that nasty porn or child porn is unsuitable for kids (and adults), the equivalent live sex is too. For example, viewing masochistic sexual conduct would seriously confuse most children about the nature of human sexuality. But forcing children away from *every* type of visible lustful expression is unjustified. Because the idea that all visible sex harms children is so powerful, debate about the types of sex that children should be allowed to see has never occurred.

A rational culture would not attack sex merely because of its visibility. It would carefully define the types of public sex that caused real harm and would prohibit only that conduct. It would encourage an etiquette of disregard towards all other public sex, and discourage the intolerant meddling that is standard today.

Private Group Sex

Some youths enjoy masturbating in groups. Teen masturbation is harmless when done alone and harmless when performed in groups. But even people who have no problem with masturbation have trouble with the idea that teens gather in groups to do it.

One of my baby-boomer friends recalls a game he played many times as a fourteen-year-old youth when he and three or four of his buddies would gather in a friend's basement and see who could ejaculate closest to a coin in the middle of the cement floor. "We'd bring a mop and bucket to clean up the cum," he told me. "We'd muffle our orgasms so nobody could hear." But one day the mother of his friend did hear and barged into the room. "She flipped, and screamed at us: 'You're perverts!' Then she called my mother. I was so embarrassed I almost died. Thankfully, when I got home my folks said nothing. But I never did a circle jerk again."

Such teen sex play is probably more common today because fewer parents are in the home as much as they were in the 1960s and 1970s. The website www.allaboutsex.org has a section called "I Got Caught" which records several incidents of group masturbation. Some parental responses are very tolerant, but many are not. For example, fourteen-year-old "George" describes a masturbation session involving teen boys and girls into which an adult intruded. The result is that the group is now "in counseling." But he and his friends rejected such "therapy." "The people keep saying that masturbation should be done alone. We don't agree. We all liked doing it with more people so we are still currently doing it with more people in the group about once a week."[13]

Some adults also enjoy sex where they can see and be seen by others, even strangers. Yet even though such conduct is performed where only willing eyes see it, many antisexual individuals and social institutions oppose it, and even support laws that allow police to barge into homes, clubs, and bathhouses and arrest those who engage in group sex. The focus of their attack is the fact that the sex is visible to others.

Some group sex sessions do spread disease, but the mere visibility of the sex does not cause that harm. Group sex can be entirely safe. Indeed, group visibility can increase the chance that safe sex occurs. For example, in San Francisco, only group sex is allowed in gay bathhouses. Bylaws require that sex not be secluded, allowing attendants to ensure that partners are using condoms.[14]

Attacks on group sex are always based on vague notions of harm such as "immorality" and "the protection of society." Consider, for example, the statement made by Jean Chretien, the Prime Minister of Canada, when as Justice Minister, he refused to repeal the Canadian criminal law that forbids group sex. "It is not in the public interest, even for those above 18 years of age, to have group sex." The law, he said, was necessary to "safeguard public morals by not permitting everything to be carried out by any number of people."[15] The Canadian Association of Chiefs of Police also opposed the change. When asked who were the victims of consensual adult group sex, a Montreal police official replied: "Society."[16]

The European Court of Human Rights now recognizes that group sex prohibitions are undemocratic. It made that ruling in a case from England where the law prohibits homosexual group sex. Seven men videotaped themselves performing oral sex and mutual masturbation at a private home. Someone with a grudge gave one of the tapes to police who raided a home and seized another tape. They charged several men with "gross indecency," the same law used to convict Oscar Wilde in 1895. The sex acts were not visible to anyone other than the participants and involved no sadomasochism or physical harm. The sex would have been lawful if only two people had been present. English courts convicted the accused.

One of these "criminals" appealed to the European Court of Human Rights, contending that the law violated his right to privacy enshrined in Article 8 of the European Human Rights Convention. The court had to determine whether there was any "pressing social need" for criminal prohibitions against these private, consensual acts. English prosecutors could not show that the prohibited conduct caused any real harm. The court of senior judges from all over Europe concluded that nothing justified such an invasion of privacy. The court awarded the convicted man monetary damages for the costs of defending the unjust criminal proceedings.[17]

Similar antisexual laws are regularly used by police all over the world to invade the privacy of group sex practitioners. For example, police in Montreal, Quebec, often raid "swingers" clubs and on one occasion phoned the press prior to the bust so photographers could get photos of the arrested swingers. Forty-two people were publicly humiliated in the raid.[18] Police in Fort Lauderdale, Florida, raided two private swingers' clubs and arrested fifty-five people, including police and corrections officers and two teachers. The prosecutor justified the action because the clubs' "only reason for existing is so people can engage in open sexual activity in front of whomever may show up that night."[19] In Phoenix, Arizona, the city council has banned swingers' clubs. The ordinance prohibits businesses "in which one or more persons may view, or may participate in, a live sex act."[20]

The "organized crime" unit of the Atlanta police attended an impromptu sex party that encouraged patrons to "put on your sexiest outfit or let your imagination run wild." The cops stayed for three hours. After observing multiple sex acts they arrested over 115 people, many for "public indecency."[21]

Police sometimes use prostitution laws to ban visible sex. Consider the case of Tom and Suzanne Wahl of St Louis. The married couple performs "erotically entertaining and educational live shows" in private locations for anyone who pays their fee. Undercover police officers arranged a show and then arrested the pair when they began performing oral sex. Missouri courts convicted the couple of prostitution because they had "deviate sexual intercourse" (oral sex) for a fee. In their zeal to ban all live sexual display the Missouri legal system criminalizes consensual sex between a husband and wife![22]

Group sex at gay bathhouses is often targeted by the same intolerance. For example, after a two-month investigation police in Calgary charged fifteen men at a gay club with "bawdy house" offences on the ground that the premises were "solely designed to facilitate indecent sexual acts between males." Newspaper editors denounced the raid as "an insensitive, illiberal, destructive abuse of power."[23]

The police and the criminal courts are not the only perpetrators of such antisexualism. So are employers. Consider, for example, the case of a Florida teacher caught in the swing club in Fort Lauderdale raided by police, mentioned above. Officers alleged that the 48-year-oldforty-eight-year-old man was on a bed performing oral sex on his wife in full view of other patrons in the room. He was charged with "lewd and lascivious" behavior, but the charge was later dropped. However, a clause in his teaching contract prohibited "conduct inconsistent with the standards of public conscience and good morals." When school officials heard about his arrest they suspended him. He had taught for sixteen years and regularly received excellent scores on his performance evaluations.

Parents objected to the school board's discipline and ultimately the teacher was reinstated, but only as an adult-education teacher with less pay. The superintendent said the transfer was necessary to protect children. Yet no evidence indicated that the experienced teacher was a threat to anyone. Antisexual activists defended the school board's action. Scott Bergthold, president of the Community Defense Council, an organization that opposes any sort of open sexual display even when only willing adult eyes see it, says: "People in positions of leadership that wield such a powerful influence over our children should be held to a higher moral standard, not just a facade of morality."[24] But that argument is based on the idea that a teacher is "immoral" by engaging in group sex, and such a notion makes sense only if group sex actually causes real harm.

Attacks on private group sex waste valuable social resources, especially costly police and court time. Police typically invest hundreds of hours of undercover work before they actually raid group sex parties. Further, when they force their way into private premises, they often need an entire squad as back-up. Court proceedings consume endless more hours. Real criminals benefit from this diversion of valuable law enforcement resources.

Such intolerance also interferes with the personal freedoms of group sex practitioners and are every bit as pernicious as the raids on the private gatherings of Jews in Nazi Germany or Christians in communist China. Yet the mainstream press largely fails to protest such homegrown violations of basic democratic rights.

Stage Sex

Because so many people enjoy watching sexual conduct, the demand is enormous for live sexual entertainment, mostly in the form of stripping. *Exotic Dancer* magazine estimates that approximately 2,500 strip clubs in the United States cater to this lusty appetite.[25] Men are the main audience of strip shows. But many women enjoy seeing nude erotic performances too. While the average stripper's dance routine consists mostly of the normal movements observed on any dance floor, strippers usually include overtly sexual movements such as thrusting their crotch against the floor in imitation of intercourse or spreading their legs so that their genitals are exposed. Some male entertainers use a penis ring that allows them to maintain an erection throughout their show.

Though highly popular, such entertainment attracts social negativity despite the fact that only willing eyes can see it. The vast amount of such negativity is prompted simply by the fact that genitals are exposed for an overtly erotic purpose. Mere sexual visibility is the target of attack.

Consider the array of laws that allow stripping only if the entertainers cover their genital organs. These laws most commonly appear in municipal zoning ordinances and liquor licensing regulations. For example, the city of Erie, Pennsylvania, was the subject of an important March 2000 ruling by the U.S. Supreme Court on the issue of whether laws can control genital exposure in erotic dance shows. The Erie law required that all strippers don G-strings and pasties. A nude strip club sued for an injunction to restrain enforcement of the nudity ban, asserting the free speech guarantees in the American constitution.

The U.S. Supreme Court had to consider whether the visibility of genitals for overtly erotic purposes in a private commercial location caused any form of harm. Think about that issue. Can you imagine how the mere exposure of very specific anatomical regions of the body during a strip show could cause harm that an identical strip show with those areas concealed would not? Common sense screams: "Of course not." Lust phobia, genital phobia, and what I call *stripper phobia* are the main motives behind attacks on such stage lust.

Yet the Supreme Court upheld the law. A plurality of the court in *Pap's A.M. v. City of Erie* ruled that the law was valid on the basis of the "secondary effects" of nude strip clubs.[26] The court noted that the preamble to the bylaw indicated that nude entertainment "adversely impacts and threatens to impact on the public health, safety and welfare by providing an atmosphere conducive to violence, sexual harassment, public intoxication, prostitution, and the spread of sexually transmitted diseases." Astoundingly, America's highest court accepted this preposterous claim. The court never demanded that the municipality produce evidence of the causal connection between the exposure of nipples and genitals and the real harms asserted. The court held that such a conclusion could be drawn from previous court decisions, and that, in any event, the court would defer to local politicians in determining harm:

> The city council members, familiar with commercial downtown Erie, are the individuals who would likely have had first-hand knowledge of what took place at and around nude dancing establishments in Erie, and can make particularized, expert judgments about the resulting harmful secondary effects.[27]

This is another of the many examples of America's highest court failing to look for real evidence of harm to justify interference with sexual activity performed only by willing adults. That is an abnegation of their vital constitutional duty to ensure that laws do not institutionalize irrational prejudice. Outside the sexual domain, the court usually admirably performs that duty. The court would never defer to politicians in a white supremacist municipality who claimed that Afro-American or Chinese dance clubs (fully-clothed) created "secondary" harms. The court would demand cogent evidence linking the type of dance with the harms alleged, and the justices would do so because common sense suggests no such link can possibly exist and that the real basis for the prohibition is prejudice. But because erotophobia is largely unrecognized, and because many judges suffer from it, the idea that irrationality rather than real harm is the basis of the municipal prohibition is never seriously considered. Other members of the Supreme Court majority upheld the law on the traditional grounds that the government needs to foster "good morals," a phrase that has no objective meaning and is a common rationalization for phobic sexual attitudes.

Fortunately, two of the Supreme Court Justices did think clearly on the issue, and dissented. Both questioned the causal link between the target of the law—mere erotic visibility—and harm. "To believe that the mandatory addition of pasties and a G-string will have any kind of noticeable impact on secondary effects requires nothing short of a titanic surrender to the implausible," said Justice John Paul Stevens.

Laws against stage sex are not only the result of the stripper phobia of politicians and judges, but also of community groups, mostly with a conservative Christian point of view. A Christian academy in Sacramento expelled a five-year old girl from kindergarten simply because her mother worked as a stripper, but offered to readmit the child if the mother agreed to end her exotic dancing.[28] A pastor at the Elm Baptist Church in Detroit reflects a similar perspective. "In a Christian community," he says, "these [strip] clubs have a negative, adverse effect on the quality of life. They also have a negative impact on both adults and children, in terms of maintaining healthy attitudes and relationships within the family and the community. Strip clubs do not support healthy values."[29]

But how do strip clubs undermine "healthy values"? Patrons come to such clubs because they want to experience the sexual feelings that naturally arise as they watch attractive dancers disrobe. Strip clubs, like any form of overtly erotic entertainment, sanction those lustful feelings. But sexual arousal in itself, even that prompted by unclad dancers, causes no real harm. The truly "unhealthy values" are possessed by those who see sexuality as inherently demonic and therefore necessarily kept under lock and key.

Many communities exclude strip bars from areas near schools. The assumption is that the clubs somehow harm children. For example, a Detroit mother objects to strip clubs near schools because, "Children often encounter women going into these clubs to work." But the idea that a woman is threatening to children just because she peels off her clothes behind closed doors at a strip club is preposterous and obviously the result of stripper phobia.

The most extreme version of the same phobia comes from Israel. A small town south of Tel Aviv was plagued by a string of tragedies one New Year season. Three residents died in traffic accidents, one during childbirth, and another from a heart attack. Local rabbis told a delegation of worried residents that the tragedies were the result of a public sin committed at a New Year Eve party—a strip show. "A black cloud has covered the town because of this filth," said one rabbi. Many townspeople uttered special prayers to remove "the curse."[30] The sad irony of such superstition is that Jews have so often been the victims of similar phobic beliefs.

Lust phobia is a major factor behind intolerance toward stage sex. Because the main purpose of a strip show is to arouse the sexual feelings of the audience, folks who are hostile to lust are naturally opposed to such entertainment. Their negativity tends to decline if a nude performance has any non-lust purpose. For example, the administration of New York Mayor Rudolph Giuliani passed laws prohibiting strippers from baring their erotic organs during their dances, leading to the closure of many strip clubs. Yet nude performances and even live sex acts often occur in New York without any official attack. Audiences flocked in droves to see Nicole Kidman shed her clothes in the Broadway show "The Blue Room." Another Broadway performance, "The Judas Kiss," opened with a man performing oral sex on a woman. Burlesque, banned in New York in the 1930s, has also made a big comeback in the city.

These exposures of erotic organs are permitted because they can be justified as "art," as something more than raw titillation, in the same way that sex for procreation is more acceptable to erotophobic people than sex for mere pleasure. Of course, subtle elitist interests may also play a role in this antisexualism. As the director of the New York Civil Liberties Union put it: "It's highbrow versus lowbrow in the city, and the people who've created this new regime will allow the highbrow and censor the lowbrow."[31]

While many communities in the west do allow strip clubs in their midst, very few allow the performance of overtly sexual acts on stage, such as masturbation or intercourse. Performing actual live sex is a serious offense in almost every jurisdiction of the world. Even in one of the most sexually liberal cities in North America, Montreal, sex on stage is taboo. In May 2003 forty police officers raided a strip bar, alleging "indecency" because oral sex acts were taking place in open dance areas.[32]

Just faking live sex by using facsimiles of genital organs can provoke police into a censorious lather. A Spanish theater troupe performed a sexually explicit play in London but claimed to use sex aids rather than real organs. Police threatened the show with charges even if no actual sex occurred.[33]

Yet in many places where such live acts are outlawed, a citizen can walk into a movie theater and watch exactly the same conduct performed on the big screen. Why is celluloid sex often permitted, but not live sex on stage?

Live sex shows involve real people having sex at a known location in the community. In contrast, an explicit movie in the same proximity involves no actual sexual behavior in the locality, for the actors performed the deed far away and perhaps long ago. Further, the sex involved in the film occurs largely in private, in the presence of only those needed to capture the act on film.

To a person suffering erotophobia, these differences between live sex and media sex are important. For example, a person harboring the phobic belief that sexual performers are paragons of immorality will be more uncomfortable with their physical presence than mere images of them. Further, live sex is a more powerful advertisement for uninhibited lust than any other sort of public event, and hence people frightened by lust are most intolerant of that form of sexual celebration. Forcing entertainers to abstain from actual sex acts, and forcing them further to don G-strings and pasties, communicates sexual restraint and control, and this will comfort anyone who sees lust as inherently dangerous and anti-social.

12 / Prostitution Prohibitions

FROM TIME IMMEMORIAL members of "the world's oldest profession" have provided sexual services for cash. The business is now a multi-billion dollar industry in North America alone. Over 69,000 sex workers and several million clients engage in approximately 40 million sexual transactions every year in the United States and Canada.[1] Though hugely popular, prostitution attracts enormous informal and institutional negativity, much of which is intolerant.

By definition, "prostitution" is the provision of sexual services for a fee. The key difference between a prostitute's sexual services and any other sexual interaction is that a sex worker receives money for the service. Does the simple fact that cash changes hands make prostitution harmful?

In no other area of life is a service that is regarded as acceptable if provided for free, suddenly regarded as harmful and illegitimate if motivated by money. Other intimate services are commercialized without complaint. Doctors probe into the most private regions of our bodies, priests marry us, and morticians embalm us. They all charge a fee, and nobody attacks them for receiving money for what they do. But prostitutes are regularly stigmatized simply because they charge for sex.

Their financial motivation means that the sexual transaction involves no love, commitment, duty, or intention to procreate. Is commercial sex *necessarily* harmful because it lacks those non-sexual dimensions?

The monetary motivation does increase the likelihood of unhealthy outcomes. A commercial sexual interaction tends to be emotionally cold and even tense. A prostitute who constantly engages in sexual penetration without a sense of emotional intimacy, probably suffers psychological damage.

But not *all* prostitutes suffer such discomfort. By carefully selecting their clients and establishing rapport, or by providing services other than penetration, sex workers can avoid the psychological damage that repeated indiscriminate intercourse is likely to cause. As psychological studies confirm, many such practitioners exist, and often charge a premium for their services.[2] A prostitute's work need not be demeaning or unsafe. As one sex worker put it in an article she wrote for a national newspaper: "All in all prostitution has been good to me and I have been good to it . . . . I don't really have to work anymore, but I love the business, so I still see my regular clients. I know I am supposed to hate my job but I just don't."[3]

Some people claim that prostitution threatens committed relationships, marriage, and the family. The argument is that the "johns" who patronize prostitutes will have less incentive to enter stable relationships. But such an argument is unfounded. Committed relationships have intrinsic rewards to both men and women. Most people report that sex within a committed relationship is superior to casual sexual contact. Further, such emotionally bonding sex costs no money. Commitment also offers continuing companionship, emotional security, and the opportunity to pool economic resources and share the responsibility for children. These positive outcomes will always make committed relationships appealing to most people, even those who have access to prostitutes. Further, sex workers can provide committed couples a way to gratify needs for sexual variety without risking the emotional attachments arising from sexual affairs.

Participants in a commercial sex transaction who engage in unsafe sexual practices risk transmitting disease. Prostitutes who solicit business on the street, especially in residential neighborhoods, help cause nuisances such as noise and litter. Many prostitutes are exploited by pimps and help fund organized criminal activity. These types of prostitution are undoubtedly harmful to the community at large, as well as to those involved in the sex trade.

But none of these negative outcomes are *necessarily* produced by prostitution. Many prostitutes are fastidious in their disease-prevention techniques. Most sex work is conducted far from the street where pimps and the underworld are in charge. Prostitutes' organizations estimate that a small minority of sex workers in America are streetwalkers.[4] Most prostitutes solicit their clients and perform sexual services without causing any social nuisance.

While some people malign only the harmful types of prostitution, sex work is more commonly attacked simply because it involves sex for money. Such blanket negativity is intolerant, and the sections below show that it is prevalent in our culture.

Informal Antisexualism

Polls indicate that only 15% of men and 6% of women condone prostitution.[5] People express their hostility to sex work in many ways. Hatred of prostitutes is often openly demonstrated on radio and television interview shows, such as in one where an audience member berated a female prostitute because she was only able "to think between her legs."[6] So low is the status of a prostitute in our culture that the civil law recognizes as slanderous any false allegation that a person engages in such work. To call a person a prostitute is to automatically impugn their character in the eyes of most people. "A prostitution allegation, to say nothing of an arrest, even for being a call girl to the stars, is a scarlet letter that is almost impossible to expunge," says the biographer of Los Angeles celebrity madam Alex Adams.[7]

Prostitutes who are homosexual and thus also face the intolerance aimed at gays in our culture, describe the hostility toward sex work as even more toxic: "It's funny, I've been a lesbian all my life, and the stigma surrounding homosexuality in the middle sixties when I came out was never even half as bad as it was around being a prostitute."[8] Because social antipathy toward prostitutes is so high, most sex workers hide their occupation from friends and especially from family. New York prostitute Tracy Quan did tell her parents, and was regarded as a "weirdo" by her colleagues for doing so. In the online magazine *Salon* she reports:

> When I ask other prostitutes why they never consider telling their parents, their answers aren't about legality or physical safety. Instead they talk about prudish, neurotic mothers who are

so out of the loop sexually that they could never acknowledge any hint of a daughter's sex life—much less prostitution.[9]

Many people regard not only all prostitutes as morally suspect, but also all of their clients. Clearly, the men who buy the services of child prostitutes, or who have sex with somebody who is under the influence of a dominating pimp or addictive drug, deserve censure. But most social negativity aimed at the customers of prostitutes flows simply from the fact that they choose to pay for sex.

Consider a letter to Ann Landers headlined: "Can you trust a man who uses escort services?" The letter writer reports that during an off and on relationship with her fiancé, during a two year period when the two were separated, the man patronized escort services "and learned some new tricks." When the couple reunited the woman learned of his foray into the sex trade. "I was devastated," she writes. Her fiancé insisted he did nothing wrong because the two were unattached at the time. "I do not understand his vulgar behavior. He has apologized, but I cannot seem to get past this. Should I go ahead with the wedding, hoping I will be able to forgive him later on?"[10] The simple fact that her fiancé paid for sex while the two had broken off their relationship causes her to cast doubts on his suitability as a mate. Her response is typical. Tens of millions of people in our culture would have a similar reaction.

Many sex workers internalize the negativity directed at their work. Consider the story of Susan, a twenty-five-year-old geologist, who worked an occasional evening shift at an erotic massage studio. Her job was similar to the work of most masseurs, except that she included a client's penis in the touch. She held the two jobs to pay down her student loans. "I wouldn't tell anyone about this work, not even my boyfriend," she told me. "Everyone would regard me as the lowest of the low, and I could never live with that." But *she* also felt shame about her work: "I would not want to be with a man who could accept that I do this."

If her work caused a social nuisance, spread disease, violated her physical integrity, or made money for the Mafia, her shame would make sense. But her erotic massage involved none of that. The only difference between her work and that of thousands of body-workers who carry on their business free of social stigma and personal shame is that her touch included male genitals. There is no rational basis for her internalized negativity.

Many *clients* of sex workers also experience similar dishonor for patronizing such "fallen" women. Organized "shame the john" campaigns try to exploit these feelings. Police often publicize the names of prostitutes and their customers in the media. Many of the named individuals regard such publicity as a far more severe punishment than a fine or even jail time. A police official in Columbus, Ohio, says: "When a male is arrested for prostitution the first question they usually ask is 'Will anybody find out about this?'"[11]

The shame felt by many sex workers and their clients severely inhibits their resistance to the intolerance aimed at them. The tens of thousands of prostitutes and the millions of patrons of their service have a great deal to gain by ridding our culture of the blanket negativity toward all sex work. Yet the vast number of these people do nothing to change social attitudes. They are socially invisible and their voice is silent. Prostitutes' organizations organize marches and protests against police harassment, and only a handful of people, mostly retired sex workers, attend. The vast majority of those involved in the trade feel too disgraced to come out of the closet of anonymity.

Institutional Antisexualism

Social institutions are guilty of much intolerance against harmless sex work. Indeed, the state's modern war on all forms of prostitution will someday be remembered as one of the most pernicious forms of discrimination afflicting democratic nations in the early years of the twenty-first century.

The worst offender in this regard is the legal system. Throughout most of the world, prostitution is a criminal offense. To gain a conviction in most jurisdictions, police need only prove two facts: that genital pleasure was provided or intended, and that money was exchanged or intended to be exchanged. Police need not show that the sex was unsafe, that a pimp exploited the prostitute, that the work harmed the prostitute's mental or physical health, or involved a public nuisance. Most anti-prostitution law is thus overtly antisexual.

Consider the anti-prostitution law in the State of Washington, typical of most similar prohibitions in the western world. It makes a criminal anyone who engages in or offers to engage in sexual conduct with another person in return for a fee. It defines "sexual conduct" as any touching of sexual or other intimate parts for the purpose of gratifying the sexual desire of either party. That includes not only intercourse, but also mere touch, such as erotic massage. A professional who touches a client's back, buttocks, or legs breaches no penal law, but as soon the worker's hands move to the genital region, an offense occurs. The clear target of the law is not harm but sexual pleasure.

Because genital contact, actual or anticipated, is the key target of prostitution prohibitions, professionals who provide bondage and domination services operate without any fear of legal attack as long as they avoid genital touch. A dominatrix who ties up a customer, verbally humiliates him, and then spanks him, commits no crime if she keeps her hands away from his genitals. But almost everywhere police consider simple erotic massage for a fee to be a criminal business.[12]

In a much-publicized Canadian case a woman outfitted her bungalow with giant cribs, a torch-lit dungeon, and an examining room. Here she whipped and abused willing clients. She was convicted of prostitution solely because most of her clients had an orgasm during their visit. Had such genital release not occurred, she would have avoided the charge. A national newspaper scoffed at the absurdity in the law: "Such is the wonderful world of Canadian law, which appears to permit the keeping of dungeons where willing customers may be humiliated and have pain inflicted so long as there is no hint of sexual arousal."[13] Professionals who provide only pain in an erotic context are more acceptable in the eyes of the law than those who provide pleasure.

Every year thousands of prostitution cases are heard in the courthouses of the English-speaking world. A veritable army of police officers routinely intrudes into the private affairs of consenting adults. While some of this action is aimed at demonstrable harm, such as protecting prostitutes from exploitative pimps, or removing minors from the sex trade, most of it involves attacks on indoor sex work involving only consenting adults. Most are sting operations by police officers who arrange to have sex with prostitutes in hotel rooms or private residences, and then arrest them before any sex occurs. For example, in Sunny Isles Beach, Florida, police simply open up the Yellow Pages, look under "Escort Agencies," and ask them to send a "call girl" to a designated hotel room. When the sex worker arrives, an undercover officer asks her if she will provide sex for money and then gives her cash. Uniformed detectives then barge in from another room and make the arrest. Police can repeat the scenario several times on the same night.[14] Hundreds of such operations occur every day in America!

Sometimes police target not individual sex workers, but rather the "madam" who is the entrepreneur connecting the client and the professional. The names of such sex brokers as "Heidi Fliess" or the "Mayflower Madam" are familiar to millions of Americans because the news media gave much attention to their high-profile clients.[15] But madams with more average clients are also regularly caught in the trap of intolerant prostitution laws.[16]

Such antisexualism has many harmful effects. First, it interferes with the freedom of millions of people who want to engage in harmless commercial sex. Every year thousands of prostitutes and their customers are arrested, handcuffed, and hauled off to jail. Many will serve years in the penitentiary. Tens of millions of dollars are wasted in undercover operations, trials, and prison time. What a squandering of precious legal resources!

Second, prostitution investigations often grossly violate the privacy of the suspects. For example, to convict the operators of escort agencies, police sometimes require evidence of completed sexual acts performed by escorts dispatched by the agency. Such evidence is often very difficult to obtain because most professionals perform sexual services in private. Police in Victoria, British Columbia, came up with a unique solution to the problem: they drilled a hole in a hotel room wall and inserted a video camera which recorded on tape the sexual contact between a prostitute and a range of clients. The evidence helped convict the friendly grandmother who operated the escort agency. The local civil liberties group expressed outrage at the practice, saying it threatened "the very essence of democracy."[17]

Third, the law forces prostitution into the underground where prostitutes become easy targets for pimps, criminal gangs, and violent clients. Anti-prostitution policies also ensure that sex work is conducted entirely in secret, and this is damaging to the psychological health of the practitioners. If sex work were regulated like any other occupation, sex workers could band together, work in partnerships, form support groups, have unions or professional associations, and define ethical and health standards. When their business is illegal they can do none of that. Their work is often difficult, and they must toil apart from any social support.

The courts have yet to recognize that legal prohibitions against all commercial sex are unworthy of a rational society. Anti-prostitution laws have been challenged as unconstitutional on many occasions, but not once have the courts struck down this institutionalized antisexualism.[18]

Antisexual Motives

Several types of irrationality motivate blanket attacks on commercial sex. The most specific is *prostitution phobia*, consisting mainly of delusions about sex work. For example, many people falsely believe that all prostitution is somehow degrading to its participants simply because money is exchanged for sex. While much of the sex trade does degrade the people in it, such degradation results from factors other than the flow of cash. As indicated above, commercial sex transactions can be entirely respectful and enjoyable to both parties.

Another false stereotype of prostitution is that it is a form of male dominance of women. For example, antisexual feminist Andrea Dworkin says: "The only analogy I can think of concerning prostitution is that it is more like gang rape than it is like anything else.... The gang rape is punctuated by a money exchange. That's all. That's the only difference."[19] That statement is, of course, a gross distortion. Some sex workers are indeed dominated by men, but most are not. The average off-street sex worker is an independent operator as free of male dominance as any other bodyworker such as a massage therapist, fitness trainer, or chiropractor.

Other specific erotophobic attitudes also motivate attacks on prostitution. The fact that such sex occurs between people who are not married to each other raises the ire of anyone who suffers the delusion that all sex is "immoral" unless confined to lawful matrimony. People who believe that sex is "impure" if it occurs outside a loving relationship will also oppose prostitution.

Churches are often at the forefront of the attack on prostitution and rally their parishioners to fight any reform of anti-prostitution laws. In doing so, religious leaders are largely motivated by phobic attitudes toward non-marital sex and sex *per se*, though they often couch their antisexual dogma in a pretended concern for prostitutes.

Opportunistic motives are also involved. Sex workers make excellent targets for anyone who profits from an attack on social outcasts. Because commercial sex does not cause harm, laws against it are haphazardly enforced. While police do investigate every murder or rape, or even most reported shoplifting offenses, they often ignore prostitution for years and then suddenly attack it, then ignore it again. The key force behind that enforcement variation is not any demonstrable social interest, but rather variations in the opportunistic interests of those enforcing such laws. A politician who already has a "law and order" image may have no need to pick on call girls or madams. A politician under attack for moral indiscretions may launch an anti-prostitute campaign to divert attention from his own failings.

Several times in the history of the feminist movement some of its members have been guilty of opportunistic attacks on prostitutes. For example, in the U.S. in the 1840s anti-prostitute campaigns initiated thousands of women into the political process, as they gave speeches, organized meetings, and lobbied for criminal laws against commercial sex. One of the key motives for the initiative was a symbolic one: to attack male prerogatives. The prevailing sexual ethic imposed a powerful double standard, allowing men much sexual freedom (especially with sex workers), but denying "good" women any sexual outlet except in marriage. Making prostitution illegal ensured that men too tasted sexual prohibitions, a sad form of gender parity. Further, attacking prostitution supported the then mandatory female roles of wife and mother. Sex workers threatened such roles because they were independent women with their own income.[20] By outlawing such female freedom, women trapped in narrow social roles felt better about themselves.

The modern feminist movement is seriously divided over the issue of prostitution, with the antisexual wing of the movement entirely unsympathetic to the business. Mainstream feminism is today mostly tolerant of sex work. The official policy of the U.S. National Organization for Women supports the decriminalization of prostitution, but the group's leaders largely ignore the issue. Only a few prostitutes' rights organizations such as COYOTE, an acronym for "Call Off Your Old Tired Ethics," are working against anti-prostitute intolerance today.

Phobigenic Effects

Blanket negativity toward prostitution has powerful phobigenic effects, generating prostitution phobia and other irrational sex attitudes. For example, when a child observes a parent react with automatic alarm to the news that a relative has become a prostitute, the child will obviously form negative ideas about the general category "prostitute." Similarly, when the law attacks prostitution and when courts refuse to strike down as unconstitutional the actions of legal officials who intrude into private spaces and arrest people simply because they engage in commercial sex, the implicit message communicated to the community by these institutions is that prostitution of any sort is harmful, that there is something inherently wrong with paying for sexual pleasure.

Blanket attacks on prostitution help spread delusions about sex work through the process of stereotyping. For example, the only contact many people have with prostitutes is when they observe hookers on the street. Unfortunately, street prostitution usually attracts only the most desperate sex workers, and also creates nuisances such as litter and noise. Psychologically healthy prostitutes, who choose prostitution because they genuinely enjoy their work, usually hide it to avoid social intolerance. The result is that healthy and happy prostitutes are invisible, while the most pathetic sex workers are in the public eye.

So a popular stereotype of the prostitute is the hooker on the street with needle tracks in her arm. In many minds, the term "prostitute" is automatically associated with exploitation and degradation. But that attitude is false; not all sex work is of that type. In fact, most prostitutes are responsible people who carry on their trade away from the street and without any public nuisance. Yet because street prostitutes are the most visible, sex workers as a group are commonly stereotyped as pathetic losers and worthy of attacks by law enforcers and neighborhood vigilantes.

Note the circularity of the stereotyping process: nasty sexual expression such as street prostitution inspires stereotyped phobic beliefs about *all* sex workers which, in turn, generates support for laws prohibiting *all* commercial sex. Because prostitution is illegal in most places, only highly desperate people, such as street hookers, engage in it publicly. That, in turn, prompts the stereotyping process, and so the toxic system continues on.

A rational society would regulate commercial sex the same as any other personal service. It would forbid only harmful types of sex work: the exploitation of sex workers, unsafe sexual contacts, under-age practitioners, and nuisance marketing. But it would heap no scorn on anyone simply because they sold sexual pleasure. In this atmosphere of tolerance an extraordinary diversity of sexual services would arise. This pluralist trend is already emerging. For example, in a few urban locations the distinction between a prostitute, a sex therapist, and a spiritual teacher is already blurring, as some professionals operate as sexual surrogates or teachers of ancient erotic arts. In time, such work will be recognized as a valuable social service, as worthy of respect as any other form of "high touch" that soothes and pleasures.

13 / Homo Hatred

SUBSTANTIAL NUMBERS OF PEOPLE in most communities have some form of homosexual experience. Modern scientific surveys reveal that as many as 21% of U.S. males and 18% of U.S. females older than fifteen have been sexually attracted to members of their own gender at least once. Fewer people, 2% to 6% of the population, report at least one actual homosexual contact after puberty. Only 1% to 2% of the population is exclusively homosexual, but the figure is much higher in central residential areas of large cities.[1]

Homosexuality attracts enormous amounts of informal and institutional negativity. The vast extent of this attack is not aimed at conduct that is obviously harmful, such as homosexual rape or disease-transmitting sex, but rather homosexuality itself.

Several ideas are key to the attack on homosexuality. Most of these are highly simplistic and specify no harm. Consider, for example, the notion that homosexuality must be "unnatural" because all humans are biologically heterosexual. This argument is wrong on two fronts. First, modern scientific discoveries challenge the idea that everyone is genetically programmed to be heterosexual.[2] Even if heterosexuality is genetically pre-programmed, no evidence indicates that anyone who chooses to ignore that genetic command causes any harm. Our species can survive even though large numbers of people abstain from reproductive conduct.

Homosexuality is also often disparaged because it is condemned in the Bible. But no rational culture accepts religious dogma as a valid indicator of real harm, and as I have argued in Chapter 5, even conservative Christians reject many non-sexual biblical commands.

Homosexuals are also attacked as "anti-family." The idea is that the open acceptance of homosexual conduct undermines the traditional family consisting of a father, a mother, and children. But such an assertion makes no sense. A person can engage in homosexual acts and still be a part of a traditional family. An attraction to members of the same gender does not preclude reproductive sex or the care of children. History is replete with examples of men and women who regularly engaged in homosexual acts and who also had families. Those who attack homosexuals as a threat to the traditional family do not cast the same aspersions on celibate priests, unmarried heterosexuals, or childless couples.

Opponents of homosexual marriage often voice the "anti-family" red herring. For example, David Frum, right-wing columnist and former speechwriter for President George W. Bush, contends that initiatives in places like Vermont that permit homosexuals to register as domestic partners undermine traditional marriage. "The inevitable consequence of upgrading the legal status of homosexual partnerships will be downgrading of the legal status of man-woman marriage." He adds that "the advance toward gay marriage" has "so destabilized" intimate relationships that today fewer than half of children reach their eighteenth birthday in the same house as both their father and mother.[3] The demise of the traditional nuclear family is the fault not of heterosexual divorce, but of gays!

Homosexuality has also been attacked as a psychological disorder. For most of the twentieth century, medical authorities believed that homosexuals were psychologically sick. For example, as recently as 1964 a Committee of the New York Academy of Medicine concluded, "Homosexuality is indeed an illness. The homosexual is an emotionally disturbed individual who has not acquired the normal capacity to develop satisfying heterosexual relationships."[4] A psychoanalytic text from the 1960s described homosexuality as "an outcome of exposure to highly pathologic parent-child relationships and early life situations."[5]

The editors of the *New York Times* once held similar views. Commenting on the resignation of President Johnson's staff after a homosexual incident, the newspaper in 1964 editorialized: "Just as alcoholism and drug addiction have come to be recognized as disease, so such sexual perversion is increasingly understood as an emotional illness."[6] The United States Immigration and Naturalization Service (INS) for decades excluded foreign homosexuals on the grounds that that they were persons of "constitutional psychopathic inferiority." The INS considered homosexuals akin to "pathological liars" and "moral imbeciles."[7]

The idea that homosexuality is a form of mental illness lacks any scientific basis, and the American Psychiatric Association recognized that fact in 1973, reversing its long-standing position that gays are disordered. Attacking homosexuals in this way is no longer common, although some religious zealots occasionally utter such slander.

Homosexuals have also been scorned as pedophiles, born with the need to convert impressionable young people to the "gay lifestyle." Anita Bryant, one of the first activists to oppose the gay rights movement in the modern era, believed that anti-discrimination protection for gays would undermine the safety of children: "They can only recruit children, and this is what they want to do."[8] Jerry Falwell, leader of the Moral Majority movement in the 1980s, uttered an even wilder claim. He thinks gays are natural-born killers. He said this: "So-called gay folk just as soon kill you as look at you."[9]

To any rational person, all such blanket allegations about gays are obvious nonsense. The only characteristic homosexuals have in common is their attraction to members of the same gender, and no evidence suggests that such a sexual orientation causes anyone real harm.

Informal Homo Hatred

Exposure to intolerance toward homosexuality begins early in life. Children learn the term "fag" at a young age, from parents, siblings, and friends, and know that it is a term of derision aimed at males who are sexually attracted to other males. Boys tease each other using such words. During their key formative years, and before they know anything substantial about homosexuality, children refer to it only in negative terms.

Hostility toward homosexuality is a fact of life in most schools. Children suspected of same-sex attractions often face emotional and physical abuse. Educators report that sexual orientation is the primary source of bullying in secondary schools.[10] One youth services worker says: "Society may be making huge strides. But in schools today, gay kids continue to be the scum of the earth."[11]

More than 84% of gay students in America are exposed to anti-gay comments from students and faculty over the course of a year.[12] For example, a teacher at an Arkansas junior high school wrote a letter to a gay student telling him he would go to hell.[13] In California a teacher banned a lesbian student from a gym class on the ground that the girl's sexual orientation made other girls "uncomfortable."[14] The victimization can be so bad that suicide is not an uncommon solution for those suspected of being gay.

"Gay-bashing" on the public street is a popular pastime in many parts of the world. It is practiced mainly by young men from the suburbs, skin-heads from working class areas, or religious zealots who seek out homosexual neighborhoods or cruising areas to pick on defenseless gay men. The most famous homophobic hate crime was the killing of Matthew Shepard, a University of Wyoming student who was beaten and left tied to a fence to die because he was gay.[15]

Families are also frequently intolerant of homosexuals in their midst. Many gays and lesbians have been disowned by their families simply because they are attracted to their own gender. Even young teens experience this rejection. Consider the story of Christian Hernandez, a fourteen-year-old high school student living near Niagara Falls who revealed his sexual orientation to his parents after he was hospitalized when a homophobic gang stabbed him. His father said he would "rather have a dead son than a queer son." His mother asked the youth to leave the home. He spent two months on the street before finding a program run by a local school board catering to the needs of gay students.[16]

A rich literature now examines family intolerance towards homosexuals and strategies to cope with it. See for example, *Family Outing: A Guide to the Coming-Out Process of Gays, Lesbians, and Their Families* by Chastity Bono, daughter of the celebrity, Cher. Even though Cher had lots of gay friends, she refused to accept her daughter's sexual orientation for several years.[17]

Many homosexuals are intolerant of their own sexual orientation. For example, Chastity Bono describes how she reacted to her involuntary "outing" by the tabloid press by regressing back into the closet. "The outing was a shock that brought me to a place that I'd never been: I suddenly became aware that at some deep level I was ashamed of who I was."[18] Self-hatred is a serious mental health problem for many gays and lesbians. This is one reason the rate of attempted suicide for gay men aged eighteen to twenty-seven is fourteen times that of heterosexuals.[19]

I first encountered homosexual self-loathing in the early 1970s in New York. A friend in his early twenties was enjoying great success as an actor on Broadway. But even in that relatively gay-friendly environment he felt isolated and "queer." One day I arrived at his apartment and through a window beside the door observed him punching himself in his face, bloodying his nose, and calling himself a "faggot." He was gay-bashing—himself. The greater the social attack on gay and lesbians, the greater such tragic self-hatred.

Institutional Homo Hatred

In the nineteenth century governments throughout the world outlawed the "crime against nature." Such laws have remained on the books in many jurisdictions. For example, in Missouri, anal or oral sex is a crime if performed by members of the same gender, but not if performed by a man and a woman.[20] The Supreme Court of the United States, in *Bowers v. Hardwick*, ruled in 1986 that such discrimination does not violate the American Constitution.[21] Chief Justice Warren Burger wrote: "To hold that the act of homosexual sodomy is somehow protected as a fundamental right would be to cast aside millennia of moral teaching."

Fortunately, in June 2003, the court reversed that intolerant decision, and struck down a Texas law that prohibited "homosexual conduct." The majority ruled that gays "are entitled to respect for their private lives," and that, "the state cannot demean their existence or control their destiny by making their private sexual conduct a crime." The Texas case heralds an exciting new era for the rights of homosexuals.[22]

Law enforcers also tend to specially target homosexual literature. For example, Canadian customs agents regularly exclude a vast range of books imported by gay bookstores. Though the courts have consistently overruled such censorship, it continues almost uninterrupted.[23]

Laws regulating immigration, child custody, adoption, pensions, and marriage usually deny homosexuals the same rights as heterosexuals. Consider the 2002 child custody decision of the Chief Justice of the Alabama

Supreme Court. He ruled that homosexuality was an "inherent evil against which children must be protected" and that homosexuals were "presumptively unfit to have custody of minor children under the established laws of this state."[24]

In many jurisdictions gays and lesbians can legally be denied jobs and housing. In Wyoming, the state where Matthew Shepard was brutally murdered, the legislature consistently rejects bills proposing to outlaw discrimination against homosexuals. Colorado voters approved a law that repealed human rights protections for gays previously passed by municipal governments. Fortunately, in a rare non-erotophobic sexual ruling, the American Supreme Court invalidated the Colorado law in 1996 on the ground that the law lacked a "rational basis" and thus violated equality guarantees in the American constitution, notwithstanding that a majority of voters supported it.[25]

The military is another hotbed of anti-homosexual discrimination. For most of the twentieth century virtually all military organizations in the world excluded gays. Soldiers exposed as homosexual were summarily expelled, even though they often had long and distinguished military careers. This intolerant policy no longer exists in a few countries, such as Canada and the Netherlands. Those nations have uneventfully integrated gays and lesbians into their armed forces, giving rise to none of the problems that opponents of such integration claimed would occur.[26]

The armed forces of the United States still overtly discriminate against homosexuals. The current policy, "Don't ask, don't tell," forbids military recruiters from inquiring into a person's sexual orientation, but says that if the recruit discloses homosexual preferences, he or she can be discharged.[27] Yet harassment of gays is still rife in the military. Even though hundreds of violations of the rule not to inquire about sexual orientation have been exposed, few have been held accountable for such a breach.[28] Meanwhile, the military fires approximately 1,000 gay service members every year.[29] For example, as America was preparing for the 2003 war in Iraq and in need of translators and interpreters, the Army fired nine linguists, six trained in Arabic, simply because they refused to keep their sexual orientation a secret.[30]

Though American courts have upheld the anti-gay policies of the

American forces, the European Court of Human Rights has declared similar provisions to be a violation of the right to privacy enshrined in the European Convention on Human Rights. In a case challenging the British military ban on homosexuals, the court in 1999 rejected arguments that integration of gays into the military would cause serious problems and found that hostility to gays was based on a "pre-disposed bias" similar to negative attitudes based on race, and therefore was not a legitimate basis for public policy.[31]

School curricula in many areas prohibit any material that seeks to portray homosexual relationships as normal. Such a prohibition is official policy in Great Britain. In 1988 Margaret Thatcher's government passed the notorious "section 28" of the Local Government Act that ordered school officials not to promote "the acceptability of homosexuality as a pretended family relationship." The draconian law is still in force years into the mandate of the Labour Party, although it seems that Prime Minister Tony Blair will in 2003 finally honor repeated election promises to scrap it.

In November 2000, Oregon electors narrowly defeated "Measure 9," a proposed anti-gay law similar to the British one. Though the ballot failed, over 700,000 voters (47%) supported it. In Surrey, British Columbia, school officials prohibit books featuring same-sex parents in books for children in primary grades.[32] Educators in Madison, Wisconsin, recently banned similar material from school libraries. All of these school initiatives have a common purpose: to try to prevent children from hearing the tolerant message that homosexuals are normal members of society who deserve respect like any other person.

As noted earlier, most schools are hotbeds of hate directed at any openly gay student. To help students deal with this harassment and many other issues that homosexuals face, "gay-straight alliance" clubs have been set up in over 600 schools in the United States and Canada. But often school officials or even state legislators oppose these groups. For example, Utah passed a law prohibiting any school club that pertained to any form of "sexual activity."[33] The Salt Lake City School Board banned all non-curriculum clubs rather than accept a gay support group that complied with the state law. In Orange County, California, school officials refused to allow a gay-straight alliance of high school students to meet on school property, unless the group changed its name and refused to discuss sex.[34]

Organized religion is also a powerful purveyor of anti-homosexual action. Most churches deny homosexuals the right to serve as ministers. Some churches allow homosexuals access to leadership positions, but only so long as they abstain from any homosexual activity. Religious officials are at the forefront of campaigns opposing teaching about homosexuality in schools, against gay support clubs in schools and equal legal rights for gays. Indeed the leadership of the Religious Right today seems more concerned with attacking homosexuality than with any other social issue except abortion.

The media is also a source of anti-gay attacks. Overtly homophobic broadcasters such as Dr. Laura Schlessinger, who called gays "abnormal," "aberrant," "deviant," "disordered," "dysfunctional," and a "biological error," are relatively rare today and have even been boycotted by large advertisers and chastised by some broadcasting industry organizations.[35]

But the media mostly ignores homosexuals, partially to avoid the deluge of protest that usually accompanies any media exploration of gay issues. For example, the U.S. cable channel Nickelodeon received a staggering 50,000 e-mails and phone calls protesting its half-hour show for children about same-sex parents.[36] Only a few entertainment shows feature gay characters. News coverage of homosexuality is still largely focused on unhappy themes: crimes against gays and AIDS. The broadcast media mostly forbids commercials paid for by gay groups announcing meetings and events or promoting gay rights.

Antisexual Motives

A variety of motives prompt intolerance against homosexuals, some phobic, others more opportunistic. The most important is *homophobia*, consisting of both false beliefs about homosexuality and aversions to homosexual stimuli. The existence of homophobia has long been recognized. Jeremy Bentham, writing 200 years ago, was the first philosopher to see that rational people could hold nonsensical attitudes toward gays that lead to enormous injustice. However, homophobic intolerance was so acute in his day that Bentham had to hide his discovery of homophobic irrationality.[37] Fortunately, a vast literature now exposes such attitudes and the intolerant action they produce. Thanks to such intellectual efforts, and also the work of the gay rights movement, homophobia is the most widely recognized type of erotophobia.

Lust phobia also motivates attacks on gays. A person who believes that sex is sinful unless confined to marriage, or who holds the vague sense that sex or sexual pleasure is dirty or sinful, will also oppose homosexuality. Homosexuals are often the most vocal champions of overtly hedonistic sexuality. Some gays celebrate anonymous promiscuity and enthusiastically practice cross-dressing and sado-masochism. Anyone ambivalent about the legitimacy of consensual, adult sexuality will be repulsed by much of the gay lifestyle. The more a community is gripped with lust phobia, the greater its intolerance towards gays.

The phobia towards anal sex probably also motivates intolerance toward homosexual men. Many gay men practice anal sex. The widespread phobia about anal sex generates hostility towards those who perform it.

Phobia is not the only motive behind anti-gay action. Other more opportunistic motives are involved. Throughout history, authoritarian leaders have attacked homosexuals to obtain selfish political benefits. Creating a bogeyman is a time-honored method of rallying the troops. Taking action against a mythical threat in turn powerfully expresses decisiveness and moral rectitude.

Consider, for example, how right-wing American politicians manufactured social hysteria against homosexuals in government in the early 1950s. After a State Department official revealed that several dozen government workers had been dismissed because of their homosexuality, the Republican Party attacked the Truman administration for being soft on gays. Seven thousand Republican Party workers received a letter from their national chairman advising that "sexual perverts . . . have infiltrated our Government," and that homosexuals were perhaps as dangerous as communists. The Senate held an inquiry into the employment of "homosexuals and other moral perverts," resulting in a huge increase in the firing of homosexual government employees. One of the first acts of the new President Eisenhower in 1953 was an executive order prohibiting homosexuals in the civil service.[38]

A modern example of the same sort of opportunism is the conviction in Malaysia of former deputy Prime Minister Anwar Ibrahim on sodomy charges. He was sentenced in August 2000 to nine years imprisonment. Amnesty International considers Ibrahim a prisoner of conscience, detained and brought to trial not because of any particular alleged crime, but because of his dissenting political activities and the challenge he posed to government leaders.[39]

Consider also the story of the massive police raids on homosexual bathhouses that occurred in Toronto. The police unit conducting the raids had been formed to investigate organized crime, but it had accomplished little in that task. Because of its poor performance, the squad was faced with severe budget cuts. The unit had to do something to justify its existence. Over 150 officers carried out raids on gay bathhouses in the city. The unit claimed to the press that "American crime syndicates" were involved in these gay businesses, many of which had been in operation for over eighteen years. Another police unit, the vice squad, which is normally involved in policing sexual laws, did not participate in the raids. The real motive for the organized crime squad in attacking gay people and businesses was self interest, "the need to generate evidence (especially for the media) of zealous activity in the defense of public order," as an academic commentator put it.[40]

Intolerance against homosexuals can also be inspired by emotional opportunism. For example, many people define themselves as heterosexual, but also have homosexual impulses and feel great shame about it. One way to cope with such anxiety is to attack other homosexuals. In the movie *American Beauty*, an ex-Marine suburban family man suddenly losses control of his repressed homoerotic impulses and sexually propositions his male neighbor (played by the lead actor, Kevin Spacey). The ex-Marine hates himself for that behavior, and deals with the shame by killing the man he propositioned.

Reverend Rose Mary Denman, a former pastor of the United Methodist Church, provides a real-life example of similar displaced shame. She opposed the ordination of gay ministers until she discovered that she was a lesbian. When she admitted her sexual orientation she was defrocked. The *New York Times* reported that she attributed her vehement stand against ordaining homosexuals to her denial of her own lesbian orientation.[41]

Homosexuals are also the targets of a related form of emotional opportunism: scapegoating. A sad fact about human nature is that we can enhance our self-esteem by acting intolerantly towards others. When overt racism is no longer permissible in a racially diverse society, homosexuals make a good substitute. Much gay bashing in schools and on the street flows from this complex motive. So does much religious intolerance against gays and lesbians.

Gender roles are also implicated. One such role defines masculinity and femininity in terms of heterosexuality: men must have an exclusive sexual interest in women, and women in men. Anyone who identifies "male" and "female" according to such roles will feel threatened by homosexuality.[42] In the same way a macho man will feel uncomfortable in the presence of emotionally vulnerable men, he will also be uneasy in the presence of homosexual men. While few macho men know exactly why they are uncomfortable with homosexuals, they are aware that they are uncomfortable. This it turn can lead to rationalizing: "If I have an intense aversion to homosexuality, it must be because homosexuality is bad." And if homosexuality is bad it must be attacked.

The hostility most police and military organizations have shown towards homosexuals (and women) flows in part from rigid notions of male roles. Hierarchical, male-dominated organizations both breed and attract a macho personality. That is why drill sergeants often humiliate recruits with terms such as "sissy" or "girl." Masculinity is "pumped up" by deriding women, or deriding men who display feminine qualities.[43] No surprise that the American military still has enormous difficulty accepting gay personnel or that for decades agencies like the Royal Canadian Mountain Police attacked homosexuality as a grievous moral offense and summarily fired any gay person they discovered.[44]

Phobigenic Effects

Because homosexual intolerance is driven by so many different motives, it is very common. Such behavior, in turn, has powerful phobigenic effects.

Blanket negativity aimed at homosexuality, whether prompted by homophobia or opportunism, generates an array of erotophobic attitudes, the most specific of which is homophobia.

For example, the average child at school today will hear the term "fag" constantly used as an insult. This repetitive conditioning will help link negative feelings to not only the sound of that word, but also the mental image of the people to whom the word refers. Stimuli that elicit the mental image of homosexuals will automatically trigger the aversion and a negative response. A child conditioned in this way will react with instant distaste to anyone who expresses homosexual preferences. Because the conditioned aversion is largely unconscious, the child will rationalize the negative feeling with homophobic beliefs.

Anti-homosexual intolerance is also conducive to stereotyping. For example, largely because of social intolerance some homosexuals lead lonely lives full of self-hatred and then kill themselves. High rates of homosexual suicides prompt some people to leap to the foolish conclusion that homosexuals are inherently unstable.[45] The obvious explanation for the suicide rate is not homosexuality, but rather social antipathy toward it.

Similarly, the idea that AIDS is a "gay disease" is a popular one, leading to the phobic notion that homosexuality and disease are inherently linked. The spread of AIDS in the gay community is partly the result of discrimination against gays. Although reckless behavior on the part of many gay men helped spread HIV, much of that negligence was driven by the lack of self-esteem on the part of many gay men, which in turn resulted mainly from their social stigmatization. Another tragic example of how intolerance and AIDS are linked is found in the Catholic Church. Supposedly celibate priests are dying of AIDS at a rate at least four times that of the general U.S. population. A majority of Catholic priests surveyed in a confidential poll said that the Church failed to offer sex education in seminaries that might have prevented such an outbreak in their ranks.[46]

Similar phobigenic processes also produce the false idea that gays are pedophiles. For example, I first learned about homosexuality in the 1960s as a result of warnings from adults and peers about a male pedophile who frequented a nearby park where I played. My young mind framed homosexuality in terms of older men who preyed upon young boys. Homophobia ensured that I never heard homosexuality talked about in any normal context. Later I learned that my automatic assumption that homosexuals were pedophiles was wrong. But some people never hear such corrective information and so still believe that homosexuals must be socially repressed to prevent them victimizing innocent youth.

Phobic attitudes toward gays are undermined when gays become visible as normal members of society. When the media portrays gay people in movies and sitcoms as ordinary folk, when schools allow gay people to join clubs relating to their sexual orientation, when gay people are allowed to marry, the implicit message is that sexual orientation is an irrelevant indicator of moral character. Anyone who believes that gays are inherently immoral or sinful will be threatened by such normalizing messages. They will oppose television shows with homosexual themes, school texts that portray same-sex parents, or laws that afford gays the same rights as others. They rightly suspect that such normalization has a counter-phobigenic effect that will lower the incidence of homophobia in our culture and socially isolate people who hate gays and lesbians.

14 / Nasty Sex

SEXUAL EXPRESSION THAT TRAUMATIZES the people performing it is powerfully phobigenic. I call it *nasty sex* and it includes sexual assault, unwanted pregnancy, sexual disease, unhappy sexual initiation, genital mutilation, sexual swearing, and nasty pornography. Each type of nasty sex is a *catalyst* of the phobigenic system, breeding erotophobia independently of the infection cycle. A key reason for the prevalence of sexual fear in our cultures is the prevalence of these toxic forces.

While nasty sex causes erotophobia, the reverse is true as well. Persons afflicted with high levels of erotophobia are more likely to be involved in nasty sex, voluntarily or involuntarily, than people who lack irrational sexual fear.

Sexual Assault

Sexual assault is the most phobigenic of any of the experiences discussed in this book. A victim of forced sex suffers fear, humiliation, and often pain at the same time as he or she is exposed to erotic stimuli, such as the sound of sexual words or the feeling of sexual arousal. Sexual assault is powerfully conducive to erotophobic aversions especially when it involves physical injury, repeated abuse, or a youthful victim. Even relatively minor sexual offenses against children, such as "flashing," can cause phobigenic conditioning. An exhibitionist who frightens a child by suddenly opening his coat and exposing an erect penis causes shock and fear that can imprint in the child's mind an aversion to the sight of that organ.

Serious sexual assault suffered as a child, and long forgotten by the adult, can create powerful unconscious aversions which later affect adult behavior. Consider the story of "Carol," related by Rawn Joseph, one of the world's leading neuropsychologists. When Carol was four years old a stepfather molested her on ten or more occasions. He would stroke her hair and then force her to perform fellatio. Somehow she forgot this abuse until it surfaced in her mind as an adult. She was in bed with her lover who stroked her hair and tried to push her head toward his penis. Suddenly she became hysterical, struck out at the man, and fled the apartment. For weeks she refused to talk to him, and felt a profound aversion toward men. Counseling was no help. Only a year later did the memory of the childhood assault return to her consciousness, when she was watching a television show which depicted a father walking into his daughter's bedroom and trying to soothe her by running his fingers through her hair.

Rawn Joseph explains that the neural association between fellatio and fear had been stored in a part of her brain inaccessible to her conscious mind. When she was again confronted by similar stimuli with her boyfriend, the hidden aversion was activated, resulting in the phobic response, and one that she could not understand. Only when exposed to similar stimuli in the television show did the memory of the assault return, which helped expose the hidden aversion.[1]

An abundance of evidence indicates that serious sexual assault is dreadfully phobigenic.[2] Over half of the victims of rape report sexual dysfunction after their ordeal, including an aversion to sex, vaginismus (constriction of the vagina), and an inability to orgasm.[3] Abuse survivors may go to great lengths to avoid sex. "I intentionally married a man who was basically asexual. He was the three-times-a-year-man, and he was absolutely perfect. When we wanted to get pregnant, I took my temperature. The conception of my children was as close to artificial insemination as you can get," reports one survivor.[4]

Non-sexual phobias are also a common product of rape, especially those involving specific odors or physical characteristics associated with the attack.[5] Women who are sexually abused as adults are more likely to be sexually dissatisfied and nonsensual.[6] One study found that a third of a group of incest victims had become lesbians.[7] Because so many abused women acquire aversions to the sight of male genitals, shelters for women sometimes refuse to accommodate persons undergoing male-to-female sex changes who are still in the pre-operational stage, as their penises may be visible in showers or toilets.[8]

Male victims of sexual abuse by men also experience profound phobigenic effects. One common outcome of such abuse is homophobia. Victims are prone to stereotype all homosexuals as abusive. Psychologists report that even gay victims can acquire such a delusion, especially if the assault is one of their first sexual experiences.[9] A more generic fear of sex is also a common outcome for male victims. Mike Lew, author of *Victims No Longer: Men Recovering From Incest And Other Sexual Abuse*, describes how survivors often associate all sexuality with danger, and thus back away from their own sexual feelings. "Any attempt to add a sexual component to a relationship is met with suspicion and fear."[10]

Sexual assault is epidemic in western culture. Freud was the first social scientist to unearth the problem after he heard his female patients frequently report that they had been sexually abused as children. Such allegations so contradicted Freud's perception of social reality that he rejected the reports as false, and created preposterous theories to explain them, such as that children naturally fantasize about having sex with adults. Fifty years later Kinsey reported that almost one quarter of the females in his survey had a childhood sexual experience with an adult, but his startling revelation attracted very little attention. The easiest way for a community to deal with the horrible fact of mass sexual assault is to deny it.

Fortunately modern social science has escaped that denial and neglect. The leading expert on child sexual abuse, David Finkelhor, estimates at least 20% of girls and 5% to 10% of boys suffer sexual abuse.[11] The abuse figures rise when people who have been sexually traumatized as adults are included. Depending on the definition of "sexual assault," which ranges from rape to unwanted genital fondling, one-quarter to one-third of all females in modern western nations have been sexually assaulted.[12] Experts estimate that approximately one in six men suffer the same.[13]

The high incidence of sexual abuse of females has a phobigenic impact on all women, not only on the vast numbers of girls and women who are actually sexually attacked. From an early age all girls learn about the risks of sexual assault. They hear the stories of such attacks from peers who have been assaulted, from reports in the media, and from sex education classes which now devote significant attention to the haunting scepter of sexual predators on streets, in school yards, and even in the home. Whether or not they have been abused, large numbers of girls connect the horror of sexual assault with their own emerging sexuality. Lust phobia takes root. As Naomi Wolff puts it:

> An extraordinary number of girls, it seems from the stories that women have told me, experience it [the worry of sexual attack] young, whether or not they have actually been abused. It is an existential crisis. Many girls then associate that encounter with being sexual women. I think few boys who have not been abused associate the risk of sexual terror with becoming men.[14]

The threat of sexual attack teaches females to especially distrust the sexuality of men. Social worker Margaret Leroy, author of *Pleasure: The Truth About Female Sexuality*, says that girls learn from the prevalence of such abuse that:

> Sex is something men do to children and women, that sex is about power, that men cannot be trusted, that the male urge is overwhelming and must be given in to. For all girls, sexual danger is part of the air we breathe, part of the atmosphere in which we grow up. Child sex abuse is not a peripheral issue: sexual abuse is a persistent subtext to the sexual education of girls.[15]

Victims often are further traumatized after the assault by the phobic reactions of their family or public officials. For example, in a culture that prizes the virginity of women, an unmarried rape victim will be socially stigmatized, and that will aggravate the phobigenic impact of the assault. Rape is a common tool of military aggression in erotophobic cultures, as illustrated by the 1990s wars in the Balkan states. Rapists in such conflicts are motivated not only by sadistic lust, but also by the knowledge that their sexual abuse of "enemy" women will be as socially destructive as a land mine: the victims will become outcasts in their own community. Similarly, heterosexual male victims of rape often suffer homophobic social rejection. In the eyes of many homophobes, the masculinity of a male victim of rape is permanently compromised.

Sexual assault victims often suffer from subtle types of social negativity that enhance the phobigenic effect of the abuse. For example, author Naomi Wolff tells how she was ten years old at a summer camp when accosted by a man masturbating. Wolff immediately reported the incident to camp authorities, but because they were so disturbed by the sexual nature of the event, she received little support. Indeed the camp administrator and staff left her feeling that she was somehow to blame for the attack.[16] Because of their erotophobia she suffered greater trauma and in turn its phobigenic effects.

While sexual assault breeds erotophobia, the reverse is true as well. The greater your erotophobia, the more likely that you will be the victim of sexual assault. Many children suffer high levels of erotophobia and their resulting sexual muteness increases the chances that they will be sexually victimized. Some sexual predators actually look for children who are especially reserved about sex because they will be least likely to report the attack.[17] In families, schools, churches, and playing fields, sexual predators are able to carry on their abuse for years simply because the victims never dare disclose the crime.

Erotophobia can also foster sexual assault, especially date rape. The more shy and sexually inhibited a woman, the more that predatory men are likely to interpret her negative response to sexual pressure as "talk me into it," or "sweep me off my feet." In contrast, women who enthusiastically say "yes" to some invitations to casual sex are more likely to be believed when they say "no." Professor Mary Krueger concludes that an important antidote to date rape is the sexual empowerment of women. "The task is to create a culture in which people care as much about increasing women's access to erotic joy as they do about decreasing their risk of rape—because, particularly in the case of acquaintance rape, the former will indirectly facilitate the latter. Indeed, one will not happen without the other."[18]

Unwanted Pregnancy

Unwanted pregnancy is another phobigenic force. Conceiving a child has an enormous impact on the life of the mother, and if the child is unwanted then this impact is powerfully negative. Pregnancy involves difficult decisions about whether to abort or give birth to the child. Both an abortion and the delivery of a baby entail major physical and emotional stress.

Unless reliable contraception is used, sex always risks the unhappy outcome of an unwanted pregnancy. Rare is the person who has not participated in sexual encounters without this gnawing worry about pregnancy. Approximately half of the roughly 5.5 million pregnancies that occur every year in the United States are unintended, either entirely unwanted or simply mistimed. Half of these end in abortion. Almost half of the women in America can expect to have an unintended pregnancy some time in their lives.[19]

The fear of pregnancy has phobigenic conditioning potential because it occurs precisely when sexual energy is flowing. The pairing of fear and arousal, especially if experienced repeatedly, can breed an aversion not only to the act of intercourse but sexual feelings. Because women bear most of the burden of unwanted pregnancy, they experience the greatest phobigenic anxiety having unprotected sex.

Prior to the 1960s birth control consisted of condoms, diaphragms, the rhythm method, and external ejaculation, all of which required discipline that was often incompatible with the hot passion of sex. In the 1960s the birth control pill and IUD appeared and they required no interference with the sexual act. For the first time in history masses of men and women could escape pregnancy anxiety, and this constrained a very powerful phobigenic force. Modern birth control technology is responsible for much of the reduction in erotophobic attitudes in the modern era.

Even when birth control information is freely available, however, it is often neglected, and erotophobia plays an important role in such neglect. The more phobic a person's attitudes toward sex, the less likely they will know about contraceptive methods, and the more likely they will use such devices ineffectively.[20] Further, people who harbor negative attitudes about sex fail to take birth control precautions even though they are aware of them. For example, if a woman fears sex she is unlikely to anticipate casual sexual relations and thus unlikely to be prepared for them. Many teen girls who feel shame about sexual exploration often deliberately dampen their erotophobic impulses by drinking too much alcohol or by allowing themselves to be "swept away" by the passion of a romantic moment and an urgent man.[21] In such circumstances precautions against pregnancy (or sexual disease, as I discuss later) are ignored, and a high rate of unwanted pregnancy is the result.

The availability of access to birth control information and devices is a function of the extent of erotophobia in the community or family. For example, many erotophobic school officials deny their students free condoms or lessons on how to use them, and this increases the risk of unwanted pregnancy, which has phobigenic effects.

Abortion is a form of birth control, although far more physically and emotionally traumatic than all others. However, the availability of abortion helps reduce the trauma of unwanted pregnancy and pregnancy anxiety. Conversely, prohibiting abortion increases the risk of unwanted pregnancy and thus bolsters phobigenic fear. The more erotophobic any individual or community, the more likely abortion will be restricted or banned. There are obviously a variety of reasons to oppose abortion, such as to preserve the life of fetuses, but anyone who believes that sex is inherently "bad" or "impure" will also attack abortion in order to inhibit some sexual conduct and insure that the sex that does occur is anxiety-ridden, thereby reducing the "sinful" pleasure in the act. That many of the most vigorous opponents of abortion are also highly erotophobic, attacking all nudity, sexual entertainment, prostitution, and homosexuality is no accident. For these people, assertions of the "sanctity of life" are just rationalizations of erotophobic motives.

Sexual Disease

Genitals can be the location of much physical distress. Chronic pain and discomfort in the genital region have a phobigenic impact, reinforcing aversions towards erotic organs. Humans have had to cope with sexual disease since the dawn of civilization. The ancients called it "copulation sickness."[22] In the U.S., over a million people a year contract some form of sexually transmitted disease, and millions more suffer from chronic genital afflictions such as herpes and genital warts.[23]

Mere anxiety about sexually contracted diseases exacerbates this phobigenic effect. Many more people worry about getting herpes, chlamydia, or AIDS than actually do acquire them. The advent of HIV in the modern era has dramatically increased fear about sexual disease. Today, a single act of sexual intercourse can lead to a horrible death. Fear of sexual disease can occur over and over whenever a person has unsafe sex with someone not guaranteed to be healthy. Because this stress is experienced during sexually charged events, it can have a powerful phobigenic conditioning effect, helping the emotional mind fix a neural link between sexual arousal and fear.

The more risky the sexual behavior, the greater this effect, except in the minds of the fools who practice unsafe sex and suffer no fear. But countless others worry about risky sex, and engage in it anyway, exposing themselves not only to deadly viruses, but also a powerful phobigenic force. A person who has sex with many people and suffers anxiety about the health risks of such behavior is as prone to acquire aversions to sexual stimuli as is a religious individual who engages in pre-marital sex and worries about God's wrath for such "sin."

The generations of youths coming of age during the AIDS era are especially susceptible to this process. Many begin their sex lives with dread. For example, in an article in the New York Times, writer Meghan Daum reports, "Despite my demographic profile, despite the fact that I grew up middle class, attended an elite college and do not personally know any women or straight men with that demographic profile who have the AIDS virus, I am terrified of the disease." Yet this fear does not have much of an impact on sexual conduct. Daum says, "Our attitudes have been affected by the disease by leaving us scared, but our behavior has stayed largely the same. One result is a corrosion of the soul, a chronic dishonesty and fear that will most likely damage us more than the disease itself."[24]

The fact that a person is promiscuous does not necessarily mean he or she is free of primitive erotophobic aversions, because if the frequent casual sex is also risky and thus anxious, phobigenic conditioning is likely. Further, the fear bred by such anxious sex tends to be highly unconscious because the promiscuity at first glance suggests the absence of sexual fear. "I could not be erotophobic because I'm jumping in and out of so many beds," is the delusional reasoning I often hear. Though not strong enough to inhibit sexual behavior, unconscious sexual aversions can trigger subtle negative responses to a range of other erotic stimuli, such as images of sex or the somatic sensations of erotic pleasure.

Throughout history many highly erotophobic individuals have welcomed sexual disease as an aid in the battle against sex. Syphilis was once called "God's little ally." Even modern religious thinkers still contend that the spirochete appeared in the western world as a "judgment from God."[25] Similarly, Christian leaders such as Billy Graham, Jerry Falwell, and many others less known have described AIDS as God's punishment for immorality.[26] Alex Comfort notes that because the existence of sexual disease supports the idea that sexuality is sinful, erotophobic religious leaders oppose attempts to reduce the risk of infection.[27]

Unhappy Sexual Initiations

The events surrounding the first time we have intercourse can have a lasting impact on our attitudes to sex. Researchers call the loss of our virginity a "turning point" in the development of our sexuality.[28] A very negative sexual initiation has powerful phobigenic potential. Surveys indicate that approximately 4% of American women age eighteen to fifty-nine were initiated to sex through force. A much higher rate of females younger than eighteen are assaulted when they lose their virginity. One-quarter of all women report that while their first sexual experience was not forced, it was "unwanted."[29] Such experiences can cause life-long problems with sex.[30] Children who suffer sexual abuse tend to suffer more erotophobia later in life than do children who escape such trauma.[31]

But for several reasons even people who are initiated to willing sex can have powerfully negative experiences. First, many girls experience pain when they break their hymen during first intercourse. Consider some of the things girls say about their first sexual experience: "It felt like there was a knife going through me." "The pain was like I couldn't stand it."[32]

Second, first sexual encounters often occur without any emotional intimacy. Millions of people lose their virginity with virtual strangers, such as prostitutes or casual sexual partners met hours earlier at a party or bar. Women, especially, often profoundly regret sharing their first act of sexual intimacy with a person they do not love.

The book *The First Time* tells the story of how several people lost their virginity. One woman recounts her first sexual intercourse with a casual friend. "I felt sad because losing my virginity should have been a wonderful experience, but instead it was meaningless. I let him inside of me, we were sharing something totally sacred, and it was treated as nothing. I felt like a slut, real dirty. I've had other sexual encounters since then. I feel that because my first time wasn't special, none of the other men I'm with will love me, and they'll think I'm dirty."[33]

Shame about having sex outside marriage, even with a beloved partner, can also powerfully tarnish a sexual initiation. As already discussed in Chapter 7, religious youths who violate erotophobic rules against pre-marital sex often describe horrible guilt about their first sexual experiences.

Many sexual initiations are devoid of any body pleasure because physical gratification is often not the aim of the contact. Surveys reveal that 58% of teens lose their virginity simply to impress their friends and become more popular; large majorities of girls have sex because of pressure from their boyfriends.[34] Also, sexual initiations are often ineptly performed. Boys ejaculate soon upon penetration; the event suddenly ends before most girls are very aroused. Further, because most girls have little masturbation experience, they are largely unfamiliar with the process of becoming aroused. All of this makes their sexual initiation a disappointment. Surveys indicate that 59 per cent of women do not enjoy the first sexual experience, compared to only 14% of men.[35]

Consider the following report of a girl who had sex with a guy she had known for four years: "Afterward I felt weird around him, like it shouldn't have happened. I didn't enjoy it because of the pain, and the disappointment of wanting it to be so special and it turning out disastrously. It also seemed like my body wasn't even involved—I was numb to the whole experience."[36]

Another letdown for girls following sex initiation is being "dumped" by their boyfriends. "Girls often expect that having sex will transform an uneven relationship into a blissful fusion or transform their lover into a devotee. When, instead, he cools abruptly, their disappointment pervades the memory of first coitus," says researcher Sharon Thompson.[37]

While the first sexual act is unfulfilling to most women, it need not be. Studies reveal that about a quarter of young women report positive first sexual experiences. These are women comfortable with masturbation, who take the initiative in the sexual encounter, who acquire safe sex information and devices long before the event occurs, and who hold out for foreplay and non-coital sex before intercourse.[38] Standard sex education omits training in such sex-positive skills and helps make teen sex unfulfilling.

Genital Mutilation

For millennia cultures have used genital mutilation rituals to designate membership in a specific community, or to signify a child's graduation to adulthood, or for more sinister reasons, such as to ensure the sexual subordination of women. Female circumcision has never been popular in western culture, although it is still practiced in many African and Arab communities. The removal of the vulva and clitoris, the most erogenous tissues on the female body, has obviously devastating phobigenic effects. Because such nastiness is so rare in western culture, and recognized as such, I will not discuss it further.

Male circumcision is still universal in Jewish and most Moslem communities, both in the west and elsewhere. Male circumcision is rare in England and northern Europe, but common in the U.S. Today roughly 60% of American boys are circumcised, down from 85% in the 1960s. Over a million foreskins are deposited in American hospital waste bins every year.[39]

When not performed for religious reasons, male circumcision usually occurs simply so a boy and his father will "look the same." Whether circumcision has any medical advantage is hotly debated. The loss of the foreskin helps keep the glans of the penis dry and free of infection and perhaps other diseases. But do enough boys benefit from such preventive action to justify its costs? Amputating a piece of the body to prevent a possible infection seems a ridiculous medical strategy in an age of antibiotics. Further, such a procedure exposes the child or adult to enormous pain, either during the operation (if no anesthetic is used) or afterwards, as the wound heals. Such trauma, occurring in the genital region, must have some phobigenic impact on the child.

Further, the loss of the foreskin significantly diminishes sensual pleasure. The male foreskin protects the head of the penis and its sensitive nerve endings. The skin of the glans of circumcised men is significantly thicker than that of men who still have their foreskins. Removing the protective sheath that nature designed reduces erotic sensitivity. That is one reason why erotophobic medical and religious authorities favor genital mutilations.[40] Consider, for example, this statement appearing in the *British Medical Journal* in 1935:

Civilization . . . requires chastity, and the glans of the circumcised rapidly assumes a leathery texture less sensitive than skin. Thus the adolescent has his attention drawn to his penis much less often. I am convinced that masturbation is much less common in the circumcised.[41]

Mutilating genitals expresses the idea that the natural state of these organs is imperfect and worthy of human correction. Such a concept lays the groundwork for the further notion that our erotic desires and pleasures are similarly unworthy. Further, when circumcision is mandated by God, as many religions believe it to be, the implicit message is that genitals and sexuality are properly controlled by an external moral power.[42] That in turn helps undermine the integrity of an individual's relationship with his or her own body and sexual impulses, generating more anxiety.

Groups such as the Attorneys For the Rights of The Child are trying to stop this phobigenic process by having male circumcision banned in western countries. They contend that the non-consensual removal of a boy's foreskin is as unethical as the mutilation of a girl's genitals and that prohibiting only female circumcision, as some countries have done, discriminates against males and harms the non-consenting child.[43] On the same grounds, some men have launched civil suits against the hospitals in which they were circumcised as infants.[44]

Swearing

Uttering sexual words as a way to vent negative emotion or to disparage other persons is also an erotophobia-generating force. Exclaiming "fuck" when we cut ourselves with a kitchen knife, or calling our spouse "a cocksucker" during a quarrel, helps breed auditory aversions. The negative emotion accompanying the words elicits negative feelings in the hearer. If this pairing of negative feeling with specific sounds occurs over and over, the hearer can acquire an aversion to the sound of the word. Thereafter, hearing the word in any context will prompt discomfort.

Because most of us grew up regularly hearing sexual cussing, we have acquired a conditioned aversion to the mere sound of sexual

words, as psychologists have long recognized. The author of a study of
the psychology of swear words explains: "There develops a neurosis so
ingrained that the will is well neigh powerless against it. Even when we
come to know that there is not a proper basis for the feeling, we are
prompted by motivations so deeply planted that we have the reactions
in spite of our intellect."[45]

Using genital or sexual words as terms of derision is conducive not
only to auditory aversions, but also genital phobia and lust phobia. The
implicit message conveyed when one person calls another a "cunt" or
"prick" is that the swearer regards these body parts as low and contempt-
ible. We use sexual words to express negative meanings because we look
down upon sex, says Edward Sagarin in his book, *The Anatomy Of Dirty
Words*.[46] A child who grows up hearing such terms used in that way is
likely to conclude that genitals and sex are indeed unworthy. Negative
conduct towards mere words generates negative attitudes toward genitals
and sex *per se*.

Nasty Pornography

Another source of erotophobia is nasty pornography: sex images that depict sex in a context of violence, humiliation, or even simple unhappiness.
This material is phobigenic through two processes: conditioning, and
stereotyping. Consider the first.

Such material often refers to itself as "dirty," "disgusting," "nasty," or
"depraved." Producers of nasty porn market their material in such terms
because they sexually excite many people who feel guilty about sex, and
thereby help sales of the product. Second, the actors appearing in nasty
porn are usually depicted in anxious or angry states. Happy, smiling faces
are unknown in nasty pornography, although they are common in
friendly porn. Nasty pornography makes us feel bad because it depicts
people who feel bad. The constant pairing of negative feeling with the visual stimuli of genitals and the somatic sensations of sexual excitement
helps imprint aversions to such stimuli.

Nasty pornography also fosters erotophobic *delusions* about both sex
and pornography. Imagine a youth whose first visual exposure to sex involves a nasty porn magazine. He or she has no real idea what sex looks

like. Seeing page after page of unhappy people having rough, unloving, and often violent sex, can easily deceive a young mind, implanting the false idea that all sex is a wretched, debasing interaction.

I had those thoughts when I was about fourteen and found a sex magazine discarded in some bushes. I had never seen images of people having sex until I opened that magazine. It was black and white, and had no advertisements. The models looked extremely tense. Several images showed a woman grabbed by the hair by a leering man. Another showed a woman with a knife at her throat while she was performing oral sex. A caption below the image said: "Take this, you bitch."

Such material made me very uncomfortable, not only because it was explicit, and I knew for that reason would provoke outrage if any adult knew I had it, but also because it made me worry that sex was something noxious. I was just beginning to find girls sexually interesting, but the magazine deflated my erotic enthusiasm. I was sure I did not want to get involved in sex that looked like that, but didn't know there was any alternative.

Although the main attack on nasty porn focuses on its negative messages about women, it also deserves censure (but not necessarily censorship) because it breeds erotophobia. As D.H. Lawrence recognized in the 1920s, such media is worthy of opposition simply because it defames sexuality.[47]

Nasty porn not only misleads about the nature of sexuality and gender relations, it also produces false ideas about sexual media. For example, the magazine I found in the bushes had no artistic appeal. Its paper stock was of poor quality. Its graphics were primitive. The models were not artfully posed. I had never seen any other overtly sexual images, and my young mind concluded that such explicit material could only be ugly. A few years later I discovered *Playboy* magazine and its high quality images and editorial content. But *Playboy* in the middle 1960s was not sexually explicit. It showed only semi-nude women. The stereotype that sexually explicit material was necessarily repulsive remained in my mind.

Later in my teens when I started having sex, I realized that sex need not be unloving and abusive, but I continued to believe that sex media was innately unsavory. I reached adulthood firmly of that view, but a trip to Asia changed my mind. In the east I encountered a rich tradition of visual erotic arts, including classic illustrations of Japanese, Chinese, and Indian erotic texts such as the *Kama Sutra*, and extraordinarily explicit erotic sculptures in India and Nepal. My contact with these beautiful representations of sex helped erase from my mind the automatic association between sexual explicitness and ugliness.

Nasty porn dominated the market a generation ago when most baby-boomers were coming of age. Prior to then porn was relatively unavailable. After the late 1980s friendly porn won a large share of the market. Consequently, members of the baby boom generation were more exposed to the phobigenic effects of nasty porn than were their parents or children, and that is a key reason the porn genre is still widely stereotyped as inherently repugnant.

15 / Rigid People Fear Sex

PERSONALITY TRAITS that have nothing to do with sex also affect our sexual attitudes. These traits, characterized by different forms of physical or psychological *rigidity*, produce primitive aversions to the very feel of sex. Such lust phobia causes an individual to perceive erotic desire, arousal, and release as uncomfortable. Because these traits are so common in our culture, so is erotophobia. However, the traits are not universal; many people do not have them. But they are endemic to specific types of social environments. How those environments cause rigidity, and how rigidity in turn causes irrational sexual fear, is the focus of this chapter.

The idea that common personality traits can produce negative sexual attitudes has a long intellectual history, and four different intellectual traditions have a perspective on the issue: Freudians, Reichians, transpersonal psychologists, and personality empiricists. Each intellectual tradition offers its own insights into the nature and cause of the condition, although all are incomplete. This chapter begins with a brief introduction to the existing perspectives and then attempts to refine them with some new insights that hopefully will more precisely describe the type of personality traits that produce erotophobia.

Freud

Sigmund Freud was the first to consider the issue of personality and irrational sexual aversions. He believed that sexual anxieties are the inevitable product of a cultivated intellect and disciplined will. Freud illustrates the idea with a story of two girls who live in the same building, one the child of an aristocratic family who occupies the top floor, the other a working-class girl who lives downstairs. He contended that because the intellectual mind of the working-class girl will not become highly developed she will grow up free of sexual anxieties. In contrast, the mentally sophisticated aristocratic girl will be plagued by sexual fear in her adulthood. In Freud's words: "The differences which ensue in these two destinies in spite of the common experiences undergone, arise because in one girl the ego has sustained a development absent in the other…. This higher moral and intellectual development in her ego has brought her into conflict with the claims of her sexuality."[1]

The notion that normal mental development is conducive to sexual anxiety led Freud to another conclusion: the more advanced a culture, the more sexually neurotic it will be. The intellectual skills that an advanced society produces in high numbers of its members, especially its elites, ensure that sexual neuroses will be common.[2] Thus Freud concluded that civilization prevented healthy attitudes toward sexuality.

If Freud's view is correct then erotophobia is an inevitable consequence of a developed culture such as our own. Fortunately, Freud was only partially right. He accurately perceived that certain personality characteristics could generate sexual neuroses, but he was wrong in assuming that mental development *per se* was the cause. Writing in the early decades of this century, Freud had no access to the now enormous cross-cultural database that reveals that intellectual sophistication is not always accompanied by sexual anxiety. While such a correlation *was* common in Freud's European culture of one hundred years ago, it is not universal. For example, today many highly educated individuals engage in sexual activity such as swinging or tantra that sexually anxious people would shun. The current college-age generation is more highly educated and less erotophobic than any other.

Reich

The most famous opponent of Freud's dark view was one of Freud's students, Wilhelm Reich. Of all the thinkers to deal with the issue of personality and sexual attitudes, he contributed the most. Reich rejected the idea that moral and intellectual development led to sexual aversions. Through yoga-like therapies, he demonstrated that persons with high intellects could lose their sexual anxieties but not their mental powers.

Reich asserted that sexual anxiety is generated by two related personality conditions. The first is chronic physical tension, or what he called *body armor*. Sexual arousal and indeed all manner of playful, spontaneous experience is an expansive energy, moving from deep within the viscera to the periphery of the body. Reich observed that such out-flowing feeling causes pain when it collides with rigid muscles.

Second, he discovered that those who are chronically tense usually become psychologically attached to their armor through a complex process by which they incorporate the sensations produced by their tense body into their inner sense of self. A person with such an "armored identity" experiences the expansive flow of sexual energy as a threat, a challenge to the very boundaries of their being. Reich concluded that sexual expression caused fear only in people with armored personality traits, only to those with a body and identity that could not "let go."

The Transpersonal Perspective

As so often happens in human intellectual history, at the time that Reich introduced the concept of the armored personality, a school of thinkers independently developed a roughly similar theme. The discipline formally emerged in the 1940s, drawing on an explosive increase in cross-cultural information. It now has a rich intellectual heritage and is generally known as "transpersonal psychology." An excellent introduction to it is Ken Wilber's groundbreaking book *Up From Eden: A Transpersonal View of Human Evolution*.[3]

One of the key hypotheses of the transpersonal school is the existence of an *experiential identity*, a neural program that fixes the sense of self in terms of specific sensations and feelings. The idea is that the part of our mind that defines our sense of self can isolate specific types of experiences, often a narrow range of normal experience, and stamp them as "me," and also isolate other experiences, often normal human experiences, as "not me."

Many of the transpersonalists focus their study on a specific type of experiential identity that senses self only in a relatively narrow range of *mental* experience, involving abstract thinking or the willful pursuit of goals, or both, and not emotional, intuitive, or spontaneous mental processes. The transpersonalists use various labels to refer to this personality type, such as "the European dissociation" (L.L. Whyte),[4] or the "separated ego" (Alan Watts),[5] or "mental-egoic consciousness" (Wilber). This narrowed identity is relevant to the study of erotophobia because the transpersonalists have assembled much evidence indicating that those with such a trait will find the spontaneous energy of sex a threat, and thus will acquire an aversion to the sensations of sexual arousal.

The Empirical Perspective

Unfortunately and disappointingly, relatively little clinical research has investigated the theoretical perspectives of Reich and the transpersonalists. Further, very limited empirical work of any sort has explored the relationship between personality traits and sexual attitudes. One of the few studies in this regard is the work of H. J. Eysenck. He developed a method to determine specific personality traits and then administered questionnaires to determine the sexual attitudes of people with such personality traits. He discovered that individuals with high levels of what he called *neuroticism*, indicated by moodiness, sleeplessness, nervousness, inferiority feelings, and irritability, have many anxieties about sex. Eysenck reports that such people "have strong guilt feelings, worry about sexual activities, have fears and difficulties associated with contact with the opposite sex and often see sex as both troublesome and disgusting."[6]

Other studies show that thrill-seeking and positive sexual attitudes tend to go together, and that inhibited personalities tend to be erotophobic.[7] Another body of research identifies a correlation between erotophobia and conservative political attitudes, including racist beliefs. The most famous of these is the work of a group of psychologists in the 1950s who investigated the personality traits of anti-Semites. In *The Authoritarian Personality*,[8] Adorno and his colleagues conducted psychological surveys of thousands of people who harbored racist attitudes about Jews. Their study revealed that anti-Semites tend to be sexually anxious and that both traits tend also to appear with several other attitudes, such as conventionalism, obedience to authority, emotional toughness, and cynicism. Later studies show that negative attitudes towards sex correlate with rigid conventionality, achievement aspirations, harm avoidance, and the desire for order and hard work.[9] Women who conform to traditional feminine roles tend to be sexually inhibited.[10] So are highly dogmatic people.[11]

The rest of this chapter attempts to integrate the perspectives outlined above and add new insights into the nature of the personality traits that cause irrational sexual fears and specifically lust aversions. There are four such personality traits, one physical and the others psychological.

Physical Rigidity

Reich was the first to note that chronic muscular tension—constant holding in the jaw, throat, shoulders, belly, buttocks, limbs, and especially the diaphragm—produces sexual anxiety. Indeed Reich showed that such *physical rigidity* (he called it *armor*) produces negative responses not just to sexual arousal, but to any type of pleasurable somatic experience. Since his day, evidence from Reichian and body-centered therapists suggests that the condition does exist in many people and causes them discomfort when they perceive *any* body pleasure and especially erotic pleasure.

For example, Alexander Lowen, Reich's main protégé, examined this phenomenon in detail in his book *Pleasure: a Creative Approach to Life*, one of the few studies of the psychology and physiology of pleasure.[12] He says: "Fear of pleasure is the fear of the pain that inevitably develops when an outward-flowing expansive impulse meets a contracted and bound area of the body."[13] To explain this phenomenon, he draws a parallel between muscle tension and frostbite. A person with "frozen" fingertips usually feels no pain because the condition numbs the affected nerve endings. Pain begins when the energy-bearing fluids of the body force their way into the frozen extremity. Pleasure has the same effect on rigid muscles. "In a situation of pleasure he [the rigid person] is exposed to the warmth produced by the flow of blood to the periphery of his body through the action of the parasympathetic nerves. His body tries to expand, but the expansion becomes painful when it encounters the resistance of chronically spastic muscles."[14]

Sexual arousal highly stimulates the flow of blood to the periphery of the body, especially engorging the penis and vulva. Such vascular expansiveness will be experienced as pain in a body constantly cramped by rigid muscles. The flow of erotic pleasure, especially the powerful explosion of orgasm, pressurizes rigid muscles and de-numbs them, resulting in discomfort.

Physical rigidity thus has the same result as a conditioned lust aversion—triggering discomfort when erotic sensation is perceived. This personality trait is a more extensive mental program than the conditioned lust aversion because it is triggered by both erotic *and* non-erotic physical pleasure.

Psychological Rigidity

Three other personality traits also generate distress when sexual energy flows. Each is a type of *psychological* rigidity and involves an addiction-like compulsion for experience that sexual arousal impairs.

Cognitive rigidity

The mind processes information through several different cognitive systems. One involves the primitive emotional brain and another the more advanced reasoning and analytic systems of the neo-cortex. Advanced cognition is in turn composed of several relatively autonomous parts. For example, psychologists have discovered that the left hemisphere of the neo-cortex is specialized to perform abstract cognition such as mathematical computations, verbally describing complex ideas, or thinking ahead and planning. In contrast the right hemisphere uses much more intuitive cognition. It occurs, for example, when we gauge how far to reach to catch a ball; the right hemisphere is also the main interpreter of the emotional impulses flowing from the more archaic regions of the brain. Sexual arousal is the product of impulses flowing out of the primitive neural region, as interpreted by the right cortex.[15]

Cognitive rigidity consists of a compulsion to engage only in the abstract information-processing typical of the left brain. It contrasts with cognitive *flexibility*, the ability to move freely from one cognitive style to another as the situation demands.

Those suffering from cognitive rigidity experience distress when sexual arousal is experienced because the flow of erotic energy in the body undermines abstract left-brain cognition. A person attached to such cognition perceives sexual pleasure as a threat. Most of us have experienced the havoc sex wreaks on abstract reasoning. Thinking "straight" is very hard when we are sexually aroused. Orgasm totally shatters our mental-linear mind. In the moments immediately before, during, and after climax our mind sometimes excludes all thoughts in a rush of transcendent bliss.

This power of sex to overwhelm the rational mind has long been recognized. The first formal discussion of the mind-altering power of sex appears in the work of St. Augustine, over fifteen hundred years ago. He noted that orgasm involved a "certain submerging of the mind altogether."[16] Modern science confirms that sexual responses often provoke what a leading sexologist, Don Mosher, calls a "sexual trance," an altered state of consciousness in which the "critical functions" are relaxed.[17] Similarly, author Murray Davis, in *Smut: Erotic Reality/Obscene Ideology*, says, "Like certain psychedelic drugs, sexual arousal alters people's consciousness, changing their perception of the world. Sex, in short, is a reality-generating activity."[18]

Sexual arousal interferes with mental-linear cognition because brainpower, like any other energy, is a limited resource. Certain complex neural functions, such as abstract reasoning or willful action, require high amounts of mental energy. The brain helps provide the energy for such demanding tasks by locating the engines that perform the job in a specific area of the brain and by ensuring that other brain functions slow down while the high-energy tasks occur. Sexual arousal, a right brain and emotional function, simply transfers energy away from the left brain to the right brain and lower regions, undermining left brain cognition.

Anyone who is not attached to a specific cognitive style will not perceive as threatening the temporary impairment of abstract cognition caused by sexual excitement. Because nature designed these sensations to be innately pleasing, most people perceive them with delight. However, a person with a compulsive attachment to left brain abstract cognition will not enjoy the transfer of power to the right brain produced by sexual passion. In such a person the sensations of sexual arousal will occur at the same time as this sense of distress. Experienced repeatedly, this form of phobigenic conditioning will imprint aversions to such erotic stimuli.

The relationship between sexual anxiety and cognitive rigidity has interested several important thinkers over the last several generations. In his collection of essays in *Sex, Literature And Censorship,*[19] D.H. Lawrence observed that many people in western culture reveal a terror of sexual expression, and he explained this fear in the following terms:

> This, no doubt, is all in the course of the growth of the "spiritual-mental" consciousness, at the expense of the instinctive-intuitive consciousness. Man came to have his own body in horror, especially in its sexual implications: and so he began to suppress with all his might his instinctive-intuitive consciousness, which is so radical, so physical, so sexual.[20]

L.L. Whyte expanded on a similar theme in his 1948 work, *The Next Development in Man,*[21] a book "hailed by scholars from Mumford to Einstein."[22] Whyte argued that many people in western society had become in effect addicted to abstract cognition, to "the god of thought."[23] He showed how this "hyperintellectualism"[24] breeds an aversion to the body and sexuality. Men more than women were susceptible to this rigid cognitive style: "The curse has fallen most heavily on the male for the special functions of woman link her thought more closely to those organic processes which maintain the animal harmony."[25]

One of the most important contributions on the relationship between cognitive style and attitudes toward sexuality is that of Alan Watts. He was one of the first scholars with a background in cross-cultural psychology, and this informed his masterly *Nature, Man, and Woman.*[26] An ordained Christian minister, he eventually became one of the world's leading western interpreters of the psychology of eastern traditions such as Hinduism, Buddhism, Taoism, and Zen. This cross-cultural sensitivity gave him special insight into the cognitive style of the western mind.

Watts shows that a preoccupation with "concentrated attentiveness, with a type of thought which is analytic, divisive and selective"[27] produces an identity frightened by emotion of any sort, but especially sexual passion. To Watts, St. Augustine's hostility to sexuality is the product "of the mode of attention which grasps and orders the world by seeing it as one-at-a-time things, excluding and ignoring the rest."[28]

Undoubtedly the most detailed and sophisticated exploration of the relationship of cognitive style and sexual aversions is found in the work of Ken Wilber. In a series of books starting with *Up From Eden*[29] in 1981 through to *Sex, Ecology, Spirituality*[30], Wilber shows how cognitive rigidity affects one's sense of self and attitudes to nature, spirituality, and sex. Aversion to the feelings of sex flows from the capture of cognition by only one of its modes, that which processes information linearly, sequentially, and symbolically.

The ultimate exemplar of the cognitive style that generates an aversion to the very feel of sex is Plato.[31] This Greek genius was a classic egghead. He was a man clearly dominated by his abstract intellect. And what an intellect it was! One scholar maintains that all western philosophy is but a footnote to Plato.[32] At the core of his vision is the idea that abstract reason is superior to all other human capabilities. Plato exalted the very type of cognition at which he excelled and which absorbed his life. Yet, ironically, the very dominance of Plato's abstract mind rendered him incapable of a rational examination of sexual life. For the reasons discussed above, nobody so consumed by a mental-linear cognitive style could feel comfortable with sexuality, and Plato is no exception.

His writings reveal his hostility to the body, to physical pleasure and especially to sex. For example, Plato holds that a "true philosopher is temperate and refrains from all pleasures of the body, and does not give himself up to them."[33] He contends that "the world would benefit enormously" if sexual pleasures were starved, and in his utopian state, sex would only be practiced for purposes of procreation, or at worst, only between married couples.[34] Further, Plato sees a dangerous animal lurking in the human mind:

> When the gentler part of the soul slumbers and the control of reason is withdrawn, then the wild beast in us, well-fed with meat or drink, becomes rampant and shakes off sleep to go in quest of what will gratify its own instincts. As you know, it will cast away all shame and prudence at such moments and stick at nothing. In fantasy it will not shrink from intercourse with a mother or anyone else, man, god, or brute, or from forbidden food or any deed of blood.[35]

This philosophy by which reason is valued over feeling and pleasure is often called "dualism," and has dominated the western mind. But, ironically, it contains several analytic flaws, of which two are salient. The first error is the idea that a vast gulf separates reason and passion. While the main engines of rationality and emotion are indeed located in different parts of the brain, each neural center is intimately connected to the other; raw emotion is thus a vital constituent of thought, and the reverse is true as well.[36] The inaccurate perception of the two as completely and inevitably distinct is a natural conclusion of a mind dominated by reason.

Secondly, the devaluation of sex is philosophically unjustified, as one modern scholar explains:

> The ancient Greek dualists manifested little awareness of the sal-
> utary effects of sex on human health, its role in enhancing the
> pleasures of the 'mind,' and the possibility of prolific but not de-
> generative sexual activity. The stark contrast between mind and
> body, then, is not simply an unfortunate philosophical mistake.
> Instead, it issues in an error of social practice which wrongly sub-
> ordinates and indicts sexual activity and deteriorates into an un-
> wholesome self-denial that pits immortal salvation against bodily
> pleasure.[37]

Plato simply cannot think clearly when sex is an issue. Plato is not alone in that irrationalism. The same ironic failure is exhibited time and again by the most skilled rationalists, for the simple reason that their personal experience of sex is negative because it threatens the dominance of their abstract intellect. They then crudely assume that sex is inherently demonic and inferior to noble reason. People with more balanced cognitive styles are not subjectively threatened by sexual sensation and thus have a more accurate picture of the nature of human sexuality.

Egoic Rigidity

The concept of the *ego* has many meanings. I use the term to refer to a key part of our personalities: the sense of willful volition, of intentionality. We need a sense of willfulness to survive and thrive in a complex world, but an overly aroused ego is unhealthy. Willfulness, even in small doses, generates tension in our body. A constantly stimulated ego generates chronic tension. Health requires that at times we let go of willful self-control and surrender to the spontaneity of the moment. *Egoic rigidity* consists of a compulsive attachment to willful volition, and an inability to let go and be carried along by the flow of life.

A person with such a rigid ego will perceive sexual arousal as threatening because it undermines the sense of self-control. As sexual excitement increases, so does the sense that we are being "captured" by the experience, that we are simply surrendering to powerful sensations rather than willfully controlling the event.

Sex impulses have long been recognized as having a power independent of the ego. St. Augustine recognized this as well. Erotic passion, he said, "rises up against the soul's decision in disorderly and ugly movement."[38] Time and time again he notes that sex impulses, even when they appear in dreams, interfere with conscious human will. Speaking of his own erotic arousal, he states: "Surely I have not ceased to be my own self . . . and yet there is still a great gap between myself and myself . . . . Oh that my soul might follow my own self . . . that it might not be a rebel to itself."[39] Modern science supports such insights. Researchers confirm that the sexual trance "is not a consciously chosen decision but is experienced as the captivation of consciousness by the delights of the sexual contact episode . . . volitional concentration is left behind."[40] This relinquishment of control is often felt as an "oceanic feeling of oneness, dissolution of self-boundaries."[41]

The reason sexual arousal undermines egoic self-control is explained by the left/right lateralization of the brain. The ego is largely a function of the left brain. Sexual arousal is largely mediated by the right brain. As sexual energy rises, neural resources move to the right brain, undermining the ego, generating the "oceanic feeling of oneness" that the right brain is so adept at perceiving. An individual compulsively attached to the sense of willful self control is threatened by the right brain dominance that sexual arousal generates.

Egoic rigidity is probably the most common of the rigid personality traits. Many different types of people are in the grips of the condition. The most extreme exemplar of this group is the pathological egotist Adolph Hitler. He was a man obsessed with the controlling will in his own mind. One of Hitler's biographers, Alan Bullock, says:

No word was more frequently on Hitler's lips than "will" and his whole career from 1919 to 1945 is a remarkable achievement of willpower . It was the will to power in its crudest and purest form, not identifying itself with the triumph of a principle as with Lenin or Robespierre—for the only principle of Naziism was power and domination for its own sake—nor finding satisfaction in the fruits of power, for, by comparison with other Nazi leaders like Goering, Hitler lived an ascetic life.[42]

Befitting such a rigidly egoic personality, Hitler was largely asexual. His only substantial sexual relationship was with Eva Braun, an attractive blonde twenty years his junior. Yet their bond was more domestic than erotic in character.[43] Further, his social policy was hostile to sex: his thugs burned to the ground the world's first institute for the study of human sexuality; he banned sexual entertainment; he hounded homosexuals into concentration camps.

Egoic rigidity rarely takes such pathological form, but is common in far more ordinary folk, in people who for any one of several reasons need a sense of rigid self-control. A good example of such a personality type is the workaholic. Predictably, obsessive toilers are prone to sexual problems. Any form of intimacy and deep feeling frightens them because it threatens their attempt to maintain excessive self-control.[44]

Members of extremely conservative political parties also exhibit this personality trait. Their extreme views are often a strategy to control their high level of anxiety and need for toughness and self-control. This causes them to reject hedonistic impulses, and especially sexual pleasure. For a detailed discussion of the relationship between conservativism and anti-hedonism, see *The Psychology of Conservatism*.[45]

Finally, egoic rigidity is also found in the person described by popular vernacular as a "tight-ass," "control freak," or "kill-joy." The hostility to sexuality is just part of a larger aversion to any spontaneous feeling and movement. As one commentator puts it: "It has also been noticed that the 'kill-joy' is especially perturbed by those forms of enjoyment which call for a spontaneous release of impulse, with a minimum of conscious control, such as music, sport and above all, dancing. It is as if he could not take the risk of lifting his conscious control of his instinctive impulses for a moment, in case the dammed up impulses burst out so strongly that he could no longer control them."[46]

Autonomic Rigidity

The autonomic nervous system consists of two branches: the sympathetic side, which produces what is often called the *fight or flight response*, and the parasympathetic side, which governs what is called the *relaxation response*. The arousal of one side inhibits the operation of the other, which is why we cannot feel anxious and relaxed at the same time. *Autonomic rigidity* consists of a compulsive attachment to sympathetic stimulation, to the sensations of adrenaline in the veins, and a vague or precise sense of anxiety and danger.

Sex can be a powerful tranquilizer. Many have sex to calm down after a busy day, the same way others use a hot bath, or physical workout, or alcohol and drugs. Sexual passion, and especially orgasm, has that effect because it powerfully stimulates the parasympathetic system. Normally anxiety and stress take time to dissipate because the parasympathetic system can only gradually suppress the sympathetic side. Orgasm is a highly unusual autonomic event in that it suddenly and dramatically boosts the parasympathetic system, generating an immediate discharge of tension.[47]

Most people enjoy orgasm precisely because of this effect. But a person compulsively attached to the sensations of a dominant sympathetic system will experience the sudden loss of such dominance as threatening. Autonomic rigidity is thus another cause of primitive sexual aversions.

The Causes of Rigidity

Some people may be genetically disposed to rigid personality traits, and thus are destined for high levels of physical tension, compulsive abstract thought, willful self-control, or high anxiety. People born with such traits are more likely to acquire lust aversions than persons lacking such genes. However, the idea that genes can produce rigid personalities is speculative. Much greater knowledge of our genetic code is required before such a hypothesis can carry much weight.

But the idea that rigid personalities are *acquired* has much more supporting evidence. The hypothesis is fairly simple: rigid personalities are the natural outcome of *experientially polarized* environments, those that stimulate high levels of muscular tension and little physical suppleness, high levels of abstract mental work and little sensual enjoyment, high levels of willful self-control and little spontaneity, or high levels of anxiety and little relaxation. The polarized environments that breed rigid personality traits can be specific to an individual, group, or entire culture.

Note that if some people are born with rigid personalities, they will naturally gravitate to the environments in which they feel most comfortable. Abstraction addicts will tend to seek out universities, professions, and bureaucracies, while compulsive egoists will tend to choose positions of social control such as police forces, armies, and politics. People addicted to chronic anxiety will seek out doomsday cults or fundamentalist religions. These environments will in turn reinforce these innate personality traits, as the rest of this section shows.

Habit

Polarized environments engender rigidity largely through the process of *habit formation*: when a response occurs over and over it tends to become ingrained and habitual. We acquire a relatively fixed psychological orientation or "shape," analogous to the physical posture most of us have acquired through physical habits. In the same way that a person who types all day can get a humped back, or a professional horse rider can become bowlegged, most of us acquire a relatively enduring inclination toward specific types of experiences, and an aversion to the responses which exclude such experiences.

Consider, for example, the computer programmer who performs complex abstract tasks all day long for years. During this process specific areas of his left brain are constantly stimulated. Contrast his experience with that of a full-time mother taking care of several young children. Her constant emotional interactions with toddlers predominantly stimulate her right brain. Consider also the different environments of a professional rodeo rider as opposed to that of a village craftsman. The life of the cowboy is extraordinarily insecure. He risks serious injury every time he works. His fight or flight response is constantly stoked. In contrast, a rural artisan is more likely to lead a quiet life, rarely experiencing high stress. Each of these environments is likely to breed a relatively fixed experiential "posture," a set of experiences to which the individual is attached, and which he will seek out over and over again.

Body chemistry

There are several reasons constant activation of a response tends to breed a psychological attachment to it. Body chemistry must play a role, although little research has been done in that area. Every experience is accompanied by a specific internal chemical bath. For example, fight or flight responses produce adrenaline, while the relaxation response pumps a different concoction into our blood. Through unrelenting exposure to the same chemical bath, we probably acquire a dependence on it, and experience a form of "withdrawal" when other experiences alter the familiar body chemistry.

Attachments are probably also a product of patterns of electrical conductivity in our nervous system. When a specific type of behavior is repeated over and over, it stimulates specific parts of the brain and the nervous system; the energy constantly flowing through these specific networks makes them more conductive, and thus the responses are more easily performed with less energy loss. Less activated neural pathways have more "potholes" and "ruts," and for that reason alone will be less traveled in favor of the deeply ingrained neural "freeways."

Identity

The fascinating phenomenon of identity plays a very important role in the attachment process. Our sense of "self" operates much like the chief executive of a corporation, sitting at the top of the decision-making hierarchy in our psyche. Our identity forms during our early years, and once it anchors in our brain we develop very powerful attachments to that sense of who we are. These attachments are so strong that they can control us even to the extent of bringing enormous unhappiness. Consider a woman who through years of domestic abuse identifies with the role of a victim. So strong is her attachment to that sense of self that she will actually seek out relationships which confirm her victim status, choosing abusive men and avoiding men who show her respect.

An important but relatively unstudied part of our identity involves internal somatic experience. Through processes discussed immediately below, we come to define certain somatic responses and experiences as "me," and define other responses as "not-me," thereby acquiring an *experiential identity*, and an attachment to those experiences.

Chronic over-stimulation of an experience can promote a sense of identity with it. For example, Reichian therapists such as Nick Totton and Em Edmondson show that people who are chronically anxious—autonomically rigid—*identify* with such experience: "Our very sense of "I" is bound up with bodily tension. Like boys at an old-fashioned public school, we learn to 'get a grip on ourselves,' and to *identify* with that grip. Feeling tense becomes part of our continuous background experience, so that full relaxation seems like a threat to our existence."[48] In the words of the great transpersonal pioneer Alan Watts: "Even when lying on the floor most people will continue to make totally needless muscular efforts to retain their position, almost as if they were afraid of the organism losing its shape and dissolving into jelly."[49]

An important way we acquire an experiential identity is through the messages we receive about ourselves from other people. If I am told repeatedly that I am a boy, or an American, or stupid, or smart, I will define myself in terms of those concepts. Such "identity messages" often refer to specific experiences. For example, boys are often told, "Boys are tough, they don't cry."[50] Through this process many boys will identify with the internal experience of being tough, of clamping down on the urge to cry, of controlling the expression of feelings. Such a boy will feel most true to his self when he is in control and willful. In that way he acquires an attachment to the experience of egoic self control, such as the sensations of tightening the belly or constricting the throat or clamping down on the jaw, and a reciprocal aversion to experiences like real sexual intimacy, which threaten that egoic sense.

Similarly, a person who is constantly identified as "smart" or "logical" can internalize that message into their sense of self. Such a person will experience their "I" in thinking abstractly and in the sensations felt in the head when complex thoughts are expressed or mathematical problems solved; they will perceive the lack of such abstract mentation as "not-I." People who identify intensively with the physical sensations of abstract thought will experience sexual arousal and release as threatening.

The left brain plays a very important role in the formation of the sense of self. According to Rawn Joseph, a leading researcher in brain lateralization, the left hemisphere governs our conscious self-concept: all the traits and experiences "that we consciously view as comprising our essential character."[51] That may bias human identity in favor of left brain experiences such as willfulness and abstraction, rather than other experiences such as intuition and emotionality that are mediated by the right brain. Excluded from the conscious self-concept, right brain functions appear dangerous and threatening. Over-stimulation of the left brain enhances this effect. In the words of Rawn Joseph:

> Since the invention of complex spoken language and the advent and eventual dominance of linguistic consciousness, many functions mediated by the right half of the cerebrum and the limbic system have been viewed as dangerous, sinful or irrelevant. Indeed so autocratic and presumptuous is the left half of the brain that not only does it try not to be conscious of many of these natural abilities, impulses and inclinations, but it often attempts to suppress or discard them as useless and unimportant.[52]

The more heavily stimulated the left brain, the more likely it is that identity will form around left brain experiences, and sexual impulses will be perceived as dangerous and worthy of suppression.

Rigidity traits are mutually causal

Once an environment breeds one type of rigidity, the other types will tend to take root as well. Consider a few examples. A person with an attachment to abstract cognition will constantly engage in that form of thought. As any advanced meditator knows, abstract thinking involves a form of stress. It tightens the body. A person who is constantly engaged in abstract cognition is likely to acquire a chronically tense body. Cognitive rigidity thus helps generate muscular rigidity.

Egoic self control also generates physical tension. Constant willful volition is thus also conducive to muscular rigidity. Chronic physical tension helps stimulate the sympathetic autonomic system, and if that constantly occurs then autonomic rigidity is the likely result. One rigid personality trait thus tends to appear with others, all ultimately breeding lust aversions.

Polarized environments

Consider a few examples of polarized environments that would breed rigid personalities and in turn erotophobia. The environment of rigid social hierarchies is highly polarized. Police forces, armies, many corporations, caste systems, and most religions have such a power structure. Hierarchies tend to define very specific roles and power inequalities between genders, generations, races, and social classes. Roles require individuals to conform to patterns of behavior that are often at variance with natural human impulses, necessitating egoic control. The more roles that we are forced to play, and the narrower the roles, the greater our egoic self-control, and the greater our aversion to sexual responses.

Second, a hierarchy is by nature goal-oriented, such as fighting a war, producing more goods and services, or pleasing a jealous god. Members of hierarchies must constantly strive to attain such goals. This requires the constant exercise of will.

Third, hierarchies are often the product of abstract ideology. A key part of the *esprit de corps* necessary for the survival of hierarchical organization is some form of dogma, usually religious or political in nature. The on-going emphasis of dogma constantly stimulates the conceptualizing left brain.

Fourth, hierarchies are stressful. Everyone is subject to the whims of their superiors and must constantly control their subordinates. Relaxed, intimate relating is impossible where relationships are regimented. All of these forces breed rigidity and an aversion to the spontaneity of sex.

Within a hierarchy, the environment at the top is the most rigidifying. With high power comes high stress. Competition for a top job is always intense. The maintenance of power requires constant anxiety and self-control. Social intimacy is impaired. All of this is conducive to rigidity. Generally speaking, the higher your social status the more likely you will have rigid personality traits. The fascinating result is that the people who control the levers of social power tend to be the most erotophobic.

In *A Sexual Profile of Men in Power*, the authors examined the sexual preferences of the powerful men residing in Washington D.C. A common personality trait they found was a powerful need to dominate. Powerful men have to repress their feelings, abandon playfulness and fantasy, demonstrate "habits of orderly, systematic, goal-directed thinking."[53] These are the characteristics of rigidity.

What type of sex do such people enjoy? The authors report:

In our interviews with prostitutes and call girls we heard the same story over and over again: the urgent demand for hostile, often dangerous, and always highly aggressive sex, often played out in incredibly elaborate scenarios in which the men get tied up, beaten up, urinated and/or defecated upon, sodomized with dildos or cut up with knives, or else do these things to the woman.[54]

A famous example of this orientation is reported by the prostitute who serviced the televangelist Jimmy Swaggert. She told the media that the charismatic God-fearing minister was not so much interested in sex as in humiliation and abasement.[55]

Sado-masochistic sex is attractive to people who suffer aversions to sexual pleasure. It allows them to avoid taking responsibility for the sexual sensations they feel. It focuses their attention on pain and on the minute details of the roles of dominance and submission, rather than the spontaneous flow of sexual energy in their body. It affirms their sense that sexuality is dirty and depraved.

Fundamentalist culture, political or religious, also engenders rigid personality traits. Fundamentalists tend to live in fear, frightened of wrathful gods or ideological opponents. They obey simplistic, well-defined codes of conduct, spelled out in religious texts or political manifestos, to mitigate this fear. Such codes heavily constrain impulsive action. Fundamentalists must develop self control to a very high degree to conform to such codes. Further, their rules are highly abstract. Bible-toting evangelists or Maoists with their Red Books are constantly interpreting their doctrine and that stimulates mental-linear experience. Rigid personality traits tend to run very deep in fundamentalists and thus so does erotophobia.

The classic historical example of an environment conducive to rigid personality traits is the Puritan culture of seventeenth century England. The Puritans opposed festivals and the theater. They demanded total sobriety. Irritability was a sin. Max Weber, in his *Protestant Ethic and the Spirit of Capitalism*, describes Puritanism as subjecting "man to the supremacy of the purposeful will, to bring his actions under constant self-control with a careful consideration of their ethical consequences."[56] Historian Edmund Leites reports, "The Puritans did not limit this concern to a few areas of life. In marriage, public life, commerce, child-raising, religious behavior and even war, they demanded emotional steadiness and self control."[57]

The Puritan culture is legendary for its fear of sex. H.L. Mencken often referred to the "Puritan distrust of whatever is bodily pleasant."[58] Indeed, the term *Puritanism* is often used as a synonym for sexual fear. Interestingly, Puritan dogma was not hostile to *all* sexual pleasure. Edmund Leites, in *The Puritan Conscience And Modern Sexuality*, shows that Puritan moralists actually supported sexual passion as long as it was confined to the marriage bed.[59] Puritan leaders in fact encouraged their followers to "keep up your Conjugal Love in a constant heat and vigor."[60]

But such sex-positive advice had little influence on real-life Puritans. Leites shows that they were sexually inhibited even in the marriage bed. "The unintended outcome of the Puritan ethic," says Leites, "was the prudery of Richardson's Pamela, who is dismayed by the animality of sensuality and its temporary abandonment of sobriety and self-control. The integrative ideal which the Puritans called for in marriage could not hold."[61] The average Puritan, saddled with the rigid personality traits and lust aversions that they acquired from their culture, simply could not follow their leaders' limited sex-positive advice.

Some modern fundamentalist religions tout the same narrow sex-positive view, encouraging sexual delight, but only between married people. Yet those same religions also produce rigid personalities; the encouragement of marital sexual pleasure is as unrealistic as that of the Puritan moralists. To anyone with a personality-driven aversion to the very feel of sex, marital sex is nearly as distressing as any other kind.

Highly unstable social or even natural environments can also breed rigid personalities. For example, in a culture afflicted by war, or rapid technological change, or even plague or famine, most people suffer from high chronic anxiety, and this in turn generates powerful aversions to sex. Several historians have examined this correlation of social instability and erotic anxiety. For example, Jayme A. Sokolow shows in *Eros and Modernization: Sylvester Graham, Health Reform and Origins of Victorian Sexuality in America* how in the mid 1800s self-styled "purity reformers" such as Sylvester Graham (inventor of the cracker that bears his name) adopted rigid antisexual morality as a way to find security in a society in which traditional religious and secular institutions were losing authority.[62]

While experientially polarized or unstable environments tend to create rigid personalities, *experientially balanced* environments tend to produce people free of such traits. The environment of the primitive hunter-gatherer society is an example. It offers very modest levels of stimulation to the ego or abstract mind, and relatively little stress. Anthropological evidence suggests that hunter/gatherer societies were far more comfortable with body processes and sexual responses than most people are today.[63]

The life of a woman in a traditional female role in modern culture, heavily focused on nurturing children, is also experientially balanced. Such an environment stimulates the emotional centers of the right brain, requiring no dominance of abstract thought and highly focused action. Intensely involved in the spontaneous rhythms of the bodies of children, and their own menstruating, lactating, and child-bearing bodies, the powerful impulses of sex will be far less foreign to these women than to a person dominated by mental-linear thought and focused willful action. This explains why men in conservative societies perceive women as more carnal and sensual; compared to the men, the women *are* much more relaxed about the body and its processes, including its sexual responses. This attitudinal difference between men and women in such cultures is largely a product of the different on-going experiences that traditional society provides for men and women. If men stayed at home all day bathing children, cooking meals, and interacting cooperatively with peers, and women went out into the world, fought wars, struggled with a career, and repressed their feelings throughout, then traditional men would be far more comfortable about sex and women would perceive sex as something alien and intimidating.

Dominant social groups often perceive social under-classes as more sexually animalistic than themselves. Generations of American white men hold to the idea that black men are sexually voracious.[64] The middle class in most cultures views the working class to be the same.[65] While their perceptions are exaggerations, they also express some truth. In general, social under-classes occupy more experientially balanced environments, which are less conducive to rigid personality traits.

The environment occupied by artists, athletes, and musicians also tends to be antithetical to rigidity. These occupations provide intense somatic experience, yet at the same time are disciplined and controlled. Artists and their ilk tend to live highly individualistic lifestyles, free of the inhibiting social roles that constrain people who work as politicians or police officers. No wonder then that the bohemian world is famous for its tolerance of sexual expression. People inhabiting a more experientially balanced world perceive erotic arousal as a source of inspiration rather than a threat.

The modern affluent world is making the same sort of balanced experience available to more and more people. The "information age" offers immense asymmetric stimulation to the abstract willful mind, resulting in powerful domination of the left brain. However, the modern era also offers a counterbalance in freeing many people from narrow traditional roles, and in providing new opportunities for powerful emotional and sensual experience, thanks to travel and leisure, psychological therapy, psychedelic and prescription drugs, and many other factors.

Erotophobia helps breed rigidity

While rigid personalities generate lust aversions, the reverse is also true. Erotophobia helps produce rigid personalities. This is a complex process, but consider briefly how it works. Once any erotophobic attitude is acquired—and remember that this can occur by non-personality processes—it will provoke stressful negative responses to sex. This increases the general level of tension that an individual experiences. If erotophobic attitudes are very potent and produce chronic stress, the result can be physical and autonomic rigidity.

Erotophobic attitudes will also tend to impair sexual pleasure and thus prevent the tranquilizing effects of sex. As mentioned above, sexual gratification is very effective in shedding physical and emotional tension, and thus is an antidote to physical rigidity and autonomic rigidity. A person who acquires erotophobia can less easily avoid rigidity.

As noted earlier in this chapter, one of the personality traits that often appears along with erotophobia is authoritarianism. For example, people who harbor racist attitudes or favor authoritarian leaders are more likely to have irrational fears about sex than people with more democratic political values. Part of the explanation for these correlations is that erotophobia helps cause authoritarianism. A man who feels great shame about his sexuality because of religious misinformation, and who suffers low self esteem because of that shame, can find some relief by demonizing social minorities. By viewing them as inferior, he feels better about himself.

Because of all these factors, a highly erotophobic person is more likely to have rigid personality traits than a person lacking irrational fears about sex. Erotophobia helps cause the very forces that produce more of it. Such an internal self-perpetuation system explains why erotophobia is so difficult to eradicate once it takes root, both in individuals and in cultures.

16 / The Politics of Lust

WHILE EROTOPHOBIA is prevalent in some communities, religions, and institutions, it is minimal in others. This variation is no accident. The ultimate cause of erotophobia is a specific type of political structure, *hierarchy*, that exists to differing degrees in different social groups. Hierarchic pecking orders produce large volumes of three types of phobigenic forces: opportunistic antisexualism, nasty sex, and rigid personality traits. Such *catalysts* breed sexual fear independently of the infection cycle. They are not so rife in democratic social groups, and hence erotophobia is less common there.

Hierarchy exists in several formats. The most common is *patriarchy*, in which men and women, adults and children are segregated into separate worlds and men dominate women and adults dominate children. Also common is *ethnic hierarchy*, where power flows through status divisions based on race, nationality, or religion. *Religious hierarchy* consists of ideology that perceives the relationships of God, mankind, and nature in stratified terms. In a hierarchic spiritual tradition, God is identified as an omnipotent "Father" or "Lord," who must be humbly obeyed and deeply feared by lowly, sinful humans, who in turn dominate and subdue the forces of nature. All modern cultures have a fourth type of hierarchy: *bureaucracy*, by which institutional power flows through religious or secular officials of various ranks, and then out to the wider community.

While hierarchy helps cause erotophobia, the reverse is also true. I shall show that irrational fears about sex help produce social inequality. This chapter explores the intriguing mutual causality of sexual attitudes and political structures.

Patriarchy and Erotophobia

Patriarchy exists in both domestic relationships and institutional policies. In a patriarchal family, the man holds the levers of power, and his wife and children submit to his commands. Institutional patriarchy is found in laws or religious traditions that deny women the same rights as men or that authorize the indoctrination or physical abuse of children.[1]

The degree of patriarchy in any culture, group, or family can be roughly gauged by determining the relative rights and powers of men compared to women, and adults compared to children. A culture that denies women the right to hold public office or even drive a car, as does Saudi Arabia, is obviously far more patriarchal than modern western culture where such official discrimination against women is largely (not totally) unknown. Similarly, the average family in modern western culture is today far less patriarchal than two generations ago when a television show like *Father Knows Best* was a hit. Families from that era were in turn less patriarchal than the families in which the generation of today's seniors were raised, when relations between genders and generations were far more formalized and less intimate than they would later become.

Rigidity

Patriarchy is especially conducive to erotophobia for several reasons. First, it helps breed rigid personalities. Patriarchy requires that men and women, adults and children, conform to social roles. For example, as psychologists Tomkins and Mosher write in their article "Scripting the Macho Man," the role of the patriarchal male requires that he express only "masculine" feelings such as anger and contempt, and that he repress any sentiments associated with femininity, such as compassion or empathy.[2] This exacts an enormous toll on the macho man, inhibiting his natural feelings and fostering the dominance of his will. Further, such a role generates high anxiety. Anyone required to maintain a role must constantly worry that they are not performing well. All of this promotes personal rigidity and, in turn, erotophobia.

Patriarchy is also rigidifying for the subordinates in a patriarchal system. Women and children must also comply with arbitrary roles, although their emotional life is less repressed than that of males. But they must cope with the absolute and often oppressive power of repressed men, and that extra fear also helps breed rigidity.

In contrast, where gender and age have minimal impact upon social status, human relationships are more relaxed and expressive. The willful mind need not be so controlling. The social environment is less experientially polarized. Less personal rigidity is the result. Because patriarchy breeds rigid personality traits, which in turn cause erotophobia, irrational sexual fear is more common in patriarchy than in more egalitarian and less rigidifying families or groups.

Opportunistic antisexualism

Patriarchy is also highly conducive to opportunistic sex intolerance, which in turn breeds erotophobia. Arbitrary sexual prohibitions are a powerful tool of any stratified social system. While status "symbols" such as crowns or uniforms are often used to designate positions on a pecking order, stratified cultures have for millennia also imposed sexual restrictions as a way to define social boundaries. A common example discussed several times in this book is the process of expressing the inferior status of children by denying them access to sexual experience and information. When an adult intervenes into the private life of a child and punishes masturbation or sexual play with peers, the adult expresses power over the child. Sexual prohibitions communicate the message "I have control over you," and this helps make the victim of the prohibitions more pliable, not only with regard to sex, but also in the non-sexual course of life. Similarly, the lowly status of women is defined in part by "double standards" that deny females the same sexual rights as males. Such rules overtly express the superior social status of men.

Because opportunistic antisexualism enhances patriarchal power it is much more prevalent in patriarchal families and communities than in non-patriarchal groups. People within patriarchy, especially women and children, are more exposed to this type of intolerant action than people in more egalitarian communities. Higher levels of opportunistic attacks on sex breed higher levels of erotophobia.

Nasty sex

Sexual assault, a highly phobigenic force, is also rife in patriarchy.[3] The lower the status of women and children, the more likely that their superiors will sexually abuse them. Consider a few reasons this occurs.

In a patriarchal culture, marital rape is not a crime. A wife's role requires her to be sexually submissive to her husband; if she refuses his advances he can legally force sex on her. Similarly, in a patriarchal culture a woman's testimony is of little value. If she complains of rape at the hands of a non-spouse she is not likely to be believed. Cross-cultural evidence indicates a high probability of rape and violence against women within male-dominant societies.[4] Further, in patriarchies a woman will be shamed for being raped because now she is "damaged goods" for her future or present husband. Because of the importance of male lineage in a patriarchal culture (and for other reasons) female virginity is highly prized, so rape victims suffer not only at the hands of their attackers, but also from their loss of virginity.

Children too are vulnerable to sexual assault in patriarchal culture. Where children must submit to the commands of adults, the more likely they will obey commands to engage in sex. The lower the status of children, the less likely their report of sexual assault will be believed. The lower the status of women, the less likely that mothers will intervene to prevent the abuse of their children. Several common features of patriarchal home environments—parental conflict, harsh punishment, and emotional deprivation—correlate with high levels of sexual abuse.[5] Psychotherapist Carolyn Heggen, author of *Sexual Abuse In Christian Homes And Churches*, says, "As long as patriarchy is supported and male dominance is considered the appropriate model for human relationships, sexual abuse of children will continue. It is impossible both to stop sexual abuse and support a patriarchal family model."[6]

Patriarchy also generates high risks for unwanted pregnancy, which is highly phobigenic. Denying women the right to control their fertility is a way to subordinate them. Much, though not all, opposition to contraception and abortion flows from the patriarchal desire to wrest decision-making authority about human fertility from the women who must bear and then nurture children. In a non-patriarchal culture women have far greater control over reproduction, and thus suffer far less phobigenic effects.

Further, normal sexual relationships within patriarchy tend to be unhappy, and this too is phobigenic. For example, patriarchal double standards prohibit girls from any sexual exploration until marriage. They must quell their natural sexual desires for years, a repression that is not easily released when they are finally betrothed, as the Puritans discovered and as modern sex therapists know. Further, male dominators have little concern for the sexual pleasure of their partners. Their sexuality is entirely selfish. In patriarchy, sex is all about quick release for the man, leading to sexual frustration and even erotophobic aversions in the female.

In a culture in which men dominate women in and out of bed, both genders learn to eroticize male dominance and female passivity in a sexual context. As Riane Eisler discusses at length in *Sacred Pleasure*, patriarchal societies breed men who want to inflict sexual pain and women who want to receive it.[7] When sex is not boring in patriarchy, it is rough and abusive, and this ultimately is unsatisfying as well, as each party plays out a sexual role rather than enjoys the spontaneous flow of sexual energy. Either way, the result is that normal sexuality in a patriarchy will be unhappy for both partners, and constant frustration in a sexual context is phobigenic.

Finally, patriarchy is also conducive to nasty rather than friendly pornography. Patriarchy produces ugly, male dominant sex media, which in turn has the phobigenic effects discussed in Chapter 14.

Empirical correlations

The amount of antisexualism (phobic or opportunistic) in any group or community is a rough indication of the amount of its erotophobia, because such behavior ultimately breeds that condition. Formal studies and anecdotal evidence show that antisexual responses and patriarchy tend to occur together. The patriarchy/antisexual link is discussed in detail in *Sex in History* by G. Rattray Taylor[8], *Saharasia* by James DeMeo[9], and *Beyond Power: On Women, Men and Morals* by Maryiln French.[10] In *Sex and Reason* the jurist and social theorist Richard Posner provides many examples of how sexual prohibitions are closely correlated to the status of women.[11] Other more specific research projects show that the more patriarchal a culture, the greater the avoidance of social nudity, erotica, or erotic variety.[12]

Consider more anecdotal correlations drawn from American culture over the last several generations. As mentioned above, the degree of patriarchy in modern America has declined throughout the twentieth century. So has the average amount of erotophobia, as indicated by the significant decline in the prevalence of antisexualism. For example, during the 1920s and 1930s, schools provided virtually no sexual education. Youth organizations such as the Boy Scouts condemned masturbation. The media contained little sexual information. The criminal law prohibited explicit sexual entertainment. Access to birth control and abortion was minimal. Every mainstream religious organization attacked non-marital sexuality as a serious sin. Virtually every child coming of age during that era was exposed to this unrelenting barrage of antisexualism, and thus could not help but acquire significant erotophobia.

Contrast that environment with that of a person born in North America in the baby-boom era between the late 1940s and early 1960s. Most children of that generation were exposed to at least rudimentary sex education in schools and enormous amounts of sexual information in the media. Youth organizations suspended their overt attacks on childhood masturbation. Sexual entertainment slowly emerged into the mainstream. Antisexual rhetoric in most churches declined. Although much institutional antisexualism remained, it was much less common than that faced by the parents of the baby boomers. The level of erotophobia of the average baby boomer is thus lower than that of their parents. And the children of the baby boomers are growing up exposed to still lower antisexualism. As inequality between genders and generations declines in western culture, so will erotophobia.

A similar pattern emerges when one compares the amount of antisexualism (and the corresponding amount of erotophobia) in Saudi Arabia, a highly patriarchal culture, with those in Sweden, a highly egalitarian society. In the conservative Moslem nation public nudity is unknown. Sex education is non-existent. Female genital mutilation is common. Sexual entertainment does not exist. Homosexuality is a crime.

Adulterers are executed. Such intense antisexualism produces much erotophobia. In contrast, institutional sex intolerance in Sweden is very low. Sex education begins when children are in kindergarten. Condoms are easily available to teens. There are few restraints on sexual media. Homosexuals are protected from discrimination. Public nudity in recreational areas is common. Erotophobia is minimal.

Ethnic Hierarchy

Political inequality is also commonly based on ethnic divisions. The greater such social stratification, the greater the erotophobia. Examples of such a correlation abound. Compare, for example, the sexual policies of the former apartheid South Africa with those of modern multicultural South Africa. The racist regime prohibited almost any form of sexual entertainment. Even *Playboy* magazine was forbidden entry to the country. Homosexuality was a crime, and so was miscegenation. In contrast, contemporary South Africa is one of the most tolerant nations in the world with respect to sexual expression and rights.

A similar pattern is evident in America. In the race-stratified American south, institutional erotic intolerance aimed at sexual media, sexual entertainment, sex education, and homosexuality has always been much greater than in the less racially divided northern states.

The reasons for the relationship between ethnic stratification and erotophobia are similar to those I have already examined in relation to patriarchy. First, ethnic hierarchy is more conducive to rigid personality traits than ethnically integrated communities because it produces high levels of racial tension. Chronic stress breeds autonomic rigidity.

Second, ethnic divisions breed more opportunistic erotic intolerance. The most obvious example is the prohibition on inter-breeding between ethnic groups. The greater the ethnic stratification of a community the greater will be the prohibitions against sexual contact across ethnic boundaries. Further, one way to guarantee that no cross-cultural sexual expression occurs is to forbid men or women sexual relationships outside marriage. Ethnically divided communities need phobigenic sexual prohibitions that integrated communities can avoid. The history of the American south presents a classic example. After the end of slavery many states passed laws prohibiting interracial sex; both men and women were sent to prison for violating such laws.[13] The "purity" of the southern belle was required, in part, to ensure no mixed-blood offspring.

Third, ethnic stratification often breeds a complex form of antisexualism by which low-status groups are viewed by high-status groups as highly sexual and thus worthy of domination. For example, the Nazis often described Jews as lascivious, highly sexed animals out to destroy the honor of Aryan women.[14] Generations of American whites perceived black people as sexually ravenous.[15] Because such racist ideology links sexuality with a hated group of people, it is phobigenic to the dominant culture. It tarnishes sexuality with the unworthiness of the outcast group.

Fourth, in highly stratified ethnic communities, sexual assault and unwanted pregnancy are more common, especially for the women of subordinate groups, who are victimized by the men of dominant groups. The most extreme example of this phenomenon is slavery, such as was common in the American south in the eighteenth and nineteenth centuries. Female slaves have few rights. They are the property of their master, and must obey his commands. Lacking any social power, a female slave must submit to the sexual demands of her owner. The greater the ethnic stratification, the greater this phobigenic force within the minority group.

For these reasons, ethnic hierarchy tends to produce more erotophobia than a less ethnically divided culture. The extra phobigenic forces that occur in racially divided culture help explain why the American south is still significantly more erotophobic than elsewhere in the nation.

Religious Hierarchy

Today as in the past, most people in most cultures have a religious orientation, and highly value their relationship with "God," however they define it. Like human relationships, the human/God connection has a political component, and it varies enormously from person to person, culture to culture. In many traditions, the relationship with God is perceived in hierarchic and sometimes even patriarchal terms: God is an omnipotent "Father" who lords over humans, demanding obedience and fear, punishing with eternal damnation those who do no submit. In that hierarchic worldview, man ranks below God but above the natural world. Fundamentalist and orthodox religions of all stripes share this hierarchic perception of God.

In contrast, egalitarian traditions perceive God not as a distant power above people and nature, but rather as the essential constituent of all things. There is no hierarchic rank in this worldview, because God inhabits everything. All people are therefore equal, and the natural world deserves the same reverence as human life. This egalitarian perception of God is typical of many tribal societies and is in fact the inner core of all the major religions.

Many complex forces determine the political structure of an individual's relationship with God. How we relate in our main *human* relationships is a very important factor affecting our bond with God. For example, highly patriarchal cultures such as those in Saudi Arabia tend to produce a very hierarchic spiritual perspective, such as fundamentalist Islam.

Hierarchic religious traditions breed erotophobia, for many reasons. First, they generate much fear. Hierarchic religion is "God-fearing" and adherents of such traditions often overtly describe themselves as such. If an omnipotent, jealous God is a major force in your life, you will live with a high level of fear. Such anxiety is conducive to the personal rigidity that in turn causes erotophobia.

Further, a religious tradition that sees nature as inferior will look down on sexuality because our carnal lusts flow from our animality. Also, jealous Gods need propitiation, usually through a sacrifice. Renouncing the pleasures of sex as a way to curry favor with a controlling God is a common practice in many hierarchic spiritual traditions.

Such religious perspectives also help generate erotophobia by fostering hierarchic human relationships. The way we relate to God obviously must influence the way we relate to each other. Social stratification is the natural social order in a culture that perceives God as "Lord." Hence priestly elites are a common feature of hierarchic spiritual traditions, and so is patriarchy. Those hierarchic structures in turn breed more erotophobia.

Contrast the political and sexual attitudes of on the one hand, Christianity represented by fundamentalist interpretations of the Bible, and on the other, Shivism and Tantrism. Traditional Christianity is classically hierarchic, framed in the patriarchal terms of "God the Father." It is also classically erotophobic. Christ taught that merely to look upon another person with sexual desire could be a sin. His apostle Paul said "nothing good" dwells in the flesh. Traditional Christian teaching highly values celibacy and rarely says anything positive about sexuality even when confined to marriage. The erotic arts are completely absent from this tradition.

In contrast, the early Indian nature religion of Shivism and the later highly sophisticated Tantric tradition, as well as pagan Dionysian cults in Europe, were highly egalitarian and highly sex-positive. They perceived God as a divine force within all things, and revered the natural world. They avoided moralistic self-control in favor of ecstasy and self-abandon. In Shivism, the human form of God is highly sexual, a seducer, a masturbator. The Tantric tradition produced one of the most advanced forms of erotic spirituality the world has ever known. Dionysian "orgiastic" rites also celebrated sexuality, and often homosexuality.[16]

Father Gods thus tend to engender erotophobia, while egalitarian Gods encourage erotic celebration. Reciprocally, a religion's sexual perspective casts much light on its political and spiritual orientation. As sex journalist Susie Bright wisely observes, sexual values provide much insight in evaluating any faith.[17]

Bureaucratic Hierarchy

While democratic societies can eliminate most patriarchal and ethnic inequality, they cannot do without bureaucratic hierarchy. Every non-tribal society needs to create a bureaucracy to run its legal system, military, media, industry, and religion, and the people who run these organizations have to have special rights and powers that ordinary people lack. Every modern society needs to stratify itself to the extent of having an executive bureaucracy. The internal structure of bureaucracies tends to be hierarchic; power flows top-down through status divisions. Such structure breeds erotophobia, not only in the members in its ranks but also the general society.

Consider, for example, a rigidly hierarchic organization such as the U.S. military. All relationships are based on rank; status gradations influence almost every social interaction. Such a pecking order tends also to be patriarchal. The U.S. military is notoriously sexist, both unofficially, in the informal responses of the macho men that military organizations attract, and officially, in the denial of combat roles for women. Predictably, all sexually explicit media is banned from retail outlets on military bases. Oral sex, even between married partners, is an offense. So is adultery. Merely disclosing homosexual conduct is grounds for discharge.

In contrast, consider a non-bureaucratized culture such as a gatherer-hunter tribe. Such social structure prevailed for hundreds of thousands of years and therefore is the cultural crucible for whatever is innate in our psyche. The !Kung tribe of Africa is a remnant of such a culture. It survived in its natural state to the 1970s and received much anthropological attention. An excellent introduction to this culture is *Nisa: The Life and Words of a !Kung Woman* by Marjorie Shostak.[18] The !Kung are highly egalitarian. They have no rank of seniority based on social position or even skills. They regard bragging or arrogance as highly inappropriate. They have no army, police force, or religious elite. While men and women have separate roles (men hunt, women gather) the status of women is high. Children are highly nurtured.

The lifestyle that gave birth to our gene pool is predictably sex-positive. !Kung children are not required to cover their erotic organs. Their sexual privacy is highly respected. Sex play is common. Many youths are able to observe adults having sex. There is no value on virginity. Talking about sex is as common as talking about food. While romantic love and marriage are common, so are affairs, and an elaborate protocol regulates such non-exclusivity.

Modern societies vary in their degree of hierarchic bureaucratization. China is highly bureaucratized compared to the United States. Powerful administrative agencies control vastly more of an individual's life in China than in "do your own thing" America. Further, Chinese bureaucracies are far more authoritarian, and are unrestrained by democratic institutions that allow Americans some control over their government agencies. The higher degree of hierarchic bureaucratization in China is one reason why erotophobia is much higher there than in the U.S. (as evidenced by much higher rates of antisexualism).[19]

Bureaucratic hierarchies breed high levels of erotophobia within their ranks and this motivates institutional antisexualism, which affects the general population. For example, the judiciary plays a major role in crafting sexual laws. The hierarchic structure of the judiciary is conducive to erotophobia in the minds of judges, and their erotophobia cannot help but influence their rulings, which in turn affect everyone in the community.

How does hierarchic structure in a bureaucracy generate erotophobia in its ranks? First, bureaucratic stratification requires high levels of self-control on the part of bureaucrats. Consider the self-discipline a police officer must exercise in the face of an abusive member of the public, or upon finding the body of a murdered child. Generally speaking, the greater an official's bureaucratic power, the greater their stress, the greater their actions must be willful and controlled, and the less they can be spontaneous. All of this is conducive to a rigid personality. Further, rigid individuals are by nature attracted to the power and order of the bureaucratic world. Surrounded by rigid people, an individual within a bureaucracy is likely to acquire the same traits.

Second, bureaucracies tend to impose sexual punishments on their ranks as a way to define their special status, penalties the general population never has to face. An example is the celibacy enforced on monks in traditional Buddhist temples. A monk's formal abandonment of sex is part of the symbolic process, along with his robes, by which he defines himself as separate from the general population. The masses often require sexual abstemiousness from its executive class for the same reason. Chastity is a sign of rigid self-control that underlings often demand of their leaders. Thus asexuality has always been a virtue for someone seeking high office. Bill Clinton was the first modern American president to recklessly violate such an antisexual tradition, and he almost lost the world's most powerful position because of it. This double standard—imposed on bureaucrats but not the general population—also generates higher erotophobia levels within the hierarchy.

Third, the maintenance of order in bureaucratic organizations often requires prohibitions on sexual activity between members of different ranks to prohibit the sexual coercion that is endemic in social pecking orders and to prevent the formation of sexual bonds and loyalties that interfere with hierarchical command. Military rules against sexual or non-sexual "fraternization" are an example of such segregation. People outside the bureaucracy do not have to cope with such rules. If two authors or sales clerks have an affair, they violate no employment rule and do not fear losing their jobs. The extra sexual prohibitions of the hierarchy, though valid and rational, have an extra phobigenic effect on the people within the bureaucracy.

Fourth, bureaucratic hierarchies, like other stratified relationships, are especially conducive to sexual exploitation. "If there is a single truth on which virtually every expert on child sexual abuse agrees, it is that abuse thrives in hierarchical, authoritarian institutions—particularly sexually repressive ones," say Elinor Burkett and Frank Bruni, authors of *A Gospel Of Shame: Children, Sexual Abuse, and the Catholic Church*.[20] For example, residential schools operated by authoritarian religions are hotbeds of sexual abuse. All over the world, children who attended such schools are coming forward with reports of systematic sexual abuse by caretakers and religious officials. Some of these victims are suing the religious organizations involved, and the total damages could run in the billions of dollars. In the litigation that has occurred to date the courts have found that a key factor behind the abuse is the hierarchical structure of the institutions.[21] Children trained in a rigid pecking order, where obedience to school officials was mandatory, remained silent when they were abused, often for years. In many cases, mass abuse was exposed only decades after the event.

Sexual predation is also common in military organizations. Sexual harassment is epidemic in the U.S. military. Two thirds of 20,000 female personnel surveyed reported harassment, and 5% said they had been raped.[22] Perhaps typical of these complaints is that of Kelly Flinn, the first female bomber pilot, who was sexually assaulted during her training at the Air Force Academy.[23] In 2003 dozens of women at the academy revealed their abuse and complained that military officials had sabotaged their efforts to get justice.[24] Women at West Point report similar problems.[25]

As a result of all these factors, bureaucratic hierarchies such as military organizations, law enforcement agencies, and political and religious elites tend to be inhabited by highly erotophobic people. The people with the most power in society and who write institutional sexual policies thus have a special emotional agenda to draft intolerant sexual regulations. As Alex Comfort puts it, the "least sexually adapted and most inhibited element" in society "expresses and ventilates its maladaption in the codifying of laws restricting the activity of others."[26] Such action, in turn, affects the sexual attitudes of the rest of the population.

Finally, hierarchic bureaucracies have opportunistic motives to impose phobigenic sexual rules on everyone. The ability to regulate the private sexual affairs of the common person in society is a powerful symbol of the dominance of any bureaucratic agency. When customs officers can censor what an individual reads, when a police officer can spy into the bedroom of a prostitute, when a Hollywood studio executive can demand the deletion of an image of a penis in a film, this expresses their authority, and that in turn enhances their power outside the sexual domain.

Further, the shame that normally results from erotophobia also advances bureaucratic power. As discussed several times in previous chapters, sex prohibitions tend to generate erotophobic shame in anyone upon whom they are imposed. Shame is uncomfortable; it seeks relief. A common way to try to fill the void that shame creates is to curry favor with social superiors, to please them by conforming to their dictates.[27] Jeremy Bentham recognized that process two hundred years ago:

> The more fear in the breasts of the subject, many the more power in the hands of the ruling few. When the people are in a shivering fit, the physician of their souls is absolute.[28]

Wilhelm Reich explores this link between sexual anxiety and social conformity in more detail than anyone else, but many other authors have perceived it too.[29] For example, George Orwell, in his masterful study of modern totalitarianism, *1984*, contends that dominant groups (like the "Party" in his novel) deliberately create sexual shame to further their own power:

> The Party was trying to kill the sex instinct or if it could not be killed, then to distort and dirty it . . . . For how could the fear, the hatred, and the lunatic credulity which the Party needed in its members be kept at the right pitch, except by bottling down some powerful instinct and using it as a driving force.[30]

The Catholic Church has long applied the same technique. Catholic attacks on masturbation, premarital sexuality, and many other harmless sexual activities cannot help but generate enormous shame in ordinary believers. But the Catholic institution of the confession box offers relief. Generating erotophobia is thus conducive to the fortunes of the Catholic Church. Catholic bureaucracies directly profit from their antisexualism. As Alex Comfort says:

> Christianity has always placed the regulation of sexual conduct in the forefront of its ethical system. It has always relied, sometimes deliberately and sometimes unconsciously, on the calculated generation of sexual anxiety as a source of its authority. Indeed, no pornographer has ever 'exploited' sex so thoroughly.[31]

Further, cultivating such irrational fears helps distract everyone from the heinous social injustices of which bureaucratic elites are often guilty. Reay Tannahill, author of *Sex in History*, shows how the development of the concept of sin in the Christian Church beginning in the medieval period, diverted attention from terrible crimes committed in the name of God:

> By some mysterious alchemy, sexual purity came to neutralize other sins, so that even the moral oppression and physical barbarity that became characteristic of the Christian church in the later medieval and Renaissance times scarcely appeared as sin at all in comparison with the sins of sex and heresy. It was, indeed, a remarkable achievement.[32]

A form of that process survives to the present day. Italian author Giordano Guerri visited Catholic priests in confession boxes in his native country, and told them of a range of fake sins he committed. He discovered that priests responded far more negatively to sins of sex such as adultery or prostitution, than to actual crimes such as murder or selling contaminated food.[33]

The upshot of such opportunistic intolerance is to generate high levels of erotophobia in those who must obey bureaucratic commands. The greater the need for bureaucratic agencies to maintain dominance in a culture, the more they will engage in sexual prohibitions, which has phobigenic effect on everyone.

Because bureaucratic hierarchies are an inherent threat to social equality, advanced democratic cultures impose limits on bureaucratic power, mainly through a system of constitutional rights. The greater these controls, the less likely that the antisexualism of the bureaucracy will infect the outside population. The Catholic Church or the Chinese Communist party have little democratic structure to restrain their antisexual policies; western democracies have some safeguards to protect against the antisexualism of the police and army, but not private organizations such as the media or religions. And even public bureaucracies get away with much antisexual policy, for ultimately they are supervised by other bureaucratic organizations, such as the courts, which share the same erotophobic values. As several examples in this book reveal, the American Supreme Court has been as erotophobic in the modern day as it was racist in the nineteenth century.

Pockets of Hierarchy

Even in a democratic culture that has largely abolished patriarchy and ethnic hierarchy, some pockets of hierarchy—and the erotophobia it causes—are inevitable. Public and private bureaucratic organizations are one such pocket, but so are fundamentalist religious groups, immigrants from traditional societies, and right wing pressure groups, many of which have an overtly patriarchal agenda. These hierarchic groups will generate high levels of erotophobia in their members, and the infection cycle will help the condition spread to others outside the group. This occurs informally through casual social relations, but also formally through antisexual social activism. Highly erotophobic groups have special motives to publicly attack harmless behaviors that less erotophobic people would ignore, and such attacks can have a phobigenic effect on everyone.

For example, as we have seen, people highly averse to the sight of nudity have a special reason to ensure that laws prohibiting nudity are obeyed. They will complain to officials when they observe public nudity and will oppose any repeal of anti-nudity law. People lacking phobic feelings toward the sight of the naked body will simply ignore public nudists and register no public comment. Because only the erotophobic voice is heard, nudity remains a crime, and that helps breed genital phobia in everyone.

Erotophobia is endemic (though to differing degrees) in most societies because most nations have either culture-wide or localized hierarchies. For example, in the United States a highly hierarchic form of Christianity has taken deep root in the culture, represented by powerful institutions such as the Southern Baptist Convention and the Catholic Church, as well as a vast network of independent Christian ministries, colleges, publishers, and broadcasters. These conservative religious groups have an intensely hierarchic worldview on two fronts. First, their social relationships tend to be patriarchal. They tend to exclude women from leadership positions, they see the father as the master of the household, and they impose strict rules on children. Second, and more importantly, they conceive of the dominant relationship in their life, that with God, in hierarchic terms. Such an ideology is powerfully conducive to personal rigidity and erotophobia. This highly erotophobic constituency is responsible for much of the erotophobia prevalent in America today.

Erotophobia Causes Hierarchy

While political inequality causes erotophobia, the reverse is true as well. Erotophobia helps segregate society into patriarchal, ethnic, and bureaucratic divisions. For example, as already discussed, erotophobia produces shame, which in turn undermines a person's self esteem. One way to deal with this loss of self-esteem is to look down upon or even victimize other people. Low self-esteem generates social prejudice and the need for social stratification.[34] High erotophobia levels thus help build an appetite for a social pecking order.

Further, the shame flowing from erotophobia seeks relief in social obedience to parents, religious leaders, corporate advertisers, or anyone who is dominant. People low in self esteem are vulnerable to external control.[35] Hierarchy requires such deference to external authority. While Reich, Orwell, and others discovered the relationship between sexual shame and social obedience two generations ago, feminists have been the most important modern exponents of the idea. "A woman's lack of sexual confidence overflows into the rest of her life: it makes her passive, dependent," says Carol Cassell, author of *Swept Away: Why Women Fear Their Own Sexuality*.[36] Women who have trouble reaching orgasm tend also to be submissive, obeying conventional feminine roles. Orgasmic women, in contrast, tend to be assertive.[37]

Erotophobia also promotes patriarchal relationships between men and women, adults and children. For example, a man highly averse to his own sexual impulses will tend also to be averse to any woman who stimulates such shame-provoking feelings.[38] This is why the great women-haters of the early Christian Church also hated sexuality. Tertullian, a father of the Christian Church, exhorted his followers to chastity; predictably, he regarded women as "the devil's gateway."[39] The more potent your erotophobia, the more likely you will perceive members of the other gender as a threat.

The same process affects relationships between the generations. The greater the erotophobia in a culture or family, the less intimate are relationships between adults and children. Children are naturally inquisitive, especially about sex. Adults who are afraid of sex are more apt to lie about the subject, conceal sexual information from their children, and impose intolerant sexual prohibitions. Children resent such behavior. Erotophobia enhances the distance between the generations.[40]

As many anthropologists have noted, the human body is a natural symbol of society. According to Mary Douglas, an authority on natural symbols, "The relation of head to feet, of brain and sexual organs, of mouth and anus are commonly treated so that they express the relevant patterns of hierarchy."[41] Erotophobic shame provides a hierarchic sense of self, which perceives genitals and sexual impulses as "lower" than the rest of the self. When we relate to the parts of our self in hierarchic terms, when our own identity is constructed on a pecking order, we are more likely to relate to other people in the same way. Thus the more we fear our genitals and sexual urges, the more likely we will embrace hierarchic political groups, religions, and family structures.

Because erotophobia and political inequality are reciprocally causal, evidence of the existence of one in an individual or culture means that the other can be inferred as well. Thus we can reliably predict that a person who is highly erotophobic will also favor hierarchic social relationships. Conversely, a person with such a hierarchic political orientation will usually also harbor much erotophobia. Attitudinal surveys confirm this relationship. People with high erotophobia tend to favor rigid roles for men, women and children, the segregation of races, hierarchic religions, law and order, militarism, and demagogue politicians.[42] Our sexual attitudes influence our political perspective.

The same erotophobia/hierarchy relationship can be observed on an institutional or even cultural scale as well. The greater the erotophobia in any group or society, the more likely it will embrace patriarchy, racism, and bureaucratic hierarchy. The less erotophobia, the more democratic the organization or culture. By determining the dominant sexual attitudes of any group of people, we can predict their political structure as well. Conversely, the nature of that political structure allows us to predict their sexual attitudes.

Political scientists are just beginning to understand this correlation. The work of American scholars Ronald Inglehart and Pippa Norris is notable in this regard. Inglehart is the director of the World Values Survey, which has accumulated a huge database on values and beliefs in more than seventy nations encompassing over 80% of the world's population. Examining relationships between sexual values and democratic structure, Inglehart and Norris conclude: "A society's commitment to gender equality and sexual liberalization proves time and again to be the most reliable indicator of how strongly that society supports principles of tolerance and egalitarianism."[43]

Because erotophobia threatens democratic values, anyone who supports democratic relationships in families, religion, or government should favor social policies that reduce irrational sexual fear. The first task must be to rid our society of the single most phobigenic force, the scourge of sexual assault. Western cultures have already made great progress on that front, although much work remains to be done. In the 1990s the international community recognized both the social significance of sexual assault and the need to eliminate it, in a series of formal human rights declarations beginning with the World Conference on Human Rights in Vienna in 1993, and the declaration passed in the same year by the General Assembly of the United Nations on the issue of violence against women. International conferences on population and development in Cairo in 1994 and on women in Beijing in 1995 again declared that freedom from sexual violence is a basic human right.[44]

Antisexualism is the other major phobigenic force, and any true democrat must seek its elimination too. The greater the intolerant attacks on sex in any society, the greater the erotophobia and the weaker the democratic structure. A key strategy in overcoming sex intolerance is the recognition of sexual rights as human rights. The World Association for Sexology, an international group of sex educators, therapists, and researchers, and the International Planned Parenthood Federation have each drafted model declarations of sexual rights. For example, the latter provides:

All persons have the right to be free from externally imposed fear, shame, guilt, beliefs based on myths, and other psychological factors inhibiting their sexual response or impairing their sexual relationships.[45]

Unfortunately, the concept of sexual rights is only just beginning to be recognized. Prior to 1993 sexuality was not recognized as a relevant part of human rights in international discourse. The notion of sexual rights first appeared in the Vienna Declaration on Violence Against Women. In Cairo in 1994 international delegates to the population conference recognized a right to "sexual health" and the importance of "a satisfying and safe sex life." The conference on women in Beijing in 1995 asserted that the human rights of women include "their right to have control over and decide freely and responsibly on matters related to their sexuality." These provisions were drafted in such general terms to mollify conservative delegates, such as those from the Vatican who attacked more specific sexual rights as the product of "a hedonistic mentality unwilling to accept responsibility in matters of sexuality" and "a self-centered concept of freedom."[46]

More specific sexual rights, such as freedom from discrimination on the basis of "sexual orientation," are just beginning to enter the international human rights agenda. In April 2003 the United Nations Human Rights Commission considered a historic motion to protect sexual minorities. While most of the democratic world supported the policy, delaying tactics by conservative Islamic nations, the Vatican, four Latin

American countries, and the United States prevented the adoption of the motion.[47] Here again, the sexual policies of the Bush Administration have far more in common with repressive regimes than democracies.

Though the pace of change is slow with respect to international agreements, sexual non-discrimination provisions are beginning to appear in human rights laws in many western countries. South Africa was the first country to incorporate such a clause in its constitution. Anyone who understands the relationship between democracy and sexual tolerance will readily comprehend why a nation trying to make a clean break from an oppressive past would be the first to enshrine sexual rights in its supreme law. Similar "sexual orientation" provisions are now found in several western countries although not enshrined with constitutional authority, and have been applied almost exclusively in issues involving homosexuality. However the concept of "sexual orientation" encompasses much more than gay rights and in the future will be invoked to protect many types of consensual sexual expression now commonly prohibited, such as comprehensive sex education, young people's access to sexual media, private commercial sex, group sex, and even some forms of public sexuality.

As the world democratizes it will more fully embrace the concept of sexual rights. The many forms of institutionalized antisexualism described in this book will be less prevalent. A new era of sexual tolerance will weaken the phobigenic system. Erotophobia will decline, and this, reciprocally, will nourish the psychological roots of democratic values. Only in the death of erotophobia will democracy be secure.

Notes

Introduction

1   Steven Carter and Julia Sokol Coopersmith, *What Really Happens In Bed: A Demystification Of Sex* (New York, Evans and Company, 1989) 37.

2   John Money, *The Destroying Angel: Sex, Fitness And Food In The Legacy Of Degeneracy Theory, Graham Crackers, Kellogg's Corn Flakes And American Health History* (Buffalo, Prometheus, 1985) 132.

3   Floyd Martinson, *The Sexual Life Of Children* (Westport, CT, Bergin & Garvey, 1994) Chapter 7, "Sexuality Education."

4   See "Clitoris: Still A Forbidden Word," in *Contemporary Sexuality* (1989) 21(2) 3; Margaret Leroy, *Pleasure: The Truth About Female Sexuality* (London, HarperCollins, 1993) 36-38.

5   Martinson, 32.

6   Edward O. Laumann et al, *The Social Organization Of Sexuality* (Chicago, University of Chicago, 1994) 85.

7   Seymour Fisher, *Sexual Images Of The Self: The Psychology Of Erotic Sensations And Illusions* (Hillisdale, NJ, Lawrence Erlbaum Associates, 1989) 41.

8   For example, author Wendy Shalit contends that most people are now free of sex insecurities. See *A Return to Modesty: Discovering The Lost Virtue* (New York, Simon & Schuster, 1999) 26.

9   Bernie Zilbergeld, *The New Male Sexuality* (New York, Bantam, 1992) 43.

10   Elaine Yates, in Jean-Marc Samson, *Childhood and Sexuality: Proceedings Of The International Symposium* (Montreal, Editions Etudes, 1980) 368.

11   The best introduction to the subject is William Fisher et al, "Erotophobia- Erotophilia As A Dimension Of Personality," *Journal of Sex Research 25* (1988) 123-151. See also the important 1984 essay (updated in 1992) by Gayle S. Rubin, "Thinking Sex: Notes For A Radical Theory Of The Politics Of Sexuality," in H. Abelove et al (eds.), *The Lesbian And Gay Studies Reader* (New York, Routledge, 1993) 3-44.

12   J. Brockner, "Low Self-Esteem And Behavioral Plasticity: Some Implications For Personality And Social Psychology," in L. Wheeler (ed.), *Review Of Personality And Social Psychology*, vol. 4 (Beverly Hills, CA, Sage, 1984) 287.

13   David Allyn, *Make Love, Not War: The Sexual Revolution, An Unfettered History* (Boston, Little, Brown, 2000) 300.

14   2 Genesis 25, *New English Bible.*

15   3 Genesis 7.

16   Ibid.

Chapter 1

1   See the Boston Women's Health Book Collective, *Our Bodies, Ourselves For the New Century* (New York, Touchstone, 1998) 269-270.

2   Kathryn Cox et al (eds.), *The Good Housekeeping Illustrated Guide To Women's Health* (New York, William Morrow, 1995).

3   Boston Women's Health Book Collective, 269-270.

4   Christiane Northrup, *Women's Bodies, Women's Wisdom: Creating Physical And Emotional Health And Healing* (New York, Bantam Books, 1998) 260.

5   For a fascinating discussion of the reflexive nature of the emotional mind by the foremost researcher in this area, see Joseph Ledoux, *The Emotional Brain: The Mysterious Underpinnings*

Of Emotional Life (New York, Simon & Schuster, 1996). See also A. Ohman, "Fear And Anxiety As Emotional Phenomena: Clinical Phenomenology, Evolutionary Persepctives, And Information Processing Mechanisms," in M. Lewis & J.M. Haviland (eds.), *Handbook Of Emotions* (New York, Guildford Press, 1993).

6   These experiments are discussed by Felicia Pratto, "Consciousness And Automatic Evaluation," in P.M. Niedenthal and S. Kitayama (eds.), *The Heart's Eye: Emotional Influences In Perception And Attention* (New York, Academic Press, 1994).

7   J.B. Watson and R. Rayner, "Conditioned Emotional Reactions," *Journal Of Experimental Psychology* 3 (1920) 1-14.

8   Ronald Kleinknecht, *Mastering Anxiety: The Nature and Treatment Of Anxious Conditions* (New York, Plenum Press, 1991) 39.

9   For a recent outline of research into the causes of phobias see: Harald Merckelbach et al, "The Etiology Of Specific Phobias: A Review," *Clinical Psychology Review* 16 (1996) 337-361.

10 Helen Singer Kaplan, *Sexual Aversion, Sexual Phobias, And Panic Disorder* (New York, Brunner/Mazel, 1987) 3. See also Catherine Fogel and Diane Lauver, *Sexual Health Promotion* (Philadelphia, Saunders, 1990) 527.

11 Daniel Goleman examines that issue in detail in *Vital Lies, Simple Truths* (New York, Simon & Schuster, 1985).

12 See Gabbie E. Smith et al, "Sexual Attitudes, Cognitive Associative Networks, And Perceived Vulnerability To Unplanned Pregnancy," *Journal of Research in Personality* 30 (1996), 88-102.

13 Goleman, 107.

14 Ibid. Emphasis in original.

15 Thomas Gilovich, *How We Know What Isn't So: The Fallibility Of Human Reason In Everyday Life* (New York, Free Press, 1991) 77.

16 A. Arntz et al, "If I Feel Anxious, There Must Be Danger: The Fallacy of Ex Consequentia Reasoning in Inferring Danger in Anxiety Disorders," *Behavior Research and Therapy* 33 (1995) 917-925.

Chapter 2

1   See, for example, a survey conducted in Britain sponsored by The Naturist Study Group and others: http://www.combes.swinternet.co.uk/rec54/docs/pubrpt.pdf.

2   Polls reported in paragraph 111 of the article "205 Arguments And Observations In Support Of Naturism" found at the Naturist Society website www.naturist.com/resources/205_107.htm

3   Ann Landers, "Freedom-loving Dad Needs to Cover Himself in Front of Children," syndicated column, 6 April 2000.

4   Cited by Mark Storey in "Why This Dread Of Nakedness? We Should Ask That Of Drs. Freud & Spock," *Nude & Natural: The Quarterly Journal of Clothes-Optional Living* 18.3 15 March 1999, 71.

5   Paul Okami, "Childhood Exposure To Family Nudity, Parent-Child Co-Sleeping And 'Primal Scenes': A Review Of Clinical Opinion And Empirical Evidence," *The Journal of Sex Research* 32 (1995) 53.

6   D. Finklehor, "The Sexual Climate in Families," (unpublished paper), Family Violence Research Laboratory, University of New Hampshire, 1980, cited in Ronald and Juliette Goldman, *Children's Sexual Thinking* (London, Routledge, 1982) 325.

7   Robert Lawlor, *Voices Of The First Day: Awakening In The Aboriginal Dreamtime* (Rochester, Vermont, Inner Traditions, 1991) 83.

8   Ramón A. Gutiérrez, *When Jesus Came, The Corn Mothers Went Away: Marriage, Sexuality, And Power In New Mexico, 1500-1846* (Stanford, Stanford University Press, 1991) 72.

9   Benjamin Spock and Steven Parker, *Dr. Spock's Baby And Child Care* (New York, Dutton, 1998, 7th edition, 460-461.

10 See Lois Shawver "Sexual Modes, The Etiquette Of Disregard, And The Question Of Gays And Lesbians In The Military," in M. Herek et al (eds.), *Out In Force: Sexual Orientation And The Military* (Chicago, University of Chicago Press, 1996) 234.

11   See Jack Morin, *The Erotic Mind: Unlocking The Inner Sources Of Sexual Passion And Fulfillment* (New York, HarperCollins, 1995) 55.

12   See S. Rachman, "Sexual Fetishism: An Experimental Analogue," *The Psychological Record* 16 (1966) 293-296.

13   Gary Brooks, *The Centerfold Syndrome: How Men Can Overcome Objectification And Achieve Intimacy With Women* (San Francisco, Jossey-Bass, 1995) 107-120.

14   See, for example, Freud's comments in T*he Standard Edition of the Complete Psychological Works of Sigmund Freud*, James Strachey (ed.), (London, Horgarth, 1974) vol. 9, 218.

15   See Okami.

16   Charley M. Johnson and Robert W. Deisher, "Contemporary Communal Child Rearing: A First Analysis," *Pediatrics* 52 (1973) 325.

17   M.D. Story, "Factors Associated With More Positive Body Self-Concepts In Preschool Children," *The Journal of Social Psychology* 108 (1979) 49-56.

18   "First Time Reports," www.netnude.com/main/newn1.html.

19   Thomas Gilovich, *How We Know What Isn't So: The Fallibility Of Human Reason In Everyday Life* (New York, Free Press, 1991) 112.

20   Bernie Zilbergeld, *The New Male Sexuality* (New York, Bantam, 1992) 43-44.

Chapter 3

1   Miriam and Otto Ehrenberg, *The Intimate Circle: The Sexual Dynamics Of Family Life* (New York, Simon & Shuster, 1988) 46.

2   Ruth Westheimer, *Sex and Morality: Who Is Teaching Our Sex Standards?* (Orlando, Harcourt, Brace Jovanovich, 1988) 71.

3   Ibid. 70.

4   D. Finklehor, "The Sexual Climate in Families," (unpublished paper), Family Violence Research Laboratory, University of New Hampshire, 1980, cited in Ronald and Juliette Goldman, *Children's Sexual Thinking* (London, Routledge, 1982) 325.

5   See Aileen Goodson, *Therapy, Nudity, And Joy* (Los Angeles, Elysium Growth Press, 1991) 210-214.

6   "Success Story: Kansas House Bill 2726 (2000)," Naturist Action Committee website: www.nac.oshkosh.net.

7   Reported by, of all people, Ann Landers, "Good Judgment Shown In Case Of Nudist," *Vancouver Sun* 12 June 1997.

8   "Stuck In Stripes," www.foxnews.com 10 August 2000.

9   *New York Penal Law* 245.01.

10   *Canadian Criminal Code* Section 174.

11   This rule is often referred to as the "Cahill Policy," named for the park Superintendent who created it in 1977. See *The Nude and Natural Newsletter* August 1999, 4.

12   Duwayne Escobedo "Naverre Strips Beach's Nudity," *Northwest Florida Daily News* 13 April 1999, A1. See also *The Nude and Natural Newsletter* August 1999, 4.

13   "At Black's A Line In The Sand," *The Nude and Natural Newsletter* August 1999, 4.

14   "City Proposes Sweeping Anti-Nudity Ordinance," website of the Naturist Action Committee www.nac.oshkosh.net.

15   Advisory of the Naturist Action Committee www.naturistsociety.com/NAC, August 9, 2000.

16   John Sullivan, "Court Rules Nude Photo Can Be Taken On The Street," *New York Times* 20 May 2000 B4.

17   *Mark v. State of Oregon* 158 Or. App 355 (Oregon Court of Appeals, 17 Feb 1999).

18   "The Girl From Ipanema Goes Walking And The Police Say, 'Uh, Uh'," *Vancouver Sun* 11 February 2000 A17.

19   "Court Convicts, Jails Topfree Great-Grandmother," *The Nude and Natural Newsletter* Sep/Oct 1999 4.

20   Chris Wattie, "You're Not Naked If You Have Shoes On," *National Post* 22 September 2002.

21   "Should Going Topless On Public Beaches Be Legal?" *Cosmopolitan* June 1998, 54.

22   "Bare Breasts Do Not Equality Achieve," *National Post* 28 June 2000, A18.

23   See Max Stackhouse, *Creeds, Society And Human Rights: A Study In Three Cultures* (Grand Rapids, Michigan, Eerdmans, 1984).

24   See *The People v. Santorelli et al* 80 N.Y. 2d 875 (New York Court of Appeals, 1992).

25   Jules Crittenden and Ellen J. Silberman, "Women bare breasts in Hub seeking right to go topless," *Boston Herald* 19 May 2001.

26   "Women's Group Demands Law Against Females Going Topless," *Vancouver Sun* 10 February 1998.

27   "Religious Group, Legislature Target Mazo Beach," *The Nude and Natural Newsletter* Sep/Oct 1999 1.

28   S. Mineka et al, "Observational Conditioning Of Snake Fear In Rhesus Monkeys," *Journal Of Abnormal Psychology* 93 (1984) 355-372.

Chapter 4

1   "UF Researcher: Erotic Photos Deter Some Women From Breast Self-Exams," *UF News* www.napa.ufl.edu/98news/erotic.htm (17 April 1998).

2   Terry O'Neill, *Tri-City News* 26 January 2000.

3   Internet Content Rating Assocation, www.icra.org

4   Quoted in the *F.C.C. Memorandum In the Matter of WPBN/WTOM*, 11 January 2000 found at www.fcc.gov/eb/Orders/fcc0010.html.

5   Unfortunately I lost the clipping of the tabloid and the date of the issue in question. The story received national coverage in Mexico. Some newspapers did publish uncensored images of the naked strikers. See, for example, *La Jornada* 9 January 1997, 1.

6   *Vancouver Sun* 20 August 1999 B1.

7   *Vancouver Sun* 17 June 2000 A3.

8   *National Post* 15 March 2000 A16.

9   *National Post* 15 November 1999.

10   *Rolling Stone* 25 November 1999 48.

11   *New York Times Magazine* 30 January 2000 36.

12   "The Prizes Of War," *Maclean's Magazine* 25 April 1994.

13   From the "The Language of the Sexes," in "*The Human Sexes*" series, aired on TLC 14 October 2000.

14   See the Frontline website: www.pbs.org/wgbh/pages/frontline/shows/porn/etc/two.html

15   "Documentary Makers In Search Of Money," *National Post* 4 May 2000.

16   The SPJ Code of Ethics; see www.spj.org/ethics/code.htm.

17   RTNDA Code of Ethics; see www.rtnda.org/ethics/coe.shtml.

18   Brandon Tilman and Milton Hollstein, "Journalism Faces A Serious Technological Threat," *Journal of Undergraduate Research* (University of Utah) 7(1) (1999) 51-58,

19   Adam Buckman, "Penis Puppeteers Told To Zip It," www.foxnews.com 8 October 2002

20   Stephen Holden, "Hollywood, Sex And A Sad Estrangement," *New York Times* 3 May 1998 20.

21   David Bianculli, "Cable Channel Lets It All Hang Out," *New York Daily News* 11 June 2002.

22   "Film-Maker Wouldn't Bow To Prurience," *Vancouver Sun* 17 March 2000.

23   See "Advertising Complaints Report," Advertising Standards Canada.

24   *Premiere* March 2000 79.

25   See, for example, the bus advertising policy of the Greensboro North Carolina transit authority: www.ci.greensboro.nc.us/gdot/public_trans/busads.htm

26   Michael Fancher, "'Sex and Lucia' Flap: Why Ad and News Decisions are Separate," *Seattle Times* 25 August 2002. Communication with Donna Tuggle, Display Advertising Director, *Seattle Times*, 23 September 2002.

27   Richard Marusa, "American Prudery, And Its Opposite," *New York Times*, 19 Feb 2000 15.

28   "Is It Really Art Or Is It Obscene," *New York Times* 11 July 1999.

29   David Shaw, *The Pleasure Police* (New York, Doubleday, 1996) 172.

30 *Virginian-Pilot Online* 6,11, 20 September 2000 www.pilotonline.com.
31 The painting can be viewed online at: www.earlyamerica.com/review/fall96/crossing.html.
32 Reported by the Thomas Jefferson Center for the Protection of Free Expression 13 April 2000: www.tjcenter.org/muzzles.html#sims.
33 "Freedom of Expression or Public Obscenity," *The Daily Californian* 11 November 1996 5.
34 David Shaw, "Nine Nudes, Few Objections," *The Post Standard* (Syracuse, NY) 7 June 2003.
35 Colleen Mastony, "School Tries To Patch Up Student Art Controversy," *Chicago Tribune*, 10 May 2003
36 See Marcia Pally, *Sex and Sensibility* (Hopewell, New Jersey, New Ecco Press, 1994) 7, and Nat Hentoff, "Sexual Harassment by Francisco Goya," *Washington Post* 27 Dec 1991.
37 Eugene Volokh, "Freedom of Speech and Appellate Review in Workplace Harassment Cases," 90 NW. U. L. Rev. 1009 (1996), www.law.ucla.edu/faculty/volokh/apprevie.htm#24, citing "It's Art Vs. Sexual Harassment," *The Tennesseean* (Nashville), Mar. 1, 1996, 1A.
38 Nicole Miller, "Is Nude Rude? The Great Federal Coverup," *Washington Post*, 24 October 2002 C05.
39 "Its What's Up Front That Got Painting Tossed Out," *Philadelphia Daily News* 20 September 1999.
40 "Artist Questions Removal Of Painting From Illinois State Fair," *Associated Press* 21 August 2000.
41 See for example the U.S. Supreme Court decision in *Manual Enterprises v. Day* 370 U.S. 478 (1962).
42 18 U.S.C. S 2256(8).
43 Andrew Jacobs, "Grandmother, Nude Photos And Charges," *New York Times*, 13 Feb 2000, 6. Debra Galant, "Anger and Pain Over Nude Photos," *New York Times*, 30 July 2000, 7.
44 "Mother Speaks About Being Accused Of Taking Lewd Photos Of Her Child," *Associated Press* 18 April 2000. www.freedomforum.org/news/2000/04/2000-04-18-05.asp.
45 "Child Porn Charges Withdrawn Against Dad," *Ottawa Citizen*, www.thecitizen.com/city/000413/3925097.html; "When Picture Is Worth A Thousand Worries," www.nudity.com/articles/nudity/society/hst246html.
46 David Clouston, "Wal-Mart Sued For Calling Police," *The Salina Journal* (Kansas) 12 December 2002.
47 Quoted in "Corporate Image vs. Right to Privacy," *Insight Magazine* online edition 19 June 2000 www.insightmag.com.
48 *Ibid.*
49 Email communication from Lisa Carparelli, Manager Public Relations, The New York Times Company 24 February 2000.
50 Marcia Pally 135.
51 "Naked Came The Rider," *Indiana University School of Journalism Ethics Cases*: www.journalism.indiana.edu/ethics/naked/html.
52 New York, Times Books, 1999.
53 See report by F.C.C. researcher Douglas A. Galbi, "Communications Policy, Media Development, and Convergence" 18 January 2001, available at: http://users.erols.com/dgalbi/telpol/media2.pdf.
54 Manish Bhatia, Nielsen Media Research, "TV Viewing in Internet Households," March 2000, www.mrcc-online.com

Chapter 5

1 Helen Singer Kaplan, *Sexual Aversion, Sexual Phobias, And Panic Disorder* (New York, Brunner/Mazel, 1987) 52.
2 Raymond J. Lawrence Jr., *The Poisoning Of Eros: Sexual Values In Conflict* (New York, Augustine Moore Press, 1989) 14.
3 Ibid. 127.

4   Quoted in Peter Gardella, *Innocent Ecstasy* (New York, Oxford University Press, 1985) 6.

5   Immanuel Kant, "The Philosophy of Law," in *Morality and Moral Controversies*, John Arthur (ed.), (Englewood Cliffs, N.J., Prentice-Hall, 1993) 254.

6   See, for example, Raymond A. Belliotti, *Good Sex: Perspectives On Sexual Ethics* (Lawrence, University Press of Kansas, 1993) 18-19.

7   Heinrich Zimmer, *Philosophies Of India* (Princeton, NJ, Princeton University Press, 1951) 434.

8   See, for example, Miranda Shaw, *Passionate Enlightenment: Women In Tantric Buddhism* (Princeton, NJ, Princeton University Press, 1994).

9   Christine Gudorf, *Body, Sex and Pleasure: Reconstructing Christian Sexual Ethics* (Cleveland, Pilgrim Press, 1994); Marvin Ellison, *Erotic Justice: A Liberating Ethic Of Sexuality* (Louisville, Kentucky, Westminster John Knox Press, 1996).

10   Peter Brown, *The Body and Society: Men, Women, and Sexual Renunciation in Early Christianity* (New York, Columbia University Press, 1988) 242.

11   Michelle Fine, "Sexuality, Schooling, and Adolescent Females: The Missing Discourse of Desire," *Harvard Educational Review* 58 (1988) 29.

12   Paul Robinson, *The Modernization of Sex* (New York, Harper Colophon, 1976) vii.

13   See Rosalind P. Petchesky, "Sexual Rights: Inventing A Concept, Mapping An International Practice," in Richard Parker et al (eds.), *Framing The Sexual Subject: The Politics Of Gender Sexuality And Power* (Berkeley, University of California Press, 2000) 94.

14   For the effects of shame, see John Bradshaw, *Healing The Shame That Binds You* (Deerfield Beach Forida, Health Communications Inc, 1988) and Stephen Pattison, *Shame: Theory, Therapy, Theology* (Cambridge, Cambridge University Press, 2000).

15   Edward O. Laumann et al, *The Social Organization Of Sexuality* (Chicago, University of Chicago Press, 1994) 85.

16   John H. Gagnon and William Simon, *Social Conduct: the Social Sources of Human Sexuality* (Chicago, Aldine, 1973) 56.

17   Lonnie Barbach, *For Yourself: The Fulfillment Of Female Sexuality* (New York, Doubleday, 1975) 39.

18   Carol Cassell, *Swept Away: Why Women Fear Their Own Sexuality* (New York, Simon & Schuster, 1984).

19   Nancy Friday, *My Secret Garden* (New York, Simon & Schuster, 1998) xvi.

20   Mary Krueger, "Sexism, Erotophobia, And The Illusory 'No': Implications For Acquaintance Rape Awareness," *Journal of Psychology and Human Sexuality* 8 (1996) 109.

21   Morton Hunt, *The Natural History Of Love* (New York, Knopf, 1959) 127.

22   Stella Resnick, *The Pleasure Zone* (Berkeley, Conari Press, 1997).

23   Russell Vannoy, *Sex Without Love* (Buffalo, Prometheus Books, 1980) 97.

24   Kinsey, A. C., Pomeroy, W. B., and Martin, C. E., *Sexual Behavior in the Human Male* (Philadelphia, W. B. Saunders, 1948).

25   According to Dr, John Dean, MB, BS, MRCGP, a Medical Sexologist in Plymouth, writing in the July 1999 issue of *One In Ten*, a publication of the British Impotence Association, available at www.sda.uk.net.

26   *JAMA* vol 281 No 6 10 February 1999.

27   Zilbergeld, op cit. 117.

28   David Snarch, *Passionate Marriage: Love, Sex, and Intimacy in Emotionally Committed Relationships* (New York, Henry Holt, 1997) 99.

29   David Shaw, *The Pleasure Police: How Bluenose Busybodies And Lilylivered Alarmists Are Trying To Take All The Fun Out Of Life* (1996, Doubleday, New York) 163.

30   Dr. Jean Marmoreo, "Sex Once A Year? You're Not Alone," *National Post* 13 March 2001 B1.

31   Seymour Fisher, *Sexual Images Of The Self: The Psychology Of Erotic Sensations And Illusions* (Hillisdale, NJ, Lawrence Erlbaum Associates, 1989) 41.

32   Max Caulfield, *Mary Whitehouse* (London, Mobreys, 1975) 96.

33   Gay Talese, *Thy Neighbor's Wife* (New York, Dell, 1980) 420.

34   Ibid.

35   Martin Kantor, *Homophobia: Description, Development And Dynamics Of Gay Bashing* (Westport,

CT, Praeger, 1998). See Chapter 8 "Paranoid Homophobes."

36   Riane Eilser, *Sacred Pleasure: Sex, Myth, And The Politics Of The Body* (New York, HarperCollins, 1995) 206.

37   Sibylle Artz, *Sex, Power And The Violent School Girl*, (Toronto, Trifolium Books, 1998) 80.

38   D. H. Lawrence, *Sex, Literature And Censorship* (London, Heinemann, 1955) 205.

39   Ellen Bass and Laura Davis, *The Courage To Heal: A Guide For Women Survivors Of Child Sexual Abuse* (New York, Harper & Row, 1994) 273.

40   Jack Morin, *The Erotic Mind: Unlocking The Inner Sources Of Sexual Passion And Fulfillment* (New York, HarperCollins, 1995) 84.

41   Ibid 92.

42   Sigmund Freud, "On The Universal Tendency To Debasement In The Sphere Of Love," *The Standard Edition of the Complete Psychological Works of Sigmund Freud*, James Strachey (ed.), (London, Horgarth, 1974) vol. 11, 179.

43   See Morin 196.

44   18 Leviticus 23, and 20 *Leviticus* 13.

45   20 Leviticus 10.

46   11 Leviticus 5-12.

47   20 *Leviticus* 9.

48   5 Matthew28

49   For example Vern and Bonnie Bullough in *Sexual Attitudes: Myths And Realities*, (Buffalo, Prometheus, 1995), Chapter 1 "Why The Hostility To Sex?" identify Greek and Christian morality as the root cause of negative sexual attitudes in the modern day.

50   John Boswell explores this issue in detail in *Social Tolerance And Homosexuality* (Chicago, University of Chicago Press, 1980).

Chapter 6

1   Wendy Shalit, *A Return To Modesty: Discovering The Lost Virtue* (New York, Simon & Schuster, 1999) 230.

2   Susan Jacoby, "Great Sex: What's Age Got To Do With It?" *Modern Maturity* Sept-Oct 1999 www.aarp.org/mmaturity/sept_oct99/greatsex.html.

3   "Casual Sex Loses Its Appeal For Youth" *The Bergen Record* 8 Dec 1999.

4   See A.H. McLean, "What Kind Of Love Is This?", *Sciences* (1994) 34, 36-48; Galindo, D. and Kaiser, F.E., "Sexual Health after 60," *Patient Care* (1995) 29, 25-30.

5   Lisa Anderson, "Caregivers Addressing Sex Among Elderly," *Chicago Tribune* 2 June 2002.

6   4 Thess 3-7.

7   Milligan College, Student Guidelines: www.milligan.edu.

8   Dan Egan, "A Moral Dilemma: Julie, BYU and 'The Real World'" *Salt Lake Tribune* 9 July 2000.

9   "Hoop Star's Dad Hopes His Son Learns A Lesson" *The Province* 13 March 2000 A3c.

10   Ethan Bronner, "Lawsuit On Sex Bias By 2 Mothers, 17," *New York Times* 06 August 1998, 14.

11   CNN.com "Southern Baptists Vote Against Women Pastors," 14 June 2000 www.cnn.com/2000/US/06/14/southern.baptists.02/

12   Richard Posner and Katherine Silbaugh, *A Guide to America's Sex Laws* (Chicago, University of Chicago Press, 1996) 101.

13   Megan Boldt, "N.D. Law Forbids Unmarried Cohabitation," www.KansasCity.com 3 April 2003

14   Posner and Silbaugh 6.

15   Ibid. 12.

16   Bill Rankin, "High Court Strikes Sex Law," *The Atlanta Journal-Constitution* 14 January 2003.

17   Quoted in Carol Cassell, *Straight From The Heart* (New York, Simon and Schuster, 1987) 95.

18   James Brooke, "An Old Law Chastises Pregnant Teen-Agers," *New York Times* 28 October 1996, A10.

19   Eric Frazier and Gary Wright, "Halt Cohabiting Or No Bail," *Charlotte Observer* 4 April 2001.

20   Linda Hirshman and Jane Larson, *Hard Bargains: The Politics Of Sex* (Oxford, Oxford University Press, 1998) 261.

21   Seymour Fisher, *Sexual Images Of The Self: The Psychology Of Erotic Sensations And Illusions* (Hillisdale, NJ, Lawrence Erlbaum Associates, 1989) 41.

22   Several studies show that trend. See, for example, W. Griffit, "Sexual Intimacy In Aging Marital Partners," in J. Marsh and S. Kiesler (eds), *Aging: Stability And Change In The Family* (New York, Academic, 1981).

23   Bernie Zilbergeld, *The New Male Sexuality* (New York, Bantam, 1992) 60.

24   Raymond A. Belliotti, *Good Sex: Perspectives On Sexual Ethics* (Lawrence, University Press of Kansas, 1993) 43.

25   Ibid. 44.

26   "Halliwell Offers," *Vancouver Sun* 16 June 1999.

27   Belliotti 45.

28   Richard Posner, *Sex and Reason* (Cambridge, MA, Harvard University Press, 1992) 324-41.

29   Audrey Leathard, *The Fight For Family Planning: The Development Of Family Planning Services In Britain 1921-74* (London, Macmillan Press, 1980) 222.

30   See Angus McLaren, *Birth Control In Nineteenth-Century England* (London, Croom Helm, 1978).

31   Quoted in John D'Emilio and Estelle B. Freedman, *Intimate Matters: A History Of Sexuality in America* (New York, Harper & Row, 1988) 244.

32   William H. Masters and Virginia E. Johnson, *Human Sexual Response* (Boston, Little, Brown, 1966) 133.

33   Lonnie Barbach, *For Yourself: The Fulfillment Of Female Sexuality* (New York, Doubleday, 1975).

34   Christine Gudorf, *Body, Sex and Pleasure: Reconstructing Christian Sexual Ethics* (Cleveland, Pilgrim Press, 1994) 16.

35   See the *Oxford English Dictionary* (Oxford, Oxford University Press, 1971).

36   Edward O. Laumann et al, *The Social Organization of Sexuality* ((Chicago, University of Chicago, 1994)81.

37   Barbach 90.

38   Ibid.

39   Laumann 85.

40   Ibid.

41   Anonymous, "The Sex Sin He Won't Confess," *Cosmopolitan Magazine* January 1999 90.

42   Lynn Ponton, *The Sex Lives of Teenagers: Revealing the Secret World of Adolescent Boys and Girls* (New York, Dutton, 2000).

43   Ibid. 61.

44   Laumann 81.

45   June Singer, *Androgyny: Toward A New Theory Of Sexuality* (Garden City, N.Y., Anchor Press, 1976) 303;

46   Fisher 84.

47   E.J. Haeberle, *The Sex Atlas* (New York, Continuum, 1981) 202; Rene Spitz, "Authority and Masturbation," *Psychoanalytic Quarterly* (1952) 21 490.

48   Elaine Yates *Sex Without Shame: Encouraging the Child's Healthy Sexual Development* (New York, Quill, 1982) 28.

49   "New Light Shed On Normal Sex Behavior In A Child" *New York Times* 7 April 1998 7.

50   Yates 105.

51   Ibid.167.

52   www.allaboutsex.org/IgotCaughtDisplay.cfm?A_Z=ASC.

53   Thomas C. Fox, *Sexuality And Catholicism* (New York, Braziller, 1995) 257.

54   Tim LaHaye, *Sex Education Is For The Family* (Grand Rapids, Zondervan Publishing, 1985) 81.

55   Belliotti 101.

56   Roger Scruton, *Sexual Desire: A Moral Philosophy of the Erotic* (New York, Free Press, 1986).

57   Vern Bullogh, *Science In The Bedroom: A History Of Sex Research* (New York, BasicBooks, 1994) 20-23.

58   Yates 27.

59   Yates 28, quoting Dr. Haim Ginott.

60   Quoted by Edward Rowan, *The Joy of Self-Pleasuring: Why Feel Guilty About Feeling Good* (Amherst, NY, Prometheus Books, 2000) 133.

61   Ibid. 135.

62   Ibid.

63   Ibid. 136.

64   Ibid. 137.

65   Betty Dodson, *Sex For One: The Joy of Selfloving* (New York, Crown, 1996).

66   See Barbach.

67   Joani Blank (ed.), *First Person Sexual: Women and Men Write About Self-Pleasuring* (San Francisco, Down There Press, 1996).

68   "Elders Practiced 'Unsafe Speech'" *Miami Herald* 16 December 1994.

69   Joani Blank and Marcia Quackenbush, *A Kid's First Book About Sex* (Burlingame, CA, Yes Press, 1983).

70   Margaret Leroy, *Pleasure: The Truth About Female Sexuality* (London, Harper Collins, 1993) 36.

71   Anonymous, "The Sex Sin He Won't Confess," *Cosmopolitan Magazine* January 1999 90.

72   "Sex Files To Push Envelop," *The Expositor* (Brantford, Ontario) 7 October 2000.

73   "Britain Orders Lingerie Adverts To Come Down," *Agence France Presse* (English) 20 October 2000

74   Mark Fleisher and John Shaw, "Celibacy in American Prisons," in Elisa Sobo and Sandra Bell (eds.), *Celibacy, Culture, and Society* (Madison, The University of Wisconsin Press, 2001) 230.

75   See *Rodgers v. Ohio Dept. of Rehabilitation and Correction*, 91 Ohio App. 3d 565, 632 N.E.2d 1355 (1993).

76   Sally Wendkos Olds, *The Eternal Garden: Seasons Of Our Sexuality* (New York, Times Books, 1985) 41.

77   D'Emilio and Freedman 268-70.

78   Ibid. 336.

79   Posner and Silbaugh 67.

80   "LA High Court Upholds Sodomy Law," www.PlanetOut.com 07 July 2000.

81   Ibid.

82   Philip Blumstein and Pepper Schwartz in American Couples, (New York, William Morrow, 1983) have an interesting section on oral sex inhibitions 233.

83   *Bowers v. Hardwick*, 478 US 186 (1986).

84   *Lawrence v. Texas*, 539 US (2003). See also Linda Greenhouse, "Justices, 6-3, Legalize Gay Sexual Conduct in Sweeping Reversal of Court's '86 Ruling," *New York Times* 27 June 2003.

85   See Jack Morin, *Anal Pleasure And Health: A Guide For Men And Women* (San Francisco, Down There Press, 1998).

86   Ibid.

87   *Susie Bright's Sexual State Of The Union* (New York, Simon & Schuster, 1997) 144.

88   *Williams v. Pryor* 240 F.3d 944 (11th Circuit Court of Appeals) 31 January 2001.

89   Kim Chandler, "Lawmakers Won't Repeal Sex Toy Ban," *Birmingham News* 30 April 2003.

90   John Lynch, "Police Find 17 Sex Toys In Local Woman's Car During DUI Traffic Stop," *Longview News Journal* 21 November 2002.

91   Derrick Penner, "U.S. Bank Gives Vancouver Sex Shop The Cold Shoulder," *Vancouver Sun*, 19 February 2003.

92   Kevin Griffin, "Bard Rejects Sex Shop Ad," *Vancouver Sun* 3 May 2003.

Chapter 7

1   Ira Reiss, *An End To Shame* (Buffalo, N.Y., Prometheus Books, 1990) 42.

2   CDC, 2001 Youth Risk Behavior Surveillance System, Sexual Beahviors.

3   Susheela Singh and Jacqueline E. Darroch, "Trends in Sexual Activity Among Adolescent American Women: 1982-1995," *Family Planning Perspectives* 31(5) September/October 1999

4   Lillian Rubin, *Erotic Wars: What Happened To The Sexual Revolution?* (New York, Farrar, Strass & Giroux, 1990) 61.

5   Sharon Thompson, "Putting A Big Thing Into A Little Hole: Teenage Girls' Accounts Of Sexual Initiation," *Journal of Sex Research* (1990) 27(3) 358-61.

6   The Alan Guttmacher Institute, "Teenage pregnancy: Overall Trends And State-By-State Information," *Teenage Pregnancy Statistics*, April 1999, www.agi-usa.org/pubs/teen_preg_stats.html.

7   CDC, op cit.

8   Elaine Yates, *Sex Without Shame: Encouraging the Child's Healthy Sexual Development* (New York, Quill, 1982) 209-210.

9   John Money, *Love and Love Sickness: The Science of Sex, Gender Difference and Pair-bonding* (Baltimore, Johns Hopkins University Press, 1980) 55.

10 Sally Wendkos Olds, *The Eternal Garden: Seasons Of Our Sexuality* (New York, Times Books, 1985) 46.

11 Peter S. Bearman and Hannah Brückner, "Promising the Future: Virginity Pledges and First Intercourse," *American Journal of Sociology* 106(4) (2001) 859.

12 Floyd Martinson, *The Sexual Life Of Children* (Westport, CN, Bergin & Garvey, 1994) 39.

13 Olds, 46.

14 Elaine Yates, 196-7.

15 "Sex And The Single Teen," *Maclean's* 28 December "1998 48.

16 National Campaign To Prevent Teen Pregnancy, "The Cautious Generation? Teens Tell Us About Sex, Virginity, and 'The Talk'," 27 April 2000 www.teenpregnancy.org.

17 Laurie Goodstein, "Teen-Age Poll Finds A Turn To The Traditional," *New York Times*, 30 April 1998, 20.

18 *Rubin*, 24.

19 Ibid. 70-1.

20 Emily White, *Fast Girls: Teenage Tribes and the Myth of the Slut* (New York, Scribner, 2002) 116. See also Leora Tanenbaum, *Slut!: Growing Up Female With a Bad Reputation* (New York, Seven Stories Press, 1999).

21 Mary Krueger, "Sexism, Erotophobia, And The Illusory 'No': Implications For Acquaintance Rape Awareness," *Journal of Psychology and Human Sexuality* 8 (1996) 111. Emphasis in the original. Quoting Audre Lorde, "Uses Of The Erotic: The Erotic As Power," in *Sister Outsider: Essays And Speeches* (Trumansburg, NY, Crossing Press, 1984) 53-59.

22 Mary Piper, *Reviving Ophelia: Saving The Selves Of Adolescent Girls* (New York, Grosset/Putnam, 1994) 210.

23 "Clitoris: still a forbidden word," *Contemporary Sexuality* 21(2) (1989) 3.

24 Coleen Kelly Mast, *Sex Respect: The Option of True Sexual Freedom* (Bradley, Ill, Respect Incorporated, 1997).

25 Sharon Lerner, "Just Say No To Sex; Just Say Yes To Big Bucks," *Salon.com* 23 September 1999.

26 Ron Haskins and Carol Statuto Bevan, "Abstinence Education under Welfare Reform," American Enterprise Institute, 1997, www.aei.org/sw/swhaskinsbevan.htm.

27 Advocates for Youth, "Administration to Dump More Taxpayer Money Into Unproven Abstinence-Only-Until-Marriage Programs," www.advocatesforyouth.org 31 January 2003.

28 Doug Sanders, "Compromise Saves UN Deal," *Globe and Mail* 11 May 2002.

29 "Sex Abstinence Becomes Rule At US Schools," *Sunday Times* 16 December 1999.

30 See Mauldon, J. & Luker, K., "The effects of contraceptive education on method use at first intercourse," *Family Planning Perspectives* 28 (1998) 19-24.

31 Reiss 73.
32 Ibid. 125.
33 Reported by Marty Klein, *Sexual Intelligence* June 2002 www.sexualintelligence.org.
34 SIECUS, "What's Wrong With Abstinence-Only Sexuality Education Programs?" 2002.
35 See SEICUS, *Policy Update*, April 2002 www.siecus.org/policy/PUpdates/pdate0013.html.
36 Marty Klein, *Sexual Intelligence* May 2002 www.sexualintelligence.org.
37 Janice M. Irvine, *Talk About Sex: The Battles Over Sex Education in the United States* (Berkeley, University of California Press, 2002).
38 Christina Larson, "Pork For Prudes," *Washington Monthly* September 2002.
39 Ibid.
40 "Survey Finds Parents Favor More Detailed Sex Education," *New York Times* 4 October 2000.
41 Human Rights Watch, "Ignorance Only: Hiv/Aids, Human Rights And Federally Funded Abstinence-Only Programs In The United States. Texas: A Case Study," September 2002 http://www.hrw.org/reports/2002/usa0902/index.htm.
42 See Naomi Wolff, *Promiscuities* (New York, Random House, 1997) 170-171; Carol Cassel, *Straight From The Heart* (New York, Simon & Schuster, 1987) 84-85; Karen Bouris, *The First Time: Women Speak Out About "Losing Their Virginity"* (Emeryville, CA, Conari Press, 1993) 196-203. Olds, 40, 70.
43 Sharon Thompson, op. cit.
44 See Daniel Goleman, *Emotional Intelligence* (New York, Bantam, 1995).
45 Thompson 355.
46 "Elders Practiced 'Unsafe Speech'," *Miami Herald* 16 December 1994.
47 S. Guttmacher et al, "Condom Availability in New York City Public High Schools: Relationships to Condom Use and Sexual Behavior," *American Journal of Public Health*, 87:9 (1997): 1430, 1428. See also: D. Sellers, S. McGraw, and J. McKinlay, "Does the Promotion and Distribution of Condoms Increase Teen Sexual Activity? Evidence from an HIV Prevention Program for Latino Youth," *American Journal of Public Health*, 84:12 (1994): 1952-59; F. Furstenberg, Jr., L. Geitz, J. Teitler, and C. Weiss, "Does Condom Availability Make a Difference? An Evaluation of Philadelphia's Health Resource Centers," *Family Planning Perspectives*, 29:3 (1997): 123-27; M. Schuster, R. Bell, S. Berry, and D. Kanouse, "Impact of a High School Condom Availability Program on Sexual Attitudes and Behaviors," *Family Planning Perspectives*, 30(2) (1998): 67-72.
48 "Condoms At Schools Still Limited," *New York Times* 03 October 1999 24.
49 Shannon Back, "Senior's Gift Of Condoms Goes Awry," *The Tampa Tribune* 25 May 2001.
50 "Teacher Fired For Condom Stunt," *Saskatoon Star – Phoenix* 1 February 2003.
51 Quoted in Naomi Wolff, *Promiscuities* (New York, Random House, 1997) 170.
52 Joe White, *Pure Excitement: A Radical Righteous Approach to Sex, Love, and Dating* (Colorado Springs, CO, Focus on the Family, 2000), see excerpt: www.family.org/lote/loteline/articles/a0013066.html.
53 Tim LaHaye, *Sex Education Is For The Family* (Grand Rapids, MI, Zondervan Publishing, 1985) 135.
54 www.nyscatholicconference.org/bishops/condom.html
55 "Condoms At Schools Still Limited" *New York Times* 03 October 1999 p 24.
56 Alan B. Spruyt, "User Behaviors And Characteristics Related To Condom Failure" by , *Family Health International*, 1999, www.fhi.org/en/fp/fpother/conom/conmon5.html
57 James Dobson, "Ask the Doctor: Why Should I Wait?," ww.family.org/lote/lotelive/articles/a0009650.html.
58 Bruce Rind et al, "The Clash of Media, Politics and Sexual Science," presented to the Joint Meeting of AASECT and SSSS, 6 November 1999, St. Louis, Missouri.
59 Judith Levine, *Harmful To Minors* (Minneapolis, MN, University of Minnesota Press, 2002).
60 Robert R. Worth, "Renegade View on Child Sex Causes a Storm," *New York Times*, 13 April 2002.

61   Melissa August et al, "Child Sexuality: Challenging The Taboos," *Time* 15 April 2002.
62   California Penal Code s.261.5.
63   *In re T.A.J.* (1998) 62 Cal.App.4th 1350 [73 Cal.Rptr.331]. Court of Appeal, First District, Division 2. See: www.courtinfo.ca.gov/programs/cfcc/resources/caselaw/delinque/delinq-13.htm.
64   *State of Oregon v. Justin Thorp* (CR97-00753; CA A101900) April 19, 2000 www.publications.ojd.state.or.us/A101900.htm.
65   "Springer Guest Arrested," *Beloit Daily News* 28 February 2001. See:
66   Philip Jenkins, *Moral Panic: Changing Concepts Of The Child Molester In Modern America* (New Haven, Yale University Press, 1998) 227.
67   Dalma Heyn, *The Erotic Silence of the American Wife* (New York, Random House, 1992) 69.
68   Laura Carpenter, "From Girls Into Women: Scripts For Sexuality And Romance In Seventeen Magazine, 1974-1994," *Journal of Sex Research* 35 (1998) 158-168 at 167.
69   Elizabeth Larsen, "Censoring Sex Information: The Story Of Sassy," *Utne Reader* July/August 1990.
70   See, for example, the Mehinaku of Brazil, described by Helen Fisher in *Anatomy Of Love: The Natural History Of Monogamy, Adultery, And Divorce* (New York, Norton, 1992) 266.
71   See, for example, the !Kung peoples of the African Kalahari, described by Marjorie Shostak in Nisa: *The Life And Words Of A !Kung Woman* (Cambridge, MA, Harvard University Press, 1981).
72   Philippe Aries, *Centuries of Childhood: A Social History of Family Life* (New York, Knopf, 1962).
73   Tim LaHaye, 49.
74   Ibid. 100.
75   Yates 197-8.
76   *Testimonies, True Love Waits* www.truelovewaits.com/test.htm
77   Sharon Lamb, *The Secret Lives of Girls: What Good Girls Really Do—Sex Play, Aggression, and Their Guilt* (New York, The Free Press, 2001) xiii.
78   Rubin 24.
79   Yates 201.
80   Seymour Fisher, *Sexual Images Of The Self: The Psychology Of Erotic Sensations And Illusions* (Hillsdale, NJ, Lawrence Erlbaum Associates, 1989) 41.

Chapter 8

1   Michele Mandel, "The Naked City: Sex Survey Gets Up Close And Personal," *The Toronto Sun*, 20 September 1999; Doskoch, P. "The Safest Sex," *Psychology Today* September 1995 46-49; Ellis, B. J., & Symons, D., "Sex Differences in Sexual Fantasy," *The Journal of Sex Research*, 27 (1990) 527-555. Jones, J. C. & Barlow, D. H., "Self-Reported Frequency of Sexual Urges, Fantasies, and Masturbatory Frequency in Heterosexual Males and Females," *Archives of Sexual Behavior* 19 (1990) 269-279.
2   Bernie Zilbergeld, *The New Male Sexuality* (New York, Bantam, 1992) 169.
3   Keith Mulvihill, "Most Fantasize About Sex Outside Relationship," *Reuters* 25 June 2001.
4   J. Mann et al, "Satiation Of The Transient Stimulation Effect Of Erotic Films," *Journal of Personality and Social Psychology* 30 (1974) 729.
5   William F. Fitzgerald, *SEX: What Every Young Woman Needs to Know* (San Jose, CA, Menequil Press, 1999).
6   See www.sexdoc.com/quess8.html.
7   David Snarch, *Passionate Marriage: Love, Sex, and Intimacy in Emotionally Committed Relationships* (New York, Henry Holt, 1997) 243.
8   Ibid. 243-244.
9   Kathlyn and Gay Hendricks, *The Conscious Heart: Seven Soul-Choices That Inspire Creative Partnership* (New York, Bantam, 1997) 47.
10   5 Matthew 28.
11   Weekly audience October 8, 1980, quoted in Snarch 272.

12 Barbara De Angelis, *Are You The One For Me?* (New York, Island Books, 1992) 230.

13 Ibid. 232.

14 See "Dr Phil On Adultery," February 2002 www.oprah.com.

15 Anne Stirling Hastings, *Discovering Sexuality that Will Satisfy You Both: When Couples Want Differing Amounts And Different Kinds Of Sex* (Tiburon, CA, The Printed Voice, 1993) 39.

16 See Donald Symons, *The Evolution of Human Sexuality* (New York, Oxford University Press, 1979) Chapter 7 "The Desire for Sexual Variety."

17 Helen Fisher, *Anatomy Of Love: The Natural History Of Monogamy, Adultery, And Divorce* (New York, Norton, 1992).

18 Robin Baker, *Sperm Wars: The Science Of Sex* (New York, 1996, Basic Books) 54.

19 Baker xxiv.

20 Pamela C. Regan and Ellen Berscheid, *Lust: What We Know About Human Sexual Desire* (Thousand Oaks, CA, Sage, 1999) 103.

21 Dalma Heyn, *The Erotic Silence of the American Wife* (New York, Random House, 1992) 25-30.

22 Terry Gould, *The Lifestyle: A Look at the Erotic Rites of Swingers* (Toronto, Random House, 1999) 150, 162.

23 David M. Buss, *The Dangerous Passion: Why Jealousy Is As Necessary As Love And Sex* (New York, Free Press, 2000).

24 Snarch, 312, emphasis in original.

25 Raymond Lawrence, *The Poisoning of Eros: Sexual Values In Conflict* (New York, Augustine Press, 1989) 63.

26 16 Luke 18.

27 Gould 225.

28 Ibid. 9.

29 Ibid.

30 Ibid. 86-87.

31 See, for example, the *Time* article by John Cloud, "Henry & Mary & Janet & . . . Is Your Marriage A Little Dull? The 'Polyamorists' Say There's Another Way," 15 Nov 1999.

32 See Richard Posner and Katherine Silbaugh, *A Guide to America's Sex Laws* (Chicago, University of Chicago Press, 1996) 103.

33 Michael A. Woronoff, "Public Employees Or Private Citizens: The Off-Duty Sexual Activities Of Police Officers And The Constitutional Right Of Privacy," *University of Michigan Journal of Law Reform* 18 (1984) 195.

34 For the full story of her ordeal see Kelly Flinn, *Proud To Be: My Life, The Air Force, The Controversy* (New York, Random House, 1997).

35 See Flinn 242-244.

36 Christine L. Williams et al, "Sexuality In The Workplace: Organization Control, Sexual Harassment, And The Pursuit Of Pleasure," *Annual Review of Sociology* (1999) 25: 73-93

37 "Fotheringham, Maclean's Guilty Of Libel," *Globe and Mail* 22 January 1986.

38 John Cloud, "Henry & Mary & Janet & ...Is Your Marriage A Little Dull? The 'Polyamorists' Say There's Another Way," *Time* 15 Nov 1999.

39 Ibid.

40 See www.lovemore.com/lmmagazine.html.

41 Deborah Anapol, *Polyamory: The New Love Without Limits*, (San Rafael, CA, Intinet Resource Center, 1997).

42 Dossie Easton and Catherine A. Liszt, *The Ethical Slut: A Guide to Infinite Sexual Possibilities* (Emeryville, CA, Greenery Press, 1998).

43 Stephen and Ondrea Levine, *Embracing the Beloved: Relationship As A Path Of Awakening* (New York, Anchor Books, 1995) 163-4.

44 See Lonnie Barbach, *For Yourself: The Fulfillment of Female Sexuality* (New York, Signet, 1975) 23-26.

Chapter 9

1   See, for example, Patricia Anderson, *Passion Lost: Public Sex, Private Desire in the Twentieth Century* (Toronto, Thomas Allen, 2001) 192.
2   Seymour Fisher, *Sexual Images Of The Self: The Psychology Of Erotic Sensations And Illusions* (Hillsdale, NJ, Lawrence Erlbaum, 1989) 15, citing Ronald and Juliette Goldman, *Children's Sexual Thinking* (London, Routledge, 1982).
3   BBC News Online – Friday, March 12, 1999
4   June M. Reinisch and Ruth Beaslay, *The Kinsey Institute New Report On Sex: What You Must Know To Be Sexually Literate* (New York, St. Martin's, 1990). See also Tom W. Smith, "A Critique Of The Kinsey Institute/Roper Organization National Sex Knowledge Survey," *Public Opinion Quarterly* 55 (1991) 449-457.
5   Bernie Zilbergeld, *The New Male Sexuality* (New York, Bantam, 1992) 152.
6   Richard Posner, *Sex and Reason* (Cambridge, MA, Harvard University Press, 1992) 203-204.
7   Childhood sex education expert Meg Hickling, quoted by Camilla Cornell in "The Sex Complex: Parents May Loathe The Subject But Kids Need To Know The Naked Truth" *Today's Parent*, June 1999 70.
8   Margaret Leroy, *Pleasure: The Truth About Female Sexuality* (London, Harper Collins, 1993) 32.
9   Ibid.
10   "Fonda Admits 'Vagina' Fear," *The Daily Telegraph* (Australia) 22 September 2002.
11   Marty Klein, "Oprah Still Promoting Sexual Anxiety," *Sexual Intelligence* July 2002 www.sexualintelligence.org.
12   Ibid. 33.
13   Quoted in Cornell 68.
14   B. M. King and LoRusso, J., "Discussions In The Home About Sex: Different Recollections By Parents And Children," *Journal of Sex and Marital Therapy, 33,* (1997) 52-60.
15   Ibid.
16   Miriam and Otto Ehrenberg, *The Intimate Circle: The Sexual Dynamics Of Family Life* (New York, Simon & Shuster, 1988) 66.
17   Ibid.
18   Diana Schemo, "Study Finds Mothers Unaware of Children's Sexual Activity," *New York Times* 5 Septpember 2002.
19   Lillian Rubin, *Erotic Wars: What Happened To The Sexual Revolution?* (New York, Farrar, Strass & Giroux, 1990) 22. See also Sally Wendkos Olds, *The Eternal Garden: Seasons Of Our Sexuality* (New York, Times Books, 1985) 49.
20   See Neil Postman, *The Disappearance of Childhood* (New York, Delacrote Press, 1982) for a discussion about how withholding information helps segregate adults and children.
21   Rubin 16.
22   Stephanie S. Covington, *Awakening Your Sexuality: A Guide For Recovering Women* (New York, HarperSanFrancisco, 1991) 28.
23   "Survey Says Patients Expect Little Physician Help On Sex," *Journal of the American Medical Association* 16 June 1999 281.
24   Steven Carter and Julia Sokol Coopersmith, *What Really Happens In Bed: A Demystification Of Sex* (New York, Evans and Company, 1989) 15.
25   Ibid. 14.
26   Midwest Institute of Sexology, "Sexual communication with partners," *Sexual Research Surveys* Fall1999/winter2000 available at www.mwsexual.com/sex-research-surveys/1-communication-results.htm.
27   Carter and Coopersmith 19.
28   Ibid. 140.
29   Somini Sengupta, "Teacher Who Assigned Graphic Poem Says He Made Mistake," *New York Times* 23 October 1997, 6.
30   See *Boring v. Buncombe County Bd. of Educ.*, 136 F.3d 364 (4th Cir. 1998).

31 Karen Arenson, "Furor Over A Sex Conference Stirs SUNY's Quiet New Paltz Campus," *New York Times* 8 November 1997.

32 Daryl Lange, "PA. House Votes to Cut PSU Appropriation," *The Daily Collegian*, 25 April 2001. Lynn Thompson and Missy Mazzaferro, "Sex Faire Had Educational Intentions," *The Daily Collegian*, 8 February 2001.

33 Electra Draper, "College Drops Class on 'Poetics of Porn'," *Denver Post*, 1 December 2001.

34 Christopher Chow, "Fort Lewis College Offers Pornography Class," *Accuracy in Academia* December 2001 www.academia.org/news/porn.html 3 December 2001.

35 Emily Fredrix, "KU Funding Threatened Over Sexuality Class," *Associated Press* 27 March 2003.

36 The experience of Imogen Stubbs is discussed by Jill Lewis in "Sex Talk And Daily Life," in Lynne Segal (ed.) *New Sexual Agendas* (London, Macmillan, 1997) 240-241.

37 Milton Diamond, "The Field Of Sex Research: Responsibility To Ourselves And To Society," *Archives Of Sexual Behavior* (2000) 29 389.

38 See www.freeexpression.org and www.indexonline.org.

39 Joani Blank and Marcia Quackenbush, *A Kid's First Book About Sex* (Burlingame, CA, 1983 Yes Press).

40 "No Joy Of Sex In Magazines' Articles, Says Expert," *Ananova.com* 31 March 2001: www.ananova.com/news/story/sm_261427.html?menu=news.weirdworld.sexlife.

41 Allen Read in the introduction to *The Anatomy of Dirty Words* by Edward Sagarin (New York, Lyell Stuart, 1962) 10.

42 "Bottom Line vs. Top Story," *The Synergy Report*, Institute for Alternative Journalism, www.independentmedia.org/congress/synery.html.

43 "Kroger Decides To Put 'Cosmo' Behind Blinker Racks," News Release from Morality in Media, Inc. at www.moralityinmedia.org/krogeryes.htm.

44 David Carr and Constance Hays, "3 Racy Men's Magazines Are Banned By Wal-Mart," *New York Times*, 6 May 2003.

45 ASA Adjudications October 2000 www.asa.org.uk/adj/adj_5211.htm.

46 Carrie Budoff, "When Is It OK To Say The, Uh, V-Word?" *The Hartford Courant* 27 February 2001.

47 See Vern Bullogh, *Science In The Bedroom: A History Of Sex Research* (New York, BasicBooks, 1994) 3.

48 Edward O.Laumann et al, "A Political History Of The National Sex Survey Of Adults" *Family Planning Perspectives* (1994) 26(1) 36.

49 Bullogh, 288.

50 Erica Goode, "Certain Words Can Trip Up AIDS Grants, Scientists Say," *New York Times* 18 April 2003.

51 John Money, *The Destroying Angel: Sex, Fitness And Food In The Legacy Of Degeneracy Theory, Graham Crackers, Kellogg's Corn Flakes And American Health History* (Buffalo, N.Y., Prometheus Books, 1985) 159.

52 Victor C. Strassburger, "Tuning In To Teenagers," *Newsweek* 19 May 1997 18-19.

53 Julia A. Ericksen, *Kiss And Tell: Surveying Sex In The Twentieth Century* (Cambridge, Harvard University Press, 1999) 229.

54 "HBO Seeks Basic 'Sex'," *Variety*, reported in new.excite.com 29 October 2000.

55 See Press Release of the Parents Television Council reported at www.mediaresearch.org/press/ent/pr19990818.html.

56 Parents Television Council www.parentstv.org/publications/reports/sr20001016f.html.

57 Eileen Loh-Harrist, "The 'V' Word," www.bestofneworleans.com/dispatch/2001-12-04/news_feat3.html 12 April 2001.

58 Sonia Sharigian, "TV's Last Taboo," *The American Prospect Online*, 7 May 2001.

59 See the survey of the Kaiser Family Foundation, "Public and Networks Getting Comfortable with Condom Advertising on TV," June 19, 2001 http://www.kff.org/content/2001/3135/; See also Chris Collins, "Dangerous Inhibitions: How America Is Letting Aids Become An Epidemic Of The Young," Harvard AIDS Institute, February 1997,

60 Thomas Walsh, "TV's Condomphobia," in the online television guide *www.gist.com* 01 December 1996.
61 Lillian Rubin quoting Foucault, 9.
62 "Bishops Come Down Hard On Condom Ads," *Philippine Daily Inquirer* 17 March 2000.
63 "Chinese Condom Ad Goes Back In Box," *Asian Economic News* 6 December 1999.
64 James R. Petersen, *The Century Of Sex: Playboy's History Of The Sexual Revolution 1900-1999* (New York, Grove, 1999) 459.
65 See 8 FCC Rcd. 3228 (1993) Letter from Donna Searcy, to the Rusk Corp quoted by Milagros Rivera-Sancez in "How Far is too Far? The Line between 'offensive' and 'indecent' speech," found in the *Federal Communications Law Journal* March 1997.
66 See F.C.C., *In the matter of Emmis FM License Corp. of Chicago*, 6 April 2001: www.fcc.gov/Daily_Releases/Daily_Business/2001/db0406/da010870.txt.
67 *Susie Bright's Sexual State Of The Union* (New York, Simon & Schuster, 1997) 17.
68 For information about this rule see the MPAA website at www.mpaa.org/movieratings/about/index.htm.
69 See: http://www.leg.wa.gov/pub/billinfo/1997-98
70 See, for example, a Wisconsin proposal requiring warnings for concerts by groups that had received parent advisory warnings in the last five years: http://www.thehollandsentinel.net/stories/060799/new_warnings.html
71 Petersen 458.
72 "'Talking Dirty' On Phone Has Police In Lather," *The Province* January 16, 1984.
73 See *Sable Communications of Cal. Inc. v. F.C.C.* 492 U.S. 115 (1989).
74 See Bonnie Bullough et al (eds.), *How I Got Into Sex* (Amherst, N.Y., Prometheus, 1997).
75 Rachel Maines, *The Technology of Orgasm: Hysteria, the Vibrator and Women's Sexual Satisfaction* (Baltimore, MD, The Johns Hopkins University Press, 1998).
76 Kathryn Robinson, "Sins Of The Poet," *Seattle Weekly* 7 May 1997.
77 Quoted in *Salonmag.com* "Your Boss May Be Monitoring Your E-Mail," 12 December 1999 http://archive.salon.com/tech/feature/1999/12/08/email_monitoring/
78 Charles Bermant, "Fired For E-Mail Offenses, Workers Overstepped Limits," *Seattle Times* 20 February 2000.
79 William H. Honan, "Professor Ousted For Lecture Gets Job Back," *The New York Times*, 17 September 1994.
80 James L. Graff, "It Was A Joke: An Alleged Sexual Harasser Is Deemed The Real Victim," *Time* 28 July 1997.
81 John Cloud, "Sex And The Law," *Time* 23 March 1998. See also Daphne Patai, *Heterophobia: Sexual Harassment And The Future Of Feminism* (Lanham, MD, Rowman & Littlefield Publishers, 1998).

Chapter 10

1 See, for example, Edward Donnerstein et al, *The Question of Pornography: Research Findings and Policy Implications* (New York, Free Press, 1987).
2 For an important study of pornography and the false harms attributed to it, see: F.M. Christensen, *Pornography: the Other Side* (New York, Praeger, 1990).
3 *Regina v. Hicklin* [1968] L.R. 3 Q.B. 360.
4 Frederick F. Schauer, *The Law of Obscenity* (Washington, D.C., The Bureau of National Affairs, 1976) 13.
5 Quoted in John D'Emilio and Estelle B. Freedman, *Intimate Matters: A History Of Sexuality in America* (New York, Harper & Row, 1988) 284.
6 "7-Eleven Stops Sale Of Girlie Magazines," *Vancouver Sun* 11 April 1986.
7 See the 1970 USA Federal Commission on Obscenity and Pornography, the 1979 British Williams Committee, the 1985 Canadian Fraser Commission, and the 1986 USA Meese Commission.

8   Stephanie Dolgoff, "Boing! Be An Instant Lust Object" *Glamour Magazine*. Date unknown.
9   Daniel Linz et al, "Estimating Community Standards: The Use Of Social Science Evidence In An Obscenity Prosecution," *Public Opinion Quarterly* 55(1991) 107.
10   Ibid. 107.
11   Don Mosher, "Moralistic Intolerance," *Journal of Sex Research* 26 (1989) 492-509.
12   William E. Brigman, "Pornography As Political Expression," *Journal Of Popular Culture* 17 (1983) 129.
13   John Heidenry, *What Wild Ecstacy: The Rise and Fall of the Sexual Revolution* (New York, Simon & Schuster, 1997) 151-3. Linda Lovelace, *Ordeal* (Secaucus, N.J. Citadel Press, 1980).
14   "Hockey Legend To Marriage Counselor," *National Post* 11 November 2000 B1.
15   *Luscher v. Deputy Minister, Revenue Canada, Customs and Excise*, [1985] 1 F.C. 85.
16   *Miller v. California* 413 US 15 (1973).
17   Ibid. at 25.
18   *Roth v. United States* 354 U.S. 476 487 (1957).
19   *Miller v. California* 22-25.
20   *Paris Adult Theater I v. Slaton*, 413 US 49 (1973).
21   Mike Brassfield, "All Eyes Watching Polk Porn Suit Sage," *St. Petersburg Times* 26 June 2000.
22   See 18 U.S.C. 1464, 47 CFR Section 73.3999 and Media Bureau Publication 8310-100.
23   See, for example, *Action for Children's Television v. Federal Communications Commission* (30 June 1995) No. 93-1092, United States Court of Appeals, (District of Columbia).
24   Child Online Protection Act, s.231.
25   See, for example, *Cyperspace Communications Inc. v. Engler* 55 F. Supp. 2d 737 (E.D. Mich. 1999) involving the Michigan law.
26   "Oops, Wrong Switch; Porn Show Played To Wrestling Fans," *Canadian Press* 29 February 2000.
27   David Kamp, "Hey, Kids, Suck On This," *Gentlemen's Quarterly*, February 2000 87.
28   Adult Entertainment Survey, DCP, NYC, 1994.
29   TSBID "Adult Use Establishments and Property Values" available at: http://hellskitchen.net/issues/tsbidsex/propval.html.
30   *Stringellow's of New York, Ltd. v. The City of New York* 91 N.Y.2d 382, 694 N.E.2d 407, 671 N.Y.S.2d 406 (1998).
31   Steve Gorman, "Censoring Stanley Kubrick's Eyes Wide Shut," www.melonfarmers.co.uk/inuseyes.htm.
32   Internet Content Rating Association, www.icra.org.
33   "Woman Fired For Posting Nude Picture Of Herself On 'Net'," *News Herald* (Panama City, Florida) 9 September 1999.
34   "Cyperporn Nurse: 'I Feel Like Larry Flynt'," MSNBC July 16, 1999.
35   "Clearbrook Students Suspended," *Vancouver Sun* 31 Jan 1985.
36   *Board of School Trustees v. John and Ilze Shewan*, 30 Jan 1986 British Columbia Supreme Court A851691.
37   10 USC 2489a.
38   Quoted in *General Media Communications, Inc. v. Cohen and the Department of Defense*, 21 November 1997, Court of Appeals, 2nd Circuit, 97-6029.
39   Ibid.
40   Va. Code Ann 2.1-804-806.
41   *Urofsky v. Gilmore*, 23 June 2000, Court Of Appeals, Fourth Circuit, No. 98-1481.
42   For the details of the 1998 event see Jeffrey Rosen, *The Unwanted Gaze: The Destruction of Privacy In America* (New York, Random House, 2000).
43   Available online at:http://ag.org/enrichmentjournal/9903/078_pornography.cfm.
44   Gloria Steinem, "Erotic and Pornography: A Clear and Present Difference," in Laura Lederer, ed., *Take Back the Night: Women On Pornography* (New York, Bantam, 1980).
45   Letters from a War Zone: writings 1976-1989. An excerpt is available at www.igc.org/womensnet/dworkin/WarZoneChaptIa.html.
46   Andrea Dworkin, "Why So-called Radical Men Love and Need Pornography," in Lederer, 141.
47   Ibid. 151.

Chapter 11

1   B.D. Schmitt, *Your Child's Health* (New York, Bantam, 1991) quoted at:
    http://www.janela1.com/vh/docs/v0002356.htm.
2   Archives of The Sex Ed Mom are available online.
3   Helen Singer Kaplan, *Sexual Aversion, Sexual Phobias, And Panic Disorder* (New York,
    Brunner/Mazel, 1987) 51.
4   Richard Posner and Katherine Silbaugh, *A Guide to America's Sex Laws* (Chicago, University of
    Chicago Press, 1996) 93.
5   *Playboy* June 2000 62.
6   "District Justice Charged With Public Indecency," *Citizens Voice* (Wilkes-Barre, PA) 20
    August 1998.
7   See the Windcrest Police Department website:
    www.ci.windcrest.tx.us/wc_police/wcpd_menu.htm, and
    www.flash.net/~wndcrest/wcpolice/Windcrest_Texas_Police_Department_Significant_Cases.
    htm
8   "All The Way Out: George Michael," *The Advocate* 19 January 1999.
9   See *Goodwin v. Canada Trustco Mortgage Company* reported in *Lawyers Weekly* (Toronto) 28
    February 1986.
10 *The Independent* (London) 11 April 1998.
11 "Why Should Gays Have The Right To Public Sex?" *Sunday Times* 30 July 2000.
12 Elaine Yates, *Sex Without Shame: Encouraging the Child's Healthy Sexual Development* (New
    York, Quill, 1982) 74.
13 www.allaboutsex.org/IGotCaughtDisplay.cfm
14 Evelyn Nieves, "San Francisco Is Urged To Allow Secluded Sex In Bathhouses," *New York
    Times* 29 May 1999 A9.
15 Statement in the House of Commons re Bill C-53 June 1982.
16 "Police Chiefs Opposed Changes In Sex Laws," *The Province* 6 May 1982 A10.
17 See *A.D.T. v. The United Kingdom* European Court of Human Rights 35765/97 31 July 2000.
    In 2003 the British Parliament debated amendments which would repeal this discriminatory
    law.
18 See Terry Gould, *The Lifestyle: A Look At The Erotic Rites of Swingers* (Toronto, Random
    House, 1999) 87.
19 Pat Jordan, "Teacher's Pet: Should Cavorting In Front Of Strangers Cost You Your Job?"
    Playboy Magazine June 2000.
20 David Holthouse, "Civil Liberties: The Battle Over Phoenix's Groundbreaking Sex-Club
    Ban Moves Into Federal Court," *Phoenix NewTimes*,
    http://www.phoenixnewtimes.com/issues/1999-03-18/feature2.html.
21 Jeffry Scott, "115 Jailed At Atlanta Party With Live Sex," *Atlanta Journal-Constitution* 7 July
    2002.
22 State of *Missouri v. Wahl* ED79631 Missouri Court of Appeals 16 April 2002.
23 Editorial, "Bawdy-house Charges Unwise," *Edmonton Journal* 30 December 2002.
24 "Debate Raging Over Teachers' Behavior," *FoxNews.com* June 12, 2000.
25 "Adult Businesses Creating Problems, Work For Lawyers," *Lawyers Weekly USA* 3 May 1999.
26 120 S. Ct. 1382 (2000).
27 Ibid.
28 Kate Zernike, "School Readmits Stripper's Child," *New York Times* 22 May 2002.
29 "Many Students And Parents Object To Presence Of Strip Clubs Near School," *Detroit Free
    Press*, 02 June 1998.
30 "Tragedies Linked To Striptease Show," *Globe and Mail*, 21 January 1986
31 Clyde Haberman, "Live, Nude And O.K. With City Hall," *New York Times* 15 Dec 1998 B1.
    Angela Tribelli, "Burlesque's Back, A Step Ahead Of The Law," *New York Times*, 4 October
    1998.

32 Mathew Hays, "Is Taboo Taboo?" *Montreal Mirror* May 2003.
33 Tim Cooper and Richard Holiday, "Stage Sex: Yard Inquiry," *Evening Standard* 23 April 2003.

Chapter 12

1   These figures are based on studies that estimate that there are about 23 prostitutes for every 100,000 people in the United States and that each prostitute has a client list of 694 male sex partners per year. See: Paul Recer, "Discrepancy Found In US Sex Survey," *Associated Press*, 10 Oct 2000.
2   Richard Green, *Sexual Science And The Law* (Cambridge, MA, Harvard University Press, 1992) 192.
3   Valerie Scott, "I Love Sex And I'm Good At It," *Globe and Mail* 17 March 2001.
4   See for example the statistics compiled by the Prostitutes' Education Network, available at www.bayswan.org/stats.html.
5   "Sex, Lies And Destiny," *Maclean's* 4 January 1999.
6   See Frederique Delacoste and Priscilla Alexander (eds.), *Sex Work: Writings By Women In The Sex Industry* (San Francisco, CA, Cleis Press, 1987) 122.
7   Alex Adams and William Stadiem, *Madam 90210: My Life As Madam To The Rich And Famous*, (New York, Villard Books, 1993) vi.
8   Sharon Kaiser, "Coming Out of Denial," in Delacoste and Alexander 104.
9   Tracy Quan, "I Cannot Tell A Lie: What Happens When A Hooker Confesses To Her Parents," *Salon.com* 15 October 1999.
10 Ann Landers, "Can You Trust A Man Who Uses Escort Services?" *Vancouver Sun* 16 November 2000.
11 Jim Woods, "Hookers, Patrons To Show Up On TV," *Columbus Dispatch* 17 February 1999.
12 Allan Richter, "Oldest Profession In New Suburban Digs," *New York Times* 3 November 2002; Martin Kasindorf, "Feeling The Squeeze, Sex Trade Infiltrates Professional Shops," *USA Today* 18 November 2002.
13 Editorial, "Kitten With A Whip" *The Globe and Mail* 27 March 2000.
14 Morgan Winsor, "Police Stage Prostitution Sting, Arrest Four," *Miami Herald* 6 May 1999.
15 Sydney Barrows with William Novak, *Mayflower Madam: The Secret Life Of Sydney Biddle Barrows* (New York, Ivy Books, 1986).
16 Arian Campo-Flores, "A Crackdown On Call Girls," *Newsweek* 2 September 2002.
17 Sarah Cox, "Police Use Of Videos Under Fire," *Vancouver Sun* 25 June 1986.
18 Green 196-203.
19 Andrea Dworkin, "Prostitution and Male Supremacy," a presentation at a symposium entitled "Prostitution: From Academia to Activism," sponsored by the Michigan Journal of Gender and Law at the University of Michigan Law School, October 31, 1992. See: http://www.nostatusquo.com/ACLU/dworkin/MichLawJourI.html.
20 John D'Emilio and Estelle B. Freedman, *Intimate Matters: A History Of Sexuality in America* (New York, Harper & Row, 1988) 139-45, 149-56, 208-215.

Chapter 13

1   An excellent summary of the data is found at the website of the Kinsey Institute: http://kinseyinstitute.org.
2   For an interesting discussion of both sides of the argument see Chandler Burr, *A Separate Creation: The Search For The Biological Origins Of Sexual Orientation* (New York, Hyperion, 1996).
3   David Frum, "Blurring The Lines Of Marriage," *National Post* 20 January 2001.
4   Quoted in Charles W. Socarides, *Beyond Sexual Freedom* (New York, Quadrangle Books, 1975) 83-4.
5   I. Bieber et al, *Homosexuality: a Psychoanalytic Study of Male Homosexuals* (New York, Basic Books, 1962) 173 quoted in Richard Green, *Sexual Science And The Law* (Cambridge, MA, Harvard University Press, 1992) 263.

6   Socarides 84.
7   See Green, Chapter 5 "Immigration and Homosexuality."
8   John D'Emilio and Estelle B. Freedman, *Intimate Matters: A History Of Sexuality in America* (New York, Harper & Row, 1988) 347.
9   Ibid.
10   "Bullying Rules Don't Work," *Xtra West* 29 June 2000.
11   Victor Dwyer, "Class Action: Fighting Homophobia At School," *Maclean's* May 1997.
12   Editorial, "The Rights Of Gay Americans," *New York Times* 27 March 2003.
13   Ibid.
14   Judith Lewis, "Lesbian In The Locker Room," *L.A. Weekly* January 10-16 2003.
15   Howard Chua-Eoan "That's Not A Scarecrow: A Brutal Assault In Wyoming And A Rise In Gay Bashing Fuel The Debate Over Sexual Orientation," *Time* 19 October 1998.
16   Dwyer 10.
17   Chastity Bono with Billie Fitzpatrick, *Family Outing* (Boston, Little, 1998).
18   Ibid. 143.
19   C. Bagley and P. Tremblay, "Suicidal Behaviors In Homosexual And Bisexual Males," *Crisis*, 18 (1997) 24-34.
20   See for example the Annotated Statutes of Missouri 566.090 (enacted 1977!): "A person who has deviate sexual intercourse with another person of the same sex is guilty of sexual misconduct."
21   *Bowers v. Hardwick*, 478 US 186 (1986).
22   Linda Greenhouse, "Justices, 6-3, Legalize Gay Sexual Conduct in Sweeping Reversal of Court's '86 Ruling, *New York Times* 27 June 2003.
23   *Little Sisters Book and Art Emporium v. Canada (Minister of Justice)* [2000] 2 S.C.R. 1120.
24   Kevin Sack, "Judge's Ouster Sought After Antigay Remarks," *New York Times* 20 February 2002.
25   *Romer v. Evans* 517 U.S. 620 (1996).
26   See, for example, RAND, "Analagous Experience of Foreign Military Services," in *Sexual Orientation and U.S. Military Personnel Policy: Options and Assessment* (Santa Monica, CA, RAND, 1993). See also the reports by Aaron Belkin and Jason McNichol of the Center for the Study of Sexual Minorities in the Military, at the University of California at Santa Barbara, concerning the integration of homosexuals into the military of Canada, Australia, and Israel.
27   See "Don't Ask, Don't' Tell, Don't Pursue," Digital Law Project at the Robert Crown Law Library at Stanford Law School at: http://dont.stanford.edu/commentary/index.htm.
28   See the annuals reports on the application of the "Don't ask, don't tell" rule by the SLDN (Servicemembers Legal Defense Network), www.sldn.org.
29   "Military Discharged Fewer Gays In 2002, Report Finds," *New York Times* 25 March 2003.
30   "Gay Army Linguists Say They Were Ousted," *New York Times* 15 November 2002.
31   Terence Shaw, "Forces Ban Violates Rights Of Gays," *Daily Telegraph* 28 September 1999.
32   "Parents, Religious Leaders Back Book Ban, Trustees Say," *Vancouver Sun* 19 February 1998. The Supreme Court of Canada eventually overruled the ban as unreasonable: see Mark Hume and Janice Tibbetts, "Ban On Books Unreasonable, Court Rules," *National Post* 21 December 2002.
33   Section 53A-3-419; see: www.code-co.com/utah/leg/96/special/sbs1003.htm.
34   For more information about the gay clubs controversy see: NEED WEBSITE
35   "Dr. Laura Too Anti-Gay For Canada," *National Post* 11 May 2000.
36   Julie Salamon, "Children, Gay Parents and Synthetic Storms," *New York Times* 18 June 2002.
37   Louis Crompton, *Byron and Greek Love: Homophobia in 19th Century England* (Berkeley, CA, University of California Press, 1985) 255.
38   D'Emilio and Freedman 292-3.
39   See Amnesty's press release: http://web.amnesty.org/appeals/index/mys-011100-wwa-eng.
40   John Alan Lee in "Some Structural Aspects Of Police Deviance In Relations With Minority Groups," in Clifford D. Shearing (ed.), *Organizational Police Deviance: Its Structure And Control*, (Toronto, Butterworths, 1981) 66.

41   Marshall Kirk and Hunter Madsen, *After The Ball: How America Will Conquer Its Hatred And Fear Of Homosexuals In The '90s* (New York, Doubleday, 1989) 127.

42   See *Susie Bright's Sexual State of the Union* (New York, Simon & Schuster, 1997) 59.

43   Linda Bird Francke, *Ground Zero: The Gender Wars In The Military* (New York, Simon & Schuster, 1997) 155.

44   See John Sawatsky, *Men in the Shadows: The RCMP Security Service* (New York, Doubleday, 1980) 125.

45   See, for example, Socarides 94.

46   "Catholic Priests Are Dying Of AIDS, Often In Silence," *Kansas City Star* 29 January 2000, www.kcstar.com/item/pages/home.pat,local/37743133.129,.htm.

Chapter 14

1   Rawn Joseph, *The Naked Neuron: Evolution And The Languages Of The Body And Brain* (New York, Plenum Press, 1993) 348-349.

2   See, for example, C.C. Nadelson et al, "A Follow-Up Study Of Rape Victims," *America Journal Of Psychiatry* 139 (1982) 1266; Elizabeth Waites, *Trauma And Survival: Post-Traumatic And Dissociative Disorders In Women* (New York, Norton, 1993); Ellen Bass and Laura Davis, *The Courage To Heal: A Guide For Women Survivors Of Child Sexual Abuse* (New York, Harper & Row, 1994).

3   Nancy Engels, "Sexual Assault," in Catherine Fogel and Diane Lauver, *Sexual Health Promotion* (New York, W.B. Saunders, 1990) 527.

4   Bass and Davis 58.

5   Engles 526.

6   M.G. Bartoi and B. Kinder, "Effects Of Child And Adult Sexual Abuse On Adult Sexuality," *Journal Of Sex And Marital Therapy* 24 (1998) 75-90.

7   Cited in Engles 545.

8   Irene Darra, "The Penis As Enemy," *Xtra* (Toronto) 25 January 2001.

9   See the website of psychologist Kali Munro at www.kalimunro.com

10   Mike Lew, *Victims No Longer: Men Recovering From Incest And Other Sexual Abuse* (New York, HarperCollins, 1990) 187.

11   David Finkelhor, "Current Information On The Scope And Nature Of Child Sexual Abuse," *The Future Of Children* 4 (1994) 31-53.

12   Margaret Leroy, *Pleasure: The Truth About Female Sexuality* (London, Harper Collins, 1993) 41.

13   See the material at the website of male sexual abuse expert Jim Hopper: www.jimhopper.com/male-ab/.

14   Naomi Wolff, *Promiscuities* (New York, Random House, 1997) 33.

15   Leroy 62.

16   Wolff 32-33.

17   Camilla Cornell, "The Sex Complex: Parents May Loathe The Subject But Kids Need To Know The Naked Truth," *Today's Parent* June 1999 quoting child sex education expert Meg Hickling.

18   Mary Krueger, "Sexism, Erotophobia, And The Illusory 'No': Implications For Acquaintance Rape Awareness," *Journal of Psychology and Human Sexuality* 8 (1996) 114.

19   Stanley Henshaw, "Unintended Pregnancy in the United States," *Family Planning Perspectives* 30(1)(1998) January/February 1998 www.agi-usa.org/pubs/journals/3002498.html.

20   G.E. Smith et al, "Sexual Attitudes, Cognitive Associative Networks, And Perceived Vulnerability To Unplanned Pregnancy," *Journal of Research in Personality*, 30 (1996) 88-101.

21   See Carol Cassell, *Swept Away: Why Women Fear Their Own Sexuality* (New York, Simon & Schuster, 1984).

22   Reay Tannahill, *Sex In History* (Briarcliff Manor, NY, Scarborough Books, 1980) 65.

23   U.S. Department of Health and Human Services, Public Health Service. Division of STD Prevention. Sexually Transmitted Disease Surveillance,1997.

24   Meghan Daum, "Safe-Sex Lies," *New York Times* 21 January 1996 32.
25   See, for example "God's Judgment For Sin In History," by Christian scholar Richard Riss
      www.grmi.org/renewal/Richard_Riss/evidences2/06sin.html.
26   Graham later recanted his remarks. See also the Times Square Church Pulpit Series
      www.tscpulpitseries.org/english/1990s/ts930823.txt
27   Alex Comfort, *The Anxiety Makers: Some Curious Preoccupations Of The Medical Profession*
      (London, Nelson, 1967) 77.
28   See Sally Wendkos Olds, *The Eternal Garden: Seasons Of Our Sexuality* (New York, Times
      Books, 1985).
29   E.O.Laumann, "Early Sexual Experiences: How Voluntary? How Violent?" in M. Smith et al,
      (eds.), *Sexuality and American Social Policy*, (Menlo Park, CA, Henry J. Kaiser Family
      Foundation, 1996); and K.A. Moore, C.W. Ncrd, and J.L. Peterson, "Nonvoluntary Sexual
      Activity Among Adolescents," *Family Planning Perspectives*, 21(3) (1989) 110-114.
30   C.R. Browning and E.O. Laumann, "Sexual Contact Between Children And Adults: A Life
      Course Perspective," *American Sociological Review*, 62(4) (1997) 540-560. J.L. Stock et al,
      "Adolescent Pregnancy And Sexual Risk-Taking Among Sexually Abused Girls," *Family
      Planning Perspectives*, 29(5) (1997) 200-203 & 227. B.C. Miller et al, "The Effects Of Forced
      Sexual Intercourse On White Female Adolescents," *Child Abuse and Neglect*, 19(10) (1995)
      1289-1301.
31   Robyn Walser and Jeffrey Kern, "Relationships Among Childhood Sexual Abuse, Sex Guilt,
      And Sexual Behavior in Adult Clinical Samples," *Journal of Sex Research* 33 (1996) 321-326.
32   Sharon Thompson, "Putting a Big Thing into a Little Hole: Teenage Girls' Accounts of
      Sexual Initiation," *Journal of Sex Research* (1990) 27(3) 341 at 345.
33   Karen Bouris, *The First Time: Women Speak Out About "Losing Their Virginity"* (Emeryville,
      CA, Conari Press, 1993) 14.
34   Nancy Gibbs, "How Should We Teach Our Kids about Sex?" *Time* 24 May 1993 53.
35   Bouris 86.
36   Ibid. 67.
37   Thompson 347.
38   Thompson 350-357.
39   For circumcision statistics see CIRP (Circumcision Information and Resource Pages)
      www.cirp.org/library/statistics/USA/.
40   Robert Darby, "The Masturbation Taboo And The Rise Of Routine Male Circumcision: A
      Review Of The Historiography," *Journal of Social History* Spring 2003.
41   R. W. Cockshut, "Circumcision," *British Medical Journal*, 2 (1935) 764.
42   Terry Gould makes that point in *The Lifestyle: A Look at the Erotic Rites of Swingers* (Toronto,
      Random House, 1999) 93.
43   See the International Coalition for Genital Integrity www.icgi.org.
44   Gersh Kuntzman, "Sex Life Not Good? Sue! Lawyer David Llewellyn Is the Johnnie Cochran
      Of The Circumcised," *Newsweek.com* 26 February 2001.
45   Allen Reid, "An Obscene Symbol," *American Speech* 9 (1935) 264.
46   Edward Sagarin, *The Anatomy Of Dirty Words* (New York, L. Stuart, 1962) 161.
47   D. H. Lawrence, *Sex, Literature And Censorship* (London, Heinemann, 1955).

Chapter 15

1   Sigmund Freud, *A General Introduction To Psychoanalysis* (New York, Pocket Books, 1970)
     362-63.
2   See *Civilization and its* Discontents (Norton, New York, 1989).
3   Ken Wilber, *Up From Eden: A Transpersonal View Of Human Evolution* (Boulder, Shambala,
     1981).
4   L.L. Whyte, especially *The Next Development In Man* (New York, Henry Holt, 1948).
5   Alan Watts, *Nature, Man, And Woman* (New York, Vintage, 1958).
6   H. J. Eysneck, *Sex And Personality* (London, Abacus, 1976), 236.

7   Michael Hutchison, *The Anatomy Of Sex and Power* (New York, Morrow, 1990), 207-9.
8   T. Adorno, E. Frenkel-Brunswick, D. Levinson and R. Sanford, *The Authoritarian Personality* (New York, Harper, 1950).
9   W. Fisher, Donn Byrne, Leonard White, and Kathryn Kelley, "Erotophobia-Erotophilia As A Dimension Of Personality," *Journal Of Sex Research* 25 (1988) 123-151.
10 Seymour Fisher, *Sexual Images Of The Self: The Psychology Of Erotic Sensations* And Illusions (Hillisdale, NJ, Lawrence Erlbaum Associates, 1989) 86.
11 Ibid. 52.
12 Alexander Lowen, *Pleasure: A Creative Approach To Life*, (New York, Penguin, 1970)
13 Ibid. 76.
14 Ibid.
15 R. Joseph, *The Right Brain And The Unconscious: Discovering The Stranger Within* (New York, Plenum, 1992) 73.
16 Saint Augustine, *Against Julian* (Matthew Schumacher, (trans.) and J. Defferrari (ed)), (New York, Fathers of the Church, 1957) 228.
17 Donald L. Mosher, "Three Dimensions Of Depth Of Involvement In Human Sexual Response," *Journal Of Sex Research* 12 (1980) 2.
18 Murray S. Davis, *Smut: Erotic Reality/Obscene Ideology* (Chicago, Chicago University Press, 1983) 3.
19 D. H. Lawrence, *Sex, Literature And Censorship* (London, Heinemann, 1955).
20 Ibid. 144.
21 Op cit.
22 Says Wilber in *Up From Eden* 192.
23 In *The Next Development In Man* 93.
24 Ibid. 123.
25 Ibid. 57.
26 Op cit.
27 Watts 56.
28 Ibid. 144.
29 See Wilber.
30 Ken Wilber, *Sex, Ecology, Spirituality* (Boston, Shambala, 1996).
31 Arthur Evans, *The God Of Ecstasy: Sex Roles And The Madness Of Dionysos* (New York, St. Martin's, 1988) 50.
32 Referred to in J.M. Roberts, *The Pelican History of the World* (New York, Penguin, 1980) 209.
33 *Phaedo* 82b8-82c3, quoted in Raymond A. Belliotti, *Good Sex: Perspectives On Sexual Ethics* (Lawrence, University Press of Kansas, 1993) 18.
34 Raymond J. Lawrence, Jr., *The Poisoning of Eros* (New York, Augustine Moore Press, 1989) 14, citing *The Laws* sect. 841.
35 Plato, *Republic* 9.57ic2-57id3, quoted in Belliotti 17.
36 Antonio Domasio, *Descartes' Error: Emotion, Reason And The Human Brain* (New York, Grosset/Putnam, 1994).
37 Belliotti 19.
38 Quoted in Elizabeth Abbott, *The History Of Celibacy* (Toronto, HarperCollins, 1999) 58.
39 *Confessions* 10.30.41-42:796-797, quoted in Peter Brown, *The Body and Society: Men, Women, and Sexual Renunciation in Early Christianity* (New York, Columbia University Press, 1988) 406-7.
40 Mosher 13-14.
41 Ibid. 14.
42 Alan Bullock, *Hitler: A Study In Tyranny* (New York, Bantam, 1953) 333.
43 Ibid. 344.
44 See Barbara Killinger, *Workaholics: The Respectable Addicts* (Toronto, Key Porter, 1991).
45 Glenn Wilson (ed.), *The Psychology of Conservatism* (London, Academic Press, 1973).
46 G. Rattray Taylor, *Sex in History* (New York, Vanguard, 1970) 73.
47 Julian M. Davidson, "Psychobiology Of Sexual Experience," in Julian M. and Richard J. Davidson (eds.), *The Psychobiology Of Consciousness* (New York, Plenum, 1980) 313-6.

48 Nick Totton and Em Edmondson, *Reichian Growth Work: Melting The Blocks To Life And Love* (Bridport, Dorset, Prism Press, 1988) 12, emphasis in original.
49 Watts 78.
50 Bernie Zilbergeld, *The New Male Sexuality* (New York, Bantam, 1992) 23.
51 R. Joseph, *The Right Brain and the Unconscious*, 180.
52 Ibid. 301.
53 Sam Janus, Barbara Bess, and Carole Saltus, *A Sexual Profile Of Men In Power* (Englewood Cliffs, New Jersey, Prentice Hall, 1977)14-15.
54 Ibid. 12.
55 Karen Armstrong, *The Battle For God* (New York, Knopf, 2000) 358.
56 Quoted in Edmund Leites, *The Puritan Conscience And Modern Sexuality* (New Haven, Yale University Press, 1986) 2.
57 Ibid.
58 M.E. Rodgers (ed.), *The Impossible H.L. Mencken* (New York, Doubleday, 1991) 443.
59 See Leites.
60 Leites, 13 quoting Puritan moralist Richard Baxter.
61 Ibid. 16.
62 Jayme A. Sokolow, *Eros And Modernization: Sylvester Graham, Health Reform, And Origins Of Victorian Sexuality In America* (Rutherford, NJ, Fairleigh Dickinson University Press, 1983). Charles E. Rosenberg makes the same point in "Sexuality, Class And Role In 19th Century America," *American Quarterly* 25 (1973) 149.
63 Evelyn Reed, *Woman's Evolution: From Matriarchal Clan To Patriarchal Family* (New York, Pathfinder, 1975). See also Marjorie Shostak, *Nisa: The Life And Words Of A !Kung Woman* (Cambridge, MA, Harvard University Press, 1981).
64 See Elisabeth Young-Bruehl, *The Anatomy Of Prejudices* (Cambridge, Mass., Harvard University, 1996) 486-507.
65 See John D'Emilio and Estelle B. Freedman, *Intimate Matters: A History Of Sexuality in America* (New York, Harper & Row, 1988) xvi.

Chapter 16

1   For a detailed discussion of patriarchy see Gerda Lerner, *The Creation Of Patriarchy* (Oxford, Oxford University Press, 1986) and Marilyn French, *Beyond Power: On Women, Men and Morals* (New York, Summit Books, 1985).
2   Donald Mosher and Silvan Tomkins, "Scripting The Macho Man," *Journal of Sex Research* 25 (1988) 60-84.
3   See J.C. Brown and C.R. Bohn (eds.), *Christianity, Patriarchy, And Abuse* (Cleveland, Pilgrim Press, 1989) for a series of essays exploring the relationship between patriarchy and abuse.
4   Peggy Reeves Sanday, "The Socio-Cultural Context Of Rape: A Cross-Cultural Study," *Journal Of Social Issues* 37(4) (1981) 5.
5   David Finkelhor, "Current Information On The Scope And Nature Of Child Sexual Abuse," *The Future Of Children* 4 (1994) 31-53.
6   Carolyn Heggen, *Sexual Abuse In Christian Homes And Churches* (Scottdale, Pennsylvania, Herald Press, 1993) 87.
7   Riane Eisler, *Sacred Pleasure: Sex, Myth And The Politics Of The Body* (San Francisco, HarperSanFrancisco, 1995)
8   G. Rattray Taylor, *Sex in History* (New York, Ballantine Books, 1954, 1970).
9   James DeMeo, *Saharasia, The 4000 BCE Origins of Child Abuse, Sex-Repression, Warfare and Social Violence, In the Deserts of the Old World* (Ashland, OR, Natural Energy Works, 1998).
10 Op cit.
11 Richard Posner, *Sex and Reason* (Cambridge, MA, Harvard University Press, 1992).
12 See Ira Reiss, *Journey Into Sexuality: An Exploratory Voyage* (Englewood Cliffs, NJ, Prentice-Hall, 1986) 189.

13   John D'Emilio and Estelle B. Freedman, *Intimate Matters: A History Of Sexuality in America* (New York, Harper & Row, 1988) 106-107.

14   Alan Bullock, *Hitler: A Study In Tyranny* (New York, Bantam, 1953) 16.

15   Elisabeth Young-Bruehl, *The Anatomy of Prejudices* (Cambridge, MA, Harvard University Press, 1996) 486-507.

16   Arthur Evans, *The God Of Ecstasy: Sex Roles And The Madness Of Dionysos* (New York, St. Martin's, 1988) 69-81.

17   *Susie Bright's Sexual State Of The Union* (New York, Simon & Schuster, 1997) 31.

18   Marjorie Shostak, *Nisa: The Life And Words Of A !Kung Woman* (Cambridge, MA, Harvard University Press, 1981).

19   Eric Widmer, "Attitudes Toward Nonmarital Sex in 24 Countries," *The Journal of Sex Research* 35(4) (1998) 349-358.

20   Elinor Burkett and Frank Bruni, *A Gospel Of Shame: Children, Sexual Abuse, And The Catholic Church* (New York, Viking, 1993) 231.

21   See for example *Mowatt v Clarke*, 2000 BCSC 0096, August 30, 1999 (British Columbia Supreme Court) per Dillon J.

22   Linda Bird Francke, *Ground Zero: The Gender Wars In The Military* (New York, Simon & Shuster, 1997) 157.

23   Kelly Flinn, *Proud To Be: My Life, The Air Force, The Controversy* (New York, Random House, 1997) 41-43.

24   Diana Jean Schemo, "Air Force Academy Seeks To Prosecute Cadet In Rape," *New York Times* 15 May 2003.

25   Diana Jean Schemo "Women At West Point Face Tough Choices On Assaults," *New York Times* 22 May 2003.

26   Alex Comfort, *Barbarism and Sexual Freedom* (Brooklyn, Haskell House, 1977) 19.

27   Rollo May discusses this phenomenon in *Love and Will* (New York, Norton, 1969) 200.

28   Quoted by Louis Crompton in *Byron and Greek Love: Homophobia in 19th Century England* (1985, University of California Press, 8) 40.

29   Such as Freud, in *Civilization And Its Discontents* (Norton, New York, 1989); Herbert Marcuse, *Eros and Civilization* (Boston, Beacon Press, 1966), and Alain Danielou, *Shiva and Dionysus* (London, East-West Publications, 1982).

30   George Orwell, *1984: A Novel* (New York, New American Library, 1961).

31   Alex Comfort, *Sex In Society* (New York, Citadel Press, 1966) 64.

32   Reay Tannahill, *Sex In History* (Briarcliff Manor, NY, Scarborough Books, 1980) 161.

33   "Fake Confessions To Priests Are 'Sins' Among Catholic Clergy," *Vancouver Sun* 17 March 1994.

34   The issue is fully discussed by John Duckitt in *The Social Psychology of Prejudice* (Westport, CT, Praeger, 1994) Chapter 8.

35   J. Brockner, "Low Self-Esteem And Behavioral Plasticity: Some Implications For Personality And Social Psychology," in L. Wheeler (ed.), *Review Of Personality And Social Psychology*, vol. 4 (Beverly Hills, CA, Sage, 1984) 287.

36   Carol Cassell, *Swept Away: Why Women Fear Their Own Sexuality* (New York, Simon & Schuster, 1984) 24.

37   Seymour Fisher, *Sexual Images Of The Self: The Psychology Of Erotic Sensations And Illusions* (Hillisdale, NJ, Lawrence Erlbaum Associates, 1989) 50.

38   Steve Allen makes this point in *Steve Allen on the Bible, Religion, & Morality* (Buffalo, Prometheus, 1990) 392.

39   Peter Brown, *The Body and Society: Men, Women, and Sexual Renunciation in Early Christianity* (New York, Columbia University Press, 1988) 153.

40   Seymour Fisher 32. See also John Money, *Love and Love Sickness* (Baltimore, John Hopkins University Press, 1980) 145.

41   Mary Douglas, *Natural Symbols: Explorations In Cosmology* (New York, Vintage Books, 1973) 70-71.

42   See, for example, Theodor Adorno, *The Authoritarian Personality* (New York, Science Editions,

1964, 1950), and Glenn Wilson (ed.), *The Psychology of Conservatism* (London, Academic Press, 1973).

43   Ronald Inglehart and Pippa Norris, "The True Clash of Civilizations," *Foreign Policy* November-December 2002; *Rising Tide: Gender Equality and Cultural Change Around The World* (New York, Cambridge University Press, 2003).

44   United Nations, *Report Of The International Conference On Population And Development*, Cairo, Egypt September 1994; *Platform For Action Of The Fourth World Conference On Women*, Beijing, China September 1995.

45   International Planned Parenthood Federation, *Charter On Sexual And Reproductive Rights*, s. 2.5, available at: http://mirror.ippf.org/charter/intro.htm. The Declaration of the World Association for Sexology is found at: www.tc.umn.edu/~colem001/was/wdeclara.htm.

46   For a detailed discussion of the politics of sexual rights in the international arena, see Rosalind P. Petchesky, "Sexual Rights: Inventing A Concept, Mapping An International Practice," in Richard Parker et al (eds.), *Framing The Sexual Subject: The Politics Of Gender, Sexuality And Power* (Berkeley, University of California Press, 2000) 94.

47   Ahmar Mustikhan, "U.N. Postpones Historic Gay Rights Vote," *www.PlanetOut.com* 25 April 2003.

Acknowledgements

Research for this book began two decades ago and over that period a large number of people contributed to the project in many different ways. I regret that I cannot acknowledge all of them.

Generous with their time and suggestions were the staff at the three libraries where I focused my research efforts: the Robarts Research Library, University of Toronto, the Walter C. Koerner Library, University of British Columbia, and the Central Branch of the Vancouver Public Library.

Many people read portions of the manuscript as it evolved. I am especially grateful for the detailed responses of Dan Rennie, Bruce Haden, Shirley Ince, Andrew Jordan, Marcus Bowcott, Steve Graham, Colin Yardley, and David Scott. The comments of Geoff Inverarity, Paul Zysman, Gary Gallagher, Vera Zyla, Gloria Roth, Hedi Kottner, Geoff Ince, and Dinesh Mader are also much appreciated.

Bill Hushion, Kevin Williams, Howard White, and Nick Hunt provided valuable insight into the publishing world. The diverse talents of David Scott at Pivotal Press have been very helpful. The fine editorial eye of Linda Field enhanced the manuscript and Patty Osborne guided the galleys with a steady hand. Vida Jurcic, who designed the covers, was a fountain of creativity.

I am inspired by the work of these colleagues who have taken courageous steps to help heal our culture's erotic wound: Joani Blank, Ray Stubbs, Tom Luscher, Martin Guderna, Tanya Seltenrich, and Dana Williams.

My life and work over the last three years has benefited greatly from the weekly gatherings and wilderness retreats with six bold and soulful men, Richard, Gary, Pete, Paul, Hal, and Dan. I wish every man could know such fellowship.

I owe a huge debt to my parents Shirley and Geoff for their decades of emotional nourishment and helpful critiques of my ideas on politics and sexuality.

Finally, thanks to the adventurous and wonderful Vera Zyla for founding The Art of Loving with me and for brightening my world with her love.

Index